BIONOMICS

MICHAEL ROTHSCHILD

BIONOMICS

THE INEVITABILITY
▪ OF CAPITALISM ▪

A JOHN MACRAE BOOK

HENRY HOLT AND COMPANY ▪ NEW YORK

Library of Congress Cataloging-in-Publication Data
Rothschild, Michael.
Bionomics : the inevitability of capitalism / Michael
Rothschild.—1st ed.
p. cm.
"A John Macrae book."
Includes bibliographical references and index.
ISBN 0-8050-1068-8
1. Capitalism.   2. Free enterprise.   3. Competition.
4. Evolution.   I. Title.
HB501.R763   1990
330.12'2—dc20   90-4712
CIP

Henry Holt books are available at special discounts
for bulk purchases for sales promotions, premiums,
fund-raising, or educational use. Special editions
or book excerpts can also be created to specification.
For details contact:
Special Sales Director, Henry Holt and Company, Inc.,
115 West 18th Street, New York, New York 10011.

First Edition

Designed by Victoria Hartman
Printed in the United States of America
Recognizing the importance of preserving the written word,
Henry Holt and Company, Inc., by policy, prints all of its
first editions on acid-free paper. ∞

1   3   5   7   9   10   8   6   4   2

Figure 19.1, "Fruit Pigeons of New Guinea," is here reprinted with permission of Macmillan Publishing
Company from *The Science of Ecology* by Paul R. Erlich and Jonathan Roughgarden. Copyright © 1987
by Macmillan Publishing Company.

For my parents and teachers

CONTENTS

ILLUSTRATIONS

PREFACE

The market is not an invention of capitalism. It has existed
for centuries. It is an invention of civilization.
            —*Mikhail Gorbachev* (June 8, 1990)[1]

C apitalism, or the market economy, or the free-enterprise system—
whatever you choose to label it—was not planned. Like life on
earth, it did not need to be. Capitalism just happened, and it will
keep on happening. Quite spontaneously. Capitalism flourishes whenever it is not suppressed, because it is a naturally occurring phenomenon.
It is the way human society organizes itself for survival in a world of
limited resources.

A capitalist economy can best be comprehended as a living ecosystem.
Key phenomena observed in nature—competition, specialization, cooperation, exploitation, learning, growth, and several others—are also
central to business life. Moreover, the evolution of the global ecosystem
and the emergence of modern industrial society are studded with striking
parallels.

Briefly stated, information is the essence of both systems. In the biologic environment, genetic information, recorded in the DNA molecule,
is the basis of all life. In the economic environment, technological information, captured in books, blueprints, scientific journals, databases,
and the know-how of millions of individuals, is the ultimate source of
all economic life.

As mankind's ability to copy and exchange information improved,
first with the invention of the printing press and more recently with the
creation of the computer, the accumulation of scientific knowledge
quickened and then accelerated again. Today, a staggering profusion of
companies—from fast-food chains to microchip makers to international

airlines—convert fragments of this vast body of knowledge into goods and services that satisfy human needs and desires. Each organization strives to survive in its niche of the economic ecosystem.

Though the pace of economic change is amazingly rapid, its basic mechanics are remarkably similar to those found in nature. In fact, the chief distinction between the biologic and economic forms of evolution is speed. Technologic change happens roughly one million times as fast as genetic change. Imagine two copies of the same movie being projected onto the left and right halves of a theater screen. With the image on the left zipping by a million times faster, the audience never realizes it's watching the same story.

To make the necessary speed adjustments, the introduction sketches the landmark events in the twin histories of genes and knowledge. Part I elaborates by tracing the development of our present ideas about organic evolution and economic change. For the last two centuries, from Darwin's predecessors to his current disciples, the *idea* of evolutionary change has itself undergone tremendous change. Today's version of Darwin's theory elegantly explains what would otherwise be a bewildering array of contradictory evidence.

By contrast, two centuries after the Industrial Revolution got rolling, economists are still baffled by the forces that propel economic change. To get their models to work, orthodox economists must assume that technology does not change. Unable to shed this absurdity, conventional economic theory has lost all touch with economic reality. Now, with technical innovation accelerating radically, an intimate understanding of the processes of economic change is more crucial than ever. But without an evolutionary perspective borrowed from modern biology, such comprehension is impossible.

After presenting an historical overview of evolutionary change in part I, each of the book's subsequent seven parts explores a single theme crucial to both biologic and economic life. Juxtaposing descriptions of organisms and organizations, these sections of the book are part nature show, part tour of the modern business jungle—with appropriate forays into the world where economics meets politics.

In closing, the postscript fully distinguishes bionomics from social Darwinism and its modern incarnation—human sociobiology. For now, it is enough to say that social Darwinism was a deeply flawed attempt to apply the theory of evolution to human social questions. Ultimately, its perverted logic led to one of the greatest tragedies in human history— the Nazi Holocaust. Because of this horrifying result, biology became a taboo subject for economic thinkers. Many still close their minds to the idea that the insights of modern biology, properly applied, might explain the complexities of the economy.

In recent years, the notion of a relationship between biology and social questions has become even more confused by the rise of human socio-biology. Human sociobiologists employ far more sophisticated language than old-fashioned social Darwinists, but the core allegation is the same—people are born to behave the way they do. Proponents of human sociobiology see the diversity of human cultures as rooted in differences within the human gene pool. For them, culture does not emanate from the mind, but from the genes.

In sharp contrast, bionomics holds that economic development, and the social change flowing from it, is not shaped by a society's genes, but by its accumulated technical knowledge. Technology, not people, holds center stage in this view of economic life. Indeed, wherever advanced technologies have penetrated, cultural chasms once thought unbridge-able have narrowed to the vanishing point. Europe's current unification is but one example of this common process. Throughout human history, profound cultural change has been driven by the evolution of techno-logical information, not the evolution of genetic information.

The central concept proposed here—that a parallel relationship exists between an ecosystem based on genetic information and an economy derived from technical information—is fundamentally different from that argued by social Darwinists and human sociobiologists. In their view, human culture is not parallel to, but an extension of, human genetic information. For them, the tree of cultural evolution grows from genetic roots. In bionomics, genes and knowledge are not connected; they are parallel. Our genes do not program us to become capitalists. Capitalism is simply the process by which technology evolves.

By way of analogy, bionomics argues that, on a day in–day out basis, biologic and economic life are organized and operate in much the same way. Of course, when an analogy is purely coincidental and superficial, nothing can be learned from it. But if an analogy is close, detailed, and has a sound logical foundation, it may reveal a great deal about the hidden nature of things. The more precise the parallels, the more con-vincing the analogy becomes.

For the analogy between ecosystem and economy to be useful, it need not be perfect. Street maps are not exact replicas of cities, but they do help us find our way around in unfamiliar territory. Then again, streets are sometimes rerouted and maps occasionally have flaws that cause us to get lost. Though the analogy between genetic and technologic evo-lution is powerful, it is not perfect.[2]

The analogy drawn here observes that organizations, like organisms, are built in complex hierarchies. One is made up of cells within tissues within organs within organisms within populations, while the other is comprised of work teams inside departments inside divisions inside businesses inside industries. Some organisms and some organizations, like bacteria and single-person offices, are minuscule but found in huge numbers and varieties, while others, like blue whales and IBM, are massive and few.

To persist, regardless of size, every form of life tends to become specialized, developing a particular way of getting by that only a few direct competitors in its niche can match. Avoiding head-on competition—in the wild and in the marketplace—leads to diversity, which, in turn, promotes interdependence. Mutually beneficial relationships, common among species in nature, are echoed in business, where the vast majority of affiliations are based upon mutual profitability. Taken over time, the twin phenomena of competition and cooperation have yielded the diversity and abundance of the earth's ecosystem in one realm and the complexity and productivity of the global market economy in the other.

The most difficult concept to accept about the natural world is that it runs itself. No conscious force is needed to keep the ecosystem going. Life is a self-organizing phenomenon. From the interplay of hormones in the human body to the expansions and contractions of the great Arctic caribou herds, nature's intricately linked feedback loops automatically maintain a delicate, yet robust balance. Markets perform the same function in the economy. Without central planning, buyers and sellers constantly adjust to changing prices for commodities, capital, and labor. A flexible economic order emerges spontaneously from the chaos of free markets.

Needless to say, this thinking bears little resemblance to conventional economics. Two centuries of economic thought, both capitalist and socialist, are based on the concept of "economy as machine" rather than "economy as ecosystem." Nonetheless, history has demonstrated that no economy behaves like a simple, cyclical machine. Like ecosystems, economies are spectacularly complex and endlessly adaptable.

Consequently, it is bionomics—which studies economic relations among organisms and their environments—that offers the best vantage point for a total rethinking of the received economic wisdom. Sprinkled throughout the book, wherever appropriate, the bionomic approach is distinguished from those of traditional capitalists and socialists. But the acid test for any economic view is not how it differs from its predecessors, but how it would work if applied in the "real world."

As such, the closing chapters in parts II through VIII rely on the bionomic perspective to assess several of today's most pressing—and seemingly unrelated—economic questions: Why does America save and invest too little? How did Japan grab world economic leadership from the United States? Why did America lose the War on Poverty? Why does pollution get worse even as we spend more to stop it? Why are so many of America's public schools so awful? Why *exactly* did capitalism flourish while socialism collapsed? And, more important, given the underlying bionomic forces at work, which new policies can harness these forces and provide genuine solutions to these dilemmas?

For readers ideologically wedded to either end of the political spectrum, the answers to these questions will be disconcerting. While certainly not "pro" socialist, the argument made here is not "pro" capitalist in any conventional way. It regards capitalism as the inevitable, natural state of human economic affairs. Being for or against a natural phenomenon is a waste of time and mental energy. Like it or not, the sun rises in the east. Meaningful economic issues always boil down to, given that capitalism exists, how can it be made better?

In short, this book calls for a profound change in our expectations of government, for a new understanding of how it can and cannot be used to foster prosperity. Bionomics does not deny the need for a social safety net, but it compels a rethinking of the net's design. The traditional notion of government's economic role—pushing the buttons and twisting the dials of society's economic machinery—is replaced by a vision of government as the astute cultivator of society's economic ecosystem, patiently nurturing the natural processes of growth.

Bionomics is not a new "theory"—some new doctrine or ideology. There's already been entirely too much of that. Instead, this book offers a fresh new perspective, a new way of observing the facts before us. When you adjust the focus on a microscope, blurry images pop into vivid detail. In all its marvelous complexity and beauty, a world invisible to the naked eye suddenly becomes intelligible.

In a way, the bionomic perspective is an infinitely adjustable *macroscope*—an instrument for the mind's eye—able to scan the panorama of the global economy or zoom in on its finest details. It is an observational technique that, once learned, comes easily. Complexities that confound traditional approaches yield to its insights. At a time of stunning change in the world, when the inadequacies of long-accepted points of view have become obvious, a new way of looking at old problems may be just what is needed.

ACKNOWLEDGMENTS

This book took far too long to write. But without help from friends and family, it would never have been written at all. Most of those who helped are not even aware of having done so, but each one of them made a difference. My thanks go to Dana Monosoff, Paul Miller, Sylvie Lemmet, Don Wood, Jennifer Trainor, Joanne Hively, John Boswell, Patty Brown, Flavia Nonis, Lewis Levin, Nori Nisbet, John Seely Brown, Barb Grehan, Kip Sheeline, Don Davis, Marge Bushman, Winifred Arbeiter, Chris Kocher, Paul Lawrence, Esther Dyson, and Fred Lee Smith, Jr.

My appreciation also goes to the Aspen Community Institute Committee for a scholarship to an Aspen Institute seminar during the book's formative stage. The library staff of the University of California at Berkeley and the people at Dialog Information Services also contributed to the effort. Mark Donahoe, who designed and programmed my bibliographic database, deserves special praise. Without it, keeping track of thousands of source documents would have been impossible.

For a book of synthesis such as this, the greatest debt is owed to the experts and specialists, the scholars and reporters, on whose research this argument rests. Their writings are cited in the notes to each chapter. Other contributors—academics, businesspeople, journalists, and government officials—offered their knowledge through personal interviews. Their kindness is also mentioned in the notes, but among them I would especially like to thank Bernardo Huberman and Bernd Heinrich.

My gratitude also goes to those directly involved in turning a few rough chapters into a polished publication. Robin Dunnigan, my research assistant, made an incalculable contribution. Without her warm spirit and hard work, I am certain that this book would not have been finished. I also thank David Fuller for doing a terrific job on the illustrations. My agent, James A. Levine, provided deft editorial guidance and boundless creative energy in all phases of this project. My publisher, Jack Macrae of Henry Holt, took a gamble on a new writer with an unconventional idea. Then, with his splendid editorial sense, Jack reshaped the manuscript into its finished form.

Just a step removed from the day-to-day grind of research and writing, a project like this must have a core group of supporters who comment on drafts, argue about ideas, and commiserate when progress is slow. Over the years, I have turned again and again to my friends James Collier, Scott Oki, Joel Feigenheimer, Max Feigenheimer, Norman Beil, Andrew Schwartz, Bob Moss, Allan King, and Gloria King. I thank them all. And for their strangely irrepressible enthusiasm and vision of what might be, special thanks go to Andrew Jacobs, Jack McMullen, and Mark Edwards.

Finally, I want to thank my wife, Leigh Marriner. For all five years of our marriage, she has steadfastly supported my work. A few years ago, when the path ahead still seemed impossibly long, when "going back to work" was the only sensible choice, she urged me to keep writing. Later, as our resources dwindled, Leigh juggled hard-nosed clients and soft-nosed babies to keep the book alive. My debt to her can never be repaid. But for all that, I thank her most of all for Adam and Emma, and for our sweet life together.

San Rafael, California
May 1990

BIONOMICS

INTRODUCTION:
GENES AND KNOWLEDGE

A hen is only an egg's way of making another egg.
—*Samuel Butler* (1885)[1]

S tripped to its core, a living organism is nothing more than the packet of information recorded in its genes. And yet, if the very essence of life is information, one has to wonder why a column of numbers or a line of words isn't alive. Obviously, when digits or letters are arranged in a particular sequence, they convey information. But just as clearly, information, in and of itself, is not alive.

Genetic information is special because it alone can make copies of itself. This remarkable ability is the basis of all the other differences that distinguish the living from the nonliving. Even a crystal of table salt is a form of information. Its sodium and chlorine atoms are arranged in a precise order, but a salt crystal cannot duplicate itself. Of all the substances on earth, only DNA, the molecule that carries genetic information, can orchestrate its own replication.

DNA's capacity to self-copy, as well as its ability to encode information, stems from its peculiar shape. First described in 1953 by James Watson and Francis Crick, the structure of the DNA (deoxyribonucleic acid) molecule is a double helix, a shape that looks like a long ladder twisted into a corkscrew. Each rung is a letter in a chemical alphabet limited to just four symbols. Arranged in varying but exact sequences, incredibly long strings of these four letters spell out the instructions for building and operating all living things. Every organism that has ever lived on this planet, from the greatest dinosaurs to the tiniest viruses, is a product of information recorded in its own particular version of the DNA molecule.[2]

No one knows how nature happened to settle on a coding system of four symbols.[3] The simplest possible way of recording information, called binary notation, needs just two symbols—1 and 0. Each binary symbol conveys one *binary digit*, or *bit*, of information. Like a simple yes or no answer, a bit is the smallest fragment of information one can receive and still learn anything at all. All the information flowing through the circuits of digital computers is encoded in immensely long strings of binary 1s and 0s.

Whether a chunk of information happens to be recorded by the four symbols of DNA or the two digits used by computers, the basics of information processing are much the same. Meaning is captured in a linear sequence of a few simple symbols arranged in a precise order. And even though it is somewhat more complicated than the binary system, DNA's method has worked for four billion years.

The letters in genetic code (A, T, G, and C) are read off in groups called codons, just as computers read 1s and 0s in groups called bytes. Each codon stands for one amino acid, the building block of proteins. For example, if DNA's letters are arranged in the order TGG AAG ATC, the first codon—TGG—will be interpreted by the cell's machinery to mean, "Place the amino acid tryptophan here." The next codon, AAG, codes for the amino acid lysine. And so on. One after another, like beads on a string, amino acids are assembled into the proteins that make up living tissue.

DNA's double-helix architecture also endows the molecule with the ability to make precise copies of the information it contains. Each rung in DNA's spiral ladder is actually formed by a pair of its four chemical letters—adenine (A), thymine (T), guanine (G), and cytosine (C). A and T fit each other perfectly, as do G and C. Consequently, the four chemical letters always form two rungs, AT and GC. With only two kinds of rungs, it might seem that DNA uses a two-symbol code, but, in biochemistry, physical orientation makes a difference. Viewed from the vantage point of one of the ladder's side rails, the TA rung is read as a T, while the same rung flipped over, AT, represents an A.

When a DNA molecule copies itself, its rungs split down the middle. Each A lets go of its T and each G releases its C. The side rails of the molecule zipper part, and the spiral ladder becomes two separate spirals, each with severed half-rungs hanging free. Because A will only bond to T, and G will only cling to C, the sequence of broken rungs on each of these half-molecules is a mirror image of the other. From the chemical soup floating around the replicating DNA, unattached letters link up with mates that are still hanging to the side rails. When this process is

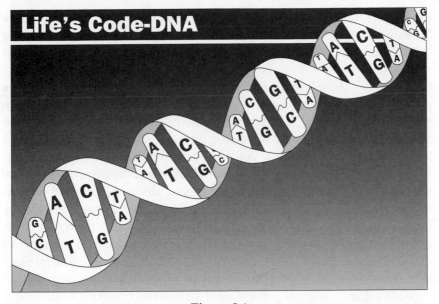

Life's Code-DNA

Figure I.1

completed, two new DNA molecules appear. Each is an exact replica of the parent molecule.

When you stop to think about it, DNA copying is an utterly amazing process. An unconscious object—a string of atoms—has the capacity to organize an exceedingly complex series of events in order to make exact copies of itself. DNA replication happens billions of times every second, all over the earth, wherever there is life. No thoughtful intervention is required. Self-copying just happens. And fortunately so, for without it, life would not exist.

In 1944, nearly a decade before Watson and Crick figured out how DNA self-copying works, John von Neumann, one of the twentieth century's greatest mathematicians, defined the minimal logical requirements for a machine to be considered alive.[4] He said that such a machine would have to carry and be able to use enough information to build working copies of itself from parts available in its environment. One can imagine a von Neumann robot clanking around in a stockroom full of parts constructing its own look-alike. The hard part is figuring out exactly how to engineer the first such robot.[5]

As the revelation of DNA's structure later showed, von Neumann's emphasis on life's ability to self-copy its design was exactly right. Since nothing lasts forever, making copies is the only route to survival. Machines wear out and break down. Buildings crumble to dust. Bodies get old and die. Given enough time, the Himalayas ultimately will slide back beneath the earth's surface and melt into red-hot lava. In a few billion years, even the sun will burn out. It's a fundamental law of nature that things tend to fall apart.

The Second Law of Thermodynamics, better known as entropy, says that order tends to give way to disorder. Organization dissolves into randomness. Given this inescapable reality, the only way to maintain any order at all is by recycling disorganized components into organized arrangements, maintaining a kind of temporary reprieve from disorder.[6]

On this planet at least, DNA and DNA alone manages to buck the universal trend toward disorder. Organisms are subject to entropy. But the bodies of living things are not life's essence. Organisms are merely temporary wrappings of tissue created by DNA solely for the purpose of supporting its own self-copying process.[7] As living beings, we tend to think of ourselves as the end purpose of all the biological activity that sustains us. But this is not so.

We humans—and all other forms of life—are merely biochemical vehicles through which DNA maintains its immortality. From the moment of conception, each of us is doomed. Our bodies decay, but our living essence—the information that defines us—copies itself across the generations into the future. It is ironical that we think of the hills and mountains as permanent and life as temporary, when just the opposite is true. The only enduring order is found in life's information.[8]

Much the same can be said of nongenetic information, otherwise known as human knowledge. Although human knowledge cannot copy itself, it can be copied. And once copied, a piece of information has a far better chance of surviving into the future to be copied again. In an age of photocopy machines, floppy disks, paperback books, videocassettes, and fax machines, we have lost all sense of how essential information copying is to modern life. But without cheap, easy, and accurate copying of complex information, society as we know it would not exist.

In fact, our emergence as the earth's dominant species depended on our ability to encode and copy vital knowledge. In the 1960s, Alexander Marshack, a science-editor-turned-archaeologist, took a close look at bone markings engraved about 32,000 years ago. Marshack saw details overlooked by previous investigators and claimed that the sequence of notched symbols matched the day-to-day changes in the phases of the moon. Mankind's first lunar calendar did not require an elaborate system of writing, but it encoded information just the same. Simple symbols were arranged in a precise order to record valuable knowledge.[9]

Anthropologists have proved that biologically modern human beings, members of the species *Homo sapiens sapiens* (doubly wise man), endowed with an anatomy indistinguishable from our own, appeared at least 100,000, and perhaps 200,000, years ago.[10] Since our ancestors possessed mental firepower equal to our own, it should come as no surprise that the oldest examples of recorded knowledge date back more than 30,000 years.

Evidence of humanity's earliest recording of knowledge has been the subject of heated controversy ever since cave paintings were first discovered a century ago in southern France. Anthropologists have debated why the paleolithic peoples went through such extraordinary effort to decorate the deep recesses of these forbidding caverns. No consensus has been reached, but one view suggests that the paintings of bison, red deer, woolly mammoths, and horses that adorn the walls of hundreds of caves were in fact more than art for art's sake.

According to this hypothesis, human beings gradually decimated the once-great herds of European bison and deer. If enough meat was to be found, hunting parties had to become better planned and more tightly coordinated. The cave paintings, which were done around 17,000 years ago, may have played a role in rituals designed to imprint the locations and tactics of the hunt on an illiterate and superstitious people. Symbols on cave walls, like the rock markings still used by Australia's aborigines, may well have served as the "tribal encyclopedia" of crucial survival information.[11]

But as we know from the workings of DNA, just being able to encode information on a reindeer antler or a cave wall is not good enough. Unless many copies are produced, entropy will ensure the eventual loss or destruction of the information. The physical process of encoding information had to be refined to the point where it no longer required enormous effort to copy something. If writing is difficult to do, not much of it is done. And, logically, when little writing is done, very little information is copied and made available to society. Even less survives to be rediscovered by later generations.

The Sumerians, an agricultural people who lived in what is now Iraq, were the first to make writing and copying relatively easy. Their earliest writings, dating back about 5,000 years, were done by taking a lump of fine, well-washed clay and shaping it into a small, smooth pad a few inches square. With the cut end of a reed stalk, the writer drew lines dividing the face of the pad into squares and filled each square with incised drawings. Left to bake in the sun, the clay became as hard as stone. Over the centuries, the pictograms in the earliest Sumerian writings were reduced to an "alphabet" of stylized symbols made by pressing a cuneiform (wedge-shaped) stylus into the clay. This method is a long way from the ballpoint pen, but it was a lot easier than scratching notches into mammoth ivory.[12]

From an economic standpoint, it makes sense that the Sumerians were the first to invent an efficient method of writing. People invent things to solve practical problems. It simply isn't worth the effort to use a tool that doesn't meet a genuine need. Before the Sumerians established the first large-scale agricultural civilization, there was little need for elaborate record-keeping.[13]

In fact, agriculture itself was an innovative solution to the most basic of all human economic problems. For the two million years of prehuman existence, our ancestors fed themselves by gathering plants and hunting animals. Their numbers were reduced from time to time by disease and starvation, but over the millennia, as our forebears accumulated the knowledge needed to survive in more challenging environments, the human population gradually increased.[14]

Then, somewhere around 9,000 years ago, the population in a few regions of the Middle East reached a critical threshold.[15] It had grown to the point where even a highly developed hunter-gatherer lifestyle was no longer a reliable means of obtaining sufficient food.[16] Roughly 100 square miles of land are needed to support a band of 25 hunter-gatherers.[17] Once the population bumped up against the limits imposed by the land's natural carrying capacity, famines became much more frequent.[18] Each round of starvation reduced the competition for food among the survivors, but it also permitted a population explosion that set the stage for the next round of disaster. Like every other species, humanity rode a boom-or-bust cycle dictated mostly by the weather.

From the same land area, primitive irrigation farming could produce about 100 times as much food as hunting and gathering. The early peoples had known about growing crops for many generations, but to take on the arduous tasks of planting, weeding, and harvesting wasn't worth the effort as long as wild foods were sufficient. Faced with an unreliable food supply, however, some abandoned foraging and began to work the soil.[19]

Over time, the shift to agriculture reduced the frequency of famines by boosting the productivity of the land. But, as is true in our own age, the solution to one economic dilemma created new social problems. The population of a single hunter-gatherer community could not grow much beyond several hundred, because the land's limited productivity kept its members widely dispersed or constantly on the move. In small tribes, social order could be maintained by tradition, family relationships, ceremony, and song.[20]

But once the Sumerians settled down to farm intensively, the population in each community could grow into the thousands. In these first cities, it must have been difficult to control disputes, particularly over rights to stored grain. Developing an efficient writing system was a response to the pressing need for better economic information.[21]

Of the thousands of cuneiform tablets now housed in the University Museum at the University of Pennsylvania, 99 percent are economic texts. In fact, most are mundane accounting records—receipts, ledgers, balance sheets, and contracts—that kept track of sheep, wool, olive oil, grain, and other commodities. One clay IOU reads, "Mr. Enlilanzu received 10 shekels of silver from Mr. Urshulpae in the month of Apindua."[22] While we'd rather know more about their history, religion, and philosophy, the Sumerians were not writing for us. They applied their breakthrough in information technology to the problems that yielded them the greatest immediate benefit.

Many writers ascribe the rise of Sumeria's complex society to its knowledge of irrigation and other agricultural techniques. But without an effective writing system, Sumerian society could not have grown large enough to require elaborate irrigation. Endless disputes over misinterpreted verbal promises would have kept people feuding constantly. Sumerian society, like any large-scale human organization, depended upon written records for order and cooperation. Economic development and a sophisticated information system were intimately interdependent.

Despite the advantages of the Sumerian writing system, clay tablets still left substantial room for improvement.[23] But two thousand years passed before the Egyptians took the next major step, finding a way to turn papyrus plants into a paperlike material.[24] It is said that the communication made possible by lightweight papyrus scrolls was the glue that held the Roman Empire together. But papyrus also had its disadvantages. It could not be folded without cracking and long papyrus scrolls were cumbersome. Looking up a particular piece of information often required unrolling the entire scroll.

This inconvenience was overcome by the Greeks, who invented a way to make parchment from the skins of sheep and goats. Unlike papyrus, parchment could be folded into pages. This innovation allowed the development of the book format, which, in turn, made information far more accessible. Centuries later, the Chinese invented paper that was even easier and cheaper to make than parchment.[25]

But whether the medium was clay, papyrus, parchment, or paper, the physical process of copying was essentially the same. A scribe, one of the few people in society trained to read and write, had to hand-copy from an original text. Anyone who has ever tried to write out an exact duplicate of a letter or a school report in longhand knows what a torturous process this is. Hand copying is not only time-consuming, it inevitably propagates errors. The more complicated the information, the less likely the copies will be identical.

Solving the intrinsic problems of copying information by hand demanded a radically new approach. And, after years of experimenting with ink formulas and tinkering with ways of forming metal into the shapes of letters, Johann Gutenberg finally overcame all the major technical hurdles involved in printing. In his first press run, which consumed the year and a half ending in late 1455, Gutenberg produced about 200 copies of the Bible.[26] It was an absurdly small edition by today's standards, but compared to the alternative of hand-copying, these machine-made books represented a monumental technological achievement.

Assuming it took a scribe six months to produce one copy of a book, Gutenberg's method was 50 times as productive. Gutenberg's printing press slashed the labor involved in copying information by 98 percent.[27] Just as important, the subtle errors that crept into hand-copied versions disappeared. Every copy was a perfect replica of the original.

It is impossible to overstate the significance of Gutenberg's invention.[28] From the time of the ancient cave dwellers, writing had made the accumulation of human knowledge possible, but the great difficulty of producing copies kept information so rare and expensive that only a tiny fraction of people ever had any direct exposure to it. Within a few decades of Gutenberg's invention, however, printing technology had spread written knowledge throughout Europe.[29]

By the year 1500, just 45 years after Gutenberg's first Bibles were printed, more than 1,000 presses had produced about 10 million copies of 35,000 different titles.[30] The extraordinary luxury of written information had been suddenly transformed into a cheap commodity. For the first time in human history, hard-won knowledge could be disseminated inexpensively and quickly.[31]

Indeed, when leafing through any history of science, one cannot help but notice that, prior to 1500, major discoveries were few and far between. Except for Gutenberg's invention of movable-type printing, scant scientific or technological progress had been made since the decline of Greece 1,700 years earlier. But after 1500, once Gutenberg's technology had become commonplace, a sudden rush of scientific achievement laid the foundations of modern knowledge.

In 1512, Copernicus first argued that the earth revolves around the sun. In the following 25 years, Anthony Fitzherbert published the first English manual on agriculture, Albrecht Dürer compiled the first German treatise on geometry, Parcelsus published the first book on surgery, Georg Agricola produced the first treatise on mineralogy, and Andreas Vesalius issued the first anatomical charts of the human body.[32]

As the trade in books grew and the channels of intellectual communication widened, science was transformed from a lonely enterprise practiced by a few isolated scholars into a cooperative social undertaking.[33] With the printing press, a scientific pioneer could disseminate exact copies of highly detailed technical information.[34] Piece by piece, tiny chunks of truth could be stitched together by many contributors.

Simply put, without printing, the Scientific Revolution at the turn of the seventeenth century could not have started. The leading lights of that era—Bacon, Galileo, and Kepler—all commented on the enormous impact of printing.[35] Indeed, if Gutenberg's invention had come along a hundred years later than it did, the Scientific Revolution would likely have been delayed by a century. And the Industrial Revolution, which turned scientific knowledge into machinery, would also have been set back. Today's world would look more like the late nineteenth century's age of steam and iron than our era of electricity and silicon.

Taken in the broadest perspective, the printing press provided humanity with a method of replicating technical information that is nearly as effective as DNA is at copying genetic information. For the first time, amazingly long strings of symbols could be replicated rapidly and without error. And even though the printing press did not allow knowledge actually to copy itself, vast quantities of detailed information could be widely distributed with relatively little human effort.

In a sense, the communication of technical knowledge allowed by printing was much like the exchange of genetic information permitted by the advent of sexual reproduction. During the eons that passed before sex began, from the time DNA first appeared in the primordial seas, all genetic information copied itself asexually. For two billion years, bacteria and blue-green algae—the simplest of single-cell organisms—were the only life-forms on earth. With the rare exceptions caused by genetic mutations, each organism was an exact replica of a single parent. Even by the sluggish standards of biological evolution, the pace of change was agonizingly slow.[36]

But roughly 900 million years ago, a modification of the cellular apparatus allowed DNA from two parent cells to be joined in one offspring. By combining slightly different versions of DNA in a single organism, sexual reproduction accelerated the pace of evolution. After billions of years of biological monotony, the communication of genetic information allowed an amazing variety of new life-forms to suddenly appear.[37]

This period, known to biologists as the Cambrian Explosion, witnessed the debut of multicelled organisms—jellyfish, sponges, and worms. The first shelled animals (primitive mollusks) and the first arthropods (trilobites)—ancestors of insects, spiders, and crustaceans—also emerged at this time.[38] After three billion years of asexual stagnation, the onset of genetic communication allowed life to burst forth in a dazzling display of diversity.

In a remarkably similar way, once printing opened up channels of human communication, the recombination of technical knowledge triggered major changes in the economy. By 1800, the traditional feudal farm economy, an economic, social, and political structure that had remained essentially unchanged since the dawn of Sumerian civilization, began to come apart at the seams. With the dawn of the Industrial Revolution, an economy composed of a few life-forms—peasant, landowner, and guild craftsman—began to sprout dozens of new occupations—mechanic, coal tender, mill worker, ironworker, and engineer. Iron foundries, textile mills, and railroads—organizations built around distinct bodies of technical information—emerged without any grand plan. In both the biological and the economic realms, communication unleashed irresistible waves of change.[39]

Today, two centuries after the onset of the Industrial Revolution, and just two decades after the invention of the computer on a single silicon chip, we are again coping with the stunning changes that flow from radically accelerated communication. In the future, as the pace of innovation quickens, the rate of economic, social, and political change will accelerate further. The phenomenon has even been given a name—the Information Explosion. But, in truth, what we are now experiencing is not *the* Information Explosion. It is only the most recent example of a process that has occurred again and again.

The first Information Explosion came with the original encoding of human knowledge—the cave paintings and notched mammoth tusks of paleolithic man. The second started in Sumer with the improvement of writing techniques. The third was triggered by Gutenberg's press. The fourth and fifth were the Scientific and Industrial revolutions that flowed

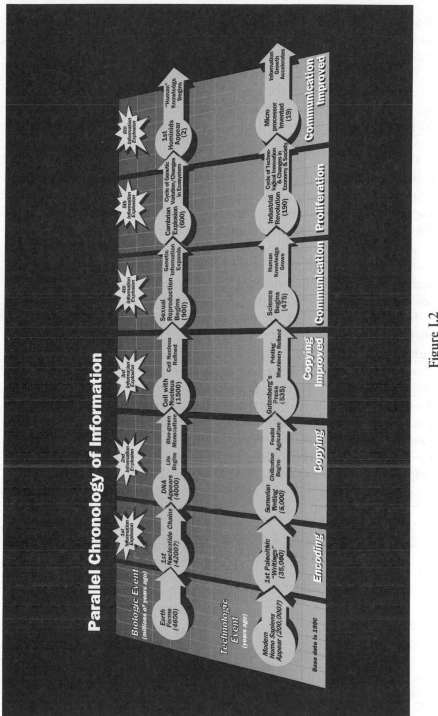

Figure I.2

from the invention of printing. In the wake of the microprocessor's invention, we are now experiencing the early decades of humanity's sixth Information Explosion.

Each Information Explosion unfolded at a much faster pace than the one preceding it. This sixth one will be no exception. In fact, because we are now learning to manipulate information in its two most potent forms—genetic and binary, the sixth Information Explosion will be the most far-reaching and will proceed at an incredibly rapid pace.

Of course, change is not without risk. The last Information Explosion—the Industrial Revolution—set off massive social restructurings. Spasms of change triggered a long series of wars and revolutions. Even today, two centuries after the Industrial Revolution began in Europe, the shift away from feudalism continues across much of the Third World. At the same time, socialism is being destroyed by its inability to make use of rapidly advancing technology. In an era of shocking change, it is well worth remembering that the agony of people whose lives are shattered by economic turmoil often turns into violence.

It is already clear that the final decade of the twentieth century will witness a stunning global transformation. And though no one can accurately predict the future, if the fundamental forces propelling economic change are like those driving biological evolution, a valuable framework can be constructed. In fact, the similarities between genetic and technological information suggest that biologic and economic life are actually parallel versions of the same basic evolutionary process. If this is true, modern biology's detailed understanding of evolution—though previously overlooked by economic and political thinkers—should be of great help in comprehending both our past and our future.

PART I

■

EVOLUTION
AND
INNOVATION

■

When a great question is first started,
there are very few, even of the greatest minds,
which suddenly and instinctively
comprehend it in all its consequences.
—*John Adams*[1]

CHAPTER
1

HINTS OF CHANGE

Farmers no longer marl their fields. But from the thirteenth century until the invention of chemical fertilizers, spreading marl—a limey soil mixed with manure—was common practice. Marling was so routine that even in the unrelenting monotony of rural village life, few events were as dull as watching workmen shovel marl from swampy lowlands. So it's safe to assume that the autumn 1800 marl dig at John Masten's farm at first attracted little attention.

But when the marl pit reached about ten feet in depth, one of the workers struck something solid. Within minutes, an enormous thigh bone—nearly four feet long and eighteen inches in circumference at its narrowest point—was wrested from the muck. More huge bones were soon uncovered, and word spread quickly that strange things were going on at the Masten place.

Farmer Masten, a frugal German immigrant, saw no gain in unearthing old bones, regardless of their size. And since his men had already dug up enough marl for his fields, he ordered them to quit work. But by then the town minister and two local physicians—the amateur naturalists of Shawangunk, a village in New York's Catskill mountains—had gotten wind of the discovery and urged him to continue the search. Finally convinced that the bones might be of some value, but not wanting to foot the expense, Masten invited volunteers to help dig them out.

Spurred on by free drink and a cheering audience, nearly a hundred men joined in the dig, competing for the adulation of the crowd. With each new find, the onlookers roared approval. After three days, the volunteers had uncovered a wide array of large bones, including several leg bones, foot bones, ribs, vertebrae, and some teeth nearly seven inches long and four inches across. The diggers would have continued, but a constant flow of spring water filled the excavation, making the work increasingly difficult. By the fourth day, despite the use of every bailing bucket in town, water had completely filled the pit.

Dr. James Graham, one of the doctors who had pressed John Masten to keep the dig going, reported the discovery in a letter to a medical journal. The following spring, Charles Willson Peale learned of the Shawangunk dig. Peale, a prominent portrait artist of the American Revolutionary War era, also was an amateur naturalist, inventor, and owner of Peale's Museum in Philadelphia. Years earlier, he had been given a few huge bones dug up in Kentucky—oddities that had attracted paying visitors to his gallery—so Peale immediately set out for Shawangunk.[2]

When he arrived in the village, Peale found the broken, battered, and incomplete skeleton of the unknown monster spread out on the floor of Masten's granary. Like other occasional visitors, Peale was allowed to look them over for a small fee. As Peale made charcoal sketches of the bones, Masten asked whether he would be interested in purchasing the skeleton. After a few days of dickering, Peale negotiated a deal for the relics and the right to dig for the missing bones in exchange for $300, a rifle for Masten's son, and dresses for each of his daughters.

Once back in Philadelphia, Peale tried to reconstruct the skeleton, soon becoming convinced that these were the bones of an extinct animal hypothesized a few years earlier by the great French anatomist Baron Georges Cuvier. Working from just a few samples sent from America, Cuvier had surmised that they were from an extinct elephant variety that he called *American Incognitum*.

Later that summer, Peale returned to Shawangunk to restart the dig. Masten's marl pit was still flooded, so the first week was spent building an enormous wooden bailing machine. The recently invented steam engine had not yet reached rural America, so the contraption—a set of buckets chained to a vertically rotating wheel—was powered by a man walking inside it.

After a few days of bailing, the Shawangunk spectacle resumed. Hundreds of men, women, and children from the surrounding farms stopped by to watch the exotic bailing machine and the crew of 25 men digging in the cold muck. Many of the missing bones were uncovered, but the lower jaw, a critical piece of evidence, could not be found.

After unsuccessfully excavating several nearby sites, one of Peale's sons struck something as he probed the ground with an iron rod. In short order, a virtually complete *American Incognitum* skeleton was dug up—only the top of the head and the tail were missing. An eyewitness recalled that

> Delight and astonishment were on every face—"the unconscious woods echoed with repeated huzzas, which could not have been more animated if every tree had participated in the joy." Gracious God, what a jaw! how many animals have been crushed with it! was the exclamation of all: a fresh supply of grog went round, and the hearty fellows, covered with mud, continued the search with increasing vigor.[3]

By Christmas 1801, Peale's "mammoths" were ready for display in Philadelphia. After a sneak preview for dignitaries and a parade through town, the public was allowed to visit Peale's Mammoth Room. Business was brisk. Peale's mammoths were a popular, as well as a scientific, sensation. A Philadelphia baker sold "mammoth bread," and the Democratic ladies of Cheshire, Massachusetts, sent a "mammoth cheese" to Thomas Jefferson, the country's recently inaugurated president. Philadelphia newspapers hailed the Shawangunk skeletons as "the ninth wonder of the world!!!"—buried since Noah's flood.[4]

The public's fascination was stimulated not only by the huge size of the animals but also by the vexing questions they raised. The skeletons stood as irrefutable evidence that an extinct species had once roamed the earth. No other interpretation was sensible. But such a conclusion flew in the face of common knowledge. As Thomas Jefferson, Peale's old friend and a highly skilled naturalist, had said, "Such is the economy of nature, that no instance can be produced of her having permitted any one race of her animals to become extinct."[5]

According to the biblical story of Creation, every living thing every species of flower, fish, and flea—was established during the first six days of life. God had crafted a marvelous living world, with each organism perfectly suited to its particular role. He had no reason to create a species only to let it die out. The extinction of a divine creation implied either that God's handiwork was imperfect or that the world had changed in unexpected ways.

The Shawangunk mammoths, later renamed mastodons by Cuvier, were not the first examples of an extinct species ever found. For centuries, since the first decades of the Scientific Revolution, fossil shells of apparently extinct sea life had been collected. But these artifacts usually were dismissed as the shells of species that were still alive but not yet gathered from the hidden recesses of the world's oceans. Peale's mastodons, on the other hand, by virtue of their incredible size and completeness, were terribly difficult to explain away.[6]

Twenty years before the first dinosaur fossils were discovered, Peale's mastodon skeletons gave compelling evidence that the world might indeed have changed since the beginning of time. The bones unearthed at Shawangunk made the unthinkable thinkable. Perhaps the world had changed. Perhaps the future would be different from the present. Slowly, these heretical ideas seeped into the nineteenth-century consciousness and began to erode mankind's conception of a perfectly static world.

From our vantage point in history, it seems incredible that any educated person ever could have believed in total changelessness. Few convictions seem more comical than an unquestioning faith in the impossibility of change. Indeed, if twentieth-century society can be characterized by any single phenomenon, it is change itself. Hardly a week passes without some slight revision to the patterns of daily life. From birth-control pills to automatic teller machines to videocassette recorders, innovations slip into routines, adjusting attitudes and broadening personal options.[7] Minor yet noticeable changes are so frequent that our view of life is, in large measure, defined by the expectation of change, by the certainty that tomorrow will be different.[8]

The pace of social change is so rapid that we find ourselves gawking at films about the Roaring Twenties, the Conservative Fifties, and the Tumultuous Sixties as if we were observing the religious rites of ancient civilizations. Language, hairstyles, clothing, music, household goods, jobs, and social mores shift so fast that "generation gaps" open between cultures separated by no more than a few years. As children of the twentieth century, we need not be convinced of the pervasiveness and inevitability of change. But until the early 1800s—until the time of the Shawangunk mastodon discovery—the very notion of directional change was patently absurd. No one had ever witnessed long-term change.

The children who visited Peale's Mammoth Room would live to see far more compelling evidence of a changing world than those huge skeletons. Their generation would grow up to witness the early days of the Industrial Revolution and would witness the rise of machines, factories, large cities, and railroads. The English poet William Makepeace Thackeray captured the experience of that generation, which straddled the agricultural and industrial eras, when he wrote, "We who lived before the railways and survived out of the ancient world are like Noah and his family out of the Ark."[9]

Two centuries have now passed since this great historical divide. Compared to one person's lifespan, 200 years is a long time, but against the roughly two million years of human evolution, two centuries of industrialization is a mere flash. Even if we ignore the evolutionary prehistory of our species and consider only the 100,000 years since biologically modern human beings first appeared, the era of rapid change driven by industrial growth is altogether new. For perspective, if we collapse these 100,000 years down to one 24-hour day, the first 22 hours (until 10 P.M.) were spent as hunter-gatherers. From 10 P.M. to 11:57 P.M., people survived by subsistence farming and crafts. All of modern industrial life has unfolded in the last three minutes. We are new to change, and it is new to us.

Perhaps the best way to grasp the enormity of the chasm separating preindustrial and modern life is by gaining some sense of what daily life was like for average people before sustained economic progress began. Unfortunately, however, we do not know a great deal about the lives of common people on the eve of the Industrial Revolution. Virtually all writers were members of the social elite, and they wrote about the upper classes. Historians have discovered only fragmentary reports about the daily lives of the common people. Consequently, our picture of English village life, just before the earliest events of the Industrial Revolution, is sketchy.[10]

However, we do know that in the late 1600s, Englishmen in the middle ranks of the social hierarchy—cottage farmers and peasant laborers— usually lived in windowless mud houses with earthen floors and thatched roofs. Their houses typically had two rooms, but those who were better off sometimes had a separate buttery or cheese room. Very few had kitchens. Cooking was done in the main room. Family possessions were limited to the bare essentials: a few pieces of furniture, some bedding, cooking utensils, and tools. Most people slept on canvas-covered straw ticks. There was no sanitation; people relieved themselves out-of-doors or in the cowshed. Water was carried home in buckets from wells, springs, or the nearby stream or pond. The staple food was bread made from barley. Sugar, spices, chocolate, and most fruits were exotic items known only by the rich.

Disease and hard work exhausted people quickly. Nearly a third of all children died before the age of 15. Life expectancy in the 1690s was 32 years. For the poor, life was even shorter. And with early deaths so common, about a third of all children were orphans. Many others were in families thrown together by the marriages of widowed parents. Despite today's high divorce rate, marriages now last longer than in the seventeenth or eighteenth century, when they were often broken by early deaths.

In 1700, London, with its 550,000 inhabitants, was the fourth largest city in the world. Even so, these urban dwellers made up less than 10 percent of England's population.[11] The overwhelming majority of people were scattered across the landscape. Roads between villages were rutted tracks, which turned into impassable quagmires in the rain. Most people lived their entire lives without ever traveling more than a few miles to the nearest market town.

Century after century, descendants of the same families toiled in the same fields and workshops with the same tools: the pick, the shovel, the plow, the flail, the scythe, the mill, and the blacksmith's forge.[12] If a time machine had transported a fourteenth-century peasant to his village in the late seventeenth century, he would scarcely have noticed the difference. To be sure, wars, famines, bountiful harvests, harsh winters, plagues, and migrations affected lives, but, by and large, the events of "history"—the machinations of the nobility—did not alter the rhythms of daily life. For scores of generations, with a stability inconceivable to us in the twentieth century, personal experience proved that life's patterns were unalterable. Human progress was a spiritual matter, not a practical one.

As if the tedium of daily life and the teachings of the Church were not enough, the static view of existence was corroborated by one of the first great achievements in the history of science. In 1687, two centuries after the Scientific Revolution germinated, Isaac Newton established modern science with his publication of *Principia Mathematica—Mathematical Principles of Natural Philosophy*. Newton's masterwork described the "System of the World"—the laws of motion of physical bodies—and laid bare the underlying mechanism of the universe. He showed that a single universal force—gravity—determined the orbits of the planets, the cycles of the moon, and the ebb and flow of ocean tides.

Newton depicted a universe of perfect predictability—a cosmic clockwork mechanism—where planets cycled endlessly along unchanging paths. Objects moved, but the "laws of motion" never changed. In the stately order of the Newtonian universe, the future was indistinguishable from the past. History was meaningless in a world of endlessly repeating cycles. Passage of time could not imply forward movement or progress. As a matter of natural law, the world and all the stars and planets in the heavens would continue exactly as they were—cycling along orbits set by God at the Creation.[13]

Without question, the Newtonian vision was the highest achievement of mankind's first two centuries of science.[14] Through the scientific method—deriving common patterns, or natural laws, from a jumble of astronomical observations—Newton cracked the secret plan by which God had organized the universe. Using calculus, his own newly invented scientific language, Newton revealed the simple elegance of the rules God had used to put the world into a state of perpetual motion and eternal equilibrium.

Propelled by Newton's success and the belief that perfect knowledge was attainable, scientific inquiry gained new prominence and urgency as the seventeenth century drew to a close. At the time, the world's leading center of scientific activity was the Royal Society in London. Chartered in 1662, while Newton was still a student at Cambridge, it was formed to lend the Crown's support to the advancement of scientific knowledge. The society's motto, *Nullius in Verba*, meant roughly, "Take nobody's word for it; see for yourself."[15] Within a few years, the Royal Society became the world's greatest forum for exchanging reports on the latest scientific experiments. Scientists throughout Great Britain and Europe sent letters and papers to be read at the society's weekly meetings. Unlike the universities whose role was to pass on ancient Greek learning, the Royal Society became the communications hub for new knowledge and the forerunner of all modern scientific societies and journals.

Just three years after Newton's *Principia Mathematica* was published, a Frenchman named Denis Papin appeared before a Royal Society meeting. Papin demonstrated a remarkable new device that dealt with the mysterious force of atmospheric pressure. We do not know whether Newton, a leading member of the society, attended that day's meeting, but even he could not have foreseen the implications of Papin's experiment. No one could have guessed that the path leading from Papin's rather trivial experiment would soon launch the world on a trajectory of accelerating change that ultimately would destroy Newton's vision of everlasting stability.

Papin was one of several scientists trying to design a mechanism that could drive a pump by manipulating the weight of the atmosphere. The idea was tantalizing because the need to pump water, though a trifling matter in the modern world, had become a crucial social problem by the late 1600s. Population growth meant that deeper wells were needed for the water supplies of expanding European cities. And after several centuries of mining, Europe's easily worked surface outcroppings of tin, copper, iron, and coal were exhausted. Miners were forced to follow ore veins underground, but as they edged deeper, flooding from seeping water became severe. Waterwheels had been used to power mine pumps since the fourteenth century, but not all mines were conveniently situated next to streams. In most cases, miners used pumps driven by horses and men. But muscle-powered pumps could not cope with the worsening drainage dilemma.[16]

The tiny gadget that Papin showed the Royal Society was a two-and-a-half-inch-diameter hollow brass cylinder that looked like a tin can with its top removed. A snugly fitting horizontal brass disk, or piston, slid up and down inside the cylinder. Using a flame, Papin boiled a bit of water in the bottom of the cylinder until expanding steam vapor drove the piston to the cylinder's top edge. With a metal catch, he locked the piston in place and then cooled the cylinder in a cold-water bath. This condensed the steam and created a partial vacuum. When Papin released the catch, atmospheric pressure plunged the piston down, providing enough power to jerk a 60-pound weight into the air.

Papin's contraption demonstrated the concept of manipulating atmospheric pressure to generate power, but it was far too tiny to do any real work. And since metalworkers did not know how to build a large-diameter piston and cylinder, Papin's device went nowhere. His ingenious method of capturing power from the atmosphere had outstripped the metalworking technology of his time.[17]

But society's need for pumping power did not disappear, and the idea of designing an atmospheric pump did not end with Denis Papin. A decade later, Thomas Savery went before the Royal Society to demonstrate his design, essentially a large kettle connected by tubes and valves to the midpoint of a vertical water pipe. Steam from the kettle forced water up the top section of the pipe, and, after the openings and closings of several valves, the condensation of steam sucked water up the bottom section of the pipe before the cycle was repeated.

Savery's engine was a bit more useful than Papin's laboratory toy, but it could not pump water more than 20 vertical feet. Attempts to boost its power by raising the steam pressure led to a series of nasty explosions. With only 20 feet of lift, Savery's engine was useless for mine drainage. So, aside from waterwheels and windmills, the world entered the eighteenth century without any self-powered machinery.[18]

In the end, the practical answer to mine flooding did not come from the elite scientific circles of the Royal Society. The solution was furnished by Thomas Newcomen, a small-town blacksmith and ironmonger who, in the course of selling tools to local tin miners, learned of their dire need for a better pump. For some reason, Newcomen believed he could solve the drainage problem. Beginning in 1698, he and his assistant labored 14 years to come up with a working atmospheric pump. Whether Newcomen knew about Papin's experiments at the Royal Society is not clear, but his final design combined Papin's cylinder and piston with Savery's boiling kettle.[19]

Newcomen had already spent ten years on the project and was on the verge of giving up when that familiar miracle of human invention, the fortuitous accident, finally broke his way. His small-scale experimental engine consisted of a kettle and a vertical brass cylinder, less than a foot wide, fitted with a piston of even smaller diameter. By sealing the gap between the piston and the cylinder wall with a leather flap wrapped around the piston's edge, Newcomen sidestepped the friction problem that had stymied Papin in his attempts to scale up his design. The entire cylinder was enclosed in a lead vessel. After steam from the kettle was piped into the bottom of the cylinder to force the piston upward, cold water was fed into the lead container to drive the piston back down. The design made sense, but the brass cylinder cooled so gradually that the piston never developed any downward thrust. It just sank slowly into the cylinder.

After countless frustrating attempts to make the model work, a drop of cold water happened to leak through an imperfection in the cylinder wall. When the water got inside the steam-filled cylinder, it immediately condensed the steam, causing the piston to plunge down with tremendous force, snapping the piston's chain and destroying the cylinder base and the kettle. Years later, one of Newcomen's friends reported that the spray of hot water and the destroyed machinery convinced "the on-lookers that they had discovered an incomparably powerful force which had hitherto been entirely unknown in nature."[20]

The workshop accident revealed the puzzle's missing piece, but it took Newcomen four more years of diligent tinkering before he was able to install a full-scale atmospheric pump that injected cold water directly into the steam-filled cylinder. Newcomen's first engine was constructed at a coal mine near Dudley Castle in Staffordshire, England, in 1712. The engine had a cylinder 21 inches across and nearly eight feet high. Able to generate approximately five horsepower, it pumped 120 gallons of water a minute from a mine shaft more than 150 feet deep.[21] Most ingenious of all, Newcomen's machine included a wooden control rod that opened and closed the engine's valves in the proper sequence. As long as the boiler was fed, the atmospheric engine kept working. Newcomen not only had invented the world's first fossil fuel engine but also had invented one that was virtually automatic.[22]

It took years to convince skeptical mine owners that the newfangled

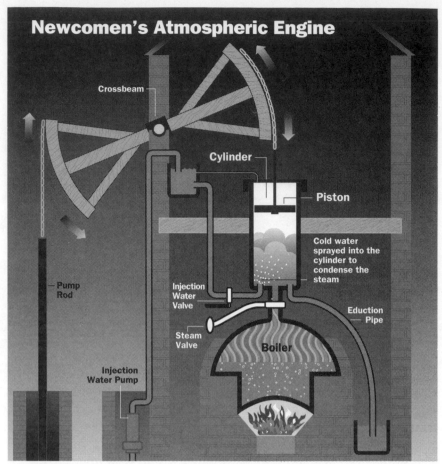

Newcomen's Atmospheric Engine

Crossbeam

Cylinder

Piston

Cold water sprayed into the cylinder to condense the steam

Pump Rod

Injection Water Valve

Eduction Pipe

Steam Valve

Boiler

Injection Water Pump

Derived from Allen and Rolt, *The Steam Engine of Thomas Newcomen,* (1977)

Figure 1.1

device could actually outperform teams of horses and men. But once the engine proved itself, owners of flooded coal mines in Durham and Newcastle began to order their own Newcomen machines. By today's standards, Newcomen's business progress was pitifully slow. Fully ten years after the first engine was installed, fewer than forty of the smoke-belching behemoths were in existence.[23] In an age long before mass production, each engine was custom-designed and handcrafted for the particular pumping requirements of its site. Erected in its own brick pump house, each of these state-of-the-art devices required an enormous investment. Records show that a 16-horsepower engine constructed in 1724 cost £1200 (roughly $100,000 in 1987 dollars).[24]

With each cycle of every Newcomen engine, the vast energy riches locked in Britain's endowment of coal became more accessible to society. Even where coal mines had not been completely shut down by flooding, the Newcomen engine began to make inroads. The sales pitch was the same simple message used to sell capital equipment today: When all the costs were figured in, the engine would save the owner money. In the 1730s, one French coal mine reported that a Newcomen engine with two men operating it 48 hours per week had replaced 50 horses and 20 men pumping all week long in round-the-clock shifts. And according to a 1752 cost comparison for a prospective English coal-mine customer, the Newcomen engine could drain mines for 30 to 40 percent less than muscle power.[25]

While today's cutting-edge technologies often become obsolete in a matter of months, the Newcomen engine remained absolutely unchallenged as the world's only self-powered machine for more than 60 years.[26] After Newcomen's death, his successors kept refining his design, gradually improving the machine's power output and fuel efficiency. By 1775, nearly 600 Newcomen engines were driving reciprocating pumps throughout Europe.[27]

But even the refined Newcomen engine had major drawbacks. Despite its advantages over wind, water, and muscle-power alternatives, it was extremely energy-inefficient. Under the best conditions, it converted less than 1 percent of the coal energy it consumed into useful pumping power.[28] This wasn't much of a problem for coal-mine owners, because they fired their boilers with small, unmarketable lumps of coal that otherwise would have gone unused. But far from the coal mines, in the tin and copper district of Cornwall and in London's public water system, the engine's appetite for coal made machine pumping economically infeasible.

Unfortunately, further refinement of Newcomen's design could not solve the problem. The engine was inherently inefficient because the cold water that condensed the cylinder's steam also cooled the cylinder. On every cycle, a great deal of energy was wasted reheating the brass cylinder.

Though Newcomen's atmospheric engine was efficient enough to drain Britain's flooded coal mines and drive down the cost of coal, it was not adequate to kick industrialization into gear. Thomas Newcomen had succeeded in building the world's first engine where others had failed, because he designed his machine around the limitations imposed by the crude materials available in the early 1700s.[29] But by the end of the century, the accumulated technical progress of the embryonic British iron industry, made possible largely by cheap coal, allowed another

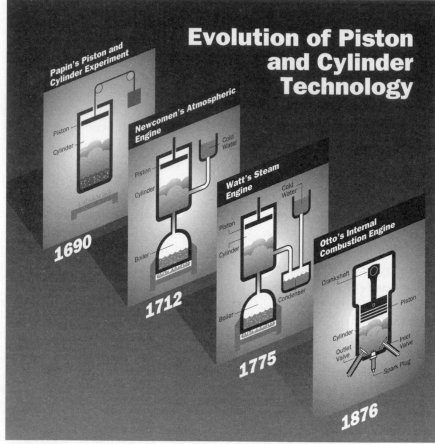

Source: Derived from Dickinson, *A Short History of the Steam Engine* (1939)

Figure 1.2

inventor to come up with a far more sophisticated engine. In a pattern that has repeated itself throughout the history of technology, the great invention of an earlier period provided the basis for an innovation that would eventually make the original design obsolete.

James Watt was a young scientific instrument maker at the University of Glasgow when he was asked by a professor to repair a scale model of a Newcomen engine.[30] As he tinkered with it, Watt realized that the cooling and reheating of the cylinder wasted huge amounts of energy, but after months of trying, he could not conceive a better solution. Then, according to Watt, while out for a Sunday stroll on Glasgow Green in May 1765, the answer came to him.[31]

In the next few days, Watt built a model engine with an additional chamber, a condenser. In his design, after the steam drove the piston up, it was drawn out of the cylinder and into the condenser, where it was cooled. After several years of further refinement, which incorporated the latest advances in metalworking, Watt secured a patent for his design, and, with his business partner Matthew Boulton, began producing pumping engines in 1775.

For the same power output, the Boulton & Watt engine used 75 percent less coal.[32] With this enormous cost advantage, Boulton & Watt began selling their engines to the tin and copper mines of Cornwall, where the cost of coal had idled more than half of the Newcomen engines already in place. The superior fuel efficiency of Watt's steam engine doomed the Newcomen engine in Cornwall, and within eight years, only one of the old engines in that region was still working.[33]

In 1784, Watt developed the rotative engine, the second of his two great improvements to Newcomen's design. By alternating steam pressure on either side of the piston and substituting a piston rod for the chain used on all earlier engines, Watt radically expanded the potential uses of machine power. Simple up-and-down reciprocating motion was fine for pumps, but to drive factory machinery, power had to be applied through rotating motion.[34]

With Watt's invention of the rotative steam engine, factory machinery no longer depended solely on the rotating power of the waterwheel, and factories no longer had to be located alongside fast-running streams. Nonetheless, waterpower was still cheaper than steam power generated by Boulton & Watt engines. It took several decades of further refinement before steam power gained a clear cost advantage.[35]

Between 1790 and 1800, more steam engines were built than in the preceding 90 years.[36] By 1800, when the Boulton & Watt patent expired, machine power reached critical mass and set off the chain reaction of the Industrial Revolution. It was to be the greatest transformation in human history since the hunter-gatherers turned to agriculture.

In little more than a century, an ageless world of perfect stability and absolute predictability had been cut loose from its historical moorings. Unquestioning belief in the absolute permanence of God's Creation, by both the scientific elite and the educated population, began fraying at the edges. Among the visitors who surged through Peale's Mammoth Room that Christmas of 1801 must have been at least a few who paused to wonder whether the massive skeletons before their eyes represented an aberration, a freak example of change in God's changeless universe, or a hint of a larger pattern of change. A few might even have wondered: If sustained change really happened, how exactly did it come about?

2

THEORIES OF CHANGE

In the paupers' section of the Montparnasse cemetery in Paris, the body of an 85-year-old man was being lowered into a long, unmarked trench. It was a couple of days before New Year's 1830, and only a few old and dear friends stood by to pay their last respects to Jean-Baptiste Lamarck. He had once been among France's most respected naturalists, the man who coined the term *biology*, and the first person to develop a coherent theory of evolution. But after ten final years of isolation, blindness, and grinding poverty, Lamarck was gone and virtually forgotten.[1]

Several years passed before Lamarck's name stirred any interest among his former colleagues. The occasion was the reading of his eulogy at a meeting of the French Academy of Sciences. It had been written by France's most honored scientist, Baron Georges Cuvier, who knew perfectly well that his assessment would strongly influence Lamarck's place in history. But instead of offering a tribute to the man who had been his intellectual adversary for 30 years, Cuvier took the opportunity to unleash a vicious attack.

In his writings, Lamarck had challenged the view—held by Cuvier and nearly everyone else—that the species were fixed, stable entities. He argued that over the course of geologic time, living things had been perfected gradually into their modern forms. Lamarck was the first to advance the subversive notion of "descent with modification," the idea that modern species are life-forms derived from primitive predecessors.[2]

One aspect of Lamarck's philosophy was his well-known theory of "acquired characteristics," which held that the actual mechanism behind gradual organic change was the tendency of each creature to make minor adjustments to its body to improve its function. He contended that, once acquired through use, physical characteristics were passed on to descendants.

For example, Lamarck claimed that by repeatedly spreading their toes underwater, web-footed birds had stimulated the development of membranes between their toes. By constantly stretching to keep above the waterline, wading birds had produced their extraordinarily long legs. Moles and blind mice lost their eyesight after living underground for several generations. And, in his most famous example, Lamarck argued that giraffes developed their long front legs and necks by reaching for foliage high in the trees of the African savanna. Lamarck wrote:

> It is not . . . the form and character of the animal's bodily parts that have given rise to its habits and peculiar properties, but, on the contrary, it is its habits and manner of life and the conditions in which its ancestors lived that has in the course of time fashioned its bodily form, its organs, and its qualities.[3]

Because animals kept adjusting to the ever-changing world around them, the very concept of a stable species was meaningless to Lamarck. Life was fluid, forever reshaping itself into new forms in response to shifting circumstances.

To Baron Cuvier—who had spent an enormously productive career demonstrating the orderly stability of the living world—such thinking was outrageous nonsense. From his research, Cuvier was certain that the earth's creatures were organized into several distinct categories that had not changed since Creation.[4]

According to Cuvier's "correlation of parts" doctrine, each feature in every animal was designed to serve a special function as part of a tightly integrated organism. For instance, hoofed animals, such as cattle and horses, invariably had grinding molars and multiple stomachs to chew and digest grasses. By contrast, animals equipped with claws, like lions and bears, always had sharp teeth, powerful jaws, and a digestive tract suited to absorbing nutrients from meat.

Cuvier believed that because each species was designed so perfectly for its role in nature, it could not possibly have been transformed from another species. The parts of an animal could not grow or shrink or be altered in any way without destroying the integrity of the whole; any significant change would be fatal. Furthermore, if organisms were so plastic, how would anatomical identification of species be possible? Each individual would be a special case, and the overwhelming similarities among individuals in each species would not be valid.

Although Cuvier held that each species was fixed, he did not deny that the natural world had undergone change. In fact, he was among the first to argue that some species, such as the American mastodons, had become extinct. He contended that violent catastrophes, caused by a series of great floods, had sporadically weeded out some of the species stocked on earth at the Creation. Change was not gradual but sporadic and cataclysmic.

Cuvier came to this view from his study of fossils in the Paris area. The region, known to modern geologists as the Paris Basin, just happened to be the site of a succession of shallow seas in past eons. The thick layers of limestone laid down by sedimentation from these seas were revealed for the first time by quarrymen working on Napoleon's lavish construction projects.

The fossils found in the quarries showed no evidence that animals gradually reshaped themselves into modern species. On the contrary, the distinct layers of rock revealed a pattern of abrupt change from one stratum of fossilized life to the next. Cuvier felt he had hard proof that Lamarck was wrong about gradual transmutation.

Cuvier reasoned that the radical differences between the species of one era and those of the next were the result of migrations that followed each catastrophe. Since the entire earth was not inundated during each flood, survivors from one area would move in and occupy the region that had just been destroyed. Later, after the next cataclysmic flood, the process of migration would be repeated, leaving behind several layers of rock, each populated by distinct types of fossil life.

If species had changed gradually, where, Cuvier asked, was the evidence to prove it? Mummified animals brought back from Egypt by Napoleon's expeditions were indistinguishable from living specimens despite the passage of several thousand years. Cuvier argued that if Lamarck was right, at least some changes should have been detected. Baron Cuvier's hardheaded approach sat well with the scientific community, while Lamarck's claim of gradual transmutation was largely rebuked.

To some extent, support for Cuvier's view stemmed from the fact that early-nineteenth-century science lived in Isaac Newton's shadow. As Cuvier described it, the world of nature, except for rare catastrophes, was like Newton's universe—stable, orderly, and knowable.[5] Cuvier believed that just as Newton had deduced the laws of motion of heavenly bodies, he had discovered the underlying laws of nature that explained the superficial complexity of life on earth.

More than anyone, Cuvier must have realized that Lamarck's ideas represented the gravest threat to his future status as "biology's Newton." He knew that if Lamarck was even partially correct about gradual transmutation of the species, his own life's work and place in history would be seriously undermined. Cuvier must have felt compelled to do everything in his considerable power to discredit the ideas of the first man to envision an organic world of unceasing and unguided change.[6]

Cuvier's vicious campaign succeeded, and Lamarck's scientific reputation was not rehabilitated until early in the twentieth century. Even so, Cuvier's views contained the seeds of their own destruction. His brilliant anatomical studies demonstrated how exquisitely attuned each species was to its "conditions of existence." But this raised a new question: Could God really have crafted so many species so perfectly suited to modern conditions if they had had to survive several catastrophic transitions during the course of history? Cuvier had argued his case too convincingly.[7]

In the end, the bitter feud between Lamarck and Cuvier is memorable because these scientists laid out the two broad alternatives—gradual versus sudden—for a theory of organic change. But nothing was settled. Neither mechanism—willful transmutation or violent catastrophes— ultimately was convincing. Oddly enough, the essential element in the explanation of biologic change was to be borrowed from another brand-new field—economics.

Economics was new because it had not been needed before. In the past, philosophers had not concerned themselves with the mundane problems of the world of work. In villages scattered across the countryside, people raised crops, made their clothes and tools, had children, and died. There were no baffling agricultural conundrums to occupy the minds of the great philosophers.[8]

But by the late 1700s, the gathering forces of industrialization had reached critical mass. After three centuries of gestation, the accumulation of technical information made possible by Gutenberg's printing press had spawned many crucial innovations. In England, new methods of cultivation had dramatically boosted wheat yields.[9] By the 1770s, the first large-scale waterwheel-powered textile factories began operating.[10] And ever since 1712, Thomas Newcomen's atmospheric engines were literally priming the pump of European industrialization by draining flooded coal mines. With cheap coal, ironmaking technology was radically improved, making possible a proliferation of precision-made machines, including James Watt's steam engine.[11]

The surging momentum of what was later labeled the Industrial Revolution was beginning to upset centuries of rural stagnation and isolation. For the first time, international trade in grain, sugar, tea, cotton, cloth, and machinery had reached the point where it was becoming vital to the well-being of the average Englishman. This change raised crucial new questions. Should England buy grain from and rely upon foreigners to feed its skyrocketing population? Or should it protect its farmers with high tariffs and strive for self-sufficiency?

Dr. Samuel Johnson, the renowned lexicographer, said, "There is nothing which requires more to be illustrated by philosophy [science] than trade."[12] Were there Newtonian "laws of motion" that regulated the economy? Could an economic Newton reveal the simple design underlying the apparent chaos of economic activity?

This was the mind-boggling task that the original "worldly philosophers" set for themselves. Adam Smith, a Scottish philosophy professor, was the first of this small group to grapple seriously with the basic questions of economic life. Not surprisingly, Smith was influenced by Newton's model of the physical universe as he searched for the "natural order" of the economy.[13] Where Newton explained that gravity was the central force holding the universe together, Smith argued that individual self-interest held human society together.

Adam Smith did not arrive at his belief in the primacy of self-interest through abstract reasoning. He was a philosopher, but he was also a well-traveled man of the world. The central role of self-interest in his system of economic thought grew from his personal observation of human behavior. In the first great treatise on economics, *An Inquiry into the Nature and Causes of the Wealth of Nations*, published in 1776, Smith wrote one of the most famous passages in all economic literature:

> It is not from the benevolence of the butcher, the brewer, or the baker, that we expect our dinner, but from their regard to their own self-interest. We address ourselves, not to their humanity but to their self-love, and never talk to them of our own necessities but of their advantages.[14]

In setting forth his "law of universal gravity," Isaac Newton never troubled himself with whether or not gravity ought to exist. Newton simply observed that gravity did exist. Similarly, Adam Smith did not build his analysis of the economy on how he thought people *should* act; he constructed his theory from observations of how they *did* act.

Smith argued that self-interest causes people to make good use of another common human trait. For a variety of reasons, some people are more adept at certain activities than others. As Smith explained, even in a primitive tribe, a person more skilled in making bows and arrows than in hunting would tend to specialize in those tasks and become the tribe's armorer, exchanging his wares for the game hunted by other members of the group. The hunters, the armorer, and all the members of the tribe benefited by their specialization and interdependence.[15]

In this way, the inherent diversity of individual talents, combined with the innate human desire to satisfy self-interest, leads members of society to organize themselves to perform tasks for which they are particularly well suited. Guided by the self-adjusting exchange ratios of market prices, producers trade their wares for the products of others. Paradoxically, when individuals pursue their special aptitudes in an effort to satisfy their selfish desires, the end result is social harmony.[16]

Following this logic, Adam Smith argued against laws restricting free trade. He contended that free trade widens the relevant market and allows a more intensive division of labor, greater productivity, and social betterment. This was the optimistic essence of Smith's *laissez-faire* economic philosophy.

Though Smith wrote on the very eve of the Industrial Revolution and knew inventors like James Watt personally, he did not foresee the burst of new technologies, the explosive growth of factories, the rise of huge cities, or any of the other radical changes that were about to transform society.[17] When he peered into the future, Smith saw more of the same. Broader free markets would allow a greater division of labor, which in turn would yield larger quantities of familiar products.[18] Like its Newtonian model, Smith's economy was essentially stable. Smith described the machinery of the market economy, but he did not foresee that the mechanism itself was about to undergo dramatic change.

Adam Smith was by no means alone in this regard. Even though they were writing several decades after *The Wealth of Nations* was published—and well after the Industrial Revolution began—the two other founding fathers of classical economics, David Ricardo and Thomas Malthus, also saw the economy as a closed and unchanging system. Ricardo, a fabulously successful stockbroker-turned-economic-philosopher, published his *Principles of Economy and Taxation* in 1817. In it, he described the economy as what we would now call a "zero-sum game." Only a fixed amount of goods are available to go around, so whatever one group in society gains, the others must lose.

By this logic, Ricardo predicted a struggle between workers and factory owners that would benefit neither. He argued that as the population expanded, food prices would rise, and landowners, who controlled the farmland, would wind up with all the wealth. Ricardo believed that the market system would inevitably produce extremely wealthy landlords and horribly impoverished workers and peasants. Thirty years later, Ricardo's ideas were to become central to Karl Marx's economic thinking.

Ricardo's bleak prognosis grew out of the simple but terrifying logic of Thomas Malthus's 1798 *An Essay on the Principle of Population.* Malthus argued that the natural rate of human population growth is geometric (1–2–4–8–16—exponential, in today's terminology) and always exceeds the arithmetic (1–2–3–4–5—linear) rate of increase in food production.[19] He contended that famine, disease, and war were the only way the population could be kept in balance with the food supply. His message was profoundly depressing, and it was, in fact, after reading Malthus's famous essay that the writer Thomas Carlyle labeled the emerging field of economics "the dismal science."[20]

Single-handedly, Malthus shattered Adam Smith's bright vision of inevitable prosperity.[21] For Malthus, the "iron law" of economics meant struggle and hardship leading to disaster. The implications of limited resources and rapid population increases were inescapable. "To prevent the recurrence of misery, is, alas! beyond the power of man."[22] Nature had doomed mankind to a cruel fate.

Malthus did not know it, but the rapid rise in England's agricultural productivity had begun to slow by 1760, just as population growth began to explode.[23] These fundamental factors—along with the expense and turmoil of the Napoleonic wars and several poor harvests—triggered a sustained rise in the price of bread. As unforgettably portrayed in Charles Dickens's novels, the streets of England's cities in the early 1800s were teeming with destitute paupers. The plain facts of everyday life seemed to verify Malthus's straightforward argument.

Amid the general misery, no aspect of English society was more appalling than life in the factories that had sprung up during the world's very first industrial boom. Working conditions had always been harsh. Well before the advent of machine power, workers using hand looms endured long hours for mere subsistence pay. But, as the first decades of the nineteenth century unfolded, conditions steadily deteriorated.[24]

In the days of the waterwheel, large textile mills were sprinkled about the countryside, wherever a stream provided a reliable source of power. Workers, who always included pauper children, had to be reasonably well treated because there were not enough of them in remote areas. Children taken on as apprentices were housed, fed, and clothed at the mill owner's expense. Conditions were by no means lavish, but they were reasonable, given the standards of the time.

But with the introduction of Watt's rotative steam engine in the 1790s, manufacturing spread to the cities, where the population boom had created an enormous labor pool of pathetically impoverished children and adults. Any entrepreneur who could raise enough money to outfit a shed with a steam engine and textile machinery could become a mill owner. With a virtually unlimited labor supply and feverish price competition among these tiny manufacturers, the unmitigated exploitation of workers, particularly children, became key to driving down manufacturing costs.

Ramshackle, unventilated urban factories were jammed with dangerous, deafeningly loud machinery. The air was saturated with dust and fibers. In 1832, witnesses testifying before a committee of the House of Commons investigating the working conditions of factory children cited examples of young workers dying because their bronchial passages were clogged with cotton dust.[25]

By the age of five or six, and sometimes as young as four, children began working in the mills. The 11-hour workday typical of the 1790s stretched to 16 hours by the 1820s. Work began at five in the morning and ended at nine at night—six days a week. When youngsters were unable to keep pace with the machinery, they were beaten by the adults they assisted. When they stumbled or fell from exhaustion, they were often injured. By the time they reached their teens, many were too crippled to keep working. Their limbs were deformed by having manipulated the same machine through the same cycle for years on end. Experienced mill workers could tell from a child's deformity which machine he or she had operated.

By 1833, after nearly 30 years of investigation, debate, and political chicanery, the first serious restrictions on the use of child labor became law.[26] Workers under 18 years of age were limited to 69-hour work weeks. Children under 11 were limited to 48 hours. Still wretched by today's standards, the legislation marked the first effort to establish a minimum level of industrial decency. It became the base from which comprehensive protection for workers in all industries was achieved.

Among those most adamantly opposed to these reforms were England's economists. Unbothered by the horrific facts of industrial life, they argued for complete freedom of contract between employers and workers. Leading economists also resisted the reform of the Poor [Welfare] Laws passed in 1834. They adopted Malthus's position that higher levels of government support for the unemployed poor would only lead to more mouths and worse starvation in the future. Malthus's population principle was as controlling as Newton's law of gravity. Why try to avoid the inevitable?

CHAPTER

3

DARWIN'S VISION

I n October 1836, while British economists pondered the inevitable doom of mankind, the HMS *Beagle* docked in Falmouth harbor after a five-year voyage. The ship's mission had been to chart the waters along the South American coastline for the British navy. But the importance of the surveying expedition would ultimately pale beside the consequences of a whim of the *Beagle*'s captain, Robert Fitzroy. Captain Fitzroy wanted an educated gentleman aboard the *Beagle* to provide conversation and companionship during the monotonous months at sea. The 22-year-old amateur geologist and naturalist he selected was Charles Darwin.

Whenever the *Beagle* was in port, Darwin set off for the interior on collecting expeditions. From the jungles of Brazil, the pampas of Argentina, the mountains of Chile, and the Galápagos Islands, he gathered an amazing collection of living and fossil species then largely unknown to European science. By the time he returned to England, young Darwin had become one of the world's most knowledgeable students of nature.

In his work, Darwin went far beyond mere observation. He tried to bring some conceptual order to the profusion of life he encountered. He began the voyage believing, like everyone else, that species were individually designed and placed in their habitats by the Creator. But as he traveled through the continent, he noticed two troubling oddities. First, the animals of South America were radically different from those living in the same climate in Africa. Why, Darwin asked himself, would God have created such different species for the same roles in climatically identical but physically distant environments?

Second, during one expedition to the interior, Darwin's group caught

and ate a rhea, South America's version of the ostrich. Darwin realized
that the animal was a distinct species—not the common rhea he had
seen farther north.[1] This was surprising, because there was no obvious
physical boundary, no mountain chain or desert, separating the ranges
of the two rhea species. The birds coexisted over an intermediate area
between their home territories. If God had designed distinct species for
separate locations, why did different yet similar species live in the same
spot?

The questions raised by Darwin's careful observations of South American species were further stimulated by a pioneering geology text he read
during the *Beagle*'s voyage. Charles Lyell's just-published *Principles of
Geology* made the argument that erosion, volcanoes, earthquakes, sedimentation, and other geologic processes observable in modern times had
been going on throughout the earth's incomprehensibly long history,
gradually reshaping the landscape. Lyell's book left Darwin facing the
most profound question of all: If the earth changes constantly and keeps
destroying habitats and their species, how are replacement species introduced?[2]

Unable to square the doctrine of the Creation with his own observations and the arguments of Lyell, Darwin slowly and reluctantly abandoned the conventional view of the immutability of species. By the spring
of 1837, six months after his return to England, Darwin was convinced
that species changed.[3] Having come to this conclusion, he decided to
discover exactly *how* they changed.

With this commitment, Darwin landed right in the middle of the
bitter controversy left unfinished just a few years earlier when Baron
Cuvier unleashed his final denunciation of Lamarck. Darwin knew that
if he were to convince anyone that species could change, he would have
to propose an explanation far more plausible than Lamarck's willful
transmutation or Cuvier's global catastrophes.

To crack the species question, Darwin began two years of effort that
he later described as the most intensive period of work in his life. But,
curiously, he did not try to solve his problem by redoubling his field
research. Instead, he took the unusual approach of reading widely, particularly in disciplines unrelated to biology and geology—such as psychology, philosophy, social theory, and political economy.

The exact process by which Darwin developed his theory of evolution
and its core principle of natural selection will never be known. It is
impossible to unravel the idea threads of a concept woven together in
the mind of a creative genius. Nonetheless, Darwin's evolutionary theory
has become so fundamental to the modern view of the world that Darwin

scholars have spent decades attempting to reconstruct precisely how he developed his bold new concept. In what they themselves fondly refer to as the "Darwin industry," scholars differ on the relative importance of certain ideas in this crucial period of Darwin's life. But they agree that Darwin's study of economics was vital to his formulation of the concept of natural selection.[4]

Like any student of economics at that time, Darwin began by reading Adam Smith's *Wealth of Nations*. Smith's argument that economic prosperity resulted from the interaction of self-interest and the division of labor helped convince Darwin that the unguided activities of diverse individuals can generate a coherent overall trend. Appreciating the importance that Smith placed on individual differences later proved to be central to Darwin's thinking, but, as Darwin recalled in his autobiography, the pivotal insight came:

> In October [actually September 28], 1838, that is, fifteen months after I had begun my systematic inquiry, I happened to read for amusement Malthus on Population, and being well prepared to appreciate the struggle for existence which everywhere goes on from long-continued observation of the habits of animals and plants, it at once struck me that under these circumstances favorable variations would tend to be preserved, and unfavorable ones to be destroyed. The result of this would be the formation of a new species. Here, then, I had at last got a theory by which to work.[5]

By applying Malthus's "iron law" of human economics to the world of nature, Darwin discovered the plausible mechanism of evolutionary change that had eluded every previous student of the species question. In truth, Darwin's idea was very simple.

Natural selection holds that because parents tend to produce more offspring than can be supported by the environment's limited resources, and because every individual is genetically different from every other individual, those offspring who are born with physical characteristics giving them even a modest edge in life's competition for food, space, and security stand a better chance than their siblings of surviving long enough to have their own offspring. Over time, as one generation follows another, the effects of the probabilities accumulate and nature selects those creatures most suited to their environment.

Inventing the principle of natural selection involved much more than simply transferring Malthus's population principle to the realm of biology. According to Malthus, whole classes of people—beginning with "the poor"—would be wiped out by disease and starvation. Learning from Adam Smith, however, Darwin saw that competition took place not between classes of identical beings but among diverse individuals. His contemporaries believed each organism was a standard example of its species, varying only in insignificant detail, but Darwin knew from his years of painstaking observation and his study of animal breeding techniques that the tiny distinctions among individuals were crucial. To dismiss these differences as unimportant and to treat individuals as if they were identical copies was to ignore diversity—an elemental fact of nature.

By penetrating to a finer level of detail, by going beyond the simple assumptions of "class" or "type" thinking, Darwin was able to see that most competition in the struggle for survival occurs among individuals within a given species, not between different species. Variations, as Darwin called them—the minute, often unnoticeable, inherited differences among individuals—are the raw material of evolutionary change.

According to Darwin, natural selection is a sorting device that acts upon variations, giving historical direction to evolutionary trends. As geological processes change the earth's habitats, natural selection tunes the average characteristics of a species population by "selecting in" traits useful to survival and "selecting out" traits no longer appropriate. Over vast stretches of time, the accumulation of traits gradually transforms one species into its descendant species.

Darwin's insight into the species problem—then called the "mystery of mysteries"—was so simple and so powerful that one could expect he would have witten up his theory immediately for publication. But Darwin realized that his practical explanation of life's evolution would ignite a firestorm of opposition. If true, his theory would obliterate the universally held view that God had crafted each species for its special role in nature. To propose a fact-based explanation for life's marvelously intricate diversity would amount to an atheistic assault on the very idea of God. Having personally experienced a spiritually painful conversion from creationism to evolutionism, Darwin was well aware of the profound moral issues his theory would raise.

Twenty-one years passed from the autumn day in 1838 when Malthus's *Essay on Population* helped Darwin crystallize the concept of natural selection until the day he published his theory of evolution in *The Origin of Species by Means of Natural Selection*. Darwin spent those years gathering evidence for and refining the concepts of his revolutionary thesis. He so dreaded a violent reaction from the scientific community, the religious leadership, and the public that he probably would have waited even longer, but when Darwin learned that Alfred Russel Wallace, another fine naturalist, had independently arrived at the idea of natural selection, his hand was forced. Darwin realized that all his years of work on the species problem would go unrecognized if he did not publish before Wallace.

The November 1859 release of *The Origin of Species* set off precisely the maelstrom of controversy that Darwin had long feared. The religious and the scientific establishments attacked Darwin and his book with unremitting hostility. But Darwin, true to his nonconfrontational style, rode out the storm by staying put at his home in the English countryside. He never once engaged in a public defense of his ideas. As far as he was concerned, *The Origin* was "one long argument" that had to speak for itself. The decades of procrastination had given Darwin the time and the ammunition to anticipate and rebut virtually every legitimate attack.[6]

By marshaling a massive amount of factual detail behind tightly woven arguments, Darwin's treatise eventually managed to win over his opponents. Within a decade of its publication, *The Origin*'s capacity to explain concisely so many previously incompatible facts made reluctant believers out of the vast majority of the scientific establishment as well as much of the educated public.

By the time Darwin died in 1882, his theory of evolution had become the central organizing principle of all biological thought, as it remains to this day. By giving coherent meaning to the scattered facts of taxonomy, anatomy, geology, and paleontology, Charles Darwin established the modern science of biology. Recognizing the enormity of his contribution, Britain's political leaders overlooked their theological misgivings and buried Darwin next to Isaac Newton in Westminster Abbey. Darwin—not Cuvier or Lamarck—had become the Newton of biology.[7]

Between them, Newton and Darwin had constructed two fundamental and fundamentally different systems of scientific thought. Newton's universe was stationary, cycling without change through all eternity, perfectly knowable and completely predictable. In Darwin's world, history mattered. The shape of the future depended on the outcome of past events. No elegant equations could predict the future of even a single organism, because chance itself is inherent in life. Newton and Darwin erected two utterly different conceptions of nature: one for lifeless objects, the other for living things; one for stability, the other for change.

Today, little more than a century after Darwin's death, most people—scientists and nonscientists alike—still have not accepted the notion that Darwinian thought is just as valid as Newtonian thought.[8] After all, it is the *theory* of evolution as opposed to the *law* of gravity. There are no eyewitnesses to evolution, but everyone experiences gravity all the time. We do not even know how many species exist in nature, but Newton's equations have taken us to the moon and back.

The staggering scientific achievements of the twentieth century have given nonscientists the impression that real scientists are all-knowing and thus able to predict the future with absolute certainty. Since biology cannot even predict the birth weight of a couple's next child, it seems fuzzy and "unscientific."[9] Newton's science, by contrast, yields exact, unequivocal answers and appears to be the only true "hard" science.

Biology is also handicapped by its youth.[10] The eighteenth- and nineteenth-century arguments over Newton's work belong to history, but the scientific debate over Darwin's ideas is still vigorous. Because controversies over certain aspects of Darwin's theory are widely reported by the popular press, and frequently distorted by religious fundamentalists, many nonbiologists have the impression that evolution itself is still in question. In its finer points, yes; there are many unanswered questions about evolution. But in its fundamental structure, no; the evolution of life is as established a fact as science ever has.[11]

Many of the disputes over evolution have grown out of conflicting interpretations of the fossil record. Paleontologists often disagree about the relationships among fossils of long-extinct creatures. There is no way to settle these arguments absolutely, because life-forms are not related through their skeletons and shells but rather through the DNA in their genes.

Because of this, it has only been in the last few years that the most compelling piece of evidence for Darwin's theory has fallen into place. Biologists recently developed a way to compare the similarity of DNA from different species. Now, scientists can trace the branching pattern of descent among species that evolved from each other by measuring the differences in their genetic instructions. The greater the DNA difference, the more distant the evolutionary relationship.

Unfortunately, fossils rarely contain intact molecules of DNA, so this method cannot settle the confusing family tree of extinct species. Paleontologists must continue to rely upon the physical characteristics of shells and bones. But the evolutionary relationships among thousands of living bird species have already been established. Recently, we have learned that humans and chimpanzees are indeed very close biological relatives—we share nearly 99 percent of our genetic information.[12]

Because it has taken 130 years since the publication of *The Origin* to pin down enough hard evidence to turn evolutionary theory into natural law; because religious fundamentalists still vigorously oppose its teaching in many areas of the United States; and because the theory of evolution must contend with all the complexities of the whole expanse of life present and past, the impression that evolution is "still just a theory" will abide for decades to come. Nonetheless, Darwin's evolution is as real as Newton's gravity.

4

THE MYTHICAL MACHINE

The long-delayed acceptance of the evolutionary concept has had a devastating impact on the development of economic thought. Economics—the study of how one peculiar species manages to survive in the world—would seem to have an inherently close connection to biology. It was, after all, the profound similarity of economic and biologic questions that allowed Darwin to crack the species problem with ideas borrowed from Adam Smith and Thomas Malthus. But economists, with a handful of recent exceptions, have never borrowed concepts from biology.[1] Starting with Smith, Malthus, and Ricardo, economists constructed their system of thinking with concepts borrowed from Newtonian physics. Writing in the late eighteenth and early nineteenth centuries, they had no other choice. The only science was Newton's science.

But even after Darwin came along, economists, like most nonbiologists, never fully appreciated the significance of evolutionary thought. As a result, today's economics remains wedded to the classical Newtonian paradigm. Sadly, several generations of economists have spent the last century elaborating a system of thought that tries to explain the intricate relationships of economic life with concepts invented to describe the motion of planets.[2]

If economics were just a branch of philosophy, its mechanistic outlook would not matter, but basic ideas about how the economy works directly affect the lives of millions. For good or ill, government policies generally conform to the received economic wisdom of the era. As John Maynard Keynes, perhaps the twentieth century's most influential economist, so elegantly put it,

[T]he ideas of economists and political philosophers, both when they are right and when they are wrong, are more powerful than is commonly understood. Indeed, the world is ruled by little else. Practical men, who believe themselves to be quite exempt from any intellectual influences, are usually the slaves of some defunct economist. Madmen in authority, who hear voices in the air, are distilling their frenzy from some academic scribbler of a few years back.[3]

Theories are useful only inasmuch as they help organize observable facts into coherent, recognizable phenomena. When an accumulation of new facts saps the explanatory power of a theory, it should be revised or abandoned. When any theory is treated as sacrosanct, its proponents assume the role of high priests, and strange things happen in the name of "science."

Because the intellectual superstructure of modern Western economics was erected on the foundation of Newtonian physics, it has become unstable. Today's best economists are quite unable to use modern theory to draw coherent and consistent conclusions from the stream of incoming data. Economists disagree among themselves so completely that their advice to political leaders amounts to little more than a spectrum of conflicting opinions. Consequently, momentous policy decisions hinge upon political mood swings and raw intuition, unaided by any deeper comprehension of how an economy works.

The weakness of modern Western economic theory has implications that go far beyond our inability to eliminate poverty, provide full employment, or meet foreign competition. When all the superficial trappings are stripped away, it becomes clear that the cold war grew out of a fundamental disagreement about the essential nature of human economic activity. And, despite wishful thinking to the contrary, as long as there is no global consensus on the basic nature of human economic existence, there can be no lasting resolution of the East–West conflict.

Until 1989, with the breaching of the Berlin Wall, most people believed that resolving this great contest was impossible. Just as seventeenth-century Europeans believed that the differences between Catholics and Protestants could never be settled, twentieth-century observers of world politics accepted that capitalist and socialist societies could *never* come to terms. Unaware of the historical roots of this ideological conflict, many people assume that the animosity between Left and Right, socialist and capitalist, has always existed.

But this contest of ideas is actually quite young. The conflict between rich and poor may predate the beginnings of property in the first agricultural civilizations of Sumer, but the great split between socialists and capitalists goes back only 150 years, to England in the 1840s. It was during this period, while Charles Darwin patiently gathered facts and polished arguments in the protective isolation of his country home, that more worldly men struggled to find a way out of the intellectual dead end that Malthus and Ricardo had constructed.

Throughout the 1830s and 1840s, the unrelieved misery of the working poor, regarded as living proof of the inevitable population crisis, haunted every aspect of social and economic thinking. The Malthusian dilemma seemed so inescapable that it became the necessary point of departure for any new economic idea.

Logically, economic thinkers had only three possible ways of dealing with Malthus's population principle. First, they could propose ways to alleviate its cruel consequences. Despite their many differences, this was the common theme of socialist reformers and communist revolutionaries. The second choice was to ignore the inevitable tragedy and hope that the population bomb would somehow defuse itself. This "head-in-the-sand" approach was pursued by capitalist economists. The third alternative, showing that Malthus was simply wrong—that production increases could outpace population growth—has never been seriously pursued by any school of economics.[4]

The first response to Malthus, trying to remedy the severe social problems generated by accelerating industrialization and population growth, was not a simple matter of one person or group leading a well-organized reform program. The English political system spawned an astonishing variety of reform movements (populist radicals, Tory radicals, Utopian socialists, agrarian socialists, Ricardian socialists, republicans, trade-union militants, atheists, and radical reformers)—all set in motion by "a motley, confused, jarring miscellany of irreconcilable theorists."[5]

These groups pursued overlapping goals, and among the ideas that eventually became British law were proposals to shorten the workday, abolish child labor, legalize trade unions, mandate universal education, and broaden the right to vote. Each movement had its own particular rationale and emphasis, but there was a widely shared belief that an enlightened, well-treated working class would voluntarily slow its reproduction rate and avert the calamity of mass starvation and social revolution.

Of course, not everyone believed that reform of the existing system would relieve the nightmare of industrialization. By far the most influential thinkers to take this position were Karl Marx and Friedrich Engels.

Marx, the son of a wealthy lawyer, edited a liberal German newspaper until he was expelled by the Prussian government for his radical political activities. Engels, who was Marx's financial supporter, coauthor, and editor for four decades, was the son of a rich manufacturer who owned factories in Bremen and Manchester.

The most widely read of their joint efforts was *The Communist Manifesto*, a pamphlet published in German in February 1848. In fewer than 20 pages, the *Manifesto* announced a new theory of economic history and a program of political revolution. Over the years, it was translated into many languages, and by 1888, five years after Marx's death, Engels wrote a new preface to the *Manifesto* in which he hailed it as "undoubtedly the most widespread, the most international production of all Socialist literature, the common platform acknowledged by millions of workingmen from Siberia to California."[6]

As Engels summarized it, the "fundamental proposition" of the *Manifesto* is this:

> That in every historical epoch the prevailing mode of economic production and exchange, and the social organization necessarily following from it, form the basis [of] the political and intellectual history of that epoch. . . . [T]he whole history of mankind . . . has been a history of class struggles, contests between exploiting and exploited, ruling and oppressed classes. . . . Nowadays, a stage has been reached where the exploited and oppressed class—the proletariat—cannot attain its emancipation from the sway of the exploiting and ruling class—the bourgeoisie—without at the same time, and once and for all, emancipating society at large from all exploitation, oppression, class distinctions and class struggles.

In the decades that followed publication of the *Manifesto*, Marx and Engels, together and separately, created a vast literature of social thought. Marx, in his three-volume *Capital*, the most important of these writings, developed an entirely new theory of economics to support his theory of history. *Capital* has been dissected, reinterpreted, canonized, and damned in literally thousands of books. But the intricacies of Marx's economics are not relevant here.

What is important is that Marx was the first person to propose *any* theory of how economies change over the course of history. The economists who preceded him—Smith, Malthus, and Ricardo—only considered the workings of the economy at a given point in time. The classical economists simply did not deal with long-term development. But Marx's theory was built upon his concept of change. In Engels's view, Marx's theory of historical economic change was "destined to do for history what Darwin's theory has done for biology." Even though experience has shown that Engels's analogy was wrong, it is true that just as Cuvier and Lamarck were the first to propose theories of historical biologic change, Marx was the first to suggest a theory of historical economic change.

The intellectual roots of Marx's theory of change can be traced back to two key sources: (1) a theory of the history of ideas proposed by the German philosopher G. W. F. Hegel and (2) the dismal economics of Malthus and Ricardo. Hegel's dialectical principle attempted to describe how new ideas are born out of the conflict of old ideas. The popular statement of Hegel's dialectical principle is that any idea or thesis stimulates an opposing view—the antithesis. The conflict is resolved in a compromise, or synthesis. This synthesis starts the idea cycle all over again.

Simply put, Marx blended this notion of change-through-conflict with the teachings of Malthus and Ricardo. Marx considered himself Ricardo's intellectual heir. His prediction of a worsening position for the working class flowed directly from Ricardo's acceptance of Malthus's population principle. Malthus's "surplus population" became Marx's "reserve army of labor."[7]

Despite making several complimentary references to Darwin, Marx borrowed none of Darwin's ideas. In fact, most of Marx's writings, including the first draft of *Capital*, were completed before *The Origin of Species* was published. Marx's ideas grew out of his study of philosophy, history, and economics, not biology.[8]

Although Marx and Darwin both proposed theories of historical change within a few years of each other, a critical difference distinguishes their ideas. Darwin's theory of natural selection states that the mechanism of organic change is the gradual reshaping of a species through competitive sorting among distinct *individuals* within a species population. In Marx's theory of class conflict, changes in "productive relations" (technology) lead to changes in the economic relations between *classes* of people, which, in turn, ultimately lead to class conflict and political restructuring.[9] Where Darwin emphasizes competition among unique individuals, Marx stresses conflict between homogeneous classes.

Darwin's objectives were purely scientific. He offered a theory to explain seemingly incompatible observations of nature. Marx's goals were primarily political. He wanted to relieve the suffering of the working class, and, after outlining his theory of economic history in *The Communist Manifesto*, he went on to propose a program of radical political and economic change. To emancipate society from all further exploitation and bring an end to class struggle, he called for the abolition of private property, the revolution of the working class, and the centralization of all instruments of production (land, machines, and factories) in the hands of the state.[10]

Marx's conception of how the economy changed through history has served as the theoretical underpinning of every socialist society. By implication, this raises the question, "What theory of economic history undergirds nonsocialist societies?" In short, there isn't one. Western capitalist economics never developed a coherent theory of change comparable to Marxism. Instead, non-Marxist Western economists have focused on the near term—how the economy works in the here and now, not how it changes over time.

Most important, this approach to economics was pursued by John Stuart Mill, the philosopher who published his hugely successful *Principles of Political Economy* in 1848, just a few months after *The Communist Manifesto* was first released. Thus, the publication of these two crucial documents ended the period of classical economics, which had started 70 years earlier with Adam Smith's *Wealth of Nations*. When Karl Marx and J. S. Mill charged off in opposite theoretical directions, they tore open the great ideological chasm between Left and Right that still defines the modern political landscape.

Although J. S. Mill's *Principles of Political Economy* is not nearly as famous today as *The Communist Manifesto* or *Capital*, it was an immensely important book. Mill's treatise was so comprehensive and readable that it remained the "undisputed bible of [non-Marxist] economists" until early in the twentieth century. Mill shaped the ideas of the two generations of economists who served as the intellectual bridge between the eighteenth-century classical thinking of Smith, Malthus, and Ricardo and the twentieth-century neoclassical theories of modern Western economists.[11]

Mill was a leading British reformer quite sympathetic to the goals of the socialists. But unlike the socialists, who argued that private ownership was the root of all economic evil, Mill believed in the necessity of private property, the profit motive, and business competition. He argued that the problem of how goods are produced is wholly separate from how those goods ought to be divvied up. Mill believed that the distribution of output among individuals was governed by changeable laws and social customs, while the actual physical processes of production obeyed the unalterable "law of diminishing returns."[12]

In keeping with this economic "law," if a farmer doubles the labor expended cultivating a plot of land, his crop will increase, but it will not double. If labor is doubled again, the crop will increase again but proportionately less than it did on the first doubling. According to Mill, "This general law of agricultural industry is the most important proposition in political economy. Were the law different, nearly all the phenomena of the production and distribution of wealth would be other than they are."[13]

Like virtually every other economist of his time, Mill firmly believed in Malthus's population principle.[14] He realized that technical progress could push back the limits of agricultural productivity to some degree, but, like his contemporaries, he never imagined the huge leaps in farm productivity that would occur in the late nineteenth and twentieth centuries. For him, the "law of diminishing returns" meant that mankind would always struggle against starvation, that a growing population would only make that struggle more brutal. At his most optimistic, Mill hoped that technical progress in farming and a voluntary lowering of the birthrate would lead to a static economy that would meet the basic needs of a stable population.[15]

By looking to the stationary economy as the ideal, Mill neatly sidestepped the problem of historical change. If the world could be brought to the point of economic equilibrium, there was no need to think about the distant future. The business cycle would cause inevitable fluctuations in well-being, but long-term economic change would be irrelevant.

The disciples of John Stuart Mill—including virtually the entire establishment of Western economic thought to the present day—followed in his footsteps and more or less decided not to think about historical development. Instead, Western economics became obsessed with the concept of equilibrium.

Beginning in the 1870s, a group of British, Austrian, French, Swedish, Italian, and American economists transformed classical economics into a system of thought familiar to any modern student of economics. Known as the "marginalists," they relied on the idea of "decreasing marginal returns" as the building block of modern equilibrium, or neoclassical, economics.

Fundamentally similar to the "law of diminishing returns," the concept of "decreasing marginal returns" deals with the problem of economic choices. For example, the farmer producing both wheat and corn has to decide what mix of the crops will earn him the highest income. Working with a fixed amount of land, labor, fertilizer, and machinery, he has to trade off between marginally more corn and marginally less wheat, or vice versa. The various mixes of wheat and corn that will yield him the same total income can be plotted on a graph as a supply curve.

Similarly, a consumer with a limited income faces a choice between spending marginally more on food and marginally less on other goods. The various combinations of food and other consumer goods that will yield him the same overall level of personal satisfaction can be plotted as a demand curve. With the new tools of supply and demand curves, the marginalist economists began to erect an abstract mathematical universe. The intersection of the supply and demand curves was the point of equilibrium, where, at a predictable price, the amount of each product equaled the volume consumed.

Equilibrium economics did not appear full-blown; it was erected over several decades. Without question, its most influential proponent was Alfred Marshall. Marshall began his career teaching mathematics at Cambridge University, where he planned to become a physicist, but in 1867, out of a desire to do good for society, he switched to economics.[16]

Like the rest of his generation, Marshall learned economics by reading J. S. Mill.[17] First at Cambridge, then at several other universities before ultimately returning to Cambridge, Marshall lectured in economics for 20 years. With his superb skills as a mathematician, he gradually pieced together his own system of economic ideas, and in 1885, he began work on his great treatise, *Principles of Economics*. Published in 1890, it received instant acclaim in England, and by the turn of the century, Marshall's work had replaced J. S. Mill's 50-year-old text as the "bible" of economists.

Ironically, even though Marshall once wrote, "The Mecca of the economist lies in economic biology," his elegant system was based on Newtonian physics.[18] Intersecting supply and demand curves glided about, automatically determining prices, allocating resources, and setting incomes. As any present-day student of microeconomic theory can appreciate, Marshall's perpetually self-adjusting mechanism is intellectually seductive. His most famous student, John Maynard Keynes, described Marshall's economic vision as "a whole Copernican system, by which all the elements of the economic universe are kept in their places by mutual counterpoise and interaction."[19] Apparently the economic "laws of motion" first pursued by Adam Smith had at last been revealed by an economist trained as a physicist.

But to make Marshall's lovely theoretical system function, certain absolute rules had to be obeyed. First and foremost, time had to stand still. Every calculation started off with a given quantity of resources, a stable population, and a fixed state of technology. The equations of the equilibrium model could come up with the solution to an economic question—if, and only if, none of the input factors changed during the computation. In effect, to allow Marshall's beautiful mathematical model to work, economic theory had to be divorced from the rude realities of economic life.[20]

For the last century, Western academic economists have clung to Marshall's static model. They are fully aware that their model does not reflect the bewilderingly complex, dynamic reality of the economy, but, as one British economist put it, "If the world is not like the model, so much worse for the world."[21]

To any scientist, such a sentiment is profoundly disturbing. The sole purpose of a theoretical model is to help explain reality. If testing of a model shows that it does not jibe with observable facts, the theory should be jettisoned and the search begun for a more representative paradigm.[22]

But economists, both Marxist and Western, never adopted the rigorous testing standards of natural science.[23] Perhaps the traditional disregard for reality stems from the fact that both schools of economics were established before reliable economic statistics became available. For example, recent research indicates that by 1820, the falling living standards of English workers had bottomed out. From that time on, rising productivity and slowing population growth began to raise the prosperity of the average Englishman.[24] But these data were unavailable to Marx or any other nineteenth-century economist. Had these facts been known, one of Marx's central predictions—that of ever-worsening working-class misery—would have been dealt a severe blow.

In fact, it was not until 1919 that the first organization dedicated to gathering detailed economic statistics—the United States' National Bureau of Economic Research—was established.[25] And it was not until the 1960s that computers made the data practically useful. Unlike Newton (who constructed his theory after studying observations recorded by astronomers) and Darwin (who derived his theory from specimens collected by naturalists), Marx and the Western economists fabricated their theories unhindered by nettlesome facts.

Even today, when massive government computer systems churn out mountains of statistics, the majority of academic economists still do not test their models against economic data. In a 1970 presidential address to the American Economics Association, Wassily Leontief, winner of the 1973 Nobel Prize in Economics, criticized his profession's "preoccupation with imaginary, hypothetical, rather than with observable, reality."[26]

In 1982, Leontief surveyed the previous four years of articles published in America's most prestigious economics journal, *The American Eco-*

nomic Review. He found that more than half the articles were mathematical models without any data whatsoever, and nearly one-fourth drew inferences from statistics gathered for some other purpose. Of the articles, only one-half of 1 percent—one article—used direct analysis of data gathered by the author. That lonesome article was about utility maximizing behavior in pigeons.

Freed of the most basic restraint of science—testing theory with facts—modern Western economics has completely lost its way.[27] The theories of academic economists are utterly divorced from the grubby reality of daily commercial life.[28] Amazingly enough, John Kenneth Galbraith, one of America's most famous and least theoretical economists, has written, "To the best of my recollection, I have never inspected a factory in a serious way in the United States."[29] Could a credible biologist freely admit that he had never bothered to take a "serious" walk in the woods?

Unable to explain the awesome complexities of real economic life as experienced by workers and businesspeople, where history matters and change is constant but largely unpredictable, Western economists have barricaded themselves inside their obtuse mathematical models.[30] Now equipped with immensely powerful supercomputers, top academic economists put their energies into making the descendants of Alfred Marshall's model ever more complicated instead of proposing truly different, and more revealing, models of reality. As Lester Thurow, a well-known American economist and dean of MIT's Sloan School of Management, has written, "If Newton and his contemporaries had behaved as the economics profession is now behaving and had access to the modern computer, it is likely that the law of gravity would never have been discovered."[31]

Although his point is correct, Thurow's reference to Newton is symptomatic of the basic problem. Western economists still think that physics equals science.[32] Most still conceive of the economy as if it were the stable clockwork mechanism of the heavens described by Newton. Adherents of Marxist ideology are no better off. If it can be compared to anything, Marx's belief in spasmodic change through class conflict is an unwitting economic version of Cuvier's catastrophism.

Both Marxist and Western economics were established before Darwin published *The Origin of Species.* To date, neither side has ever seriously considered evolutionary biology as the paradigm for an entirely new kind of economic thinking. Consequently, neither side has yet resolved the central dilemma of how the economy changes.[33]

CHAPTER

5

LIFE'S PULSE

No one has ever seen a living trilobite. The last of these ugly little hard-shelled animals died 245 million years ago in the great Permian extinction that killed off about 90 percent of all species.[1] But despite their long absence from life's stage, trilobites are one of the most exhaustively studied of all extinct life-forms.

Trilobites first appeared about 570 million years ago, during the Cambrian Explosion, and were among the first complex organisms. Because they were hard-shelled, while most of the creatures living around them in the shallow seas were soft-bodied, the trilobites fossilized much more readily than their neighbors. Only under the rarest circumstances would the delicate tissues of a jellyfish drift to the sea floor intact, be covered in sediment, and turn into a fossil. But trilobite fossils are found in huge numbers on every continent.[2]

The trilobites' worldwide success can also be attributed to the advantage of being the first animal to have a hard outer shell. It protected them from the world's first carnivores—worms that had abandoned scavenging for hunting—and provided them with an exterior skeleton for body support and muscle attachment. Trilobites were the first arthropods, the ancestors of modern horseshoe crabs, insects, and lobsters. Over the course of 325 million years, 10,000 distinct trilobite species evolved, prospered, and vanished.

Because they were so prolific and fossilized so readily, trilobites have long been a favorite subject of paleontologists. Niles Eldredge, one of today's leading trilobite experts, was a graduate student at Columbia University in the late 1960s when he first became interested in them.

When it came time to select a dissertation topic, Eldredge chose a North American trilobite species, *Phacops rana*, as the focus of his study on the evolution of invertebrates.[3]

Eldredge, now curator of invertebrates at the American Museum of Natural History in New York, simply wanted to reconfirm Darwin's axiom that organic change happens when a species, responding to shifting environmental pressures, gradually evolves into another species. This emphasis on the gradual nature of species modification had dominated evolutionary thought ever since the publication of *The Origin of Species* in 1859. But in more than a century of research, paleontologists had failed to locate any fossil evidence to substantiate Darwin's gradualism.

Even Thomas Huxley, Darwin's staunchest supporter, had been deeply troubled by the lack of any fossils showing a smooth transition from a parent to a daughter species.[4] Although fully committed to Darwin's theory, he was terribly embarrassed by the inability of paleontologists to dig up any fossils showing gradual change. Until Huxley died in 1895, every example in the world's expanding fossil collections showed the same thing: Major physical differences existed between a parent species found in one layer of rock and its daughter species embedded in the layer immediately above it. Not one scintilla of evidence squared with Darwin's insistence on gradual change. Baron Cuvier's ghost, still insisting on catastrophism, must have been overjoyed.

Against Huxley's advice, Darwin stressed that species were modified very slowly as tiny incremental changes accumulated from one generation to the next. In *The Origin*, Darwin wrote, "As natural selection acts solely by accumulating slight, successive, favourable variations, it can produce no great or sudden modification; it can act only by very short and slow steps. Hence the canon of 'Natura non facit saltum [Nature does not make leaps].' "[5]

For Darwin, like Lamarck before him, species were not stable entities. They were droplets, frozen in fossil form, from a flowing stream of life. For most of the twentieth century, because the fossils collected did not corroborate Darwin's view, and since evolutionists were not about to abandon Darwin, paleontology—the only source of tangible facts about the history of life—was increasingly ignored.[6]

In its place, the new field of genetics, unknown in Darwin's time, became the prime hunting ground of evolutionists looking for facts supporting Darwin's belief in gradual change. But genetics also failed to supply clear-cut evidence for gradualism. As knowledge about genetics accumulated, faith in Darwin's gradualism waxed and waned. A few heretics even went so far as to argue that "macromutations"—major changes in genes—caused radical transformations of species from one generation to the next.[7]

While proponents of macromutations stirred up the "sudden or gradual" controversy once again, their view never gained wide support. And by the 1940s, a new consensus had emerged among evolutionists. Known as the "Modern Synthesis," it interpreted genetics discoveries to bolster Darwin's view that all species were steadily modified as natural selection fine-tuned organisms to their changing environments. But the Modern Synthesis was not an all-embracing scientific consensus: It still had no place for the paleontologists' inconvenient fossils.[8]

Finally, in the 1960s, a new generation of paleontologists, including Niles Eldredge and Stephen Jay Gould (a professor of biology and geology at Harvard and a world-famous authority on evolution), began working their way up the academic ladder. Their goal was clear: They wanted to make paleontology relevant again by bringing it back into the fold of evolutionary biology. To do so, they needed to find the missing fossil evidence that would support the Modern Synthesis.

In pursuit of this goal, Eldredge decided to scrutinize specimens of the trilobite *Phacops rana*, a species that lived for eight million years in a vast, shallow inland sea that covered eastern North America about 380 million years ago. Through a meticulously detailed study of this trilobite, Eldredge hoped to identify the minute evolutionary changes that previous paleontologists had overlooked.

To gather examples for his study, Eldredge spent months driving around New York, Ohio, Michigan, Illinois, Indiana, and Iowa. From small quarries, streambeds, lakeside cliffs, and railroad cuts, he unearthed and catalogued hundreds of *P. rana* specimens. Using existing studies of local geology, he identified the age of each rock layer examined and each fossil collected. As he moved vertically up a rock face, he moved forward in time. No single site contained specimens covering the complete eight-million-year expanse of *P. rana* history, but by matching fossil layers from various locations, Eldredge was able to piece together a collection that covered the species' full range through space and time.

As his collection grew, Eldredge became more and more worried. Regardless of their antiquity or location, all the fossils looked exactly the same. They came in different sizes, because individual animals died at different ages, and some showed signs of injury and disease, but the expected pattern of gradually changing physical traits simply was not there. Desperately concerned that he had no results to report in his dissertation, Eldredge measured hundreds of specimens under the microscope. He recorded 50 different dimensions for each sample: length of the head, distance between the eyes, height of the eyes, length of the tail, and so on. He ran the data through a computer, but statistical analysis showed no pattern of change.

Certain that he must have overlooked some telltale sign of change, Eldredge studied his collection yet again. This time he concentrated on the eyes of his specimens. Like modern insects that descended from them, trilobites had compound eyes. Rows of tiny lenses gathered light to the optic nerve, where the brain converted it into a visual image. At a loss for what else to do, Eldredge started counting the lens rows in each specimen. Every trilobite had 17 rows of lenses, except for one from an Ohio quarry, which had 18.

Having finally detected a shred of evidence for evolutionary change, Eldredge examined the lens rows of the rest of his collection. What he found was not encouraging. The 18-row variety, a subtype of *P. rana* called *Phacops milleri*, was found only in the lower strata in Ohio and Ontario. The 17-row version occurred everywhere else, in all layers. And, most disturbing of all, even where the 18-row variety had been found, layers of the 17-row type appeared immediately above it. In short, there was no evidence of gradual change, just a sudden jump from 18 to 17 rows in Ohio and Ontario.

Despite his extraordinary diligence, Eldredge found himself confronting the same conundrum that had vexed every sophisticated student of the fossil record. The explanation for the stability-jump-stability pattern, proposed 150 years earlier by Baron Cuvier during his angry debate with Lamarck, claimed that catastrophic floods wiped out old species from time to time and survivors from other areas migrated in to replace them once things had settled down. Cuvier's argument made sense as far as it went, but it never explained how the new replacement species were formed. Since Cuvier did not believe that new species arose from old species by modification, he had to contend that replacements were survivors from species stocked on earth at the Creation. Logically, the long series of cataclysms should have whittled nature down to a bare handful of creatures by modern times, but the incredible diversity of life undercut this explanation.

In *The Origin*, Darwin had taken a completely different tack. In the last paragraph of a chapter entitled "On the Imperfection of the Geological Record," he summarized his explanation for the obvious jumps in the fossil record and the corresponding lack of evidence for steady, gradual change.

> I look at the natural geological record, as a history of the world
> imperfectly kept, and written in a changing dialect; of this history
> we possess the last volume alone, relating only to two or three
> countries. Of this volume, only here and there a short chapter has
> been preserved; and of each page, only here and there a few lines.[9]

Essentially, Darwin's explanation was, There are many gaps in the fossil
record, and much of what the rocks seem to be saying is misleading.

But by painstakingly gathering specimens from nearly every location
and every age within the geographic range and eight-million-year lifespan
of one particular trilobite, Eldredge had all but eliminated the problem
of "missing pages" in the fossil record. Even so, the record showed
absolute stability interrupted by an undeniable jump from 18 to 17 rows
of lenses. Cuvier's explanation was useless, and Darwin's apology for
the incompleteness of the Victorian fossil record did not apply to Eldredge's *P. rana* collection. There had to be some sensible way to reconcile the conflicting evidence for sudden and gradual evolution.

The only really helpful alternative was suggested in 1942 by Ernst
Mayr, now retired from Harvard and one of the twentieth century's
great authorities on evolution.[10] He argued that a small group—such as
a flock of birds that had nested on an island at the outer edge of a large
population—might become isolated from the main group. Out of convenience, if nothing else, they might tend to reproduce among themselves
rather than to mix with the main group. Mutated genes, errant copies
of DNA, that cropped up in this small group would have a greater impact
on their offspring than if the mutations were diluted in the gene pool
of the main population.

Mayr argued further that since the environmental conditions at the
location of this offshoot group were likely to be distinct from those in
the home territory of the base population, natural selection might drive
evolution in the small group much faster than Darwin had envisioned.
A form of accelerated evolutionary change—still the product of the
Darwinian interplay of variation and natural selection—would be concentrated in small groups that had budded off from main populations.
The problem with his theory, Mayr admitted, was that it would be nearly
impossible to find fossil evidence of rapid transitions in tiny, isolated
populations. And, by the rules of science, a theory that cannot be tested
with hard facts isn't worth proposing in the first place.

But through a combination of dogged persistence and blind luck,
Eldredge found just such rare transitional fossils. The "missing pages"
in this trilobite story—transitional specimens that had somewhere be-

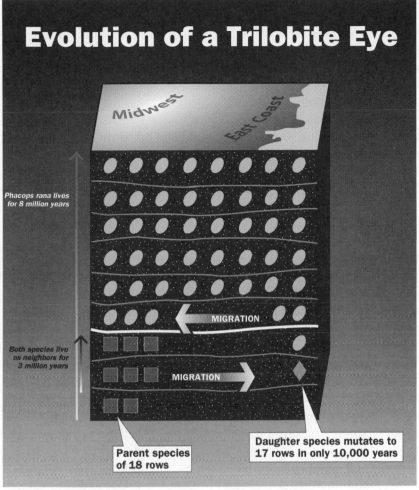

Evolution of a Trilobite Eye

Midwest

East Coast

Phacops rana lives
for 8 million years

Both species live
as neighbors for
3 million years

MIGRATION

MIGRATION

Parent species
of 18 rows

Daughter species mutates to
17 rows in only 10,000 years

Source: Eldredge, *Time Frames* (1985)

Figure 5.1

tween 17 and 18 complete rows of lenses—were discovered in a road gravel quarry dug into the hillside of a cow pasture outside the town of Morrisville, New York. The entire transitional series was embedded in a 35-foot-thick layer of sediments located in what had been the extreme northeastern edge of the ancient inland sea. The sediments had been laid down in less than 10,000 years, during the earliest days of *P.rana*'s eight-million-year existence.

Armed with this new evidence, Eldredge pieced together a plausible explanation of *P. rana*'s evolution. He argued that the 18-row version—the original parent species—lived in the western part of the inland sea, in what is now the midwestern United States. They then spread east to what is now New York. As Mayr suggested, the mutations that arose in this peripheral population led the New York trilobites to lose one row of eye lenses over the course of 10,000 years—time enough for thousands of trilobite generations, but just a brief moment in the expanse of evolutionary time.

After the transition was complete, the new 17-row version prospered throughout the East, spreading from New York down through the Appalachian region, while the parent 18-row species continued to flourish in the Midwest. For three million years, the two species lived as neighbors. Then the sea covering the Midwest dried up and killed off the 18-row parent species, leaving only the 17-row daughter species in the waters still covering the East.

After another million years, the sea inundated the Midwest once again. With the 18-row parent variety extinct and the trilobite niche in the ecosystem vacant, the 17-row daughter species expanded into the Midwest. Because there had been very little sedimentation during the dry spell, the shells of the first 17-row immigrants were deposited directly on top of the last of their 18-row ancestors. The "jump" from 18 to 17 rows found in Ohio and Ontario was not an evolutionary event at all. It was a misleading clue left by the extinction of a parent species and the subsequent in-migration of an offshoot daughter species.

In 1972, not long after the trilobite story came together, Eldredge joined with Stephen Jay Gould in publishing a scientific paper that laid out this explanation of evolutionary change. Gould had come to similar conclusions after studying an extinct species of snail that had lived in Bermuda. To describe the process of evolution as long periods of species stability intermittently disturbed by bursts of new species creation, Gould coined the phrase *punctuated equilibrium*. And even though not all biologists accept the punctuated-equilibrium version of evolution, many have become converts in the last two decades.[11]

Like all powerful theories, punctuated equilibrium explains so much so simply. It does not require belief in radical transformations from one generation to the next. And it does not insist, as Darwin did, that an entire species be modified at an incredibly slow pace—a pace that, it turns out, is too slow to account for the evolution of modern life even over 4.6 billion years of earth history.

Essentially, punctuated equilibrium says that evolutionary change happens neither overnight nor over millions of years, but rather in bursts that stretch for a few hundred or a few thousand years. It is pulsating evolution, a surge of relatively rapid change followed by a long period of stability or equilibrium. Punctuated equilibrium contends that once established, a species does not change. As long as it fits its ecological niche, there is no reason to change. If the environment changes, the species will migrate in an attempt to regain the ecological setting it needs. If the environmental shift is too extreme and migration fails, the species becomes extinct.[12]

But well before a species dies off in the normal course of events, small groups will drift away from the main population, either by getting lost during an annual migration or by simply wandering off in search of less crowded, greener pastures. If such a group is fortunate enough to find an acceptable place to live, it will survive in reproductive isolation. Over several generations, mutations will modify the physical characteristics of the group, transforming the parent species into a new daughter species.

As the environment continues to change, a daughter species may come upon an unoccupied niche in the ecosystem left by the extinction of the parent species. In such cases, the offspring species fills an ecological vacuum. In other cases, where this evolutionary process endows a daughter species with physical advantages over a parent species that is not yet extinct, the offspring may not wait for the parent species to disappear. It may invade the parent's home territory and aggressively compete it out of existence.

When the ebb and flow of evolution is viewed as a cross section cut into sedimentary rocks, the overlapping fossil layers make it appear as though change was sudden, even though it was not. By stressing the importance of change within small, geographically isolated populations, punctuated equilibrium makes sense of these confusing fossil patterns and imbues the concept of evolution with far greater explanatory power than it wielded when Darwin first proposed it. Punctuated equilibrium does not refute Darwin. It employs knowledge accumulated in the last century to refine and strengthen his epochal work.

Unlike Lamarck's theory of "acquired characteristics," Cuvier's catastrophism, or Darwin's gradualism, punctuated equilibrium does not need to ignore contrary facts. Building upon two centuries of vigorous inquiry and sometimes venomous argument about the nature of change, punctuated equilibrium neatly disposes of evolution's most troubling dilemmas. In short, this theory offers the most comprehensive and sensible explanation of organic change yet developed.

Even so, punctuated equilibrium does not answer every question about how organic change works. It's doubtful that any plainly stated concept ever will. The evolution of life is too vast and complex a subject. But in the last few years, the theory has helped biologists make better sense of evidence like Eldredge's trilobites, which did not fit previous theories.[13]

In the years since punctuated equilibrium was proposed, an array of related evidence has come in. David Raup of the University of Chicago has tracked the number of genuses (groups of closely related species) living over the course of earth history. Raup discovered a regular pattern of mass extinctions—once every 26 million years—intermixed with sporadic extinctions of less fatal power.[14]

Several competing theories have been proposed to explain the periodic global debacles. One suggests that a huge comet circles the sun once every 23 million years, causing a shower of asteroids to collide with the earth each time it goes past. Other scientists believe that clouds of dust from intense periods of volcanic activity regularly block out the sun, causing widespread death. Whatever caused these extinctions, none of them ever totally eliminated life. After each calamity, with life's slate wiped nearly clean, a dazzling array of new species burst forth from the handful that managed to survive.

The best example of this phenomenon of destruction and rebirth is recorded by the history of the ammonites, a coiled, snail-like creature of the ancient oceans. Like the trilobites, they fossilized easily and survived for more than 300 million years. In each epoch of their long history, a different group of species dominated ammonite life. And each great global extinction knocked out the vast majority of species in that family.

From the few that managed to squeak through each great dying, an entirely new ammonite family, with many subsidiary species, would sprout. Once established, these new species survived without modification for millions of years—until they too were wiped out. This pattern repeated itself until the Cretaceous extinction 65 million years ago, the disaster that finished off the dinosaurs along with the last of the ammonites.[15]

The ammonites' history shows that the tragedy of mass extinction is also the harbinger of new life. By clearing the land and the seas of most inhabitants, extinctions create wide-open ecological opportunities for the few species fortunate enough to have survived. Unimpeded by entrenched competitors, they find more food and space than they can use. Some of the mutant offspring that would have been weeded out quickly in a more competitive environment survive and reproduce.

It is as if extinctions temporarily suspend the stabilizing pressure of natural selection, permitting nature to experiment with new versions of life. Exploiting their evolutionary opportunity, these offspring repopulate the nooks and crannies of the earth's emptiness. As they do, small groups at the periphery of each population bud off, and an assortment of new species springs forth.[16]

In the past, many imagined evolution as a ladderlike progression from primitive to modern forms. But under punctuated equilibrium, particularly as influenced by intermittent extinctions, life's history seems more like a bush that has been pruned back severely from time to time.[17] After each pruning, a few branches survive. No longer shaded from the sun's life-giving energy or crowded by neighboring branches, they propagate new shoots in every direction. When the bush regains its fullness, vigorous competition resumes for nutrition and space. Growth slows and opportunities for the development of new branches diminish sharply. Mature stability characterizes the bush of evolving life until the next great dying prunes it back and restarts the cycle of organic innovation.

Although the bush may be a better metaphor for life's evolutionary structure than the ladder, some evidence suggests that a severe pruning need not precede each new form of life. In certain cases, a modest shift in the environment is enough to create a new ecological opportunity. One of the best examples of opportunistic species creation—speciation not preceded by a holocaust—occurred in East Africa's Lake Victoria. The lake is only about 750,000 years old, but it is home to 170 species of fish found nowhere else in the world. All the species are members of the cichlid genus. Some species eat only insects, others eat only fish larva, some specialize on mollusks, others just eat water plants, and some subsist solely on the scales of other fish. Each cichlid species has a mouth and digestive system optimized for its food source.[18]

The ancestral cichlid species still flourishes today. It is an unspecialized type with simple teeth that has lived unchanged in the rivers of Africa for millions of years. Apparently earth movements dammed up some of these rivers and formed Lake Victoria, one of the largest bodies of fresh water on the planet. Rather suddenly, a vast and uninhabited freshwater environment appeared out of nowhere. Unhampered by competition, the ancestral cichlids fanned out across Lake Victoria and turned wide-open ecological opportunity to their advantage.

Groups became reproductively isolated in this immense body of water, and genetic mutations interacted with distinct habitat conditions in the various parts of the lake to create an array of distinctive new species. Once Lake Victoria's potential cichlid niches were filled, natural selection strengthened, new speciation dropped off, and ecological stability was reestablished. The sudden blossoming of innovation was a natural response to opportunity.

CHAPTER
6
BRAINS AND TOOLS

When the earth formed, its superhot lava surface was exposed to the near-absolute-zero temperature of space. As it cooled, the surface congealed into a semisolid shell—think of the thick scum that forms atop a mug of hot chocolate on a winter night. The centrifugal forces of planetary spin and the moon's gravitational tug cracked the shell into segments, known as continental plates, that to this day continue to career into each other. Earthquakes and volcanoes offer terrifying proof of this ceaseless continental wandering.[1]

Africa, like the earth's other land masses, is comprised of a few of these massive plates. Roughly 15 million years ago, geologic turmoil began to lift the eastern edge of Africa. Eventually, the strain caused by the uplift ripped open a 3,500-mile-long north-south gash called the Great Rift Valley. In time, low-lying sections of this chasm filled with water and became the string of lakes that includes Lake Victoria.[2]

As East Africa rose to a higher elevation, its average temperatures declined. The steaming jungle that had blanketed the region gradually turned into a mosaic of dense forest, open woodlands, and rain-shadowed high plains. The breakup of East Africa's tropical forests accelerated again, around six million years ago, when the entire earth went through a pronounced cooling phase. Much of what remained of the rain forest became an archipelago of jungle islands scattered across an immense ocean of grasslands.

On this much, most scholars agree. But when discussion turns to the evolutionary drama that unfolded on this East African stage, the experts concur on rather little. This is perfectly understandable. Since systematic research into mankind's African origins has been underway for only about 35 years, today's collections of broken bones, skull fragments, teeth, and stone tools are far from complete.[3]

Physical evidence documenting the course of human evolution is so sparse that scientists must work like detectives reconstructing a primeval crime scene. With state-of-the-art dating techniques, scanning electron microscopes, and sophisticated statistical analyses, they squeeze tiny morsels of knowledge from mute objects. Despite the scientists' ingenuity and perseverance, a great many important questions remain unanswered. The complexity of the story and the scarcity of hard evidence allow different experts to come up with credible yet conflicting explanations of the same facts.[4]

Although no one yet knows precisely how human beings evolved from apes, the broad outlines of the story can be constructed from what *is* known. For example, by comparing DNA from humans and apes, it has been shown that our lineages split around five million years ago. About one million years later, as the fossil record indicates, the Australopithecines (southern apes) became the first primates to walk upright.[5] Perhaps they descended from apes marooned on a shrinking "island" of jungle in the midst of an East African grassland. Competition would have been intense in the jungle's interior, but along its edges, abundant food would have awaited any apes able to cope with the special challenges of a mixed forest/grassland habitat.

In an ecological niche previously uninhabited by primates, an upright stance could have been the key to survival. With hands freed to carry food, the Australopithecines would have enjoyed the best of both worlds—access to grasslands food sources unavailable to other apes as well as the safety of the forest for their young.[6]

Of the various Australopithecine species, those directly in our lineage survived until about 2.5 million years ago. It was sometime after this that Homo habilis (handy man)—the first animal considered to be a member of our genus—appeared on the East African scene. Anatomically, the Habilis differed from their forebears in several ways. The Australopithecines were only four feet tall, while the Habilis stood about a foot taller. Moreover, in the transition, the protruding snout of the Australopithecines became somewhat flattened, giving the Habilis a much more humanlike appearance.

But, without question, the most important change was the far larger brain of the Habilis. Australopithecine brains were only 30 percent of the size of a modern human brain, making these creatures about as intelligent as chimpanzees. Habilis brains, by contrast, were nearly half the size of modern brains. Greater brain mass, and the increased information-processing power it provided, made possible a survival strategy that no previous species had pursued—relying on tools to overcome innate biological limitations.[7]

In all likelihood, the earliest inventions were devices for carrying things. Pouches made of animal hide or trays made from tree bark would have made food carrying far more efficient. But unfortunately, because animal skins and wood do not leave fossils, we will never know when these crucial inventions occurred.

Stone tools, on the other hand, are virtually indestructible. Consequently, these ancient objects provide the bulk of the evidence on our ancestors' technologies. Through their variety and degree of specialization, and the sophistication of the techniques used to fabricate them, stone tools reveal how much technical knowledge our forebears possessed. Just as bones and shells are the fossilized remains of the genes they once carried, discarded tools are the fossilized form of the knowledge used in their manufacture.[8]

The very first stone tools—crudely but deliberately chipped rocks and pebbles—were made by the Habilis. Until recently, it was thought that the Habilis used tools to butcher hunted animals, but the present view is that man's early ancestors were scavengers, not hunters. After a pride of lions finished feasting on a kill of wildebeest or antelope, our forebears would move in, fending off the hyenas, jackals, and vultures. Often making their tools on the spot from stones found near the carcass, they used flaked stones to slice through the animal's hide and heavy rocks to crack open its marrow-filled bones.[9]

The Habilis survived for nearly one million years—roughly 70,000 generations. Their descendants, the *Homo erectus* (upright man), appeared around 1.6 million years ago, and were much like the Habilis. But, as in the previous transition from the Australopithecines, there was a major jump in brain size. Many anthropologists believe that the erectus—with brains 75 percent of the modern size—were intelligent enough to have language. But since the spoken word leaves no fossils, we probably will never know. It is certain, however, that the Erectus used fire, hunted small animals, and crafted stone tools that were far more sophisticated than the crude implements of the Habilis.[10]

The Erectus vanished roughly 500,000 years ago, when our immediate ancestors, the archaic *Homo sapiens* (wise man), made their debut. This species, whose brains were as large as ours, used stone tools that were even more elaborate than those of the Erectus. After several hundred thousand years, the Sapiens were supplanted by two daughter species. The dates of these transitions are hotly debated, but it seems that the

Neanderthals (*Homo sapiens neanderthalensis*) arose sometime before 230,000 years ago, while our own species—*Homo sapiens sapiens* (doubly wise man) emerged between 290,000 and 140,000 years ago.[11]

At present, the nature of our species' relationship with our closest evolutionary relatives is murky. For perhaps as long as 200,000 years, our ancestors and the Neanderthals lived in overlapping regions of Africa, Europe, and Western Asia, although they might not have inhabited these areas at the same times. Then, about 35,000 years ago, the Neanderthals suddenly disappeared from their last territories in Europe. The demise of our sister species coincides with our own invasion of Europe.[12]

Some believe that we killed off the Neanderthals. Others suggest that we outcompeted them in the hunt for big game. Although the Neanderthals had slightly larger brains, our higher foreheads gave us an enlarged frontal lobe, the area of the brain responsible for thinking ahead. Perhaps, in times of hardship or famine, this modest anatomical rearrangement provided us with a crucial competitive advantage.[13]

Of course, this view cannot explain why we shared the Old World with the Neanderthals for so long without destroying them. In this connection, it is worth noting that although many Neanderthal encampments have been studied carefully, no evidence of Neanderthal art has been found. Symbolic representations—whether animals drawn on cave walls or lunar calendars notched into animal bones—are associated exclusively with our species.

Perhaps that minor tweak of our brain's shape, along with some "rewiring," endowed our ancestors with a type of intelligence—the ability to comprehend visual symbols—not possessed by the Neanderthals. Once this latent intellectual potential was exploited by the invention of symbolic communication—say, 35,000 years ago—we would have quickly gained an overwhelming technological edge.[14]

When looking back over the course of human evolution, one can hardly miss the close relationship between brain development and technological change. Neither the biological nor the technological record shows a smooth and steady slope of progress. Instead, both seem to follow the punctuated-equilibrium pattern of evolution characterized by rapid bursts of change followed by long periods of stability.

With their dramatically enlarged brains, the Habilis were able to invent stone-tool technology, but, once invented, this tool kit shows no trend of gradual refinement. Instead, despite the passage of hundreds of thousands of years, both the Habilis's brain size and tool technology remained constant. Perhaps the invention of crudely chipped stones exhausted the intellectual potential of the Habilis.

With the appearance of the Erectus, stone-tool technology leaped to a new level of sophistication. But, once again, these tools show little sign of improvement, despite the passage of one million years. The next step up in technology awaited the emergence of the even-larger-brained archaic Sapiens. And finally, these tools remained virtually unmodified until the handiwork of our own species first appeared.[15]

Not surprisingly, the parallel patterns of "jump-stability-jump" in brain size and stone-tool sophistication have been the subject of much debate. One view holds that the intelligence and hand-eye coordination allowed by bigger brains were needed to manufacture better tools. Improved tools, in turn, gave our ancestors access to more and better food. According to this thinking, a self-reinforcing feedback loop—bigger brains, better tools, more food—drove forward the process of human evolution.[16]

For those who imagine the human species raising itself to global dominion by dint of intelligence, ingenuity, and hard work—a kind of Horatio Alger of the apes—the "brain–tools–food" logic is enormously attractive. And indeed, once this positive-feedback loop got going, being more intelligent proved to be a winning evolutionary strategy. But this view cannot explain why our predecessors' brains began to expand in the first place. The original makers of stone tools, the Habilis, had to have their enlarged brains *before* they could begin using them to make tools. Tool use could not have caused the first and most radical jump in brain size. Something else must have initiated the cycle of brain growth and tool use that ultimately spawned our species.[17]

According to Yale University's Elisabeth Vrba, that trigger was a wave of cold weather. Around 2.5 million years ago, about the time the Habilis appeared, the earth was at the peak of another massive cooling phase. East Africa's forests were fragmenting again, while the dry grasslands expanded. Many African mammal lineages, particularly the various families of antelope, underwent a simultaneous pulse of new species creation. According to Vrba, the Habilis were just one more new mammal species spun out by an ecosystem adjusting to a blast of frigid weather. Falling temperatures may be a less dramatic evolutionary stimulus than the evaporation of the trilobite's ancient North American sea or the flooding of the cichlid fish's Lake Victoria, but apparently it was stimulus enough.[18]

Professor Vrba has also speculated that the cold wave of 2.5 million years ago influenced the anatomical changes that transformed the Australopithecines into the Habilis. A new species cannot be too different from its immediate ancestor. Evolution is conservative. If a mutant offspring is to survive, it must represent only a slight modification of a proven genetic design.

Consequently, among closely related species, their differences often are merely variations in body size. The species living in colder climates tend to be larger than their warm-weather cousins. Large animals have proportionately less surface area for their body volume. This translates into energy savings, since fewer calories are lost to the environment as body heat. Simply put, larger animals are cheaper to maintain in cold weather.[19]

Of course, becoming physically larger has its drawbacks. First of all, it takes longer to reach full adult size. For this to happen, the entire sequence of life-cycle events—from infancy through puberty to senility—must be stretched out. If the body's genetically programmed "internal developmental clock" is not slowed, sexual maturity is reached too soon, before the animal has grown to full size. To avoid this, the animal must retain the physical attributes of a growing juvenile for an extended period. When the animal's growth finally stops, it tends to look remarkably like an overgrown, adolescent version of its ancestral species.

All of the amazingly intricate steps in an organism's development—worked out over millions of years of evolution—unfold in the normal order. No bold (and almost certainly fatal) genetic experiments are necessary. Only the timing of life's milestone events is altered. Mutation of the few genes regulating developmental timing allows nature to proliferate an array of species, each suited to different environmental conditions.[20]

With these facts in mind, describing the emergence of human beings as an example of evolution by punctuated equilibrium requires little imagination.[21] In a small, isolated population of Australopithecines, mutations cropped up in the genes controlling the developmental clock. Because this group happened to live in a particularly lush, underpopulated niche, they flourished despite the added costs of an extended childhood and delayed reproduction. After several thousand transitional generations, the adults in this group of early Habilis looked much like overgrown, juvenile versions of their Australopithecine forebears, complete with flattened faces and disproportionately large brains.[22]

As the cold spell of 2.5 million years ago reached its peak, natural selection increasingly favored these large-bodied animals. Natural selection drove the Australopithecines to extinction. But the Habilis, aided by a more energy-efficient body and crude tools, managed to survive. Ultimately, they migrated into areas formerly occupied by their Australopithecine ancestors.

Jolted onto a new evolutionary trajectory by frigid weather, our lineage began to be shaped by the feedback loop of bigger brains—better tools—more food. Over hundreds of thousands of years, incessant migrations must have spun off countless small bands that became genetically isolated. Nearly all of them perished. But for at least one group in each era, the process that generated the *habilis* repeated itself. Ever-larger, more juvenilized forms with spectacularly outsize brains became better makers and users of technology. Whenever selection pressure intensified, these creatures tended to survive more readily than their smaller, dim-witted cousins.

From the Habilis to the Erectus and on to the archaic Sapiens, the story of human evolutionary "progress" was, ironically, one of developmental retardation—of becoming ever more like our juvenile ape predecessors. A photo of a baby chimpanzee—with its high, domed forehead and flat face—always evokes a gasp of recognition. Of all the creatures on earth, we look most like nearly hairless, jumbo versions of infant chimpanzees.[23]

Remarkably, though, our most profound connection to immature versions of remote ancestors is not our looks but our behavior. Konrad Lorenz, the legendary Austrian-born ethologist, wrote that as we evolved and retained more of our juvenile forebears' physical characteristics, we also took on more of their behavioral traits. We became more inquisitive and less set in our ways. We became what Lorenz called a "creature of curiosity."

Curiosity supposedly "killed the cat," but it turned out to be a winning evolutionary strategy for our ancestors. Lorenz wrote,

> All purely material research conducted by a human scientist is pure inquisitive behaviour . . . it is *play behaviour*. All scientific knowledge—to which man owes his role as master of the world— arose from playful activities conducted in a free field entirely for their own sake. [Italics in original.][24]

By retaining the unquenchable curiosity of young apes throughout an ever-lengthening lifespan, our ancestors acquired the intellectual potential for discovery. But, of course, curiosity, in and of itself, did not lead to our "mastery of the world." After some playful rock smashing by a bored, young Habilis revealed a stone's sharp inner cleavages, someone had to pick up the shattered stone and use its edge to slice through an otherwise-impenetrable hide. An elephant's carcass, with its tons of meat and marrow, has no value to a starving man with only his fingertips for tools. For our species to survive, each step of playful discovery had to be followed by a step of purposeful innovation—using new knowledge to create value.

The "purpose" driving our ancestors' innovative behavior was not a striving for progress toward some cosmic goal. Our capacity for innovation did not make us a "better" or "higher" species. In biology, such terms hold no meaning. Because our genes evolved under different environmental pressures, we are simply different from chimps.[25]

Like every other biological phenomenon, innovative behavior has as its purpose survival itself. Given the earth's limited resources, every long-surviving lineage becomes more bionomically efficient, better adapted to the conditions of its environment. As a lineage evolves, its members waste less energy getting food and keeping warm. Their savings are put into producing more offspring—more copies of their genetic program. In biologists' jargon, this goal-directedness is called *teleonomy*—where the purpose of a genetic program is its own reproduction.[26]

Our lineage is unique because our anatomy allowed our ancestors to supplement their genetic evolution with technological evolution. Through creativity and innovation—behaviors made possible by the vastly enlarged brains of a strain of juvenilized apes—our ancestors were able to satisfy their most fundamental economic needs. The brains of our forebears became a living bridge connecting the ancient process of genetic evolution with the brand-new process of technological evolution. Up to this point in the earth's history, the only form of living information was nature's—the mechanism of DNA. But once the Habilis brain, itself a product of DNA, began to innovate, it launched an entirely new realm of living information.

Of course, none of this would have happened if the wobble in the earth's orbit that set off a cold snap 2.5 million years ago had triggered a heat wave instead. If intelligent, innovative creatures had ever evolved on earth, they would not be human beings. It is serendipitous that we are here. But here we are, nonetheless.

CHAPTER
7

TECHNOLOGY'S RHYTHM

Once recognized, the parallel pattern of biological and economic evolution that emerged with the appearance of the human lineage raises several questions. Why didn't the human brain continue to grow when technology rose above the primitive level of the hunter-gatherer age? If brain size and technical sophistication were linked for two million years, why were they disconnected in the last few thousand? How could the outer bounds of human knowledge suddenly be freed from the constraint of the brain's limited information-storage space and processing power? The answers must be related to our ability to store and process information outside our bodies.

One scholar has argued that when the amount of knowledge required to survive exceeded that which could be learned by a single individual, there was less selective pressure for individual increases in intelligence.[1] Once this threshold of accumulated knowledge had been crossed, natural selection began to act more upon groups than upon individuals. Survival no longer hinged on an individual's physical traits, but on the group's ability to discover and apply knowledge to life's problems. If this hypothesis is correct, it seems obvious that the ability to record information, even with the crudest symbols, would have played an important role in the lost events of prehistory.

Unfortunately, even though sophisticated writing systems existed throughout the agricultural era, detailed records of the history of technology were not kept. Even if literate people were aware of technical improvements in crop irrigation or animal husbandry, they were most unlikely to write about peasants' work. And although archaeologists know when various types of pottery, metal utensils, and other tools emerged, and how widely they spread, these objects by themselves cannot tell us how they came to be invented.[2] Only written records carry this kind of detailed information, and they were not kept until the early 1700s, with the first murmurings of the Industrial Revolution.

We know, for example, why Thomas Newcomen invented the atmospheric engine. Miners could not get at valuable ores without a better mine pump. We also know that the essence of his design, the piston and cylinder, probably was derived from experiments conducted by Denis Papin. Finally, we know that once Newcomen stumbled upon the secret of a powerful engine, its basic design did not change for 60 years, even though it was refined modestly.

For the economic need that the atmospheric engine was intended to satisfy, it performed quite well: Newcomen's engine fit its economic "niche." It employed state-of-the-art technology to meet a pressing economic need. At the time, no radical redesign was possible or necessary. Although laughably primitive by today's standards, the know-how of Newcomen and his associates, as embodied in the atmospheric engine, was appropriate for the economy of that time and place.[3]

In biological terms, we might think of a machine as a fossil representing the state of technological information at the time it was made, just as a shell or bone is a remnant of the state of genetic information at the time it was formed. Old machines, like ancient stone tools, crystallize the knowledge used in their design and manufacture. These artifacts, whether organic or economic, were themselves never alive. They are the durable by-products of the only thing that is ever truly alive—coded information.

It was the growth of knowledge during the decades between the Newcomen and Watt breakthroughs that allowed James Watt to redesign Newcomen's machine. By then, metallurgy and metal-machining techniques had advanced enormously, and scientific understanding of heat and energy was much improved. Catalyzed by Watt's creative genius, this enhanced body of human knowledge came together in the invention of the energy-saving steam engine.

Not surprisingly, Watt's initial commercial success was in the copper mines of Cornwall, where, because of high coal costs, Newcomen engines could not pay for themselves. The gross inefficiency of the Newcomen machine had confined it to the coalfields, where fuel was literally dirt cheap. In the language of punctuated equilibrium, Watt's engine budded off at the periphery of the Newcomen engine's economic range. In fact,

Watt was unsuccessful when his firm first tried to sell its engine to coal operators. The parent species was quite healthy and firmly entrenched in its home niche.[4]

Watt's invention of the condenser was a "mutation" of the information embodied by the Newcomen design. The radical improvement in energy efficiency provided by the steam engine allowed this new species of technical information to invade niches of the economic landscape that Newcomen's engine could never inhabit. But Watt's steam engine was not confined for long to these previously uninhabited niches. A few years after Watt's penetration of Cornwall's copper mines, a refined Watt engine—with even better fuel efficiency, power, and reliability—invaded the home territory of its parent technology and displaced Newcomen machines in one coal mine after another.

Eventually, no more Newcomen engines were built. The few atmospheric engines that continued operating did so only at coal mines whose economics were particularly insensitive to fuel costs. Finally, near the beginning of the twentieth century, the last Newcomen engine was taken out of service. The world's first self-powered machine had become extinct, competed out of existence by its daughter species.

From the beginning of the Industrial Revolution—as far back as we have precise information about economic matters—the record shows that technological progress is not smooth and gradual, but sporadic and disjointed.[5] Periods of stability and modest refinement are shattered by radical inventions that germinate at the outer edge of a technology's range of economic viability. From the stone tools of the Paleolithic era to the engines of the Industrial Revolution to the computers of the Information Age, technology seems to have always evolved in fits and starts. Like the genetic information embedded in trilobites, cichlid fish, and prehumans, the knowledge embodied in our technology may have no other way of changing.

For the past 60 years, economic historians have pummeled each other with arguments about the inherent pattern of economic change. Joseph Schumpeter, a prominent twentieth-century economist, claimed that innovation was sharply discontinuous, causing massive and sudden destruction of old industries by the new.[6] Schumpeter saw this "creative destruction of capital" as the central process of capitalism.[7] Others, led by A. P. Usher, pointed out that old industries usually prosper alongside new competitors for long periods of time. Usher stressed that when the great inventions are studied in detail, sudden "breakthroughs" are revealed to be little more than the final steps in a long chain of gradual technical refinements stretching over decades.[8]

Today, the experts are still choosing up sides in this debate between technologic catastrophists and gradualists. Never having studied biology, they remain unaware that punctuated equilibrium has resolved the 200-year-old debate over the pace of evolution by showing that sudden and gradual change coexist. Neither gradualism nor catastrophism allows us to understand the inherent nature of change, be it biologic or economic. In both realms, information change is cumulative. Rapid change happens at the edge, when a group of organisms becomes isolated from its main population. And it happens when a frustrated inventor grows tired of being told no, goes off by himself or with a few associates, and mutates the existing technology into something absolutely astonishing.

For those who want to understand how economic change works, the lessons of biologic and economic history are particularly instructive. Economic change driven by the syncopated rhythm of punctuated equilibrium is more powerful and pervasive in our own time than ever before. On every front, from electronics to aviation, agriculture, health care, and communications, great bursts of technological change are utterly transforming the human economy. Propelled by the computer's power to help the human brain manipulate complex information, business firms in thousands of obscure niches are participating in an awesome surge of economic speciation. In the 1990s, more new products and services are being introduced each year than were created during the entire nineteenth century.

Even though the pace of punctuated change is far faster than it once was, the fundamental processes of change remain the same. For example, engine technology did not stop evolving with the steam engine's conquest of the atmospheric engine. When Watt added rotating linkage to his steam engine, and supplemented the reciprocating motion of pumps with rotating power, a vast range of steam-engine applications opened up. Rotating linkage—considered by Watt to be his greatest invention—allowed steam engines to invade economic habitats remote from mine pumping. From factories to steamships to railroads, the concepts embodied in Watt's rotating steam engine were essential knowledge ingredients in the nineteenth-century economic revolution that reshaped human existence.[9]

But even Watt's great invention was not the answer to every need. Engine technology lurched forward again in 1876, when Nikolaus Otto, a self-taught German engineer, revised Denis Papin's piston-and-cylinder concept once more by using exploding petroleum gases instead of condensing steam to drive the piston.[10] Otto's engine was designed for circumstances not well served by the steam engine. Some users had wanted an engine that, unlike a steam engine, could be started or stopped quickly. Others had dreams of a self-powered carriage but were stymied by the tremendous weight of steam engines.[11] These needs simply could not be met given the inherent limitations of steam technology.

After decades of engineering refinement to solve the problems of fuel handling, ignition, control, and cooling, Otto's new species of the piston-and-cylinder lineage became the modern internal-combustion engine. Otto's engine did not drive Watt's engine to extinction, but steam engines are now viable in only a small portion of their former economic range. Otto's design made possible the automobile, the airplane, and hundreds of other twentieth-century "necessities." Today, in specialized applications, ceramic and "orbital" engines appear to be budding off from traditional internal-combustion engine designs. Evolution never stops.

The punctuated equilibrium of unexpected, erratic change across an immense variety of technologies is terribly frustrating for those who want to plan and control the economy. The intrinsic unpredictability of technological evolution makes a mockery of every effort to plan the future. Just as random events reshape the natural environment and cause genetic mutations that set off bursts of speciation, serendipitous discoveries launch new industries. Most recently, the world's physicists were flabbergasted by the discovery of superconductive ceramics that have almost no electrical resistance at near-normal temperatures. The rush to exploit this stunning breakthrough has just begun. Which economist can predict with certainty how the economy and society will be reshaped by this amazing new knowledge?[12]

The plain facts of daily economic life weigh heavily on the worn-out nineteenth-century economic ideologies that undergird the politics of both the Left and the Right. Even diehard Marxists now admit that what Marx wrote might not be applicable to modern economies. Similarly, many Western economists acknowledge that they have precious little to say about the role of technology in economic change. And while a few recent academic works have explored the similarities between biological evolution and economic change, for now, at least, orthodox Newtonian economics still reigns supreme.[13]

And yet, the sensational political changes now underway around the globe reveal the immutable power of economic forces that classical thinking cannot explain. After decades of bitter experience, the world's socialist countries have discovered that when people are denied the opportunity to satisfy their self-interest, the natural processes of technical advance collapse. Reluctantly, the leaders of these nations have come to realize that only by dismantling the bureaucratic superstructure of state planning will there be any hope of revitalizing their moribund economies. None of them realize it, but, by moving to capitalism, these countries are unshackling the natural phenomena of economic evolution.

A less dramatic, though related process of economic liberalization has been changing the face of Western Europe. For most of the cold-war era, these nations relied on the nationalization of key industries and strict regulation to control their economies. But, plagued by technological stagnation and persistent unemployment, the allure of conscious economic planning gradually faded. For the last decade, from Great Britain to Italy, governments have been selling off state-owned firms and relaxing regulations.

In the Third World, nations that gained their independence in the 1950s and 1960s—before the results of the cold war's "capitalist vs. socialist" economic experiment were in—are realizing that sovereignty and socialism are not synonymous. Third World leaders have watched attentively as Japan, South Korea, Taiwan, Hong Kong, Singapore, and other once desperately poor nations have risen to world prominence.[14] By now, with the collapse of Soviet and Eastern European economies, everyone knows that capitalism works better. But because the evolutionary nature of economic change is not yet recognized, no one can convincingly explain *why*.

Unless the spontaneous, unpredictable character of evolutionary economic change is understood, there is a strong possibility that many of today's economic reforms ultimately will be undone. Needless policy errors will trigger political backlashes and demands for a return to the "good old days" of heavy-handed government control. Should this happen, real human beings will lose the opportunity to improve their lives and their communities. Avoiding such pitfalls demands a full appreciation of the organic nature of the human economy.

So far, we have seen how both biologic and economic life evolved from tiny scraps of ordered information and how they each blossomed into phenomenally complex systems. We have surveyed the grand sweep of their parallel histories. But to comprehend completely the nature of the economy, we must understand how it functions as a vibrant ecosystem on a daily basis. Only after this is achieved will we gain the perspective needed to select public policies that nurture rapid and sustained economic growth.

PART II

ORGANISM
AND
ORGANIZATION

Changes in function require new forms;
new forms foster further changes in function.
—*Abbott Payson Usher (1954)*[1]

8

FORM AND FUNCTION

Buried in the back of *Linscott's Directory of Immunological and Biological Reagents*—after a hundred pages listing monoclonal antibodies, gamma globulins, enzymes, and assorted venoms—is a section entitled "Normal Human Cell Lines." If you happen to be in the market for human liver or pancreas cells, or even embryonic brain cells, you'll find they are as readily available as a pair of silk pajamas from Bloomingdale's.

Linscott's Directory is a specialized industrial catalog used by biomedical researchers. To the uninitiated, the idea of buying human cells by mail order seems a bit ghoulish. Then again, research supply houses aren't selling whole human beings, just tiny pieces of the dead. Using state-of-the-art cell-culture techniques, the cells are bathed in nutrients and stimulated to keep growing and redividing. The donors' corpses may be moldering in the grave, but their marketable cells remain very much alive.

Somehow the idea that human cells can live on after their "owner" dies conflicts with our innate sense of what a human being is. Try as we might, we simply cannot think of the fellow sitting across the aisle as an assemblage of 10,000 billion cells that just happens to be arranged in a familiar shape. Nonetheless, from the biologist's perspective, the cell is of utmost importance, because the cell is where life's real action takes place, where genetic information turns chemicals and energy into living tissue.

The same is true in the economy. A huge multinational corporation is, on close inspection, a confederacy of thousands of specialized "work cells." Just as every complex organism is comprised of cells organized in tissues and organs, large firms are composed of work cells arranged in hierarchies of departments and divisions. As in nature, all the critical life-giving functions take place inside individual cells, where people use knowledge to transform resources into goods and services.[2]

Because of their size and influence, the great corporations—the behemoths of the economy—grab the headlines. But the overwhelming majority of organizations, and organisms, are minuscule. Ice-cream parlors, hair salons, plumbing contractors, and family farms are microbes of the economy. Like single-celled creatures, such firms are incredibly numerous and diverse, but, because of their minute size, they seem unimportant to casual observers. Nonetheless, whether work cells are clumped together as complex organizations or live independently as small firms, they are all essential to economic vitality.

The biologic and economic systems owe their similarity of form to their similarity of function. In nature, organisms convert genetic information into tissues. In the economy, organizations turn technological information into products. Since both information realms are constrained by limited resources, they evolved similar ways of efficiently turning resources into more information.

Over time, the changing shapes of organisms reflect the evolution of their genetic codes. Dramatic genetic change—like the invention of sexual reproduction—led to the redesign of the entire ecosystem. In an analogous way, the evolution of technology compels the restructuring of organizations. Particularly significant technical advances—such as the invention of the microprocessor—can set off changes that reverberate throughout the global economy. Once the profound likeness of organisms and organizations is appreciated, it is easier to understand the forces presently propelling economic restructuring in the Soviet Union and elsewhere.

Until quite recently, drawing a convincing parallel between organisms and organizations was impossible because the incredibly tiny dimensions of cells prevented biologists from learning much about the inner workings of organisms. A typical plant or animal cell is just 10 to 30 microns (millionths of a meter) in diameter. The naked eye cannot detect objects smaller than 100 microns across. Until the 1880s, microscopes were not powerful enough to reveal much useful information about cells, and even then, scientists could observe only the broadest outlines of cellular life. It wasn't until the late 1950s that the electron microscope began providing biologists with a view of the ultraminiaturized chemical factory packed inside every living cell.[3]

No two cells are exactly alike in every detail. But if you could see inside an "average" cell—perhaps one located in the tip of your tongue—what you would observe would be quite typical of the action inside any cell. In fact, except for bacteria, all cells in all organisms work essentially the same way. First, every cell has a nucleus, a bubblelike membrane that floats within the larger bubble of the cell's surface membrane. The nucleus is the largest of the tiny organs (organelles), that populate a cell's interior. During cell reproduction, the nucleus orchestrates the copying of DNA. But most of the time, the nucleus serves as the cell's genetic library, preserving its precious copy of DNA.

To translate genetic code into living tissue, the protein blueprints recorded in the DNA molecule must be transmitted to the cell's protein-building machinery. But instead of shipping the cell's single original set of genes out of the nucleus, DNA uses a similar molecule—RNA—to make a partial, temporary copy of itself. Like a photocopy of a vital diagram in a book that cannot be removed from the library, each RNA molecule is a copy of a protein design embedded in a DNA molecule that cannot leave the nucleus.[4] And just as libraries have photocopying rooms, the nucleus has special areas where RNA molecules are produced.

Once the blueprint of a particular protein is copied into RNA, the molecule slips through a pore in the nuclear membrane and out into the body of the cell, headed for a protein assembly site (ribosome). At a ribosome, the linear code carried by RNA is translated into the three-dimensional shape of a protein molecule. Pure information is given physical form. Just as a pile of loose bricks is assembled into walls of specific dimension according to a blueprint, free-floating amino acids are assembled into the proteins called for by DNA. Disorder yields to order.[5]

Before protein assembly begins, raw materials brought in from outside the cell must be prepared. Food molecules—proteins and carbohydrates—are taken in through the cell's surface membrane and shipped to organelles that serve as minuscule "stomachs." Known as lysosomes, these spheres are loaded with powerful digestive enzymes.[6] Working like chemical scissors, enzymes snip long food molecules into manageable pieces. Carbohydrates are cleaved into simple sugar molecules, and proteins are disassembled into their components—amino acids.

Essentially, a cell takes amino acids recovered from food proteins and reassembles these building blocks into proteins of its own. All of life's structures and chemical reactions depend upon the interplay of proteins. The protein assembly process begins when a freshly made RNA molecule arrives at a ribosome. Much as a factory robot reads the step-by-step instructions in a computer program, a ribosome reads off the sequence of amino acids called for by the RNA's genetic code. As one end of the

Parallel Flow of Production

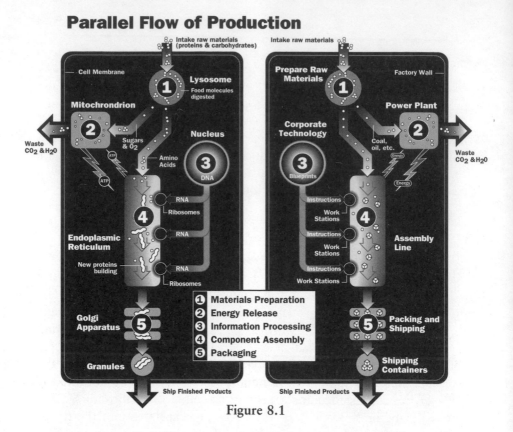

Figure 8.1

ribosome ratchets along the RNA molecule, the other end grabs nearby free-floating amino acids and snaps them onto the lengthening chain of a protein molecule. A protein generally contains between 40 and 1,000 amino acids. Depending upon the exact sequence of these acids, the protein will twist and fold itself into a unique shape.[7]

Most of a cell's ribosomes are embedded in the walls of a long, flattened tunnel called the endoplasmic reticulum (ER). Amino-acid components flow into one end of the ER and are spewed out the other as protein products. Since the thousands of ribosomes lining the walls of the ER tunnel can simultaneously read different sets of RNA instructions, they can concurrently assemble many kinds of proteins. As protein filaments are completed by the ribosomes, they drift toward the exit of the ER tunnel. After its message is communicated, an RNA molecule dissolves, leaving the ribosome vacant and ready to assemble the next design sent down by the cell's DNA.[8]

At their last stop before shipment, the proteins enter another organelle—the Golgi Apparatus. The Golgi is made up of several membrane-enclosed sacs, flattened and stacked like hollow dinner plates. Much as nearly completed products move through the final processing stations in a factory, the proteins travel from one enzyme-filled sac to the next. In each sac, they undergo chemical alterations that serve as labels, earmarking particular proteins for specific destinations. Once labeled, the Golgi sorts the proteins into batches and packs them into membrane-lined shipping containers called granules.[9]

Some granules are dispatched to distant regions of the cell where proteins are needed in the repair or replacement of worn-out organelles. In growing or reproducing cells, proteins are shipped to the sites where new construction is underway. In multicell organisms, granules often carry proteins destined for export to neighboring cells that specialize in the production of other proteins. In a reversal of the process that first brought raw materials into the cell's interior, the granules migrate to the cell's surface membrane, fuse with it, and unload their proteins outside the cell.[10]

None of these steps happens spontaneously. Every molecular manipulation requires energy. To keep the organelles along the protein assembly line working, sugar molecules are incinerated in the cell's power plants, the mitochondria. When the sugar molecules are completely burned, only carbon dioxide and water remain as wastes. The electricity released by this reaction recharges a special protein, the "organic battery" known as ATP. Freshly charged ATP molecules are shipped throughout the cell, wherever work is underway. Once an ATP molecule has delivered its energy, it is recycled back into a mitochondrion for recharging.[11]

All plant and animal cells use this suite of five organelles for information processing (nucleus), materials preparation (lysosome), component assembly (ribosome), protein packaging (Golgi), and energy release (mitochondria). The chief distinction between plant and animal cells is that plant cells are equipped with an extra set of organelles called chloroplasts. The inner chambers of chloroplasts contain chlorophyll— the protein that gives plants their green color. In an intricate series of reactions, chlorophyll snares electrical energy from sunlight and uses it to weld carbon dioxide and water into sugar molecules.[12]

With the energy of trapped sunlight flowing back and forth between them, chloroplasts build sugars up and mitochondria tear them down. Because plants provide their mitochondria with sugars made inside their own chloroplasts, they are self-feeders. By contrast, since animal cells lack chloroplasts, they are forced to gather energy by eating the sugars lodged in the tissues of plants and prey. The energy flowing between these complementary organelles drives each cell's protein-manufacturing line and makes life possible.

Because all cells are built along the same lines and work in the same way, it is hard to imagine how they form such an incredibly diverse array of organisms. By modifying the "standard" cell module, all the amazingly specialized features of living things become possible. For instance, in the human body, one set of DNA generates roughly 180 different cell types. The designs for all 180 cell types are inscribed in the genetic code carried by every cell. Somehow, as the body develops from fertilized egg to mature adult, the DNA in each cell "knows" which design to execute as it erects a cell around itself. By emphasizing the production of certain proteins and the construction of particular organelles, the same DNA builds cells of astonishing diversity.[13]

For example, the instructions for assembling a hemoglobin protein, the oxygen-carrying molecule in red blood cells, account for less than 0.0002 percent of the information encoded in human DNA. But 95 percent of a red blood cell's substance is hemoglobin. By exaggerating hemoglobin production, every red blood cell turns into a device dedicated to the transportation of oxygen.[14]

Similarly, some of the embryonic cells that wind up inside the pancreas—an organ that specializes in the production of digestive enzymes—develop unusually large and productive protein assembly lines. In fact, these ER/ribosome/Golgi complexes occupy the bulk of the space inside pancreas cells. Aside from the nucleus, a few mitochondria, and lysosomes, most of the rest of the cell is crowded with granules containing digestive enzymes ready for export.[15]

By contrast, heart muscle cells have withered protein assembly lines. Instead, they are packed with oversized mitochondria wrapped around parallel bundles of long protein fibers that stretch from one end of the cell to the other. A special feature of each cell's membrane attaches its internal fibers to those of its immediate neighbors. When energized by ATP, these protein fibers contract spontaneously. Linked end to end, billions of cardiac cells form the powerful heart muscle that pumps blood with each pulse.[16]

From human being to willow tree to grasshopper to sea slug, the same method of cell differentiation holds true. By commanding the production of different proteins and mixes of organelles in its various cells, DNA reshapes life's standard cell into structures of awesome complexity. But beneath the rampant diversity, the basic structure and the production process of every cell are the same.[17]

With few deviations, these principles of form and function apply to economic organizations. Underlying the complexity, there is a universal pattern of organization. Inside every work cell, people use tools and knowledge to turn energy and materials into products. Whatever the product happens to be, the flow of production mimics the protein-building process of organic cells: prepare the incoming materials, rearrange their components into new configurations, and package them into deliverable products.

In a simple organization, like a downtown delicatessen, the parallel to a single-cell organism is straightforward. Rye bread and pastrami are sliced, assembled into sandwiches according to a recipe, garnished with pickles, and wrapped in white paper for delivery. Energized by the electricity flowing through the deli's equipment and the labor of its workers, the process grinds out one sandwich after another.

At each sequential step, a worker using a tool (knife, slicer, scale, cash register) performs a necessary function. In effect, a worker/tool combination acts like an organelle inside an economic cell. But unlike organic organelles, human workers can pick up different tools, learn new skills, quit their cells, join others, and change their roles in the life of the economy. This flexibility, along with the rapid pace of technical evolution, endows the economy with capacity for lightning-fast restructuring.

Even in major corporations that make exceedingly complicated products, the basic pattern of production remains the same. But, as in large organisms, the work is divided up among groups of highly specialized cells, with the products of one group becoming inputs for another. On a far larger scale, but in a familiar sequence of steps, technical information reshapes materials and energy into final products. Organizations that possess the most advanced technologies make the most sophisticated products.

Today, perhaps the highest of high-technology products is the microprocessor—the so-called computer-on-a-chip. In keeping with Charles Babbage's original nineteenth-century design, a computer must include five basic components: a program input device (keyboard), an output display (video screen or printer), a controller, a memory, and a central processor. Of the five, the processor is by far the most complex. It is the heart of the beast—the place where the arithmetic and logical computations are actually performed. A *micro*processor squeezes a computer's most complicated circuitry onto a single sliver of silicon.[18]

Dozens of large organizations, scattered throughout the industrial nations, compete in the various niches of the microprocessor business.[19]

Each firm has its strengths and weaknesses, but one company, the Intel Corporation of Santa Clara, California, is probably the most highly regarded microprocessor maker in the world. Not only did Intel invent the microprocessor in 1971, it has managed to stay at the cutting edge of microprocessor technology ever since.[20]

At present, Intel's most important microprocessor product is the "386," the chip that serves as the computing engine inside millions of high-performance desktop computers. The product was introduced in 1985, but Intel began working on it three years earlier. The 386 project kicked off with a small group—just a half-dozen top engineers—charged with responsibility for resolving the major design issues. Trading off the technical constraints of chip size, power consumption, processing speed, manufacturing cost, compatibility with earlier designs, and a host of other issues, this initial work cell defined the basic architecture of the 386.

In the months that followed, this team grew to include several dozen members, all highly trained specialists in the disciplines of circuit design, logic design, layout, microcode, and computer architecture. As the design group expanded, it subdivided into small teams, each dedicated to a specific portion of the 386. These engineering cells translated the concepts of the original team into detailed product specifications. After the expenditure of 150 man-years and more than $100 million, the design group distilled its ideas into a final set of 11 blueprints.[21]

A microprocessor's blueprints are like the genetic code defining a protein. And just as DNA never leaves the cell's nucleus, the 386's original blueprints never leave Intel's tightly guarded headquarters. Instead, like the RNA molecules that carry DNA's instructions, blueprint copies—called photomasks—are used to transmit the design to the factory. To produce a photomask, a table-size blueprint is photographed and, using reduction lenses, shrunk down to the chip's actual dimensions—about the size of a newborn's fingernail. Then, 200 of these miniaturized images are laid out in a grid pattern on the glass plate of a photomask. The 386 chip requires 11 photomasks, one for each blueprint.

If a 386 chip were blown up to a size that permitted easy, walk-through inspection, it would resemble an enormous, low-slung office building covering several square miles and standing 11 stories high. Portions of each floor are dedicated to particular computing functions. Since silicon "real estate" is incredibly expensive, designers cram as many electronic "cubicles" as possible onto each floor. By juggling the locations of "elevator shafts" and "hallways," and by positioning certain computing functions near each other, designers shorten the average distance that electrons must travel as they zip around inside the chip.

Because the 386's electronic "cubicles" are so tiny, microscopic particles of airborne dust are large enough to short out the chip's circuitry. Consequently, the entire manufacturing process takes place inside "clean rooms"—hermetically sealed factories where elaborate filtration systems keep the air a thousand times purer than in the best hospital operating rooms. At Intel's newest factory, outside Albuquerque, New Mexico, technicians clothed in lint-free outfits work under extremely strict procedures to maintain an environment that is virtually particle-free. Using some of the most sophisticated, precise, and expensive manufacturing machinery in the world, these workers take incoming raw materials and turn them into chips ready for packaging.

The chip assembly process begins with a thin, circular wafer of pure silicon, about six inches in diameter. The top side of the wafer is first coated with a light-sensitive chemical called a photoresist. Then the photomask, with 200 tiny layouts of the chip's first floor, is placed over the coated wafer. Inside a special machine, an intense light is shone through the mask and onto the wafer. Wherever floor-plan features block the light, the silicon is unaffected. But in those areas exposed to the light, the photoresist becomes chemically active and eats away the layer of silicon directly beneath it. After treatment in a chemical bath, microscopic inspection reveals 200 identical copies of the chip's first-level floor plan neatly etched into the wafer's surface.

Not unlike the step-by-step protein assembly in a ribosome, the same sequence is repeated 11 times, once for each floor. As each cycle begins, the wafer is covered with a fresh layer of material, coated with photoresist, exposed to light through a photomask, and etched in a chemical bath. The blueprints are sculpted into the wafer as it builds up level by level. In the 386, the top two floors are etched out of aluminum, because these levels serve as the chip's power grid, feeding electricity into the computational "cubicles" on the lower floors. Just as the genetic code carried by RNA is converted into a protein's three-dimensional shape, the technical information encoded by the blueprints is transformed into the three-dimensional shape of a chip. In both cases, pure information attains physical structure.

The last stages of 386 production resemble the finishing steps that take place in a cell's Golgi Apparatus. In a plant located in Manila, the chips are electronically tested, wired inside ceramic packages, labeled with Intel's logo and part number, and arranged in trays for shipment. As orders are received, Intel ships its finished 386 chips to customers all over the world. At each customer site, the production sequence is repeated yet again. The 386s are combined with other incoming components and assembled into complete computers. Eventually, the computers are purchased by final customers, who use them to handle the information needed in their own production processes.

The entire global economy is comprised of work cells and organizations engaged in the interdependent production and exchange of products. Regardless of size or level of technological sophistication—from the corner delicatessen to the world's leading microprocessor firm—all organizations cope with essentially the same tasks that face a single living cell. Encoded information is developed and preserved in DNA or blueprints. Copies are shipped to ribosomes or assembly sites. After raw materials are prepared, components are reassembled in new configurations. In a series of finishing steps, these objects are packaged into deliverable products. From protein to microprocessor, the essentials of organic and economic production are the same.

CHAPTER
9

DESIGN BY COMPROMISE

With specialized organelles handling each crucial step in life's chemical rearrangements, nature seems to have come up with the ultimate architecture for life's central challenge—transforming information into physical substance and back again into more information. Form and function appear so seamlessly integrated that it's hard to imagine a better design. But, as any engineer or architect will confirm, there is no such thing as a perfect design. Every solution represents an unhappy compromise among conflicting objectives. Some designs are less inefficient than others, but none are perfect.

Because every bit of genetic code must be physically recorded by molecules, the proliferation of life is constrained by the availability of the earth's finite material resources. Consequently, if information is to flourish, it must use these resources as efficiently as possible. The structure of the cell reflects nature's efforts to squeeze the most living information from a fixed amount of chemicals.

Until fairly recently, few people thought of the cell as a chemical factory designed for optimal efficiency, because no one had the tools to examine the machinery inside the cell. Except for the nucleus, which is relatively large and easy to see under a conventional light microscope, no one knew exactly what all the other organelles were or what they did. But once the electron microscope and advanced biochemical techniques were introduced in the 1960s, biologists were able to resolve a host of previously unanswerable questions.

Of these mysteries, the most fascinating involved the evolution of the cell's complex structure. Obviously, the array of superminiaturized chemical-processing stations inside the cell did not appear full blown.

92 ·ORGANISM AND ORGANIZATION

The cell, with its collection of precisely engineered organelles, must have evolved from something simpler. But no one knew what those predecessors were or how they had turned into cells. These questions are still not resolved to the satisfaction of all biologists, but most experts now accept a theory of cellular evolution. Adapted to the economic realm, the same theory provides crucial insights into the development of economic organizations.

The modern theory of the cell's origin began by challenging a basic dogma of biology. For centuries, the "great divide" in biology classified all living things as members of either the plant or the animal kingdom. Considering the obvious differences between plants and animals, these categories seemed the logical way to begin any classification of organisms. All life-forms—except for a few nettlesome single-cell organisms with mixed characteristics—seemed to divide themselves neatly into the realms of botany and zoology. But the electron microscope showed that plant and animals cells were virtually identical—except for the presence or absence of chloroplasts. In short, plants and animals were much closer evolutionary relatives than biologists had ever imagined. Neither one could be the ancient forebear of the other.

Electron-microscope studies also revealed that the most radical differences in cell design separated bacteria (prokaryotic cells) from all other cells (eukaryotic cells). The cells of plants and animals are gargantuan—several thousand times larger than the average bacterium. And while plant and animal cells are packed with organelles, bacteria contain no organelles.[1]

The enormous differences between bacteria and all other cells led several biologists to contend that this was the true "great divide" among organisms. Relying on recently discovered fossils showing that bacteria predated the first cells by two billion years, these scientists argued further that bacteria must have been the ancestors of cells. Their case was strengthened by subsequent research that revealed close physical similarities between mitochondria and chloroplasts and certain strains of bacteria. Taken together, the evidence is now convincing that the modern cell began as a collaboration of ancient bacteria.[2]

But why did some bacteria organize into interdependent communities? After all, bacteria had survived quite nicely for more than two billion years as self-sufficient, single-cell organisms. Why bother with the complications of working together? No one can say for sure, but a reasonable guess suggests that groups of cooperating bacteria were more biochemically efficient than their independent bacterial brethren.[3]

Remember that the ultimate function of any organism is to copy the information encoded in its DNA. To do this, the cell must manipulate matter and energy. If it performs the necessary biochemical manufacturing steps ineffectively, the cell wastes precious resources. A haphazardly organized cell squanders much of the food it consumes. Scarce resources that could have been turned into copies of the cell's DNA dissipate back into the environment. Fewer DNA copies means fewer offspring and longer odds against survival. Over time, natural selection favors genes that build and operate structures that more efficiently convert resources into more DNA.[4]

When it comes to efficiency, the highly compartmentalized structure of cells gives them a big edge over bacteria.[5] A cell's organelles isolate chemical reactions that otherwise would interfere with one another, allowing each step to proceed far more smoothly.[6] The breakdown of food molecules inside lysosomes obviously requires different chemical steps than the assembly of proteins in the ribosomes. Similarly, each of the Golgi's sacs contains the special enzymes needed for labeling and packaging proteins. Chloroplasts are designed to capture the sun's energy as mitochondria are crafted to release it. Through an elaborate internal division of labor—where each organelle is tailored to perform one crucial function—the cell boosts its overall efficiency.[7]

In light of the efficiency gains provided by specialized compartments, it seems reasonable that bacteria should have evolved their own internal compartments. And although bacteria do have inner structures, no bacteria approach the complexity of a modern cell. Perhaps, given their incredibly tiny dimensions, bacteria were unable to construct sophisticated organelles that made economic sense. At such a minuscule scale, the efficiencies provided by elaborate organelles would likely have been overwhelmed by the "capital" costs of erecting such internal vessels.[8]

If bacteria were too small to boost their efficiency markedly by setting up complex internal compartments, their only alternative would have been to cooperate—a form of external compartmentalization. Over millions of years, these loose confederacies of ancient bacteria evolved into the tightly integrated system of organelles that comprise modern cells. By this reasoning, the modern cell evolved as nature's way of squeezing more gene copies from a given amount of resources.[9]

Perhaps, aided by their extra margin of efficiency, cells were able to survive in certain niches—such as tidal pools, which became a bit chilly at night—that ancient bacteria could not tolerate. If this is true, the early cell's ability to eke out a living in niches inhospitable to bacteria was a crucial development in evolutionary history, because bacteria already had fully populated the least complicated niches. Competition for resources in these long-settled habitats was extremely intense. Like seedlings on the shaded floor of a densely forested valley, the precursors of modern cells had little chance to prosper in these crowded conditions. But if chance happened to sweep a few cells to a frontier niche that was not too severe, those cells would have experienced the extraordinary opportunities for growth and reproduction enjoyed by all successful pioneers.[10]

The contrast between crowded, easy niches and vacant, challenging niches propelled an evolutionary trend toward organisms of increasing complexity. Once single-celled organisms had occupied the niches in which they could survive, the remaining open niches demanded organisms of even greater efficiency. Following the pattern first set by co-operating bacteria, some single-celled organisms gave up their independent lifestyles and stuck together to form the first multicelled creatures. Life had discovered that when it comes to efficiency, there's always room at the top.[11]

Differentiation among cells in these original multicelled organisms was almost undetectable. But, as time passed, the forces of variation and natural selection worked their evolutionary magic. As DNA evolved the technology of cell differentiation, sister cells in multicelled organisms took on dedicated roles—just as primitive bacteria had evolved into specialized organelles. Bolstered by the efficiency gains yielded by compartmentalization, these microscopic multicelled creatures were able to colonize niches that had been beyond the reach of their single-celled predecessors.[12]

To exploit fully the potential of complexity, the outer limit of organism size increased steadily. Trilobites—giants by the standards of the early Cambrian era—were dwarfed by the dinosaurs that emerged 500 million years later. But because life was buffeted by intermittent mass extinctions, climatic changes, and a host of other shocks, evolutionary history shows no simple trend in scale from tiny to immense.

Instead, multicellular life's most impressive feature has been its tendency to branch into an ever-more-amazing array of species. New species came in all sizes. As each species emerged, it created more convoluted ecologic relationships and new niches for other organisms. Endlessly shifting evolutionary pressures reshuffled collections of cells into organisms of every conceivable size and shape.

Organic tissues were molded by natural selection to fit any niche that could support the reproduction of more genetic information. From the Arctic tundra to deep ocean trenches, life proliferated into virtually every corner of the sea, land, and air. Long before the first *Homo sapiens*

Parallel Compartmental Structure

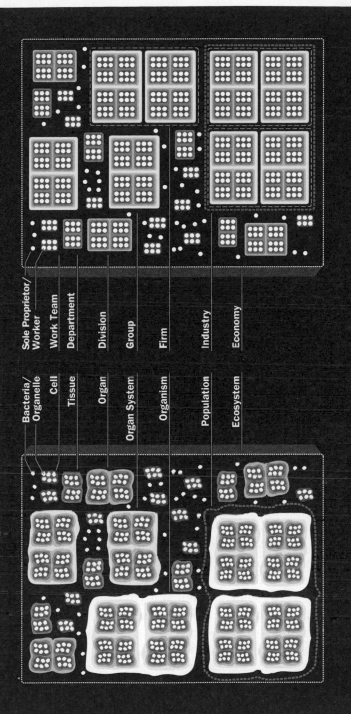

Bacteria/Organelle	Sole Proprietor/Worker
Cell	Work Team
Tissue	Department
Organ	Division
Organ System	Group
Organism	Firm
Population	Industry
Ecosystem	Economy

Figure 9.1

appeared, the trend toward increased efficiency and complexity had produced a stunningly diverse and robust global ecosystem—the result of genetic information's inexorable drive to insinuate itself into every possible opening.

Every fundamental trend eventually runs up against an equally potent counterforce. In the case of the trend toward greater complexity, the constraint was the cost of coordination. A bacterium may be a primitive life-form—little more than a bubble of "living juice" bathing a short strand of DNA—but its very simplicity is its strength. With genetic instructions and the necessary chemistry right next to each other inside a single membrane, a bacterium requires no complicated coordinating apparatus.

By contrast, a cell requires an incredibly complicated system of chemical signals to coordinate the organelles. With crucial activities physically isolated, an information-processing system must'exist. As evidenced by uncontrolled growth of cancerous cells, things can go wrong with this apparatus. At each successively higher level of organizational complexity, more can go wrong. To keep the tissues and organs of more complex organisms in synch, increasingly elaborate control systems are needed.[13]

But such coordination is costly. Nerve cells, which comprise the primary information-processing network in complex organisms, consume enormous quantities of food—an "overhead cost" that must be borne by the rest of the organism. The human brain amounts to just 3 percent of total body weight but burns up about 20 percent of all the energy derived from food.

The cost of keeping our brains fed would be far higher if the body's information processing were not decentralized. Although we tend to think of ourselves as being in complete command of our bodies, most of life's choices—like the "decision" to produce more of a certain enzyme in a particular cell—are left to that cell. Recognizing the depletion of its shippable inventory, the DNA "senses" when to restart fabrication of the needed protein. Decentralized decision-making means the cell doesn't have to wait for a command from the brain. If each of our 10,000 billion cells required direct instructions on what to do and when to do it, our brains would be impossibly massive.

But even with a decentralized design, as size increases, the efficiency gains yielded by compartmentalization begin to be overwhelmed by the rising "overhead costs" of information processing. Had the high costs of coordination not prevented it, nature is likely to have produced creatures far more massive than its greatest leviathans—the blue whales and the giant sequoias. But within the limits imposed by a fixed quantity of resources, 3.5 billion years of evolution came up with organic designs that struck workable compromises between the benefits and the costs of size and complexity.

In business, the drive for greater efficiency and the attempt to avoid the intense competition in crowded niches also propels a spontaneous evolution of larger and more complex organizations. But, as in nature, sizable organizations are vastly outnumbered by tiny ones. The economy's smallest firms employ just one person—the so-called sole proprietor. These companies are the bacteria of the economy. Like their ecologic counterparts, sole proprietors are enormously diverse and productive; they are viable in market niches that cannot support larger organizations. Ranging from auto mechanics to street jugglers to literary agents, these minute organizations are as crucial to the vitality of the economy as bacteria are to the life of the ecosystem.

But, like bacteria, sole proprietors are hamstrung by the impossibility of internal compartmentalization. The auto mechanic who does his own parts purchasing, repair work, customer relations, and bookkeeping may be able to sustain his enterprise in a tiny market niche on a paltry stream of revenues, but the lack of specialization hampers productivity. An expert on automatic transmissions is unlikely to have as firm a grasp on the general ledger. The sole proprietor's costs of coordination are nil, but his efficiency in any function is far from ideal.

Consequently, just as ancient bacteria joined together in collaborative associations that evolved into the modern cell, most individuals work in cooperative economic cells. Employing from two to about six people, these work cells are the primary organizational unit of the economy. A proprietor who gives up the solitary life and becomes part of a work team is, in effect, making a transition from economic bacterium to organelle.

Like interdependent organelles, cooperating workers enhance the overall efficiency of the cells in which they labor. The crucial difference between organelles and workers is that human workers can learn new skills and take on new duties, but organelles cannot. Even when an organization or some of its cells die, displaced workers can adapt and join organizations that are building new cells. Despite their manifest differences, workers and organelles play similar roles in the structural hierarchies of the economy and the ecosystem.

The germination phase of a new organization is an extraordinarily delicate period. Most business ideas never become operating organizations. Of the firms that are born, one-half die within five years. Of those that survive infancy, few grow beyond a handful of work cells. Small companies make products that are beyond the capabilities of sole proprietors, but the niches they inhabit cannot sustain large firms with their high coordinating costs. Small multicelled firms range from building contractors to pizzerias to architectural firms. A sixth of all Americans work in firms with fewer than 20 employees, so microscopic organizations are essential players in the economy.[14]

At the top of the organizational pyramid are the economy's titans, giant firms that simply could not perform their productive roles if they were not so large and complex. Automakers, pharmaceutical houses, and jetliner manufacturers are all huge because the inherent task complexity in these businesses overwhelms tiny firms. Intel presently employs about 25,000 people, organized in several thousand specialized work cells, because it takes a massive and sophisticated organization to handle all the duties involved in producing millions upon millions of state-of-the-art microchips. As in nature, the size and structure of an organization must be appropriate to the specific requirements of its niche.

Because conditions in every market niche keep changing, no organizational design is permanent. Large firms are reorganized endlessly because their managers keep struggling to find the right balance between the benefits of coordinated corporate action and the cost savings that flow from decentralization. Oscillating between centralized and decentralized designs, companies seek but never find the perfect organizational structure.

CHAPTER
10

AMERICAN *PERESTROIKA*

S ince technology evolves so much more rapidly than genes, organizations change shape far more quickly than organisms. The
organelle-equipped cell appeared about 1,500 million years ago,
while the economy's first work cell appeared only 2.5 million years ago,
when members of a Homo habilis family subdivided the tasks of gathering a meal. Since then, human knowledge and tools have grown immensely more elaborate, radically boosting the output of each worker.
Hunting parties and harvesting teams—the work cells of earlier economic eras—gave way to the factory crews of the Industrial Age and
the data-processing departments of the Information Age. Each advance
in technology set off changes in the form and functions of the typical
economic cell.

Of course, most technical advances lead to only minor improvements
in products and slight changes in the organization of work. A modified
condenser might boost the power of a steam locomotive, but it wouldn't
radically affect the work of the train's crew or fundamentally alter the
economic role of railroads. But, in rare cases, an especially potent new
technology will trigger a restructuring that ripples throughout the entire
economy—from the lowliest work cells to the largest organizations.
Today, as the twentieth century draws to a close, we are in the midst
of precisely this kind of massive structural transformation.

Because we lack the benefit of hindsight, we cannot fully appreciate
the magnitude of the economic restructuring we are now experiencing.
But our descendants will almost certainly judge the "computer-on-a-
chip" to be the most economically significant technical achievement of
the previous 500 years. The microprocessor will rank at the very pinnacle

of human invention because—like the printing press—it slashed the cost of encoding, copying, and communicating information. And by doing so, it has brought vast areas of previously unattainable knowledge within human grasp and has made possible a staggering array of new products. Today these products are profoundly altering the capabilities of millions of work cells in every niche of the global economy.

Less than 20 years old, the microprocessor makes possible products and services that we have already come to accept as mundane. Digital watches, hand-held calculators, video games, personal computers, word processors, automatic bank tellers, supermarket scanners, magnetic resonance imaging, direct-broadcast satellite TV, VCRs, camcorders, electronic fuel injection, antilock brakes, cellular phones, fiber optics, medical lasers, factory robots, and on and on. Not one of these innovations would have been possible without the microprocessor. In the 1990s, microprocessors—like Intel's 386 and its successors—will endow machines with the faculties of vision, hearing, and speech. In ways that remain beyond the horizon of our imagination, daily life at work and at home will be transformed.[1]

The 1971 invention of the microprocessor by Intel completed a sequence of innovations that began in the 1940s, when computer pioneers started turning piles of wire and switches into machines that could do what no machines had ever done. As remarkable as these contraptions were, the early computers were phenomenally expensive. ENIAC, the first American-made computer, cost the U.S. government about $3 million (in 1987 dollars) for less computing power than that found in today's hand-held calculators.[2]

As long as information-processing power remained so expensive, computers could not penetrate the economy. A 1948 U.S. government study concluded that no more than 100 computers would ever be purchased by government bureaus, universities, and major corporations. At $3 million each, the projection probably was accurate. Only the largest organizations, paying thousands of office workers manually to perform calculations and bookkeeping tasks, could save money by using computers. To make widespread computer use possible, the cost of computing had to be reduced.

Technically, the heart of the problem was the high cost of the computer's basic component—the on/off switch. A switch—typically called a device—is essential, because the 1s and 0s of binary code must be physically represented by an object that has two alternate states. On equals 1, and off equals 0. Each device can hold just one bit of information at a time. More complex computations require simultaneous processing of more bits. Consequently, more powerful computers need more devices, and cheap computing requires cheap devices.[3]

Less than 15 years after the ENIAC began crunching numbers, advances in device technology set off the most precipitous decline in product costs ever witnessed. The cost collapse began when the computer's original switching device—the vacuum tube—was replaced by the transistor, which is made out of semiconducting materials. Neither good nor bad conductors of electricity, *semi*conductors—such as the element silicon—are solid materials with properties that allow them to be switched on and off. A transistor is a solid-state switching device etched into the surface of silicon.

In 1959, the transistor's economic potential was unleashed by the invention of the integrated circuit, better known as the "chip." Before the chip, individual transistors had to be wired together by hand to form complete electronic circuits. With chip technology, finished electronic circuits with transistors already wired together could be engraved into a single slice of silicon.[4] Between 1947 and 1987, the transistor and the integrated circuit drove down the cost of a single switching device by a factor of 100,000. Computing power that once had cost $3 million could be had for $30.

By way of historical comparison, Johann Gutenberg is credited with the invention of the printing press, but his primary contribution was the invention of an adjustable mold for forming molten metal into letters of the alphabet.[5] For decades prior to Gutenberg, Dutch artisans had used presses to print images carved into wooden blocks. The Chinese had been using the wood-block technique for centuries. But hand-carving individual letters was extremely slow and expensive. With Gutenberg's adjustable mold, forming letters was simple, and the cost of a single piece of type—printing's basic component—plummeted. Printing presses existed before the adjustable mold cut the cost of a letter, just as computers existed before semiconductor devices slashed the cost of a switch. In both cases, innovations designed merely to cut costs wound up un leashing the awesome power of information evolution.[6]

By delivering on the promise of computer technology, the microprocessor thrust the world's capitalist economies into a new economic era— the Information Age. Robert Noyce, coinventor of the integrated circuit and a founder of Intel Corporation, wrote, "Just as the Industrial Revolution enabled man to apply and control greater physical power than his own muscle could provide, so electronics has extended his intellectual power."[7] By the mid-1970s, microelectronics had spawned categories of goods and services that were unthinkable just a few years earlier.

Almost unnoticed at first, microchip technology began to revolutionize the workplace and lay the technical foundation for the integrated global economy of the twenty-first century. Throughout the 1970s, the West's transition to the new economic era was overshadowed by the energy crisis and price inflation. But while the TV cameras were trained on gatherings of OPEC oil ministers, firms across a wide spectrum of industries—from machine tools to home appliances—began introducing products that relied on microchips to provide radically higher performance at much lower prices.

Also unnoticed at the time was the sudden upturn in the rate of new business formations. Beginning in 1975, just a few years after the first microprocessor was introduced, literally millions of small, highly specialized organizations sprang up to invade the economic niches made possible by microelectronics. At the same time, many thousands of long-established American firms remained oblivious to the fundamental environmental shifts going on around them. They plodded on as before, while the entrepreneurial upstarts and aggressive Japanese companies rushed to exploit the power of the new electronics.[8]

The promise of the new economic era could not be achieved without first breaking down the structure of the existing economy. The 1982 recession, the most severe economic downturn since the Great Depression, marked the disruptive phase of this restructuring. Thousands of ineptly managed American firms were simply too weak to adapt to the new technologies or to cope with the onslaught of Japanese and upstart domestic competitors.

By the time the recession hit bottom, imploding companies had laid off three million workers. Throughout the early 1980s, the news media reported heartbreaking stories from America's deindustrializing "Rust Belt." Desperate workers and their families were shown drifting from the once-robust American heartland to nonexistent jobs somewhere in the Sun Belt. Many commentators, particularly those on the political Left, saw the tidal wave of bankruptcies and unemployment as an unmitigated human tragedy—a prime example of capitalism's inherent weakness.

In reality, the 1982 recession was particularly severe because two otherwise-unrelated factors coincided. First, a decade of monetary mismanagement and runaway inflation was abruptly ended, triggering the sudden shrinkage of an overstimulated economy. Money inflation does to an economy what amphetamines do to the human body. When monetary policy goes "cold turkey," withdrawal pains are excruciating. Second, inflation had masked the inefficiency and technological backwardness that had become commonplace among American firms. Propelled by the microchip revolution, global economic competition had been intensifying since the mid-1970s, but until inflation was stopped, many firms managed to put off the day of financial reckoning. With inflation brought under control, the lack of competitiveness of these firms became painfully obvious.

A recession serves the same purpose as a harsh winter. Weak organizations in each industrial species are weeded out, leaving more room for the survivors to grow. Even though it is traumatic for those involved, the death of organizations is just as important to the vitality of the economy as the birth of new firms. Like death in the ecosystem, bankruptcy is an essential aspect of the economy. But—and this point is easily overlooked—while bankrupt organizations die, unemployed workers do not. In the economy, natural selection acts upon the organization, not the individual.

Workers are like flexible, durable organelles inside the work cells of organizations. The closer the match between a worker's skills and the functions needed in the economy's expanding organizations, the faster a worker will find a new job. The best protection for workers is an economic system that helps the jobless update their skills to match the needs of prospering firms.

Poorly managed organizations—those that do not provide products as efficiently as their competitors—*should* die. They withdraw more value from society in labor and materials than they return in the form of products. Executives, managers, and workers in incompetent companies *should* lose their jobs—not because they are bad people but because their skills are not used effectively. No company has an inalienable right to life.

Unemployment—a necessary consequence of allowing firms to go bankrupt—is unquestionably capitalism's roughest edge. But few people have a clear understanding of unemployment's actual impact. Many seem to believe in a "myth of the firing squad." In this nightmare, when a firm shuts down or cuts back its workforce, the unfortunate workers are marched behind the plant and economically executed, their incomes and lives destroyed. But in real life, jobless workers jump back into the labor market, where they are reabsorbed by expanding, successful firms. Workers who lose their jobs face the emotional turmoil of transition, but they do not face summary execution.

In an economy whose component organizations are constantly restructuring as they adapt to changing conditions, unemployment is a fact of life. At present, nearly 120 million Americans have jobs. Each year, about ten million quit voluntarily. Another ten million are fired or lose their jobs through layoffs.[9] Of those dismissed between 1981 and 1986 (including the 1982 recession), one-fourth found new jobs within five weeks and 60 percent were hired within six months. Less than 20 percent of job losers were out of work longer than a year.[10] Unemployment insurance, which typically pays workers about a third of their lost wages, covered 80 percent of all job losers.[11] When the dust settles, unemployment costs the average American worker about one-fourth of his or her income for the year in which the job loss occurs.

For minorities, the impact of unemployment is greater. Comparing workers with equivalent educations, discrimination makes it about 20 percent tougher for blacks and Hispanics to find new work.[12] Nonetheless, the data show that education is the single most important factor in determining the likelihood and length of unemployment. In 1987, the jobless rate for workers without high-school diplomas was almost five times that of college graduates.[13] The tragedy of long-term joblessness is caused primarily by a failed education system. It is *not* a necessary feature of a capitalist system.

No one likes unemployment. It hurts to give up even a quarter of one's expected annual income. But joblessness is not the unmitigated personal catastrophe it is widely assumed to be. More than half of all job losers wind up earning as much or more in their new jobs.[14] Some former steelworkers do indeed wind up as hamburger flippers, but in the vast majority of cases, joblessness is a brief transition between jobs of roughly equal pay. In a modern economy, temporary unemployment is a necessary condition whose costs are shared by the individual and, through unemployment insurance, by the community.

By 1987, although 11 million jobs in decimated industrial species had vanished, virtually all of those who had lost their jobs, along with seven million new workers, had found employment.[15] New, vacant economic niches created by microchip technology had set off a continuing entrepreneurial boom. Armed with personal computers and the other new tools of the microprocessor era, legions of unknown small firms sprang up to replace the fallen industrial dinosaurs.[16]

Of course, small firms were not alone in exploiting the opportunities created by microelectronics. Under intense competitive pressure from aggressive foreign rivals and nimble entrepreneurs, well-managed large firms began flattening and decentralizing their traditional vertical hierarchies.[17] Before the microprocessor had endowed each work cell with sophisticated information-processing power, large organizations had no choice but to bear heavy costs of coordination. Ever since large-scale industrial organizations first emerged in the nineteenth century, passing papers up and down the chain of command had been the only practical way to keep complex organizations under control.[18] Suddenly, the microprocessor allowed firms to boost the sophistication of their products and accelerate their responses to customer demands by decentralizing and slashing the costs of coordination.

As millions of microprocessors flooded into the economy, it was as if the information-processing power of each work cell's nucleus was abruptly and immensely multiplied. With their newly acquired personal computers, front-line managers began exercising a level of control that was previously unimaginable.[19] Production cells that had always depended upon instructions from remote headquarters cells suddenly were empowered with enough information-processing capacity to make fast, rational decisions on their own. In short, microprocessor technology radically boosted the productive potential of every work cell in the economy.[20] In a turbulent decade, with little conscious awareness of the fundamental forces at play, and without any plan, the economy spontaneously restructured itself in what amounted to an unsung American *perestroika*.[21]

CHAPTER
11

A COMMONS FALLACY

The dramatically renewed vigor of the world's capitalist economies did not go unnoticed in the Kremlin.[1] In the words of the Soviet historian Leonid Batkin, "While the Brezhnev system was reducing our country to a state of mediocrity, the world was developing lasers and personal computers and witnessing the explosion of the post-industrial revolution."[2] In 1983, when President Ronald Reagan translated the military potential of microchip technology into the threat of "Star Wars," the Soviet leadership recognized the impossibility of retaining superpower status without a twenty-first-century industrial capability.[3] To argue otherwise was to suggest that nineteenth-century France could have remained a European power without adopting the steam engine invented in England. The profound economic and military consequences of the microchip—a technology far too complex and fast moving for the Soviet system—forced the hand of the Soviet elite.

By 1985, after several years of worsening economic stagnation, even the most conservative elements in the Kremlin reluctantly agreed that the highly centralized economic system erected by Lenin and perfected by Stalin and Leonid Brezhnev had to be changed.[4] To implement the transformation, the Communist party's inner circle selected Mikhail Gorbachev, who consolidated his grip on power and then launched the policy of *perestroika*, or economic restructuring.[5] Though stoutly defended as the reinvigoration of socialism, *perestroika*'s twin goals—more private ownership and the decentralization of *perestroika*, or economic decision-making—amounted to nothing less than an assault on the central principles of Marxist economics.

Even the most fervent Communists now admit that the Marxist economic program has utterly failed. Curiously, though, no one seems to know exactly why. For most Soviet citizens, the reasons behind their country's embarrassing technological backwardness, lack of consumer goods, gross inefficiency, and suffocating bureaucracy are unimportant. Practical people want remedies for problems, not explanations for why they happened. But this hardheaded attitude is shortsighted. To fix something as quickly as possible, one must first understand *why* the failure occurred.

In the past, many Western thinkers argued that a Marxist-style economy was just one of several alternative economic systems.[6] According to this view, a decentralized market-oriented economy is no better or worse than a centralized state-controlled economy. Both systems have pluses and minuses. Both are valid, just different. Because of their distinct historical experiences, what works for Americans probably wouldn't work for Soviets, and vice versa. In this view, the structure of an economy is merely an aspect of culture—a matter of political taste.

But from a bionomic perspective, such open-mindedness cannot be maintained. If the workings of the economy parallel the functions of the ecosystem, if organizations follow the same principles of form and function that govern the evolution of organisms, then there is but one natural mode of economic organization. Disparities will, of course, exist from region to region just as variations exist among the world's ecosystems. But whether tropical rain forest, high desert, or ocean depths, the themes of organic form and function are universal. Any economy that disrupts the interplay of immutable organic forces is inherently flawed and doomed to failure.

An economic system that clashes with fundamental life processes is not just another option; it is a profound aberration from the natural way in which human economic activity spontaneously organizes itself. This is the real reason for *perestroika*. After seven decades of a system erected on nineteenth-century Marxist theories of how an economy *should* work, the Soviet leadership has concluded that these theories *cannot* work. The abject failure of Marxist economics—whether in the Soviet Union, China, or assorted other countries—is not a matter of poor implementation of a sound theory.[7] Quite the contrary, the implementation of Marxist ideology has been remarkably thorough. Marxism failed because its core elements violate processes essential to the functioning of all living, evolving systems.

The most succinct description of Karl Marx's economic program is found on the last page of *The Communist Manifesto* of 1848. In essence, Marx wanted to shift economic power from the individual to the community—hence the label *Communist*. To eliminate private economic power, Marx called for "abolition of property in land," "abolition of all right of inheritance," "confiscation of the property of all emigrants and rebels," and "a heavy progressive or graduated income tax." To establish the economic power of the community, he advocated "centralization of credit in the hands of the state by means of a national bank with state capital and an exclusive monopoly," "centralization of the means of communication and transport in the hands of the state," and "extension of factories and instruments of production [equipment] owned by the state."[8]

Over the last century, Marx's vision of an economically empowered community attracted hundreds of millions of adherents. Marx's supporters believed that by planning a common future and eliminating the waste and duplication of competing enterprises, human progress would be accelerated. Transferring economic power from self-serving individuals to the community as a whole would lead to a much fairer distribution of wealth. Intuitively, it makes sense that everyone would be better off if people worked together, as members of a community, for their common good. The conflict and competition that characterize capitalism seem so petty, mean-spirited, and counterproductive. According to Marx, only the rich benefit from capitalism, because they alone own the farms and factories used to exploit the working man for the value of his labor. If the community owned everything, such exploitation would cease. Obviously, a community would not exploit itself.

But what is intuitively obvious is often incorrect. An inescapable, pragmatic flaw undermines this notion of community. As the size of a community increases, each member's sense of personal obligation to each of the others becomes diluted. Our sense of obligation to our immediate family is naturally stronger than our emotional connection to our neighbors. Similarly, our loyalty to our neighbors is more intense than our allegiance to all our fellow citizens. The larger the community, the weaker the bonds of mutual obligation. As these bonds weaken, it becomes more likely that someone will abuse community benefits.

From the bionomic perspective, Marx's emphasis on the community contradicts the organic principle of compartmentalization. All living things are composed of small units. Efficiency in a world of limited resources demands differentiation, specialization, and diversity. No complex organisms are made of one cell that has grown immensely large. If such a design worked, 3.5 billion years of evolution would have produced it. Instead, each cell in the community of a large organism manages most of its own affairs, trading its outputs for inputs provided by other cells.[9]

Economists trace the inherent inefficiencies of overly large cells to a phenomenon called the "tragedy of the commons."[10] For example, if you go out to dinner with three friends and agree in advance to split the bill, you'll probably wind up paying close to what you would have paid had the items been charged carefully to each diner. Because you know you'll bear 25 percent of the tab, and because you want to stay on good terms with your friends, you avoid overspending and order dishes in the same price range as your companions. Everyone in your little dinner community benefits by avoiding the nuisance of complicated calculations that can spoil an otherwise-enjoyable meal.

But if you are dragged off to an impromptu dinner with 30 people from the office, the dynamics of check splitting are quite different. You'd like to stick to your budget and plan on ordering a cheeseburger. But the first three people order filet mignon, veal Oscar, and lobster tails. Knowing that you're going to wind up paying 3 percent of the total bill, regardless of what you eat, you switch to prime rib. The incremental cost to your companions is negligible, and you'll get a much nicer meal for your money. But as this process works its way around the table, the community winds up spending far more than it would have spent if people had paid individually for what they ordered, or if the group had been seated at several smaller tables. Through no one's fault, everyone winds up overeating and overspending. No one wanted to abuse the commons. Things just worked out that way. Each individual's rational decision adds up to an irrational, negative outcome for the group. In effect, the community exploits itself.

In the Soviet Union, where everybody owns everything, the tragedy of the commons runs amok. Without the self-policing behavior that grows out of self-interest, irrationality pervades the economy. Expensive farm equipment is left outside in the winter to rust. Year after year, half of the potato crop, the staple of the Soviet diet, is allowed to rot before reaching consumers. Supplies and machinery of all types disappear from factories. In a system where everyone owns an equal infinitesimally small share of everything, no one behaves like the owner of anything. Without immediate financial feedback to the self-interested compartment, there is no linkage between economic cause and effect, between cost and value, between individual effort and personal well-being.

The Soviet military and its offshoot, the space program, are well-known successes, but Soviet economists now admit that the costs of these capabilities are higher than those of equivalent American programs.[11] Even so, one Soviet space scientist recently complained that half the equipment aboard the orbiting *Mir* space station doesn't work.[12]

Lacking the efficiencies yielded by private contracting, the Soviet military-industrial complex has to be coordinated by a bureaucracy that dwarfs even the Pentagon.

The Soviets' "command-and-control" economy can churn out endless quantities of heavy armor and plutonium but not a single state-of-the-art microprocessor. Complex Information Age products can be produced only by the decentralized interactions of highly sophisticated expert organizations. Having watched microelectronics-packed Stinger missiles blow their jets and helicopter gunships out of the skies over Afghanistan, Soviet military planners came to fear a future where Western "smart weapons" would sentence Soviet tanks and ICBMs to obsolescence.[13] But without an Information Age economy, there was nothing they could do about it.

In the consumer sector, the Soviet economy has been completely devastated by the long-term effects of a bureaucratically controlled, commons-style organization. In 1989, along with its traditional huge purchases of Western grain, the Soviet government began importing millions of pairs of shoes, boots, and panty hose, along with razor blades, cassette tapes, soap powder, and toothpaste. Goods available in all but the most impoverished Third World countries simply cannot be produced by an economy designed to comply with Marxist theory.[14]

Soviet health care is free, but infant mortality is 2.5 times higher than in the United States and ranks fiftieth in the world, just behind Barbados.[15] Under the administrative rules of the health-care system, doctors must see eight patients an hour. That amounts to 7.5 minutes per patient, but studies show that five minutes of each visit are consumed by paperwork. While life expectancy in the West has continued on an upward trend, it has been declining in the Soviet Union. Across the board—in food, housing, health care, and consumer goods—Soviet products are not only scarce and poor in quality, but when measured in the number of labor hours needed to produce them, Soviet goods are among the most expensive in the world.[16]

Before *perestroika*, the inherent deficiencies of a commons-style economy were ignored. Instead, Soviet economists contended that improved planning would remedy these problems. In effect, their argument was that the coordinating apparatus of the economy had not yet been adequately refined. But even a "perfect" economic model running on the fastest imaginable supercomputer cannot define a plan for an entire economy. As new technology emerges, the optimal structure of an economy keeps evolving. No one can know in advance how these interdependent changes will play themselves out.[17]

Even the engineers developing a new technique do not know whether or when their approach will work or what its ultimate impact will be. If the experts do not know what will unfold, how can economists factor it into their models? In the mid-1800s, when industry was in its infancy and technical change was sluggish, Marx's dream of a planned economy was at least conceivable, even though it was impractical without computers. Today, computers allow incredibly complex calculations, but the economists' mathematical models simply cannot predict the structure of an economy endlessly reshaped by the chaos of innovation.[18]

By its very nature, an evolving economy cannot be planned, so the entire rationale for centralized economic decision-making collapses. Marx called for a centralized state bank with monopoly power over investable funds because he wanted to be certain that the community's resources would in fact be invested according to the common plan. Marx understood that a monopoly on all capital-investment decisions would mean that every organization in the economy would effectively become a subsidiary of the state bank. By implementing Marx's prescription for centralized planning and investment, the entire Soviet economy was welded into one incredibly massive conglomerate.

In nature, the benefits of increasing size and complexity are offset by rising costs of coordination. Among other advantages, larger organisms are vulnerable to fewer predators. But they need larger brains to coordinate their movements, and big brains consume so much energy that finding enough food becomes difficult. Each organism represents a trade-off between the benefits and the costs of size.

In a centralized economy, where virtually all economic activity is concentrated in one mammoth organization, coordination costs are ruinous. An immense bureaucracy whose futile mission is to coordinate all the economic activities of 300 million people soaks up resources that would otherwise be available to productive, independent organizations.

In 1986, under Gorbachev's *perestroika* campaign, the Soviet Union took its first tentative steps toward disassembling the superstructure of the centralized economy and began moving toward an economy populated by a variety of independent organizations. Carefully avoiding the dirty word *private*, the government rewrote laws to allow individuals to start small businesses called "cooperatives." The Soviet government's inability to run decent restaurants, hairdressing salons, and auto-repair shops convinced the leadership that small businesses simply could not function as subsidiaries of a state bureaucracy intended to control steel mills and coal mines. *Perestroika*'s lifting of the ban on small enterprises implicitly recognized the essential role of microscopic organizations in a productive economy.[19]

Even this limited easing of restrictions on private enterprise has run into bitter opposition. Many Soviet citizens fear the Law on Cooperatives will open the Pandora's box of capitalism.[20] Soviet newspapers are filled with stories of cooperatives and would-be entrepreneurs stymied by red tape and public resentment of their relatively large incomes.[21] "Eighty percent of public opinion is against us," said the founder of a coop that recycles industrial waste. "Stop anyone on the street and ask, and you will find the general opinion is that we are thieves, profiteers, and speculators."[22]

For the Soviet people, who have been schooled in Marxism–Leninism for generations, the idea of allowing some people to become richer than others is nothing short of blasphemy. One Soviet lawmaker put it this way: "It's our slave psychology. It is possible to be hungry, but everyone must be equally hungry. If one person lives well and another person lives better, this is capitalism. It's better for everybody to be hungry. This psychology puts the brakes on *perestroika*."[23] The noted American columnist Flora Lewis echoed this sentiment when she wrote, "The painful fact is that the idea of egalitarianism is about all that is left of the early vision in Communist societies. It is hard to give it up when there is nothing else on the shelf."[24]

Despite vigorous objections, the legalization of small-scale cooperatives was complemented by a 1988 Law on State Enterprises that promised to shift decision-making authority from Moscow bureaucrats to factory managers and workers. If it had been implemented, the law would have gone a long way toward dismantling the centralized economic apparatus. It would have freed many prices from central control, introduced wholesale trade as an alternative to administrative distribution of industrial supplies, and instituted a network of banks so that enterprises could borrow funds instead of relying on state grants. But decentralization would also have led to layoffs for hundreds of thousands of bureaucrats in government planning ministries whose main job is to direct production by handing down minutely detailed instructions to grass-roots factory managers. The bureaucracy would never tolerate this, so the reforms did not take place.[25]

Had the Law on Cooperatives and the Law on State Enterprises been complemented by free-market pricing, a silver stake would have been driven through the heart of the economic system envisioned in *The Communist Manifesto*. If small, private enterprises and the Soviet Union's 48,000 state enterprises were actually set free from central control, a new era in Soviet economic history would have begun. For the first time, profits would have replaced production quotas as the chief aim of each economic organization. Stagnation, waste, and bureaucracy would have been supplanted by innovation, efficiency, and competition. But without free prices, none of these changes could begin.

In the end, the Marxist ideal of a society where everyone has an equal share of the commons simply cannot be reconciled with a system that relies on competition as its primary shaping force. Competition implies winners and losers. Some firms prosper while others go bankrupt. If a firm is forced out of business, its employees lose their jobs. This reality cannot be squared with the Soviet government's guarantee of a job for everyone, a policy that has been a cornerstone of Soviet economic and social life since 1930.[26]

In fact, the fear that newly competitive state enterprises may be forced to lay off millions of unneeded workers is probably the chief reason the Soviet people are so reticent about *perestroika.* Unaware of the facts of Western unemployment, they are haunted by the "myth of the firing squad." As Bill Keller, head of the *New York Times*'s Moscow bureau, put it, "The Soviet people expect, as a matter of basic right, something most economists believe is impossible: that *perestroika* should bring them a better life without risk, without discomfort."[27]

Accidents of history ultimately will determine whether Mikhail Gorbachev hangs onto power during the transformation of the Soviet economy. But to focus on Gorbachev's fate is to miss the main historical point. With or without Gorbachev at the helm, the Soviet Union eventually will abandon Marx. The transition will not be smooth. Crucial errors already have been made—especially the failure to free prices. But, as Gorbachev himself has said, "There is nowhere for us to retreat."[28]

The Soviets are drifting toward capitalism, not because it is fashionable but because it is inevitable. The immutable, natural forces of economic evolution are too powerful to be stifled permanently. A robust economy that violates the principles of organic form and function is an impossibility. The issue has never been whether capitalism would come to the Soviet Union, but rather which style of capitalism the Soviets will adopt.

The Soviets have several styles of capitalism from which to choose, ranging from Hong Kong's laissez-faire to Sweden's government-dominated approach. Reasoning from the biological analogy, some might argue that government should have no role in the economy, that an economy true to bionomic principles would be a pure market economy. After all, in nature there is no commons, no concerted community action, and no government. Each organism struggles to survive on its own, scrounging enough resources to invest in the construction of the next generation. Life on earth is abundant, because each organism does the best it can. According to this view, an economy consistent with fundamental biological processes has no place for taxes or the public goods distributed by government.

But such a view overlooks a rather pivotal fact: Human beings *are* different from all other creatures. We are conscious beings. As social animals, we are socially conscious. Marx's ideas attracted millions precisely because our sense of community is so vital an aspect of being human. We feel compassion for neighbors whose lot is misfortune. We choose to form communities for mutual aid, support, and sharing. As a species, we have always done so. Indeed, our capacity to cooperate may well be our most powerful adaptive trait.

The issue is not whether a capitalist economy ought to have a commons, but rather what portion of an economy's output should be distributed through its commons. If the commons takes shape as a "social safety net," precisely how high should that net be? How can acknowledged community needs be met without creating unnecessary commons problems? If creating a commons is the only feasible way to cope with a particular social need, what techniques can be borrowed from the free market to manage the commons as efficiently as possible? Each nation—with its unique history, culture, and sense of community—will come to somewhat different conclusions on these questions. There are no absolute answers.

In practical terms, these larger themes translate into the detailed issues of tax policy, education, retraining, deregulation, free trade, bureaucratic waste, environmental protection, and international cooperation—issues high on the political agenda in every nation. Experience shows that another century of the Left/Right polemics that grew from classical economics cannot provide useful answers. But from the bionomic perspective, it is possible to identify proposals that will work in concert with, rather than against, the natural forces of economic evolution.

PART III

ENERGY
AND VALUE

■

The worst crime against working people
is a company which fails to operate at a profit.
—*Samuel Gompers (1908)*[1]

CHAPTER

12

SURPLUS AND GENES

When the lunar module *Eagle* landed near the Sea of Tranquillity in July 1969, its crew did not expect to find any signs of life. The scientific community was virtually unanimous in its prediction that life was impossible on the surface of the moon. The argument was that the moon's gravitational pull was too weak to hold the atmospheric gases essential for life. And without oxygen, carbon dioxide, nitrogen, water vapor, and a smattering of other elements, life could not get started. From the chemist's standpoint, life on earth is essentially a stew of these chemicals, brought to a slow simmer by the warmth of a sun floating 93 million miles away. Scientists of course knew that the moon's surface received plenty of sunlight, but they contended that energy without the right chemical building blocks could yield nothing more than hot rocks. And, as revealed by a thorough examination of the moon rocks brought back to earth, their predictions were right. There is no life on the moon.

A similar, yet far less well-known expedition took place eight years later. Instead of using a spacecraft, the explorers traveled in a tiny, three man submarine named *Alvin*. Made technically feasible by advances achieved during the American space program, the *Alvin* was designed to survive the immense water pressure in the deep crevices of the ocean floor. These troughs—some as deep as seven miles beneath the ocean surface—were the only places on the earth's surface that had not been explored before man went to the moon. Since these trenches are portions of the seams that run between the earth's continental plates, they hold great interest for geologists.

Biologists, by contrast, showed little interest in *Alvin*'s descents. The consensus of opinion among them was that life was impossible at such great depths, because sunlight cannot penetrate so much water. In fact, at depths below 1,000 feet, the sea is utterly black.[2] Conditions were exactly the reverse of those found on the moon—plenty of the right chemicals but no sunlight. Even so, the consequences were expected to be the same—no prospect of finding life.

But during a dive in 1977, near the Galápagos Islands off the coast of Ecuador, the geologist crew of the *Alvin* stumbled upon the impossible. While searching for "hot spots" in the ocean floor—places where heat from the earth's molten core seeps out of the rifts between the continental plates—their thermometer registered a sharp jump. After zeroing in on the heat signal and descending to the bottom, they flipped on *Alvin*'s headlights.[3] Before them stretched a surrealistic panorama teeming with bizarre creatures: huge white worms topped with red plumes swaying gently in the currents, surrounded by bright yellow mussels, crabs, shrimp, and gigantic clams—all gathered around a chimneylike "black smoker" spewing superhot water out of the ocean floor.

The first reports that life flourished in the deepest recesses of the ocean stunned biologists.[4] Because the energy that gives life to virtually all previously known organisms can be traced back to green plants and their remarkable ability to use sunlight to convert carbon dioxide and water into carbohydrates, few ever considered the possibility that life's energy could be derived from a source other than the sun. But despite their initial disbelief, marine biologists were delighted to have a whole new realm of life to investigate. In the decade after the discovery of the hydrothermal vent community near the Galápagos, several more communities were found in the Pacific and the Gulf of Mexico.[5]

Recent work has shown that although the mix of species populating these isolated ecosystems varies, all vent species rely upon the chemical wizardry of a special bacteria. The life process begins with the intense geothermal activity that heats seawater to over 400°C (750°F). The superhot water drives a chemical reaction that produces energy-rich hydrogen-sulfide, a toxic gas known by its characteristic smell of rotten eggs. The hydrogen-sulfide molecules are modified by chemistry inside the bacteria, and the energy released is used to construct carbohydrates from carbon dioxide and water.[6] Some of the food-producing bacteria are eaten by grazing vent creatures, just as plants are consumed by land animals, but most of the bacteria actually live inside the bodies of vent animals. In these symbiotic relationships, the animals extract raw materials (hydrogen sulfide, carbon dioxide, and oxygen) from the water and pass it along to the bacteria, which in exchange export carbohydrates back to their hosts. In a harsh environment, cooperation is crucial to survival.

The chemosynthesis process employed by vent bacteria is less common and less familiar than green-plant photosynthesis, but both are methods of capturing physical energy and storing it as food energy. Chemosynthesis uses heat to build sugar molecules, while photosynthesis uses light.[7] Neither photosynthesis nor chemosynthesis happens spontaneously. Both processes are set up and controlled by life's master molecule—DNA.

The existence of hydrothermal vent communities demonstrates that energy—and not just energy in the form of sunlight—is the universal driver of life's processes.[8] DNA may encode the instructions that organize simple chemicals into biologically useful molecules, but without an external power supply to support it, DNA is helpless and life is impossible. Quite simply, it takes work to build complex molecules (including copies of DNA) out of smaller components. Without information to channel and control it, energy is just diffuse energy. And information, without energy available to it, cannot reproduce and cannot be alive. To put it another way, life is the process of using energy to convert raw materials into information.

Because energy is as fundamental to life's existence as information, knowing exactly how much energy flows in and out of organisms is crucial to understanding what makes living things live. But quantifying energy by monitoring the flow of calories in and out of animals and plants is not a simple undertaking, especially out in the field, where the conveniences of a laboratory are unavailable. Consequently, most of the ecological research done so far has been descriptive rather than analytical. Perhaps the most notable exception to this rule is the work of Bernd Heinrich, a professor of zoology at the University of Vermont.

Heinrich's family left Germany in 1951 and settled on an old run-down farm in western Maine. There, his teenage fascination with nature grew into an all-consuming passion—the need to know how things worked. He pursued his interest in biology until he found himself, years later, in a laboratory at UCLA working toward his Ph.D. in cell physiology. It was at this point that he decided he had become too removed from his love of nature and switched his research into a new biological specialty—physiological ecology, the study of how organisms function in their environments. His specialty was insect energetics.[9]

In April 1970, shortly after finishing at UCLA, Heinrich was visiting his parents' farm when he noticed bumblebees flying about, despite the frosty morning temperature. This observation set him off on a decade-long study of how bumblebees gather and use energy. His research, summarized in a remarkable book, *Bumblebee Economics*, demonstrates that a bumblebee hive is a living system shaped by one central purpose— gathering enough energy to ensure the survival of the bumblebees' genetic information.[10]

Unlike most species of bees that live as solitary individuals, bumblebees (members of the genus *Bombus*) are social insects.[11] Depending on the species, they live in colonies of a few dozen to several hundred related individuals. None of these individuals can survive for long on their own. In a sense, individual bumblebees are not complete organisms; the colony as a whole is the real organism. In a beehive, an ant colony, or a termite nest, individual insects are more like mobile cells, parts of a larger social organism.

For bumblebees living in Maine, the social organism begins its life cycle in early April, when a single queen bumblebee, having survived eight months of underground hibernation, is awakened by the sun's warmth. A furry yellow, gold, and black ball, the queen buzzes about for several days searching frantically for the right spot, perhaps an abandoned rodent burrow, in which to start her nest. She interrupts her quest only long enough to refuel on sweet nectar from early rhododendron blossoms. After finding a suitable nest site, she lays her first batch of eight to ten eggs—the "brood clump."

For the next month, she divides her time between incubating her brood clump against the cold of early spring and foraging for supplies of pollen and nectar. Pollen grains are tiny, protein-rich capsules that carry the male genes of flowering plants; nectar is essentially liquid sugar exuded by plants to attract insects. These two substances are the only food of bumblebees. Pollen provides protein—the construction material for building more bees. And nectar, which is converted to honey, is the bumblebees' sole source of energy.

Over the course of 135 million years, bees and flowering plants have evolved interactively. In the language of biology, they "coevolved."[12] Today, their survival is intimately interdependent. A plant turns sunlight into sugary bribes for bees. By doling out only tiny rewards in each flower, the plant forces a bee to visit many of its flowers. When a bee inadvertently brushes pollen from one flower onto the female parts of neighboring flowers, the plant's reproduction process begins. Bees and flowers "exploit" each other to their mutual benefit.[13]

If the queen's food-gathering efforts are successful, she will have collected enough protein and energy to satisfy her hungry brood clump. But only if she collects the food very quickly, and is able to spend most of her time incubating the eggs from the cold, will her brood clump mature into normal adult worker bees. If everything goes right—and most often it does not—the first batch of workers will emerge on time. These workers will help the young queen by caring for subsequent broods and gathering more pollen and nectar. Before long, her offspring take over these duties completely, and the queen becomes a full-time egg-laying machine, the epicenter of an expanding colony, constantly fed and groomed by her children.

Bumblebee workers live only about two weeks, but in that brief life-span, each worker collects enough of a food surplus to raise several siblings. As spring turns into summer, the colony's growing population of workers commutes incessantly to nearby blossoms. Leaving the nest with just enough honey to fuel their flight out to the flowers, they load up on pollen and nectar and haul it back to the nest. There it is stored and drawn upon by hive workers, which incubate and feed new batches of eggs. In August, as the early Maine fall approaches and flowers disappear, the queen starts producing eggs that are fed a different diet. These eggs turn into virgin queens and males. And when the first frost kills off the last workers and the old and exhausted queen, the virgin queens and males take off on their nuptial flight. After mating in midair, the males fly off and die, while the inseminated queens seek underground shelter for the long winter ahead. Of the few dozen queens from each hive that go into hibernation, only one on average will survive to produce her own colony the following spring.

The life cycle of the bumblebee colony hinges on one economic fact— the individual worker's ability to gather more energy on each flower commute than it consumes.[14] And, as Heinrich discovered through his meticulous measurements, the energy "profit" earned on a typical flight results from the bumblebee's proficiency at maximizing energy revenues while minimizing energy costs. But reducing costs isn't easy. The wings of a flying or hovering bumblebee beat nearly 200 times a second. Such intense work burns up about one fourth of a calorie per minute. This may not sound like much, but, adjusted for the weight difference, it's about 24 times the maximum energy consumption of a world-class marathoner.[15]

But even this prodigious rate of energy use doesn't tell the whole story of bumblebee energy costs. Bumblebees cannot fly unless their flight muscles are warm. The muscles must be at least 30°C (86°F), even when it's near freezing outside. To maintain this threshold temperature without leaking too much heat, the bee's body has evolved so that hot blood recirculates inside the thorax, which contains the flight muscles, while the rest of the bee (the head and abdomen) is allowed to remain much cooler. Despite this remarkable ability to focus heat where it is needed, a bumblebee's energy consumption nearly doubles in cold weather.

To satisfy its own energy appetite and still have a surplus to bring back to the hive, a foraging worker must optimize the energy revenue of each trip. Since every minute burns energy and a worker can visit no more than 30 to 40 flowers a minute, it has to concentrate on the flowers that hold the most nectar. A rhododendron blossom, for example, puts out 11 times as much sugar as a lambkill flower. In cool weather, when energy consumption is greatest, a worker will avoid the lambkill because it cannot break even given the time needed to check a blossom. Only when the weather warms up, and the worker's energy cost-per-minute has declined, will it bother with low-yield flowers.

Even in summer, when several nectar-rich flowers compete for the attention of pollinators, individual bumblebees maximize their revenues by specializing in certain flowers. A newly hatched worker has no specialty and at first will stumble around ineptly, trying to extract food from a wide variety of flowers. But after a few trips, the worker will learn to recognize and begin to concentrate on one plant species. Plants minimize the intensity of their competition for pollination services by blooming in sequence throughout the spring and summer. With new bumblebee workers being born continuously, the handful of plants preferred by a colony's workers changes week by week. In this way, the beehive social organism adjusts its diet to stay in tune with nature's most lucrative energy payoffs.[16]

Worker specialization is also important because the flowers of each plant species have unique shapes. To collect the most pollen and nectar in the shortest amount of time, a bee must execute a precise sequence of movements inside the flower. Heinrich found that individual bees learn to be more efficient as their experience with a certain flower accumulates.[17] While inexperienced bees need an hour to collect a full load from jewelweed flowers, experienced bees need only six minutes. Obviously, a worker will develop an expertise with jewelweed flowers sooner by concentrating on jewelweed. And this is exactly what happens. The time saved by learning a specialty means more trips per day and more profit contributed to the colony.[18]

Honeybees (genus *Apis*) are famous for performing elaborate dances in the hive to indicate the location of rich food supplies. By contrast, bumblebees don't cooperate through communication. Bumblebees operate as individuals, each seeking to maximize its own profit per trip. The division of labor in a bumblebee colony might appear to be the result of organized cooperation, but it is not. The "organization" of a bumblebee hive is merely a consequence of individual specialization.

The differences between honeybee and bumblebee behaviors grow out of their distinct evolutionary histories. Honeybees evolved in the tropics, where nectar is concentrated in dense clumps of flowers such as those of blossoming banana trees. Because tropical blooms hold far more nectar than a single bee could ever haul back on its own, communicating the location of a super-rich find to hivemates aids the survival of the colony. But bumblebees evolved in northern and arctic zones, where flowers with minuscule reserves of nectar are scattered over meadows and tundra. In such a situation, there's little benefit in elaborate communication techniques for coordinated foraging.

Even so, there are some negative consequences of a system built entirely upon individual initiative. Bumblebees from the same hive may visit exactly the same flower shortly after one another. For the second bee, the visit will be a waste of precious energy, since the first bee will have sucked up all the nectar. It would seem that the hive, as a whole, would be better off if the bumblebees cooperated and arranged to visit different flowers. But because the hive of a typical northern bumblebee species only reaches a size of about 50 workers, and because workers foraging within a one-mile radius of the hive can reach 2,000 acres and about eight million flowers, the likelihood of one bee's visiting a flower shortly after a hivemate has been there is quite low. Consequently, the competition among hivemates resulting from an uncoordinated foraging system has no negative impact on the hive's economy. But the cost of coordination—such as the energy consumed in recruitment dances— would overwhelm any energy savings that might be gained by avoiding a few useless flower visits. Given the bumblebees' environment, the appropriate survival strategy is individual initiative and specialization, rather than close communication and coordination.

The greatest competitive threat comes not so much from other members of the same hive but from other bee colonies. The flowers in a single Maine meadow may supply hundreds of bees from many different species and colonies. There is a substantial likelihood that a worker from one hive will come upon a flower just drained by a forager from a neighboring hive. But, unlike their tropical cousins, northern bumblebees never attempt to defend flowers or stage mass attacks on the food supplies of others. It isn't worth the effort. No single flower is worth protecting.

Precious time is better spent gathering food. The logic of the economic environment dictates competition by scrambling for food rather than competition by territorial aggression. This is why bumblebees of different species can be found working frantically, yet peacefully, alongside each other on any northern hillside.

Just as direct competition among plants for pollination services is reduced by the staggered timing of their blooming periods, head-to-head competition among closely related bumblebee species is limited by subtle differences in their anatomies. Bees use their tubelike tongues to suck the nectar from flowers, and the workers of each bumblebee species have tongues of different lengths. For example, a *Bombus fervidus* worker usually has an 11 millimeter (mm) tongue, while *Bombus terricola*'s is only 6mm. Short-tongued *B. terricola* workers cannot reach the nectar pool inside long, tubular flowers, so they concentrate on shallow, open flowers. Long-tongued bees avoid the easy, shallow flowers because they are so heavily worked over by their short-tongued neighbors.

Even where two species have tongues of similar length—such as *B. fervidus* (11mm) and *B. vagans* (8mm)—the workers of each type will tend to avoid direct competition by foraging at different times of the day. *B. vagans* workers start foraging at the crack of dawn, despite the high energy costs of flying in cold air. Then they take the afternoon off, while the *B. fervidus* workers, with their slightly longer tongues, enjoy the lower energy drain of afternoon temperatures and the fact that nectar in the deepest flowers, lying beyond the reach of *B. vagans*, will still be waiting for them when they arrive. Just as the flower specializations learned by workers from a single hive reduce foraging overlap and maximize overall hive revenue, the flower specializations that grow out of slight physical distinctions among closely related species limit head-on competition and allow maximum survival.[19]

Ultimately, the survival of every bee species rests upon an intricate relationship between an anatomy that minimizes energy costs and a behavior pattern that maximizes energy revenues. And, despite its wonderful complexity, the energy economics of a typical bumblebee hive can be outlined easily in a simple format familiar to any businessperson—the profit-and-loss statement. A profit-and-loss statement (often called an income statement) reports the flow of dollars into and out of a business for a given period—usually one year. By substituting calories for dollars, measuring energy instead of money, the same technique can summarize the economics of a living organism. Prepared from data gathered by Professor Heinrich, the accompanying income statement depicts

Bumblebee Hive Income Statement

All Amounts in Calories (except as noted)	Cold & Rainy Days (Avg. 10°C)	Warm & Sunny Days (Avg. 23°C)	Total Per Season	As % of Total Revenue
Revenues per Foraging Minute	1.77	1.77		
Direct Costs per Foraging Minute				
Warming Up	0.15	0		
Flying	0.28	0.28		
Subtotal	0.43	0.28		
Gross Profit per Foraging Minute	1.34	1.49		
Minutes per Avg. Foraging Trip	60	60		
Avg. Trips per Forager per Day	8	9		
Avg. Number of Foragers	17	45		
Cold or Warm Days each Season	40	75	115	
Total Revenue to the Hive	577,728	3,225,825	3,803,553	100.0%
Total Gross Profit to the Hive	437,376	2,715,525	3,152,901	82.9%
Overhead Costs				
Feeding the Queen			57,200	1.5%
Feeding Worker Larvae			1,515,024	39.8%
Incubating Worker Larvae			33,600	0.9%
In-Hive Worker Heat Losses			378,000	9.9%
Dead Workers at Disposal			10,020	0.3%
Subtotal			1,993,844	52.4%
Net Profit Available to Reinvest			1,159,057	30.5%
Feeding Queen/Drone Larvae			1,134,000	29.8%
Incubating Queen/Drone Larvae			16,200	0.4%
Subtotal			1,150,200	30.2%
Profit Not Reinv. (Sugar Left Over)			8,857	0.2%
Sugar Left Over in Grams			2.21	

Sources: Heinrich, *Bumblebee Economics* (1979); Heinrich personal communication. Author's estimates

Figure 12.1

the estimated energy revenues, costs, and profits of a normal Maine hive of *Bombus terricola* during one year.[20]

The accountant's green-eyeshade view of bumblebee life may clash with the poet's image of bees buzzing aimlessly among fragrant, nectar-laden blossoms on a lazy summer afternoon. But the stark reality of bumblebee existence—and the existence of all living things—is shaped by the unrelenting drive for an energy surplus, by the overwhelming imperative to eke out enough profit to reinvest in the creation of the next generation of life.[21] Heinrich writes:

> The colony cannot merely break even economically; it must expand as rapidly as possible, until it crashes at the end of its cycle

when it no longer invests to replace worn-out machinery [work-ers]. . . . Profit is ultimately measured in terms of the number of new queens and drones that are produced before the crash.[22]

Although the profit-and-loss statement shows a small reserve of honey left unused at the time of the hive's autumn demise, these excess profits would vanish if the workers lost more than a few hours of the warm weather normally available to gather nectar. A late-spring thaw, too many rainy summer days, or an early frost would push the colony from energy surplus into deficit and force the bees to shut down almost all activity in a desperate effort to conserve energy. The profitability and the survival of the beehive organism are subject to all of nature's risks. Whether the colony will fulfill its biological mission by sending virgin queens and drones off on a nuptial flight is in doubt right up until the flight begins.

Virgin queens and drones are the carriers of the colony's genetic in-formation. They are the sex cells of the social organism. Newly insem-inated queens—the ultimate product of energy profits earned by hundreds of workers from millions of flower visits—represent the im-mortal thread of information that links all the bumblebee colonies that have ever lived or will ever live. They are proof of the fact that, despite their great beauty and delicacy, all of nature's elaborate contrivances of bumblebee anatomy and behavior come down to nothing more than a way of turning profits into information.[23]

CHAPTER
13

PROFITS AND TECHNOLOGY

B usinesses, like bumblebees, turn profits into information. In an expanding industry, a company's profit—the surplus after operating costs—usually is reinvested in new equipment, more buildings, and research and development (R&D). Whether a firm uses its profits to purchase a new delivery truck, a laboratory instrument, or a fax machine, it is buying a chunk of technological information. For example, a brand-new Xerox photocopier embodies everything the Xerox Corporation knows at that time about making a commercially viable photocopier. In the carton, Xerox ships a bundle of its most recent knowledge in image reproduction, manufacturing logistics, quality control, and marketing. Via the marketplace, all this expertise is transferred to anyone willing to pay the price Xerox needs in order to profit from the transaction.

Obviously, this kind of investment in information is considerably different from the beehive's investment of surplus calories in virgin queens and drones. The bumblebee hive has no choices. It can invest in just one kind of information, its own DNA. There may, of course, be an occasional mutation of a gene here or there, leading to changes in future bee anatomy or behavior, but this kind of deviation is not a matter of choice. It is a consequence of error, of chemically coded information copying itself inaccurately. Nature does not grant the hive the option of improving its offspring's competitiveness by incorporating the latest advances in wing design developed by a strain of Japanese honeybees. When the bumblebees' biological information changes, it changes through the random events of evolution.

By contrast, when the decision-makers in a firm choose to invest past profits in specific pieces of equipment, buildings, employee training, and R&D programs, they are deciding what fragments of information ought to be grafted onto their company's existing "genetic" core. The managers realize that their organization's survival will hinge upon whether the "genes" they select now will be appropriate for the market niche the company inhabits in the future. Whether a company buys its technology from outside suppliers, invents its own, or does some of both, it is gambling on the shape of the future competitive landscape.

Unsung but important advances in an industry often come when a worker or designer struggling with a knotty problem decides to "borrow an idea" from a completely unrelated field. For example, in the 1980s, aerospace manufacturers, in their drive to improve aircraft fuel efficiency, have started using carbon composite material instead of aluminum to make tail sections, wings, noses, and fuselages. Used in tennis rackets and skis, composite material is just as strong as aluminum but weighs only about half as much. Raw composite material is like a sheet of fabric made of epoxy and acrylic fibers that have been charred into carbon. Despite its weight advantage, composite has been used only sparingly, because it is far more expensive than aluminum and much more difficult to handle.[1]

Unless composite is kept refrigerated, the epoxy hardens before the fabric can be cut to the proper shape, and the material then is wasted. But properly refrigerating a huge aircraft production facility is no simple undertaking. It's expensive, and if it's not done right, uneven warm and cold spots appear. When production managers at Northrop, a major southern California aerospace firm, began wrestling with this practical dilemma, one of them decided to call up the refrigeration specialists at Sara Lee, the maker of frozen baked goods. All of Sara Lee's plants rely on large-scale refrigeration and one plant near Chicago has a freezer the size of a football field. Not long after Northrop contacted Sara Lee, expertise garnered through decades of experience in preserving cakes became part of modern aircraft production technology. A purposeful "genetic recombination" of useful technical know-how led to a small, but quite typical, step forward.[2]

The human capacity to imagine, to consciously pull together unrelated pieces of knowledge and produce new answers, is what makes economic evolution happen so much faster than biological evolution. Nonetheless, the fundamental process—turning profits earned today into information for tomorrow—is the same for both organisms and organizations. In both realms, profits make possible the natural process of growth and renewal.

Nor is the intimate relationship between profit and information restricted to high-technology businesses. Consider the local grocery store, which seems a simple-enough business. A supermarket provides its customer with a service. The company buys a box of Rice Krispies from Kellogg's at one price, shelves it conveniently on the breakfast-cereal aisle, awaits the customer's arrival, sells it to the consumer at a higher price, and pockets part of the difference as profit. The supermarket earns that profit in exchange for moving a box of cereal from a distant factory to a convenient neighborhood location.

The transaction is not all that different from a beehive earning an energy profit for providing pollination services to a plant. The beehive expends energy commuting out to a flower. Normally, this cost is lower than the energy price it collects in nectar. The beehive keeps the margin between price and cost as profit. And even though the beehive must "commute" to service its "customers," while the supermarket remains stationary with its customers doing the commuting, the essence of each economic transaction is the same. Needed services are provided in exchange for a profit. Whether organism or organization, calories or dollars, survival hinges on achieving a positive margin between price and cost—profit.

Fashioning a way of life that consistently earns profits is difficult, because the economic and natural environments are crowded, competitive, and risky. Achieving regular profitability requires finding ways to diminish direct competition. The common strategy employed by organizations and organisms is to develop a way of getting by that is just a little bit different from that of any other species. Long-tongued bumblebees focus on flowers with deep corollas; upscale grocery stores cater to customers with deep pockets. In the vast network of relationships that make up an economy or an ecosystem, each player tries to create for itself a unique and necessary role, a position of relative safety in an ever-threatening environment.

Even in a relatively simple business, like the grocery business, this natural tendency to differentiate in order to avoid competition is apparent. For example, just as several closely related species of bumblebees with their varying tongue lengths compete and coexist in slightly different niches of a Maine hillside, the distinct species of the genus *Grocery store*—each with its own subtle features—compete and coexist in adjacent and overlapping niches of the American food marketplace. Of the half-dozen or so grocery-store species, the more notable include the ubiquitous "24-hour convenience store," the familiar "neighborhood supermarket," and the endangered "Mom-and-Pop corner store."

The newest and least well-known species in this genus is the "super-warehouse" store. The first super-warehouse store, called Cub Foods (Cub stands for Consumers United for Buying), appeared in 1977 in the suburbs of Minneapolis/St. Paul. The super-warehouse concept was the brainchild of Jack Hooley and Cub Davis.[3] The Hooley family had been in the grocery business ever since Grandfather Hooley, an Irish immigrant, settled in the town of Stillwater, 25 miles northeast of St. Paul. In 1876, he opened a meat store that was typical of the post–Civil War era. Cattle and hogs were slaughtered right behind the store and sausages were made in a back room. A few simple grocery items, like bread and flour, were stocked on shelves out front. And since this was before refrigeration, the meat was kept cool atop a marble counter. Grandfather Hooley's meat store was a classic old-time butcher shop.

Around the time his son Matt returned from World War I, Grandfather Hooley died, so Matt decided to open his own butcher shop in Stillwater. Throughout the 1920s, the store prospered, but Matt wanted to expand and grow beyond the limits of a traditional butcher shop. In 1932, he opened Hooley's Public Provision Company on Main Street—a full-fledged grocery store carrying an assortment of canned goods, dry groceries, and produce, as well as meat. Although the store was not a rousing success, Matt managed to keep it profitable in treacherous economic times.

Throughout this period, Matt Hooley would regularly drive around the Midwest looking for a better way to do business—searching for ideas that would build his sales volume, raise his modest profits, and ensure his store's long-term survival. It was on just such a tour that Matt and his twelve-year-old son Jack came upon the answer to his quest. Up until that time, shoppers would enter a grocery store and order their items at the front counter. A clerk then would be dispatched to the back of the store to fetch the groceries. This method was not particularly efficient, but it was the way things were done.

When the Hooleys walked into Perlmutter's Market, on the outskirts of Moline, Illinois, in 1937, they witnessed a revolutionary concept—self-service. Customers were provided with wire shopping carts and asked to walk among the shelves and select the goods on their own. Matt was intrigued with the new concept, but he feared that his customers, comfortable with the traditional approach, would refuse to shop for themselves. He asked Mr. Perlmutter, "What makes you think a customer's gonna push a cart around?" To which Perlmutter replied, "You see that big pile of Tide soap over there? It's twenty-nine cents a box. You know what it is in town in a regular market? It's fifty-nine cents. When they see that kind of difference, they'll crawl over crushed glass to get to it."

Matt Hooley needed no further convincing. Immediately upon his return to Stillwater, Matt remodeled the Public Provision Company to the self-service format. Having radically reduced his labor costs, he could afford to slash prices. And, at the lower prices, sales and profits began to grow. Over the years, he copied this successful business formula by opening stores in nearby Red Wing and Hudson and a second store in Stillwater. None of his local competitors could match his low prices and keep doing business the old-fashioned, labor-intensive way. One by one, stores that failed to adopt the new self-service system went out of business.

In 1949, after several years of postwar growth, Matt Hooley moved his Main Street operation to a larger building just up the block. With more floor space, he was able to add two new sections to the market— a self-service meat department with prewrapped meats and a freezer for frozen foods. At the time, both departments were innovations. Throughout the 1950s, as Matt stepped aside and let his sons Jack and Charles take over, sales volume increased with the growth of the area. In 1961, the store was moved to a still-larger location in downtown Stillwater. The new store had more frozen-food coolers, six checkout lanes with mechanical cash registers, and a bakery. At 17,000 square feet, the 1961 store was the kind of place most Americans think of when they think about a small neighborhood supermarket.

From the days of Matt Hooley's first butcher shop, the Hooley family's business philosophy was simple: minimize costs, maximize revenues. Don't buy equipment or hire workers unless absolutely necessary. Find out what customers want and give it to them. Work as hard as you can. Keep prices as low as possible, but always wring out a narrow profit. Reinvest every penny to improve the business. The philosophy apparently worked. No local supermarket could underprice Hooley's and squeeze out enough profit to stay alive. Local competitors dropped out, unable to survive on the razor-thin margins on which Hooley's had learned to thrive.

For many companies, eliminating the last of the serious competitors means that it's time to raise prices and fatten profits. But Jack Hooley followed his father's dictum to keep prices so low that no competitor would have the incentive to move into town. Instead of raising prices, Jack and his close friend Cub Davis kept looking for ways to trim prices even more. In 1966, when one of them read a magazine article about Prairie Market, a new type of store in Watertown, South Dakota, they decided to drive out and take a look.

The Prairie Market was owned by Merle Whitwam, a wholesaler who for years had sold groceries to local independent markets. But the expansion of the supermarket chains in the 1960s had put all of his customers out of business. Since the chain stores bought their supplies through their own headquarters, Whitwam was facing certain bankruptcy. Necessity being the mother of invention, he decided to open his grocery warehouse to the public and sell off his inventory by the case at wholesale prices. The idea was an instant success. Farm families drove great distances to load up on necessities at rock-bottom prices. Much to his own surprise, Whitwam made enough money to replenish his inventory, and he became one of the first "warehouse" supermarkets in America.

Watching station wagons packed full of groceries pulling away from the Prairie Market parking lot, Jack and Cub were convinced that this new format would work in the Minneapolis area. After locating an inexpensive piece of land along a main highway in the nearby suburb of Fridley, they built a very simple, 27,000-square-foot building and opened their first warehouse supermarket—the Food Bonanza. Despite threats from suppliers that they would withhold their products if Food Bonanza resold them too cheaply, Jack and Cub stocked the new store with inventory. After a year of losses and intense effort, the store reached profitability.

Having found a successful formula, Jack and Cub added a few more stores over the next few years and changed the name to Cub Foods. The decor was barebones, with concrete floors, unpainted cinder-block walls, crude wooden shelving, no fresh meats, and almost no produce. There were no coupons, no public-address system, no Muzak, no air-conditioning, little advertising, and no bottle recycling. Labor and frills cost money and force prices up, and that was not the strategy of Cub Foods.

Management was focused totally on keeping costs, and therefore prices, as low as possible. To save labor, individual grocery items were not marked with price stickers. Prices were shown on the shelf underneath the items, and it was the customers' responsibility to mark the prices with a grease pencil on each package. At the checkout counter, a clerk totaled up the purchases, but the shoppers did their own bagging. Because the principles of self-service and scrimping on costs were taken to such an extreme, Cub Foods could offer prices that were 20 to 25 percent below those of conventional supermarkets. To a large family, that meant savings of hundreds of dollars a year. The original Cub Foods warehouse store lived by low prices and low prices alone.

But even with the successful Minneapolis-area launch of the warehouse-supermarket concept, Jack and Cub were not satisfied. They continued their search for other ways to make Cub Foods grow. Experience had shown that the low prices at Cub Foods were not enough to attract the middle-class or upper-middle-class shopper. The Spartan warehouse atmosphere, discount prices, self-bagging, and lack of fresh meats or good produce gave Cub Foods a low-class image. Status-conscious, service-sensitive shoppers in the broad middle-income customer group simply refused to walk into a Cub Foods store. To boost sales further, Cub Foods had to find a way to attract these customers without losing its base of lower-income consumers.

Jack and Cub discovered the solution to this dilemma during a 1974 trip to Los Angeles, when they walked into a Ralph's Supermarket, featuring the most massive display of fresh produce they had ever seen. More than 3,000 square feet were devoted to tables heaped with the finest available fruits and vegetables. The produce department at Ralph's exuded an intoxicating, "horn-of-plenty" feeling. The visual impact of mounds of high-quality, farm-fresh produce was so powerful that Jack and Cub were certain that such a department would instantly change the image of the Cub Foods stores. By 1977, each of the four stores had been remodeled, and the format that was to become the Cub Foods standard had emerged.[4] The message conveyed by the new format: Cub Foods has tremendous freshness, variety, and quality to go along with its low prices.

The message worked. Middle-class customers flocked in and weekly sales began to skyrocket. In fact, sales climbed so quickly that managers and staff were barely able to keep up with the workload. Customers jammed the parking lots, the store aisles, and the checkout lanes. Clearly, Jack and Cub had come up with a brand-new kind of supermarket. They had created a hybrid that blended the most powerful aspect of a warehouse store—everyday low prices—with the best features of an outstanding conventional neighborhood supermarket—freshness, quality, and variety. They had invented a new species of grocery store—the super-warehouse.

The huge size of its stores was central to the success of Cub Foods. When conventional supermarkets were building 25,000-square-foot stores, Cub built 80,000-square-foot stores— equivalent to almost two football fields. With so much space available, Cub had the room to carry

double the assortment of items carried by the average competitor—
25,000 versus the normal 12,000. Virtually any food item a customer
could imagine—from Italian anchovy paste to kosher horseradish—was
shelved somewhere in the cavernous stores. Cub carried 88 kinds of hot
dogs and dinner sausages and 1,500 different frozen-food items. There
was plenty of space for a full-scale delicatessen, a seafood section, a
scratch bakery, a butcher shop, and a pharmacy.

Extra-large, brand-new stores kept open 24 hours a day were designed
to employ all the cost-saving tricks the Hooleys had learned over the
years. For example, most Cubs posted price changes on blackboards,
saving pennies on signs. To save on utilities, heat from the refrigerator
compressors was recirculated through air ducts. Heavy plastic strips
reduced heat loss from truck loading docks and controlled the flow of
cooled air from the dairy section. Laser scanners, brand-new technology
at the time, were installed in all checkstands to accelerate checker productivity. Every aspect of the Cub Foods operation was fine-tuned for
efficiency and designed to minimize the labor needed to provide service
to the customer.[5]

The sudden success of the Cub Foods super-warehouse format took
Minneapolis competitors by surprise. They had dismissed the original
warehouse concept as a passing phenomenon appealing only to low-
income customers. But as customers increasingly abandoned their old
markets for Cub, many of Cub's competitors found themselves racking
up substantial losses. Realizing that the prospects of reversing the situation were remote, the owners of some of these conventional supermarkets decided to pull the plug and withdraw from what had become
the cutthroat game of the Minneapolis grocery world.

But not everyone abandoned the field to Cub Foods. Several conventional supermarkets managed to hang on. Generally, these were independents who decided not even to try matching Cub's low prices. Instead,
these stores advertised their friendly service, the convenience of shopping
so close to home, bagging service, and the quality of their meats and
produce. Store managers asked their butchers to start smiling at customers and start learning the names of regular shoppers. Many stores
were completely remodeled with bright colors, full-service delicatessens,
and bakeries. Supermarkets that avoided nose-to-nose competition with
Cub Foods survived the invasion of super-warehouse stores.

In retrospect, Cub Foods looked like an invincible new challenger.
The company was the first individual of a new, more vigorous species,
one better suited to the conditions of the suburban Minneapolis grocery
business than any of its competitors. But the Hooleys were not convinced

that Cub was a world-beater. The huge size of each store, with all its special laborsaving equipment, meant that an investment of $3 million was required to open a new store. The laser scanners alone cost $250,000 per store. If just one store were built at the wrong highway crossing, the Hooleys could lose everything they had built up over the decades. The risks had grown too great, and family sentiment grew for selling the business.

During this period, Super Valu, one of the nation's largest grocery wholesalers, was a supplier to Cub Foods. Headquartered in another Minneapolis suburb, Super Valu's executives had witnessed at close range the success of Cub Foods. As a key supplier to thousands of independent (nonchain) supermarkets nationwide, Super Valu wanted to offer its supermarket-owning customers something they could not buy from the other major grocery wholesalers—the expertise needed to run a successful super-warehouse store.

The wholesaler believed that the concept could be replicated across the country. It might not work in every city, but it was obviously a powerful new way to run a supermarket. With local independents financing the new stores and Super Valu supplying Cub's surefire success formula, both Super Valu and its customers would gain strength in their never-ending battle against the national chains.

In August 1980, the Hooleys sold all five Cub Foods stores to Super Valu for $10 million. The giant wholesaler hired the entire Cub Foods management team to teach it exactly how to trim costs while building sales. The secrets of Cub's business methods were turned into blueprints, training manuals, and classroom exercises for the independent owners and managers attending Cub's school for new franchisees. The Cub Foods system was reduced to a body of technical information.

These "genes" of a super-warehouse store—the product of decades of innovation and profit reinvestment—could be reproduced far more rapidly by franchising than if the Hooleys had tried to finance hundreds of new stores by themselves. To make copies of genetic information, a source of biological energy must be available. To make copies of technical information, stored-up economic energy—accumulated past profits—must be put to work.

The independent store owners who became Cub Foods franchisees committed past profits from their mature, slow-growth conventional stores. They also invested money borrowed from banks and individuals, money that represented the past profits and savings of companies and families unrelated to the supermarket industry. With dozens of independent firms investing capital to build new stores according to the Cub

Foods formula, the genes of Cub Foods were copied far faster than if the Hooleys had been forced to grow the business strictly from internal profits.

By early 1988, 55 Cub Foods stores were in operation and another 20 were under construction. Every time Cub Foods opens a new store, the competitive scenario unfolds in pretty much the same way. Even before it opens its doors for business, some of the entrenched conventional supermarkets set off a price war in a belated attempt to secure customer loyalty. But most of these supermarkets have not rigorously refined the science of minimizing costs and maximizing sales. They are not nearly as efficient as Cub at getting a roll of paper towels or a can of peaches from the factory to the customer. They cannot begin to offer the huge variety of products that Cub carries. And, with prices marked below their full costs, these stores begin to run up losses. Within months, a handful are forced out of business. In a year or two, after several more relatively high-priced and unattractive stores withdraw from the battlefield, three species of supermarkets remain in business: high-price/high-service conventionals, ultra-low-price/barebones warehouses, and low-price/wide-selection super-warehouses.[6]

Like the distinct bumblebee species working over the flowers in a Maine meadow, these three supermarket species compete with each other to some degree. Just as each bumblebee hive must gather nectar from a limited number of nearby flowers to offset the energy costs of maintaining itself, each supermarket must gather sales dollars from a limited number of nearby customers to offset the overhead costs of running its organization. But, just as the varying tongue lengths of related bumblebee species allow them to specialize in distinct plant species, the differences between these supermarket formats allow them to specialize in distinct customer groups.

Cub Foods attracts a customer group that fits right between the ultra-price-sensitive warehouse customers and the service-oriented conventional customers. A detailed independent study of the Milwaukee marketplace made shortly after Cub opened two stores in 1984 shows how Cub Foods fits into a typical competitive environment.[7] For example, the average super-warehouse customer spends more on each shopping trip ($36) than a conventional store shopper ($27) but less than a warehouse customer ($50). Responding to survey questions about levels of quality and service, shoppers rated Cub midway between the Spartan warehouses and posh conventionals. About half of Cub's sales were captured from warehouses and half were taken from conventionals. In the minds of customers, the super-warehouse, as represented by Cub

Foods, was a hybrid between the low-price/no-frills warehouse and the high-price/high-service conventional.

One might expect that family income level is the biggest factor distinguishing the customers for conventional, super-warehouse, and warehouse stores. But the Milwaukee study showed that low-income, middle-income, and upper-income customers all seemed to shop in roughly the same proportions at all three types of stores. The only glaring difference among shoppers was the number of people in their households. Warehouse shoppers had the largest families, with an average of 3.5 people living in their homes, while super-warehouse shoppers had 3.0 and conventional-store shoppers had 2.5. On reflection, this makes perfect economic sense. The larger the family, the more groceries consumed. As the volume of grocery purchases goes up, more money can be saved by shopping at a store other than a high-price conventional store.

Where a round-trip to a conventional store might take about 40 minutes, the super-warehouse trip may take 70 minutes. A shopper uses an extra 30 minutes shopping at a super-warehouse. Since shopping for most people is drudgery, shoppers must be compensated for their time. A bargain must be struck. The money saved by shopping at a super-warehouse is the payment made by the store to compensate the shopper for the extra time. It's as if flowers doled out larger portions of nectar to encourage bumblebees to fly farther from their hives.

Calculations from data provided in the 1984 study of Milwaukee supermarket competition show that for each extra hour of shopping time spent in either a warehouse or a super-warehouse store, consumers are rewarded with about $12.50 of savings. Since taxes are not taken out of this income, it works out to a wage of roughly $16 per hour. In essence, the owners of these markets pay their customers $16 an hour to shop in their stores and wait in line at the checkstand.[8]

For those with small families, the possible savings are smaller and their effective shopping wage is lower. For those whose family incomes are very high, $16 an hour is not enough to grab their attention or their patronage. Consequently, families with small households and high incomes seldom make the extra effort to go to a super-warehouse or warehouse market. If these stores enjoyed cost advantages over conventionals that allowed them to pay their customers $50 an hour, the conventional markets would be deserted. But, given the efficiencies achieved so far, $16 an hour is about the best the giant stores can offer and still earn profits that are competitive with other kinds of businesses. With the competitive alternatives faced by stores, consumers, and investors, an unspoken but "fair" division of the benefits of their collaboration

Supermarket Income Statement

All Amounts in Dollars (except as noted)	Total Per Week	Total Per Year	As % of Total Revenue
Revenues per Customer Visit	32.25		
Direct Costs per Customer Visit	27.38		
Gross Profit per Customer Visit	4.87		
Average Customer Visits	31,000		
Total Store Revenue	999,750	51,987,000	100.00%
Total Gross Profit		7,850,037	15.10%
Overhead Costs			
Payroll		3,176,406	6.11%
Facilities		1,486,828	2.86%
Depreciation		412,095	0.79%
Advertising		265,134	0.51%
Supplies		410,697	0.79%
Services		181,955	0.35%
Miscellaneous		1,070,932	2.06%
Subtotal		7,004,047	13.47%
Operating Profit		845,990	1.63%
Income Taxes (34%)		287,637	0.55%
Net Profit After Taxes		558,353	1.07%
Total Equity Invested in Store		3,000,000	
Total Debt Borrowed for Store		5,000,000	
Totl Inv. in Store (Net Assets)		8,000,000	
Return on Net Assets%			6.98%
Return on Equity Invested%			18.61%

Source: Willard Bishop Consulting Economists, Ltd., *Competitive Edge Insight Reports* (1987-88)

Figure 13.1

has been made. When new competitive alternatives emerge, the pie will be redivided.

As the history of the Hooley family grocery businesses demonstrates, the expertise—or corporate genetic information—embodied in the Cub Foods system did not emerge full-blown. This knowledge evolved over the course of a century—from the time Grandfather Hooley opened his Stillwater butcher shop in 1876 until the first super-warehouse store was "invented" in 1977. Every step in the evolution of this business required the investment of past profits. When the Hooleys built their first warehouse store in 1968, they risked all the equity value (accumulated past profits) they had built up in the business over the decades. Using the stored-up energy that profit represents, they were able to turn their ideas into a new kind of business.

Although the Hooleys' track record of business innovation is longer than that of most firms, it is by no means unique. In fact, the Hooleys' story is quite representative of how profit-seeking organizations in every industry reinvent themselves again and again. Since companies have no control over the prices their competitors charge, they have no alternative but to keep finding subtle ways to cut costs. When Cub switched from stocking individual milk cartons on shelves to wheeling dairy racks directly into store displays, few customers noticed. Such laborsaving innovations seem trivial. Patents aren't granted and TV crews don't show up to do a profile of a path-breaking dairy-department manager. But such prosaic innovations are the very stuff of economic progress under capitalism. And they keep coming about because firms struggling to eke out profits in a challenging, competitive environment have little choice but to invent ways of whittling down their costs while simultaneously improving their products.

Unfortunately, there are no fossils of bumblebee hives. If there were, the record probably would depict the history of a genus that evolved to be ever-more energy-efficient. A rather unspecialized and energy-inefficient ancestral species was transformed into dozens of distinct bumblebee species, each tuned to minimize energy usage and maximize nectar revenues in a particular ecological niche. As the last 80 million summers turned to autumn, bumblebees that inherited genes endowing better energy efficiency enjoyed higher-energy profits than their competitors. Like grocery-store species, bumblebee species probably became more narrowly specialized and cost-efficient over time.

The emergence of new species does not necessarily mean the oblivion of predecessor species. Ancestral species may not dominate vast regions as they once did, but they survive in narrow niches where their physical characteristics fit well against the selective pressures of the environment. The same can be said of the genus *Grocery store*. The once-ubiquitous family-owned butcher shop, like the one opened by Grandfather Hooley, can still be found today. But its inherent inefficiencies make its high prices attractive only in neighborhoods populated by wealthy gourmets.

The same can be said for the conventional neighborhood supermarket. Of the 30,000 conventionals that were operating in the United States in 1980, nearly half have shut down.[9] Just as these supermarkets displaced most Mom-and-Pop corner grocers in the 1940s and 1950s, they are now being displaced by convenience, warehouse, and super-warehouse stores. Even with the recent appearance of species called "superstores" and "food/drug combos," conventional supermarkets are unlikely to become extinct, but the niche within which they can survive profitably has narrowed. They continue to prosper in neighborhoods dominated by singles and small families insensitive to grocery savings; in inner cities where no sites large enough for warehouse stores can be found; and in rural areas where the volume of business is too small to support super-warehouse stores. The result of all these evolutionary processes is a business environment populated by a spectrum of seven distinct grocery species—from the 7-Eleven convenience store to the Cub Foods super-warehouse store.[10]

No one knows what the next species in the genus *Grocery store* will look like. Some industry experts say it will be the "hypermart," an idea imported from France that is a cross between a Cub Foods and a K mart. But it's too early to tell whether this species will find a niche in the American economy. The only absolute evolutionary certainty is that people working in the grocery industry today will continue to find new ways to improve performance while shaving tiny increments off the cost of doing business.

Today's most technologically advanced supermarket companies are investing their profits in complex data systems that tie checkstand laser scanners to headquarters computers that automatically reorder supplies from the computers of wholesalers and manufacturers. The producers' computers are in turn setting production schedules in manufacturing plants and planning truck routes that minimize freight costs. There is no end to the process of recycling today's profits into the technology that will define the structure of tomorrow's economy. The evolution of capitalism will continue as long as business organizations, in pursuit of elusive profits, keep searching for ways to cut costs while differentiating themselves from their closest competitors.

CHAPTER
14

SAVINGS AND TAXES

Super-warehouse supermarkets could not make profits without willing customers, and shoppers could not save on their groceries without the super-warehouses. Deep-sea tube worms cannot live without their chemosynthetic bacteria, and the bacteria, in turn, depend on the tube worms. Bumblebees cannot survive without flowers, and plants cannot reproduce without the bees. By virtue of their differences, organisms and organizations are able to establish symbiotic or mutualistic relationships—cooperative arrangements that generate benefits for both participants.

Of course, there are exceptions to any rule. Some flowering plants produce no nectar but they use rich fragrances to entice bees into entering and pollinating their flowers. Similarly, before the advent of consumer-protection laws, supermarkets were known to "bait and switch"—advertise a special price for an item and then carry no inventory of that item. Like flowers that fool bees into visiting, these supermarkets exploited their customers.

On the other hand, some bumblebees bite holes in the base of flowers to suck out the nectar without servicing the plants. And, of course, some shoppers don't pay for their groceries. Like nectar-robbing bees, shoplifters exploit supermarkets. Even in predominantly mutualistic systems, examples of unfair behavior are not hard to find.

Exploitation—where the benefits of a relationship flow in one direction—is commonplace. Cigarette companies profit while society picks up the ultimate costs of emphysema and lung cancer. Acid rain poisons lakes and forests in the northeastern United States and Canada, while Appalachian coal companies, midwestern utilities, and their customers enjoy lower electricity costs. In too many cases, employers profit and customers save at the expense of workers suffering from various forms of discrimination.

But under modern mutualistic capitalism, exploitive situations are noteworthy not only because they are unconscionable but because they are so unusual. The vast majority of economic relationships are mutually beneficial and quite unremarkable. The freedom to choose among alternative employers and suppliers keeps economic players honest. Competition imposes a harsh discipline that keeps most organizations from crossing the line that separates mutualists from parasites. Cooperative relationships generate cost savings that are shared between the partners as profits. Unfair profits—where one party gains at the other's expense—are the exception, not the rule.[1]

With only a minor portion of the profits generated in a capitalist economy deriving from parasitic behavior, profits per se do not deserve condemnation. Indeed, since most profit flows from intimate cooperation and the clever application of ideas to cut the costs of life's necessities, profit deserves a far better press than it has received. Moreover, since personal gain causes millions of workers in thousands of specialized organizations to cooperate in making complex products and services, profit is something that society ought to encourage.

In a market economy, either a mutualistic company contributes value to society or it has no customers. To be viable, a company must combine raw materials, labor, and its special expertise to produce an output worth more than the sum value of its component parts. A personal computer is worth more to its buyer than a carton of microchips, plastic, wire, and a credit for the wages of the computer's assemblers. The knowledge base of the computer firm, the company's "genes"—how best to assemble a computer—imparts real value-added to raw inputs. By applying its special know-how, by avoiding wasted materials and labor, an organization creates value.

In the broadest sense, value-added—the difference between the cost of inputs and the worth of finished products—can be thought of as *social profit*. Under modern mutualistic capitalism, each specialized economic organization—from the smallest grocery store to the largest computer maker—contributes to society's total social profit. Once produced, this social profit is divvied up through bargaining. Cub Foods cannot keep all the social profit (value-added) it creates by organizing its operations in such an efficient manner. To attract customers, a portion of its total social profit flows to its customers in the form of lower prices.

Indeed, feverish competition forces Cub Foods to charge prices that distribute the bulk of its value-added back to consumers.

In fact, only a small fraction of Cub Foods' total social profit winds up on its financial "bottom line." After the customers have been bribed with their share of the value-added, other claim-holders take their slices. Interest payments on Cub's borrowed funds flow to the depositors of lending banks. In many companies, a portion of the social profit produced is channeled into employee profit-sharing and incentive programs. Some profit may be contributed to charities in a firm's community. Finally, after all these claims on the social profit have been satisfied, income taxes are levied on what remains of the company's profits. Once these taxes are paid, whatever is left is retained by the company for investment.

Needless to say, the existence of taxes on profits is a crucial distinction between profit flows in nature and in the economy. All the profits retained by a bumblebee hive are reinvested in new queens and drones. One hundred percent of its energy profit is devoted to the next generation of genetic information. But in the American economy, nearly half of an organization's profits will be drawn off by various types of profit taxation. How would an ecosystem's vitality be affected if half of each organism's energy profits were drained from the system?

Of course, human societies are not ecosystems. They are communities of conscious beings who have established governments to deal with problems that cannot be managed effectively through private means. Like all other organizations, governments must have revenues. Taxes imposed by law meet that need. Nonetheless, since profit is the flow of surplus economic energy that pays for technical innovation, and since new technology is the ultimate source of rising living standards, does it make good sense to tax profits as the primary source of government revenue?

Students of taxation might properly point out that companies don't actually bear the ultimate burden of taxes. Through higher prices for the goods they sell, firms shift the final tax cost onto their customers. In the end, it is the people—as earners and consumers and shareholders—that bear all the costs of government. Firms serve the government as tax collectors, but they do not actually pay taxes.

Nonetheless, the American tax system is still based on the taxation of profits. But instead of corporate profits, the system actually rests on "household profits." To calculate the tax bill, total family revenues (all sources of income) are offset by various exemptions. In effect, the various allowances, exemptions, and deductions represent the government's estimate of a barebones cost of living. After these basic household costs are deducted from household revenues, whatever's left is "household profit," or in tax parlance, "taxable income." Tax rates are then applied to this amount.

At present, tax law exclusions for basic living costs work out to about $13,000 for a family of four. Four-member households pay income taxes only on revenues over $13,000, because that is when they turn "profitable."[2] To be more precise, since a household's profit could be saved if it were not taxed away, the "income" tax is, in reality, a tax on potential household savings.

In short, when all of the politically adroit camouflage is stripped away, the simple economic reality is that the federal tax system is based on the taxation of household savings. Consequently, the U.S. government's single most powerful economic policy device is designed to discourage household savings and encourage consumption. After all, once a dollar is received, there are only two things you can do with it. You can spend it now or you can save it for later. Consumption satisfies today's wants. Savings are invested to meet tomorrow's needs and desires.

Few people have much day-to-day control over their earnings. Wage levels are determined largely by one's previous investment in education and skills. But people do control how much they consume and how much they save. Teenagers decide between more stylish clothes and a larger college savings fund. Families choose between larger homes and more retirement money. Executives choose between fancier offices and more sophisticated production equipment. Congress chooses between farm subsidies and scientific research. A single consume/save decision may redirect a few dollars or a few billion dollars, but all decision-makers face the same basic trade-off: now or later. Does consumption or saving make one better off?

Of course, economic choices are rarely "all or nothing" decisions. Teenagers don't choose between no clothes and too much college savings. Few families opt for opulent mansions but no retirement funds. Economic choices are made at the margin, as decision-makers to try to find the right mix. Should your revenues be allocated 95 percent consumption/5 percent savings or 92 percent consumption/8 percent savings?

The design of the tax system is crucial to an economy's long-term vitality, because it influences countless millions of consume/save decisions. Taxing something is like raising its price. When gasoline taxes go up, a gallon's total price increases, and gasoline use declines. In the same way, a tax on savings raises the effective price of savings, making it harder to accumulate savings. When people save less, they consume more. There's nothing else to do with the money.

The American tax system was not always based on savings. Indeed, for most of American history (from 1787 until 1918) federal revenues came from tariffs on imports and taxes on consumption. There was no income tax. Taxes levied on alcohol and tobacco—along with customs duties on imports—were the primary source of government funds. Only during the Civil War, when military costs skyrocketed, did the federal government tax income. This tax was abolished shortly after the end of the Civil War.[3]

But in the late 1800s, political pressure grew for a tax on incomes. And in 1893, Congress responded with a tax targeted at the wealthy. A 2 percent tax was imposed on incomes over $4,000 (about $68,000 in today's money). The Supreme Court soon struck down this law, ruling that under the Constitution, federal taxes could only be assessed in direct proportion to population of the states.

For a time, popular demand for an income tax subsided. But in 1909, Congress passed a tax on corporate profits, and four years later, the states ratified the Sixteenth Amendment to the Constitution. This amendment empowered the Congress to impose direct income taxes.

At first, income taxes affected only the wealthiest Americans. But as federal spending grew, people further and further down the income ladder began to be taxed. Almost without notice, a tax designed for the wealthy became a tax on everyone. Over the years, tax rates were raised and lowered, loopholes were opened and closed, but inexorably, the federal government's primary revenue source shifted away from taxes on consumption to taxes on savings. By 1988, "income" taxes, together with social security taxes, comprised over 90 percent of all federal revenues.[4] A nation that began the twentieth century without taxes on household savings ended up with a government utterly dependent on such taxes.

The dire economic consequences of a system that taxed savings did not begin to emerge until the late 1960s. As spending for Great Society programs and the Vietnam War rose, the percentage of the nation's total output absorbed by the federal government began climbing. Tax rates went up, and the income tax bite got bigger. The tax shelter "industry" flourished and lobbying for special tax favors intensified beyond all previous experience.

In the 1970s, several waves of inflation swept American economy. As in every inflationary period, consumers began buying goods even before they wanted them. Delaying purchases meant much higher future prices.

In the midst of this inflation-inspired buying binge, many Americans discovered they could deduct from their taxable income (potential household savings) interest paid on borrowings. Under the rules of the tax law, interest costs took on a privileged status. The cost of being in debt was treated as if it was a basic necessary household cost, like those covered by the personal exemptions. Every dollar of interest paid by an indebted family was heavily subsidized by debt-free taxpayers.

Inflation also stimulated another powerful phenomenon known as "bracket creep." As inflation drove wages up along with prices, families found themselves reporting ever higher incomes, though in real terms, they were no better off. Surreptitiously, inflation raised the tax rate faced by the typical American family. More than ever, it made economic sense to avoid taxes by borrowing.

It took several years to get the "borrow and spend" message across to millions of independent decision-makers. But with credit-card companies, tax accountants, and banks only too anxious to point out the benefits of borrowing from the future to consume now, the American people caught on. Today, many people believe that Americans are innately spendthrifts. Few realize that before World War II, before the "income" tax system reached it present form, Americans saved a larger portion of their earnings than the Japanese.[5]

During the 1970s, many millions of Americans figured out that it was smart to be in as much debt as their paychecks allowed them to carry. And since, aside from their car, the only property most Americans can borrow against is their house, the tax shield provided by the "home mortgage interest deduction" became the central icon of American economic culture. Not surprisingly, home building and the suburban sprawl that it generates are major preoccupations of American life.

Despite the tragedy of America's homeless citizens, over 99 percent of Americans do have places to live. Tens of millions own homes that are lavish by any international standard. Indeed, conspicuous consumption of housing seems like a peculiar American cultural trait unless one appreciates the enormous stimulus to housing construction provided by federal tax law.

Of course, in any large population some families would be big spenders, take on a lot of debt, and consume beyond their means. Even without generous tax breaks for borrowing and consuming, such behavior would be common. But the big spenders would be matched by an equally fervent group of big savers. Over time, wealth would shift within the population from the consumers to the savers. Only when the tax law wildly favors consumption does the entire population's normal consumption/saving pattern become distorted.

Sadly, America's runaway consumption of housing is just the most vivid example of a vast overconsumption problem. Until the tax law was changed in 1986, all interest payments—even for credit card debt— was subsidized by debt-free taxpayers. Much of that credit card debt has since been recast as home equity debt in order to retain the protection of the mortgage deduction. The labels on the accounts have changed, but it's still debt.[6]

Surveys now show that most Americans don't save at all. With so much of their earnings deducted for various taxes before they even see their paychecks, and with rules that explicitly encourage consumption, this should hardly come as a surprise. Under the rules of the American tax game, the usual human motive for saving—having more later on by sacrificing a bit today—no longer holds true.

Of the savings that Americans do have, most of it is in pension plans. Like interest costs, money that flows into pensions gets preferential treatment under the tax code; it is not "recognized" as taxable income. Before the 1986 tax law effectively eliminated tax protection for Individual Retirement Accounts (IRAs), these accounts had become important vehicles for saving. When given the opportunity, rational people divert the flow of their scarce resources through the channels where it is least taxed.

If your potential savings is going to be taxed, but your consumption isn't, you might as well spend your money now. Only when potential savings, like pension funding, is beyond the reach of the Internal Revenue Service, does it make sense to actually save it. Otherwise, the best policy is to spend whatever you get and take on as much debt as possible. Rely on high interest payments to shield your potential savings. Even though you may have to buy more housing than you want to accomplish this goal, you might get lucky and later resell the house at a gain. Oddly enough, under the bizarre rules that Americans have come to accept as the natural order of things, being deeply in hock is the only way most families have of protecting their financial future.

In short, a tax originally intended to force the super-wealthy to pay their fair share of the nation's expenses became a system that compelled average citizens to liquidate their savings, borrow against the future, and consume. From the 1960s to the 1980s, America's savings as a percent of GNP dropped from 11 percent to 4 percent.[7] Today, the U.S. has less than half the average saving rate of the major industrialized nations and about one-fifth the saving rate of Japan.[8] And, though many commentators contend that Americans simply have an insatiable appetite for the good life, no other country's tax system so adamantly insists, "Don't save; borrow and consume!"[9]

The nation's tax system has an equally devastating impact on business behavior. The corporate takeover boom of the 1980s was, after all, fueled by "junk bond" debt. Until quite recently, interest paid on sums borrowed for takeovers was subsidized by the average taxpayer. In effect, financiers found a way to tap the equity (accumulated savings) locked inside large corporations. Just as home-equity credit lines permit homeowners to spend their net worth, a massive surge in American corporate debt allowed executives to drain equity from businesses. When the next recession hits, the weakest firms with the heaviest debt burdens will be driven into bankruptcy.

To top it all off, the savings problems of American households and businesses are vastly compounded by the federal government's own massive debt. Now over $3 trillion, federal government debt per individual American is about $12,000. At roughly 4 percent of the GNP, the federal deficit annually adds almost $900 to this invisible—but quite real—debt burden.

Making matters even worse, the federal government's thirst for resources drains them away from productive investment. With America's pool of savings so limited, massive government borrowing bids up market interest rates and makes many private investments unprofitable. The much-criticized "short-term mentality" of American business executives is an inevitable consequence of the high cost of capital. When rational investors face high capital costs, they have no choice but to focus on low-risk, quick-payoff investments. High-risk, long-term investments, the kind represented by virtually all technological innovations, can be pursued only by those with abundant savings and a low cost of capital— namely, the Japanese. America's high cost of capital is a symptom of an economy starved for savings.[10]

Together, an anti-savings tax system and gigantic federal deficits have grievously damaged America's economic future. A persistent $100 billion–plus trade deficit (because consumption exceeds total production), mounting debts to foreign lenders, pitifully inadequate R&D spending, shabby university laboratories, a stagnant average standard of living, and deteriorating conditions for America's poorest families are all consequences of an economy gradually suffocating for lack of investable funds.

In 1989, with half the population, Japan spent more than the United

States on new plant and equipment. Indeed, if Japanese and other foreign investors had not invested some of their excess savings in American facilities, the situation would have been far worse. Nonetheless, even with substantial foreign investment, how can American workers and firms compete in a global economy if they must make do with less than half as much state-of-the-art equipment?

Given the armies of economic experts that regularly appear before congressional panels, one might well wonder how we managed to paint ourselves into this corner. Why did America erect such a destructive tax system and then compound the damage with runaway deficit spending? Simply put: because traditional economics never grasped the connection between the economic present and the economic future.

Specifically, economic thought has been crippled by two fundamental errors. From the time of Karl Marx, profits have been widely regarded as inherently evil. According to Marx, profits could come only from the exploitation of workers. That surplus value could be created through mutualistic cooperation apparently never occurred to Marx. Consequently, all profit was morally tainted. Marx's remedy was a heavily progressive income tax. Such a system was seen as the best way to recapture profits that never legitimately belonged to the "exploiters." For Marx, the economy was an indestructible machine, not a living ecosystem whose continued existence depended upon the recycling of economic energy.

The second crucial error was made by John Maynard Keynes. Perhaps the most influential economist of the twentieth century, Keynes argued that recessions and depressions, particularly the Great Depression of the 1930s, were caused by too much saving and not enough consumption. Keynes imagined the economy to be an engine that could not run efficiently and keep everyone employed unless the government kept a heavy foot on the accelerator. By subsidizing the cost of private debt and spending more than it taxed, government could pump up consumption and keep the economic engine humming.

When America's Keynesian economists first came to power in the 1960s, they planned to spend in deficit only during recessions. By cleverly fiddling with this fiscal throttle, they expected to vanquish the business cycle. But for practical political reasons, things never quite turned out that way. Once a federal spending program starts, it is very hard to stop. The special interest groups that benefit from a particular program always fight like demons to keep it.[11]

Once the borrowing started, there was no easy way to stop it. And in short order, Keynes's dogma of inadequate demand had created a vast new "commons problem." Here, the commons was the pool of savings normally invested in the future economy. Since citizens not yet born or too young to vote have no political power, they have no way to defend the economy they inherit. Unrestrained by any political counterforce, the American economy had fallen into what might best be described as a "Keynesian black hole."

Now that we recognize the disastrous consequences of Marx's attack on profits and Keynes's predeliction for deficit spending, it is possible to redesign basic policies and begin America's economic recovery. Already alarmed by the explosive growth of federal debt during the 1980s, the American public and worried foreign governments demanded that America's politicians face the issue. Despite its many weaknesses, a deficit reduction plan seems to be slowly narrowing the federal budget gap. Once a balanced budget is reached, it should be locked in. Over 30 state legislatures have already called for a constitutional amendment to keep the federal budget balanced.

Redesigning the federal government's anti-savings tax system may take even longer than staunching the flow of federal red ink. Most economists recommend special tax treatment for various forms of savings and investment. Some want to revive the IRAs, while others push for a reduction in the tax rate on capital gains. Just a few years after the 1986 tax act eliminated most loopholes, the tradition of cutting loopholes into the tax code has resumed.

Too few of the experts seem to realize that if a tax system must be riddled with loopholes to make it economically functional, then perhaps its basic design is wrong to begin with. These experts forget that no law of nature requires that a government raise the bulk of its revenue from an income tax.

A sound tax system need meet only two requirements. First, it must be fair within each generation. The taxes each family pays should reflect its ability to pay. Second, a tax system must be fair across several generations. To protect the viability of the future economy, taxes must not distort the people's usual consumption/saving preferences.

The most promising idea is to create a new federal sales tax—much like a state sales tax—that is tied to the consumption of goods and services.[12] The traditional argument against consumption taxes is that they are unfair, or in tax parlance, regressive.[13] A regressive tax forces a poor family to pay a larger portion of its income in taxes than a wealthy family. Consumption taxes are seen as regressive because household necessities—food, clothing, and the like—take up a relatively larger share of a poor family's income.

Some proponents of a national consumption tax deal with the problem of overtaxing poor consumers by suggesting different tax rates for essentials and non-essentials. But the consumption tax experience in Western Europe shows this approach to be an administrative and political nightmare. Producers constantly lobby to get their goods recategorized as low-tax-rate "essentials." Other tax experts argue for exempting essentials like food and clothing altogether. But it turns out that the well-to-do families actually spend a larger percentage of their income on things like clothing than do poor families.[14]

In the end, the cleanest solution would be to tax all consumption at the same rate and then rebate the first several hundred dollars of federal sales tax each person pays on basic consumption items. After all, even the strongest proponents of a consumption tax realize that the income tax will not be abolished. This being the case, the income-tax system might as well be used to rebate taxes on basic consumption. Once one gets above the level of basic consumption, a flat-rate consumption tax is perfectly fair. People do not consume if they cannot afford to. By the very act of consuming, they demonstrate their "ability to pay" more taxes.[15]

Many consumption tax supporters endorse something called the VAT (Value-Added Tax), instead of a federal sales tax. The VAT is the common form of Western European consumption tax. Under this system, taxes are added into a product's price as it moves through each stage of production. The steel company pays a VAT on the iron ore it gets from the mining company. The automaker pays a VAT on the steel. The auto dealer pays a VAT on the car. Finally, the consumer pays for all the layers of VAT, and all the producers get full refunds.

Two problems weaken this approach. First, the VAT requires a large bureaucracy to handle the paperwork. Second, and more important, the VAT is buried in the price of final goods and services. The car buyer cannot tell what portion of the car's price is for the car itself and what portion reimburses the dealer for the VAT. In a democracy, taxes—like prices—should be clearly labeled. For a society's financial signalling system to work effectively, citizens must know how much tax they are paying for a given quality and quantity of government services.

The simplest alternative is to install a federal sales tax.[16] Forty-five of 50 states—home to 98 percent of all Americans—levy sales taxes. Virtually all businesses already calculate and report sales taxes. A federal sales tax would be easy to implement and impossible to hide from taxpayers. Some VAT proponents argue that the states don't want their sales tax "turf" invaded by the federal government, but this ignores the fact that state and federal tax collectors presently share the income-tax turf.

To eliminate the existing bias toward borrowing and consumption, federal income-tax rates should be cut as a federal sales tax is implemented. For example, a 10 percent federal sales tax with a $250 rebate to every person would raise nearly $200 billion, or almost half as much as the corporate and personal income taxes now raise. If income tax rates fell from 15/28 percent to roughly 10/18 percent, the federal government would raise just about as much money as it does now, but the incessant pressure to consume rather than save would be relieved. The right mix of tax rates on income (savings) and consumption would rebalance the economic system and revive long-term growth.

But despite the destructiveness of the present anti-savings system, a switch to a balanced tax system is unlikely to come about anytime soon.[17] Politically savvy observers argue that such a fundamental change in society's economic ground rules is impossible. But somehow change must come, because the alternative—doing nothing or cutting more loopholes into the income tax system—will not halt the demise of the United States as an economic power and world leader.

PART **IV**

■

LEARNING
AND
PROGRESS

■

Practice makes perfect.
—*Traditional adage*

CHAPTER
15

SURVIVAL TRAINING

D aily existence presents few intellectual challenges to the microscopic creatures inhabiting a drop of pond water. Single-celled animals called protozoans noiselessly graze on bacteria and algae, going about the business of growth and reproduction. For these animals, whose lifespans are measured in hours or days, life is as stupefyingly boring as it ever gets. Quite often, the very first problem a protozoan faces is its last. A passing tadpole, dragonfly, or guppy—all hideous monsters by comparison—may inadvertently swallow the entire waterdrop community. Unobserved and unmourned, countless millions of nature's tiniest animals depart the living world in the course of a lazy summer afternoon.

With life so brief and monotonous, protozoan intelligence seems an absurd luxury. Why should a microscopic animal be smart enough to learn if it is unlikely to live long enough to apply any knowledge gained? In the rigorous economy of nature, a protozoan that invests scarce resources in intelligence would seem to be at a severe evolutionary disadvantage. For the survival of the species, cellular simplicity and prodigious reproductive capacity would seem to make far more sense than having enough intelligence to learn from experience.[1]

But sensible assumptions are no match for facts. So, at the turn of this century, Herbert S. Jennings, then a young zoology professor at the University of Michigan, conducted a famous experiment to find out whether one of life's simplest beings could learn. For his work, Jennings selected the pond-dwelling protozoan called Stentor. Named after a Greek warrior whose voice could drown out 50 other men, Stentor's conelike shape resembles a college cheerleader's megaphone.

The wide end of a Stentor's body is its "mouth" and the narrow point its "foot." When the animal finds a suitable feeding spot, it attaches its foot to the surface of a decaying leaf or other debris. The rim of a Stentor's mouth is covered with tiny hairlike organelles, called cilia, that beat in undulating waves. By their coordinated rowing, the cilia create a tiny vortex that sucks particles of food—mostly bacteria and microscopic plants and animals—into the Stentor's gaping mouth.[2]

While peering through a microscope, Jennings used a thin glass tube to drop particles of carmine, a noxious red pigment, into the water above the animal's mouth. At first, the Stentor swallowed the carmine and kept on feeding, but as soon as it sensed the chemical, it bent its mouth away from the source. The carmine cloud soon enveloped the creature, so it tried another reaction. For a moment, the Stentor reversed the direction of its cilia to expel the polluted water from its mouth; then it resumed its normal feeding.

But the carmine was still present, and, after a few more tries at the reversal maneuver, the Stentor closed its mouth and squeezed itself down into a tight little ball around its foot. This successfully avoided the carmine, but it also cut off the hungry animal's access to food. So, after another half-minute, the protozoan began to extend itself to resume feeding. But this time, when the Stentor again sensed the carmine, it didn't bother with its initial repertoire of evasive maneuvers—first bending its body, then reversing the water current. Instead, it hunched down as soon as it tasted the pollutant. Each time it tried to start feeding for the next fifteen minutes, it contracted again. After every contraction, it hunkered down a bit longer, until finally, with the carmine unavoidable, the Stentor jerked its body violently until its foot let go of its attachment. Having had quite enough, the protozoan swam off to a more hospitable spot.[3]

Jennings's experiment in protozoan learning was but one brief episode in a vast twentieth-century scientific undertaking. In an attempt to discover the underlying mechanisms of human intelligence, thousands of comparative psychologists have spent their careers investigating the learning abilities of "lower" species. Legions of paramecia, octopi, worms, crayfish, honeybees, rats, goldfish, cats, pigeons, and chimpanzees have endured all sorts of exotic experiments designed to assess and rank their intelligence. But, despite the magnitude of the effort, one prominent expert recently concluded, "Comparative psychologists have spent about 100 years in the more or less serious scientific study of animal intelligence. It cannot be claimed that they have very much to show for their pains."[4]

Beyond demonstrating that animals, stretching from protozoans to humans, do indeed modify their behavior in light of previous experience, little else has been proved conclusively. In fact, even at this date, the experts cannot agree on a precise definition of the term *learning*.[5] For some, the Stentor's varied responses to carmine are not sophisticated enough to indicate "learning."[6] These psychologists reserve use of the term for more complex animal behaviors, such as that of a dancing bear in the Moscow Circus. Human learning—so intimately bound up with language—is generally put in a class by itself.

One of the few principles accepted by all the experts is that learning, whatever its complexity, depends on the accumulation of experience. Whether the learner is a "lower" animal or a human being, improved performance—the tangible result of learning—is a product of repetition. As anyone who has taken on a new task knows, the first few tries take longer, with poorer results, than subsequent attempts. Whether it's diapering a baby, adjusting a carburetor, or sinking a jump shot, practice makes perfect.

Trying to quantify the relationship between experience and learning has occupied psychologists for decades. In a famous 1922 experiment, Edward Tolman, a leading psychologist at the University of California at Berkeley, and his graduate students measured the effect of experience on learning by testing laboratory rats.[7] Their technique was simple: Place a rat in a wooden maze and record the time the animal took to find its way out. The maze had several blind alleys and one goal box. A food reward was placed in the goal box before each run. Every day for several weeks, each of the 36 rats was run through the maze once a day. Each run through the maze constituted one unit of experience.[8]

Stopwatch in hand, Tolman's graduate students patiently recorded the times of each rat on each run through the maze. The results were far from surprising, but the experiment did provide plenty of precise data on the average rat's learning rate. A graph showed that during the first few trials, the rats dramatically reduced their times to reach the reward. Then it took several more trials for the rats to achieve only slightly better performances. The general shape of the curve seemed to indicate that the rats' rate of learning gradually slowed with repeated trials.

But shaving fewer seconds with each subsequent run does not mean that the rats' *rate* of learning had diminished. To calculate a rate of learning, one must compare the *improvement of performance* to the *growth of experience*. For example, if a rat takes 50 seconds to run the maze in its second trial and 40 seconds in its fourth, the rat's performance

Maze Learning in Rats
(Linear Scale)

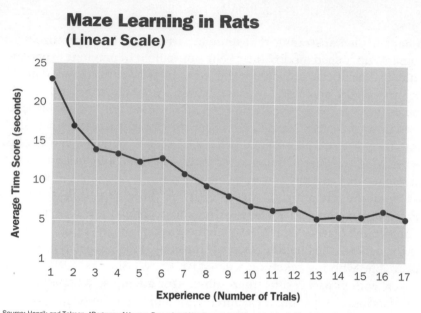

Source: Honzik and Tolman, "Degrees of Hunger, Reward and Non-Reward, and Maze Learning in Rats," *Univ. of Calif. Publ. in Psych.* (1930)

Figure 15.1

improves 20 percent (10 seconds saved out of 50), while its total experience doubles (second to fourth trial). In other words, a 100 percent addition to the rat's experience base yields a 20 percent performance improvement.

If the same rat then cut its time to 32 seconds by its eighth trial, another doubling of accumulated experience yields another 20 percent improvement. Saving eight seconds after four additional runs might not seem as impressive as the ten-second savings achieved between the second and fourth runs, but in both cases a 100 percent increase in experience generates a 20 percent improvement in performance.

When comparing two rates of change, the clearest picture of their relationship is provided by a double logarithmic graph. Despite its forbidding name, a double-log graph is perfectly straightforward. On normal graph paper, the distance between 2 and 4 is twice the distance between 1 and 2. But on a log graph, the distances between 1 and 2, 2 and 4, and 4 and 8 are the same because each of these jumps is the same percentage change, an increase of 100 percent. On log graphs, equal distances represent equal percentage differences.

Professor Tolman never plotted the data from his maze-running rats on a double-log graph, but doing so provides a more revealing picture of the rats' learning history. Even though the rats saved less time with each subsequent run, the rats' rate of learning did not gradually decrease. In fact, the results showed three distinct phases in the experiment. In the first half-dozen trials, the rate of improvement was modest (about a 20 percent time decrease with each doubling of experience) as the rats memorized the exact sequence of left and right turns from the starting gate to the goal box. During the next six runs, performance improved rapidly (50 percent time reduction with each doubling of experience) as the rats scurried to the reward as fast as possible. Then, after about the twelfth run, progress stopped (0 percent time decrease with each experience doubling). Apparently, the rats had perfected their technique and their little legs simply could not carry them any faster.

In the years following Tolman's experiments on rat learning, studies on a wide variety of species confirmed that improving performance was a direct consequence of accumulating experience. Of course, the steepness of each learning-curve slope—the subject's rate of learning—varied from experiment to experiment.[9] And, for a time, some investigators believed that by comparing learning-curve slopes of various species, they could determine the rank order of animal intelligence. Their reasoning was simple: The steeper the learning curve, the faster the learning, and thus the smarter the species.

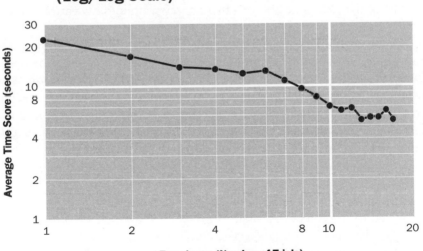

Maze Learning in Rats
(Log/Log Scale)

Source: Honzik and Tolman, "Degrees of Hunger, Reward and Non-Reward, and Maze Learning in Rats," *Univ. of Calif. Publ. in Psych.*(1930)

Figure 15.2

But even if two species are run through exactly the same experiment, their learning curves cannot be compared meaningfully. Imagine trying to get an octopus to slither through a rat maze. Rats are especially good at learning mazes, because they evolved to live in burrows.[10] Octopi, on the other hand, happen to be quite bright, but their intelligence evolved to support aquatic skills. Since no two species are identical, designing unbiased experiments is impossible. And without absolutely fair tests, the comparison of learning curves is pointless. Learning curves prove that experience drives learning, but they cannot be used to sort out the relative intelligence of animal species.[11]

Once it became clear that learning experiments would never lead to a reliable ranking of animal intelligence or to answers to crucial questions about human intelligence, a completely different approach took center stage. In 1973, H. J. Jerison, a professor of psychiatry at UCLA, published a study that compared the brain and body sizes of hundreds of specimens of both living and extinct species.[12] Jerison's work revealed several vital insights. Each class of backboned animals (amphibians, fish, reptiles, birds, and mammals) has its own characteristic brain-mass/body-mass ratio. Mammals—the most recently evolved group—have the highest brain/body ratio.[13]

Within each class of vertebrates, as body size increases from one species to the next, brain size expands in an extremely predictable fashion. But for a few aberrant species, the tight relationship between brain and body size does not hold. In these species, brain/body ratios diverge wildly from the statistical norms for their class.

Among mammals, the species with the most abnormal brain/body ratio is *Homo sapiens*. Compared to a "standard" mammal of equal body weight, humans have hideously large brains. The enormous size of the human brain is not unlike the absurdly long snout of the anteater. In both cases, one part of the animal is grossly out of proportion to the rest of its anatomy. Professor Jerison captured the magnitude of this deviation from expected brain size with an index called the EQ, short for "encephalization quotient." The EQ compares the actual brain/body ratio of a species to its predicted ratio. The human's EQ of 7.44 means that the human brain is 7.44 times heavier than would be mathematically predicted for a typical mammal of human body weight. *Homo sapiens* has the highest EQ of any species, living or extinct.

Since the brain endows an animal with information-processing ability, any excess brain tissue seemingly would allow an animal to process information above and beyond that needed for basic sensation and muscle control. The higher the EQ, the greater the brain's information-

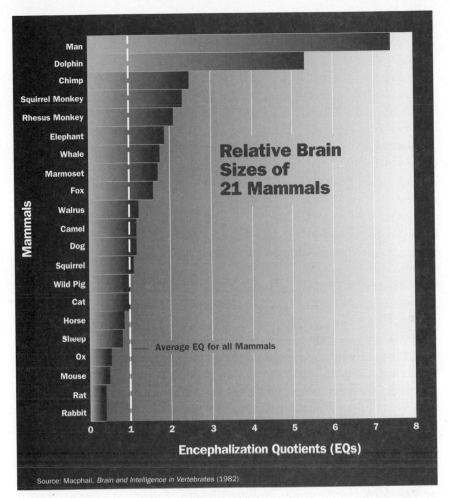

Figure 15.3

processing capacity. Since complex learning requires the capacity to process huge quantities of information, it seems that the EQ of a species could serve as a rough measure of its overall intelligence. And although controversy still surrounds the method of computing EQs, a ranking of mammal EQs jibes quite well with our intuitive sense of the relative intelligence of these animals.[14]

Of course, knowing that an animal has a certain amount of extra brain tissue says nothing about how that raw information-processing capacity is used. In fact, two species with exactly the same EQ—the same *amount* of intelligence—will have different *types* of intelligence because of differences in their ways of life.[15] Wolves and deer have just about the same EQ, but their behavior patterns are completely different. What it takes to be a competent wolf obviously is different from what it takes to survive as a deer.

Precisely the same issues confront scientists trying to compare the intelligence of humans and that of our closest intellectual rivals, the bottle-nosed dolphins (*Tursiops truncatus*). Their EQ indicates that they have nearly as much raw brainpower as humans, but dolphin intelligence is used for different purposes. The dolphins' survival hangs on their ability to eat and not be eaten in a vast and murky domain. In their watery niche, dolphins must know what is swimming around them at all times.

Because sound waves carry so well in water, these mammals evolved sophisticated sonarlike sensory systems for tracking objects in the ocean depths. Evolution also dedicated a large portion of the dolphin's massive brain to translating acoustic signals into wraparound, three-dimensional mental maps. Apes, by contrast, emerged on a mostly two-dimensional land surface, where light waves traveling through the air provided crucial information. Consequently, much of the large primate brain was committed to an enormous expansion of the visual system.[16]

Our diverse evolutionary histories help explain some of the differences between human and dolphin intelligence. But, according to most researchers, the very essence of human intelligence, the feature that so radically distinguishes us from all other species, comes from the human brain's ability to process language. One expert asks, "Do humans acquire language because they are more intelligent than non-humans, or are humans more intelligent than non-humans because they acquire language?"[17] Whatever the answer, it is clear that language is absolutely central to human learning and intelligence. Indeed, it is hard even to imagine human intelligence without language. How can anyone think without using words?

This is not to say that only humans can communicate. Individuals in many species communicate, but language is a very special form of communication. The gestures, sounds, and odors of animal communication convey relatively simple information. But with a collection of sentences, people can transmit ornately detailed information. Language allows teachers to pass learning along to students lacking in experience. By any measure, spoken language is far more flexible and powerful than other forms of animal communication.

In recent years, the popular press has reported that chimpanzees have been taught language, but no experiment has proved this claim. Chimps *are* able to learn that certain symbols carry specific meanings, but recognizing symbols does not constitute language. Having language requires the ability to translate symbols, as well as the ability to place those symbols in proper sequence. Under the rules of English syntax, "Dog chews bone" conveys meaning; "Chews bone dog" does not. The importance of sequence—or syntax, as linguists call it—seems beyond the reach of chimp intelligence.

This should not be too surprising. Although chimps are our closest surviving evolutionary relatives, they possess a far lower EQ (2.49) than humans (7.44). This EQ gap may simply be too large for chimps ever to grasp the fundamentals of sentence structure. The computational power required to digest a complete sentence may overtax the data-handling capacity of the chimpanzee brain. Without a lot more excess brain tissue, using language may be an impossible feat for a chimp.

By this logic, it seems that bottle-nosed dolphins, with their much higher EQ (5.31) might have enough brainpower to handle language. And although it has not yet been proved that wild dolphins have language, a meticulously executed experiment recently showed that bottle-nosed dolphins do comprehend sentences as long as five words.[18] For example, the command "SURFACE HOOP FETCH BOTTOM BASKET," elicits a different response from a trained dolphin than the sentence "BOTTOM BASKET FETCH SURFACE HOOP." Unlike chimps, dolphins grasp syntax as well as symbols.

Should future research with dolphins show that humans hold no monopoly on spoken language, we will be forced once again to admit the closeness of our relationship with the rest of nature's species. Even if the complexity of human speech turns out to be greater than that of dolphins, such a finding would only show a difference of degree, not a difference of kind. Where before Darwin we considered ourselves "little lower than the angels," we may finally come to see ourselves as biological freaks—the mammal with the absurdly high EQ, a statistical outlier in nature's experiments with various brain/body combinations.

Ultimately, the only absolute distinction separating humans from dolphins and all other species may be that humans alone have a second form of language—writing. Once we learn to read, it comes so naturally that it's hard to appreciate the awesome complexity of the act. Our brains somehow breathe meaning into otherwise-empty squiggles. Who has not been transported to an imaginary world created by Dostoyevski or Hemingway? The human brain's singular capacity for interpreting strings of written symbols allows people distanced by oceans of space and time to share the most intimate details of their inner lives. Even if dolphins are shown to have the power of speech, they do not have writing.

Like all of our other physical attributes, our ability to read resulted from a series of evolutionary accidents. Apparently the verbal ability of prehumans was grafted onto the superb visual apparatus possessed by all apes. The fusion of language and vision gave our brains the capacity to extract meaning from written symbols. Without this biological potential for literacy, science and technology would have been impossible.[19] Speech alone could not have propelled humanity to its present mastery of the planet. If there is a single anatomical basis for modern civilization, it is the brain's ability to convey its internal imagery to other brains through writing.

If literacy, rather than speech or the opposable thumb, is the attribute that distinguishes us from all other species, it makes sense that the use of written information is the key to our evolutionary success.[20] Ever since our ancestors painted symbols on cave walls, we have been using writing to gain an edge in the struggle for survival. As we moved from notches carved into reindeer antlers to transistors etched into silicon chips, our skill in storing and retrieving knowledge improved, but its fundamentals remained unchanged. In effect, the evolution of technology is an outgrowth of literacy—humanity's unique biological capacity.

Obviously, verbal language also played a crucial role in the development of modern society. Even today, the bulk of daily personal communication is spoken, not written. But, from an economic standpoint, writing is the magic potion because it alone allows several people to work cooperatively on exactly the same problem. Speech is the communication medium of family and friends, but writing is the medium of science and business.

As the parlor game of "Telephone" shows, speech is too easily garbled to convey the same precise meaning to several minds. Before writing existed, the prehuman hunter-gatherer bands that roamed the world for millennia were, like dolphins and every other species, prisoners of their inability to solve the most complex survival problems. It is no accident that every advanced civilization of the past, from the Sumerians to the present, had some form of writing. Only writing imparts the full power of organized intelligence to otherwise-disparate individuals.

CHAPTER
16

ORGANIZATIONAL LEARNING

Without many minds chipping away at the same problem, sustained technical progress is virtually impossible. A group solves a problem that would overwhelm a Newton or an Einstein. Through the medium of written symbols, our individual mental powers are melded into "organized intelligence." The evolutionary advantage conferred upon humanity by the brain's ability to read finds its ultimate expression in the problem-solving power of intelligent organizations. In short, our species has come to dominate the planet because a unique feature of our brains allows us to form intelligent organizations.

Logically, if an organization can be said to have "intelligence," then it ought to behave like an intelligent organism; it ought to learn from experience.[1] In the business world, an intelligent firm should show improving performance as it accumulates experience in producing its products. Just like Edward Tolman's maze-running rats, intelligent firms ought to demonstrate clear learning curves.

But how can one measure the "learning curve" of an organization? In maze running, the rat's decreasing time to the goal box is an unequivocal measure of learning. In business, what's the proof of learning? Steadily rising profitability? If so, very few firms can be called learners. The profitability of virtually every firm gyrates up and down with changing market conditions. Even the most successful companies do not widen their profit margins indefinitely. Competitors see to that.

And even if a company's performance could be quantified by something other than profitability, how can a firm's experience be measured accurately? Financial analysts compare corporate performance from one year to the next. But a year is a measure of time, not a measure of the experience garnered in that time. In the psychologist's laboratory, it is easy to measure a rat's maze-running experience. A single run through the maze is one unit of experience. But what constitutes a unit of experience for a company?

An organization gains a unit of experience each time it completes one unit of output. Just as a rat's unit of experience is a single run through the maze, a firm's unit of experience is the cycle of producing one unit of product from raw materials. Converting inputs into finished goods and services is the essential function of every economic organization. Each time a company cranks out one more unit of product, it accumulates another unit of experience in solving the problems associated with turning inputs into outputs. When measuring an organization's experience, the cumulative number of units produced to date is perfectly analogous to the number of maze trials previously run.

The performance of an organization can also be measured in a rigorous way. When a firm reduces the amount of labor and materials needed to produce a single unit of output, its economic performance improves. In effect, a firm's cost per unit of output is analogous to a rat's time per maze run. Since a rat uses up food every second, its maze-running time actually measures the energy cost of its search for a food reward. As the rat learns to avoid wrong turns and wastes less time, it cuts the cost of attaining the reward. By tinkering with its production methods, an organization trims the costs associated with earning a given price. In both organisms and organizations, performance is measured by the cost associated with a particular unit of experience.

With accurate data on unit costs and cumulative output, it should be easy to plot a firm's learning curve. But even when detailed company data are available, plotting a learning curve is not as simple as it is in the psychologist's lab. During the course of a maze-running experiment, the rats repeatedly run through exactly the same maze. Changing the maze layout in the middle of an experiment obviously would invalidate the results.

In the economy, however, companies rarely keep on producing absolutely identical products. To stay competitive, they revamp designs continually. Companies that don't, usually go out of business. But because firms keep modifying their products, the unit of production experience is unstable, making impossible any perfectly fair cost comparisons between earlier and later units. Nonetheless, some products—100-watt light bulbs, soap bars, aluminum ingots, and chicken eggs, to mention a few—rarely are modified. Unchanging commodities like these are stable units of production experience. As such, they offer the best tests of organizational learning.

But, unfortunately, even when the unit of experience is stable, the unit-measuring cost is not. Professor Tolman timed his rats with a stopwatch, but companies must measure their costs with money. Each click of the second hand marked off precisely the same amount of time, but this level of reliability cannot be claimed for the dollar, or any other form of money. For a variety of reasons, the actual economic value measured by a dollar, yen, mark, pound, lira, peso, or franc keeps changing over time.

Usually, the value represented by a given unit of money shrinks due to price inflation. For example, in 1972, the average wholesale price of a dozen chicken eggs in the United States was 31 cents. By 1980, the price was 56 cents, an increase of 80 percent in just eight years.[2] Obviously, the product had not changed, and the data show that the number of eggs produced and consumed had remained the same. For all practical purposes, the real economic value of a dozen eggs was constant. In a period of rapid inflation, the egg price rose only because the dollar's value had shrunk by 80 percent.

Money inflation has the same distorting effect as if Professor Tolman's stopwatch had kept speeding up, continually shrinking the amount of time reported by each click of the second hand. Had this happened during the maze-running trials, it would have appeared that the rats took *more* rather than *less* time to complete each successive run. Instead of showing steady improvement, the performance of Tolman's rats would have appeared to deteriorate as their experience accumulated.

With prices climbing ever upward, it appears as if the cost of everything we buy—from chicken eggs to automobiles—keeps rising. But because we measure value with an ever-shrinking unit, we cannot fairly compare today's prices with yesterday's. To allow meaningful historical comparisons, statistical adjustments must be made to compensate for inflation.

In the United States, most analysts use a statistical index called the GNP Deflator to offset the effects of inflation. They arbitrarily pick one year—say, 1987—and convert the "current dollar" prices of earlier and later years into what those prices would have been if all prices had been stated in "1987 dollars"—a stable measure of economic value called a "real dollar." The economist's "real dollar" isn't as stable as the scientist's second of time, but it's the best unit available, and it's perfectly adequate for most purposes.

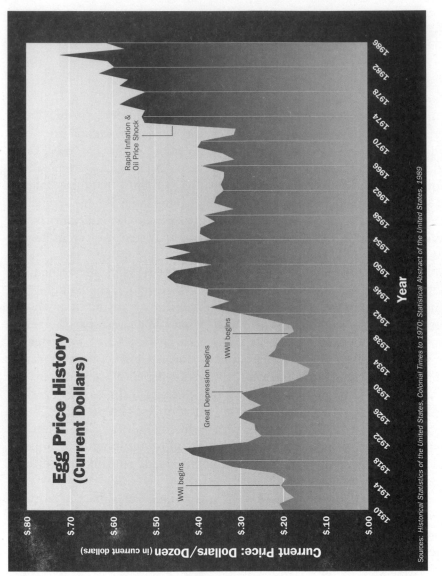

Figure 16.1

Sources: Historical Statistics of the United States, Colonial Times to 1970; Statistical Abstract of the United States, 1989

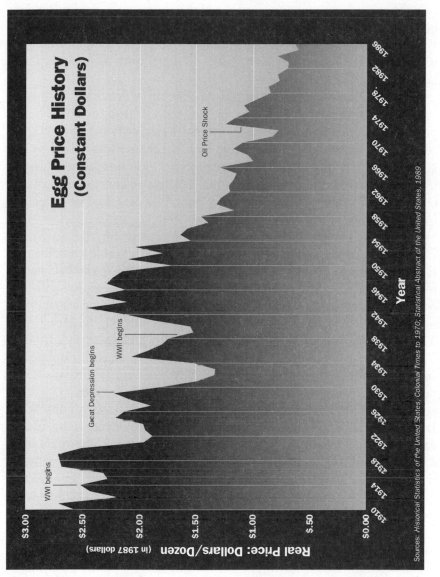

Figure 16.2

Sources: *Historical Statistics of the United States, Colonial Times to 1970; Statistical Abstract of the United States, 1989*

After converting "current-dollar" prices into a constant 1987 "real-dollar" price history, the price trend for chicken eggs looks completely different. Measured in "1987 dollars," the wholesale price of a dozen eggs was 78 cents in both 1972 and 1980. In real dollars, a constant value shows up as a constant price. More important, instead of tripling between 1910 and 1986, real egg prices actually fell about 80 percent. With inflation wrung out of the prices, it's clear that an egg purchased in 1986 cost the consumer just one-fifth as much as an identical egg cost his great-grandfather.

Since the chicken egg—the result of eons of evolutionary history—has not changed in the last 75 years, it is hard to imagine how its real price could have plummeted.[3] In the United States, eggs are a free-market commodity. American egg producers have never been subsidized by the government. To stay in business, egg farmers must earn a profit, or at least break even. Logically, prices could have dropped only if the farmers' costs fell by a comparable percentage. But an 80 percent cost reduction for exactly the same product seems impossible.

To see whether the decline in egg prices was caused by the growth of farming experience, two final statistical adjustments must be made. First, the portion of the farmer's total costs that are actually under his control must be isolated. The cost of cornmeal (the raw material that chickens convert into eggs) is not under the farmer's control. To keep his chickens in feed, the farmer has to pay the market price for corn, whatever it is. The economic function of the egg farmer is to add value to cornmeal by setting up an organized system that turns it into eggs. To isolate the cost of providing this "value-added" service, the cost of cornmeal must be deducted from the price that the farmer receives for eggs.

Second, instead of plotting the value-added data against historical time, they must be plotted against cumulative egg production. By adding each year's egg production to the combined output of all the years since 1910 (when the U.S. government began keeping egg-production data), it is easy to calculate the cumulative output of the American egg industry. Using cumulative output is crucial, because learning is a consequence of previous experience, not a function of elapsed time.

Once these adjustments are made, it is possible to plot the farmer's average cost of producing a dozen eggs against cumulative egg output. The pattern shows two distinct periods in the history of egg production. From 1910 until 1943, when total past production reached about 1,200 billion eggs, the farmers' value-added remained fairly stable at about $1.70 per dozen eggs. Except for a drop during the Great Depression, the egg farmer's value-added remained largely unchanged for 30 years.

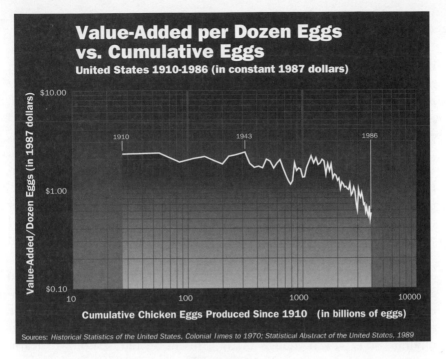

Value-Added per Dozen Eggs vs. Cumulative Eggs

United States 1910-1986 (in constant 1987 dollars)

Sources: *Historical Statistics of the United States, Colonial Times to 1970; Statistical Abstract of the United States, 1989*

Figure 16.3

If America's egg farmers were managing intelligent, cost-cutting organizations, the data do not show it.

But then, in the years after 1943, the second phase of the egg industry's history began. The farmers' value-added per dozen eggs began to decline on a remarkably steady 50 percent learning curve. Short-term swings in the prices of cornmeal and eggs caused the farmer's value-added to bounce around from year to year. But from 1943 until the present day, the average cost of producing a dozen eggs has declined in a highly predictable pattern as the industry's experience has accumulated. For some reason, after a long history of nonlearning behavior, America's egg farmers suddenly began acting like learning, cost-reducing organizations.

To be more precise, the act of learning actually takes place inside individual firms, not across an industry as a whole. An industry is a population of similar organizations just as a species is a population of similar organisms. A population does not learn; individuals do. In the chicken-egg business, a well-managed farm will experiment with new production techniques in an effort to cut costs. If a new method proves successful, the farm's competitors will adopt the innovation unless it is kept secret by the innovator.

The leakage of new technology from innovators to copiers is the mechanism of industry-wide "learning." New techniques are almost never adopted throughout an industry overnight. Even when useful new methods are widely known, managers in many firms remain skeptical, choosing to do things the old way. The prevalence of nonlearning organizations in industries that steadily improve their performance seems paradoxical, but a similar phenomenon has been explained by biologists.

For instance, individual spiders do not learn to build their webs. Web-building behavior is coded into each spider's genes and is purely instinctive. But each spider species, as a group, "learned" to build webs over the course of evolutionary time. Through the trial-and-error process of variation and natural selection, the genes of spiders that failed to build workable webs were weeded out of their species' gene pool.

In the egg business, only a tiny percentage of the farmers operating in 1943 are still in business today. The vast majority did not adopt new methods fast enough to stay competitive. The industry-wide learning curve of the commercial egg industry could be more accurately called its "evolution curve." Even though many firms in an industry fail to learn, some firms adopt innovations. Since they become the survivors, the technological "genes" of the industry change over time. The economic species as a whole evolves to fit its niche more precisely. Like a biological species, an industry has an "evolution curve" independent of the individual "learning curves" of its members. In this sense, evolution is a learning process that unfolds at a species-wide or industry-wide level.[4]

Of the 1,500 American egg farms still in business, few have been more effective learners—and none is more aptly named—than Darwin Farms.[5] Owned and operated by Darwin Lewis and his sons Spencer and Greg, Darwin Farms is a medium-size egg farm with 750,000 hens producing 30,000 dozen eggs a day. Nestled in the foothills of California's Sierra Nevada range, Darwin Farms ships its eggs to food brokers and supermarket chains serving the San Francisco area.

Until the late 1930s, when Darwin Lewis as a teenager started raising chickens, eggs were a minor sideline of the typical family farm. No one treated eggs as a serious business. Most farmers considered poultry raising beneath their dignity. Taking care of the birds and selling any eggs not consumed by the family usually was left to the farmer's wife. The family's flock, which rarely numbered more than 50 birds, roamed free in the barnyard, scratching for worms to supplement a diet of corn kernels and scraps from the kitchen table. Each day, someone would be sent out to hunt around the yard, basket in hand, delicately probing the spots where the hens usually laid their eggs. Little had changed in poultry raising since the Asian red jungle fowl, the chicken's wild forebear, was domesticated 4,000 years earlier.[6]

But with so many families forced off the land by the Great Depression, some of the surviving farmers, like Darwin Lewis, saw a new profit opportunity in chicken eggs. In an attempt to drive down their production costs, they began changing age-old farm practices. The first important innovation was building a simple shed to house the birds. With their chickens confined, farmers could find more of the eggs, and they lost far fewer birds to foraging dogs. The first chicken houses were little more than enclosed dirt floors covered with wood shavings, and since the birds wound up scratching for food in their own manure, they often were heavily infested with parasites. High rates of chicken mortality and disease accompanied the move to the chicken house, and egg production, although higher than before, was far below what it might have been with healthy birds.

To combat this problem, some egg farmers began to install wire-netting floors set just a few feet off the ground in their chicken houses. The chicken manure dropped through, leaving the birds in a far more sanitary environment. Putting chickens "up on wire" immediately reduced mortality, improved health, and boosted egg production. But because the wire floors provided too fragile a footing for workers, most farmers switched to wire cages. Using the basic arrangement still dominant in modern egg farms, the chickens were placed in long rows of cages suspended over the chicken-house floor.

Today, Unit 9 at Darwin Farms is home to 268,000 hens. The building is probably the largest and most modern chicken house in the world. Within its cavernous, darkened interior, 160 parallel rows of cages stretch 700 feet. The rows are arranged in pairs stacked ten high, and each bank of 20 rows is separated from its neighboring banks by narrow aisles. Running along the floor, down the center of each aisle, is a single rail, and atop each rail sits a rather bizarre-looking contraption—a feed-dispensing robot.

On either side of the robot, ten feed troughs, each 30 feet long, are positioned horizontally, one above the other. As the contraption rolls along its rail under computer control, the hens in cages farther down the rows crane their necks in anticipation of the trough's arrival. The trough passes by a cage in just 90 seconds, so the birds eat quickly, but the chickens are never allowed to go hungry. Hungry birds do not lay as many eggs.

The robots roll by their cages once an hour, 16 hours a day. Along with food, the robots bring light. Both sides of each robot are fitted with a single vertical bar of fluorescent lamps. Experience has shown that hens lay the most eggs if they get enough light to convince their pituitary glands that it's eternally summer. It turns out that intermittent light works just as well as constant light, and intermittent light is cheaper.

Every feature of Unit 9 at Darwin Farms is engineered to trim operating costs. Fluorescent lamps are used instead of incandescent bulbs because they consume less electricity. Almost the entire building is underground to reduce the costs of heating and cooling. Unit 9 is constructed entirely of concrete, because fumes from chicken urine corrode every metal except stainless steel. The whole building is set at a slight angle—just enough to draw drinking water through the pipes that run between each pair of cage rows. Every bird needs a constant supply of fresh water, and gravity is cheaper than electricity.

Cage floors slope down to a gap in the wire bars facing the aisle. Just beneath the gap sits a neoprene conveyor belt that runs the length of the cage row. Freshly laid eggs roll through the gap and onto the belt. Every morning at four o'clock, the computer activates the belts, sending 160 white streams coursing into a river of 170,000 eggs. After passing through a computer-controlled washer, the eggs are channeled to another machine that sorts the eggs by size and checks for defects and cracked shells. Untouched by human hands, the eggs slide into paper cartons, onto pallets, and into the back of a trailer truck.

The extraordinary level of automation in Unit 9 permits just two workers to care for more than a quarter of a million birds. Each morning, the workers climb aboard the robots, set the machines in manual mode, and ride up and down the banks of cages searching for dead birds. Only 10 percent of the hens die in a year's time, but with so many birds under one roof, that's still 75 dead birds a day. Since a disease can wipe out an entire flock in a few days, immediate disposal of dead chickens is essential.

To maintain cleanliness, rubber scrapers attached to each robot are set down on the concrete shelves that separate each cage row from the one below it. As the workers ride along, the scrapers angle the previous day's excrement into a large tub at the base of the robot. At the far end of the building, the tubs are dumped into a trough that feeds into a huge pond. When completed, a cogeneration facility will convert methane gas from the manure into electricity for sale to the local utility. Darwin Lewis figures that the methane plant will cut costs by about two cents per dozen eggs—an enormous savings in a business where one-tenth of a penny makes a major difference.

In the 50 years since Darwin Lewis built his first chicken shed, a stream of innovations in areas other than chicken housing have contributed to a gradual reduction in costs. For example, every week Darwin Farms adjusts the feed formula used in each of its 30 chicken houses. Using a personal computer, a livestock nutritionist calculates the most nutritious, lowest-cost blend of corn, soy, vitamins, meat scraps, and limestone appropriate for the flock's age and current weather conditions.

A specialized hatchery industry supplies one-day-old female chicks to egg farmers. Since males cannot lay eggs, they are processed into meat scraps and fed to the hens. The birds are bred for temperament, rate of lay, disease resistance, feed conversion, and egg size and quality. Unhappily for egg farmers, the most critical genetic trait—egg-laying rate—is linked to aggressiveness. The most aggressive hatchlings in a flock make sure they get their fill of food and water. Less aggressive hens eat less, weigh less, and lay fewer eggs.

In the tight confines of a cage shared by four to ten birds, aggressiveness is a deadly trait. Chickens, like all other fowl, maintain a rigid social hierarchy—the pecking order. Dominant hens often peck to death their cage mates. Pecking was not much of a problem in the days of the open barnyard, but on a modern egg farm, controlling pecking mortality is crucial to economic survival. Today, as they have for 40 years, virtually all farmers use a hot metal blade to chop off the point of a hatchling's top bill. "Debeaking" turns a razor-sharp weapon into a blunt instrument. Though traumatic, debeaking reduces annual pecking mortality from 30 percent to 10 percent of the flock.

At the age of five months, the birds reach sexual maturity and begin laying eggs. For the next year, the hens are on the production line. Most lay about 240 eggs during that year, or about two eggs every three days. At the end of the year, as their productivity slows and the value of their eggs drops below the cost of their feed, the birds are slaughtered. Typically, their carcasses are sold to soup companies.

Since Darwin Lewis has always kept up with the industry's state-of-the-art, it's hard even to imagine where he might find any further cost savings, but he never stops looking. Back in 1984, to finance the $2.5 million construction cost of Unit 9, he took on too much bank debt and was forced into bankruptcy when the 1985 cholesterol scare collapsed the price of eggs. Having struggled to save enough to buy back his farm, Darwin never neglects a chance to shave the cost of a dozen eggs.

In fact, intense financial pressure led Darwin Farms to be the first commercial egg producer in the world to test a radical new cost-saving technology—red contact lenses for chickens. For some reason, red light makes even the meanest fighting cocks completely docile. Under the influence of red light, hens do not peck each other and they don't waste energy pacing around their cages, flapping their wings. Red light turns even the most aggressive hens into perfect egg-laying machines.

The effects of red light on chickens have been known for decades, but no practical method for using this knowledge has been available to farmers. Humans can't see well enough in red light to work effectively in chicken houses that have red light bulbs. Red-tinted chicken goggles, not unlike swimmer's goggles, were tried, but they got caught in cage wires and wound up killing the birds. In 1987, however, after years of tinkering, a Boston-area start-up firm, Animalens, Inc., developed a patented design for red contact lenses that solved these problems.[7]

Results from the first test flock of 20,000 birds at Darwin Farms showed a 6 percent drop in feed consumption along with a slight increase in egg production. The results were so promising that Darwin Lewis put lenses on a second test flock that had not been debeaked. By using the red contact lenses to reduce feed consumption and stop pecking battles, Darwin had found a way to slash costs by about 4 cents per dozen eggs. This enormous savings helped yield enough profit for Darwin to buy back his farm from the banks.

Of course, the cost savings generated by this new technology won't translate into permanently wider profit margins. If the red contact lenses prove effective over the long term, news of their benefits will spread through the industry, and other well-managed egg farms will adopt the innovation. Eventually, the relatively high production costs of those that fail to use the lenses will force them out of business. But even the farms that adopt the new technique will gain little more than a chance for continued survival. As in the past, competition among the surviving egg farms will drive down wholesale prices to a level just above the cost of production.

Animalens estimates that by the year 2000, the red contact lens will save the worldwide chicken-egg industry (2 billion hens) about $1.5 billion a year in feed costs. Of these savings, about $500 million will be spent on lenses and the labor needed to install them. Virtually all the rest, about $1 billion, will go to consumers in the form of lower real prices for eggs. Like every other innovation that has swept through egg farming in the last 50 years, this technology will lead to lower production costs and lower consumer prices. There is no foreseeable end to the process. In the future, genetic-engineering firms may come up with chickens whose productivity dwarfs that of today's best breeds. Bit by bit, without fanfare or even customer awareness, the real cost of eggs will continue to decline as the industry's accumulating experience drives its learning.

CHAPTER
17

THE UNIVERSAL CURVE

I f egg farms were the only organizations capable of learning, the learning curve would be nothing more than an economic oddity. Even if
organizational learning occurred throughout agriculture but in no
other sector, it would have limited importance. After all, the great bulk
of modern economic activity unfolds in offices, shops, and factories—
not on farms. But the process of organizational learning revealed by the
learning curve is not restricted to egg farms or to agriculture. Organizational learning is a universal economic phenomenon.

Literally thousands of studies have shown that organizational learning
occurs in every industry. Indeed, if there are industries in which learning
does not take place, they have yet to be reported. Products and services
as diverse as motorcycles, electricity, microprocessors, long-distance
telephone calls, facial tissues, cars, and life-insurance policies all show
irrefutable evidence of the learning-curve effect. The orderly, experience-
driven decline of chicken-egg costs is not an exception; it is the rule.
Regardless of the product category, properly defined unit costs erode as
production experience accumulates. Organizations and industries, like
intelligent organisms and species, learn to become more efficient as they
gain experience in solving problems.[1]

Oddly enough, despite its power to help explain why capitalist economies grow ever more productive, the learning curve has lingered in
semiobscurity for nearly 60 years. Except for strategic planners in large
corporations, MBA students, and a handful of renegade economists, few
people have even heard of industrial learning curves. Although the phrase
"getting down the learning curve" has crept into common business usage,
few understand its roots or its full implications. Even among those who

rely upon the learning curve as a vital planning tool, few realize that learning is the prime cause of the steady rise in the standard of living.

The first careful observations of organizational learning were made in 1922 by Theodore P. Wright, a 27-year-old MIT-trained engineer at the Curtiss Aeroplane and Motor Company in Garden City, New York. In those days—just after the airplane proved its worth in World War I but before Charles Lindbergh flew the Atlantic—the aircraft business was as exciting and chaotic as any newly emerging high-tech industry. Curtiss Aeroplane was just one of several dozen upstart companies struggling to get established by winning big orders from the United States government.

Accurate price bidding was essential to success. If a company bid too high, it would lose the contract to a competitor; if it bid too low, it would go broke producing underpriced planes. To bid low enough consistently, but not too low, meant having a good handle on the cost of building the average unit. But this was no simple matter. Typically, aircraft makers built just one prototype of a new model to prove the design's airworthiness before bidding on a contract for several hundred copies.

Then, as now, aircraft were exceedingly complex machines made of thousands of parts assembled by highly skilled craftsmen. Being unfamiliar with a brand-new design, workers took far more time to assemble the prototype than they would need to build the average unit in a long production run. With assembly labor accounting for about 75 percent of a plane's total labor cost, estimating average assembly time per plane was critical to precise bidding.[2] Every aircraft maker realized this, but no one knew how to estimate accurately the labor content of a plane that had never been mass-produced.

After being promoted to assistant factory manager and becoming responsible for cost estimates at Curtiss Aeroplane, Wright asked the company's workers to fill out separate time cards for each airplane on which they worked. With this raw data, he was able to calculate the hours consumed by each unit in a production run. By plotting his data on a double-log graph, Wright discovered that the assembly labor declined 20 percent with each doubling of production experience. The sixtieth airplane in a batch required only 80 percent of the labor consumed by the thirtieth, which, in turn, had used only 80 percent of the labor absorbed by the fifteenth.

Considering the usefulness of the "80 percent curve" in competitive bidding, Wright kept his discovery quiet until 1936, when he published a short article in the *Journal of the Aeronautical Sciences*.[3] By that time,

Wright already had established himself as a leading figure in American aviation. As chief engineer and general manager at Curtiss, he had designed and built a string of famous military and commercial aircraft. In early 1943, a year after Pearl Harbor, Wright was put in command of all American aircraft production. From that point forward, the "80 percent curve" became a rule of thumb throughout the aircraft industry.

By exploiting the predictive power of the learning curve to its fullest, Wright's production planners were able to accurately estimate workforce requirements for a massive buildup of aircraft manufacturing capacity. In just three years, America's factories churned out 230,000 fighters and bombers. By the spring of 1945, when production rates were at their peak, nearly 10,000 planes rolled off the line each month. The swarms of new aircraft overwhelmed enemy air defenses and were central to the Allies' victory. Without question, Wright's learning curve played a key role in bringing America's industrial potential to its full might.[4]

After the war, the U.S. government commissioned several studies that again validated the accuracy of the learning curve.[5] But during the 1950s and early 1960s, except for a few articles in academic journals, the learning curve was largely ignored.[6] Since the statistical proof for organizational learning was drawn almost exclusively from aircraft production, apparently few executives in other industries believed that continuing cost reductions were possible in their own firms. Intuitively, the learning curve seemed to apply only in businesses where a high labor content and complex tasks made worker learning especially important.[7]

The learning curve languished in obscurity until 1966, when the Boston Consulting Group (BCG)—a recently formed consulting firm specializing in corporate strategic planning—conducted a study for a client in the semiconductor industry. BCG analysts found that, after adjusting for inflation, the unit costs of integrated circuits were dropping 25 percent with each doubling of experience. This cost erosion could not be attributed solely to improving labor productivity. Instead, the data revealed that *all* of the client's cost components—overhead, advertising, research, engineering, and marketing, as well as direct labor—declined with the accumulation of production experience.[8]

To distinguish this across-the-board cost erosion from the notion that learning only applied to labor, BCG rechristened the learning curve the "experience curve." Throughout the 1970s, as BCG grew to become one of the world's premier advisers to major corporations, the experience curve served as its creed. In confidential studies prepared for corporate clients around the globe, BCG analysts compiled historical cost data showing thousands of experience curves. Unfortunately, since a company's unit costs usually are kept secret, the great bulk of this experience-curve evidence remains buried in inaccessible documents.

Nevertheless, over the last two decades, dozens of studies—prepared by BCG and others—have been disclosed to the public. The data consistently show real cost declines ranging from 10 percent to 30 percent per doubling of experience.[9] Of course, shortages and gluts can temporarily drive costs sharply up or down, but the trends are absolutely clear. Data proving learning-curve cost declines have been published for steel, soft contact lenses, life-insurance policies, automobiles, jet-engine maintenance, bottle caps, refrigerators, gasoline refining, room air-conditioners, TV picture tubes, aluminum, optical fibers, vacuum cleaners, motorcycles, steam turbine generators, ethyl alcohol, beer, facial tissues, transistors, disposable diapers, gas ranges, microprocessors, float glass, long-distance telephone calls, knit fabric, lawn mowers, air travel, crude-oil production, typesetting, oil-refinery construction, factory maintenance, and hydroelectric power.[10]

Significantly, no study has ever identified a product or service whose costs did *not* decline with accumulating experience.[11] Bruce Henderson, BCGs founder and intellectual leader, wrote,

> The experience curve phenomenon is as real as gravity. . . . [Its] effect can be observed and measured in any business, any industry, any cost element, anywhere. . . . The reasons for the experience curve effect are not particularly important. The important fact is that the experience curve is a universally observable phenomenon.[12]

Product or service, high or low tech, fast or slow growth, foreign or domestic, labor or capital intensive—learning curves are found because they reveal a fundamental property of all competitive economic organizations. Like intelligent organisms, organizations improve performance as they accumulate experience. Because they inhabit an enormous variety of economic niches, cope with a broad spectrum of technical problems, and possess varying degrees of intelligence, firms and industries exhibit a wide range of learning-curve slopes. But whatever their rates of learning happen to be, the important point is that all organizations learn. In their pursuit of economic survival, organizations leave behind a data trail that reveals the evolutionary nature of technical progress.[13]

During the 1970s, in presentations to top executives throughout North America, Europe, and Japan, BCG relentlessly argued that adroit use of the experience-curve effect was the key to competitive success. The curve implied that the firm with the largest share of its market would gain production experience—and reduce unit costs—faster than smaller competitors. At comparable prices, the leader's cost advantage would translate into wider profits and faster growth.[14]

BCG argued that under certain conditions, a firm could seize industry leadership with a preemptive strike against its competitors. By slashing prices below costs, winning the biggest share of industry volume, and accelerating its cost erosion, a company could get permanently ahead of the pack. If its lunge for leadership was executed properly, the firm would more than recoup its up-front losses by building an unchallengeable long-term cost advantage.

After 40 years of being ignored by everyone outside the aircraft industry, BCG's efforts turned the learning curve into the centerpiece of corporate strategic thinking. In all the leading business schools, lessons drawn from the experience-curve effect became part of the core curriculum. To executives in search of a logically coherent framework for risky, multimillion-dollar decisions, the "first-strike" solution derived from the experience curve seemed to be the ultimate answer.

But by the early 1980s, several critics began arguing that grabbing market leadership did not necessarily guarantee a long-term cost advantage. They pointed out that in many industries, cost-cutting innovations spread quickly among competitors, making it impossible for an aggressive leader to hang onto its cost advantage. With managers and engineers job-hopping among competing firms and equipment makers, peddling the same state-of-the-art machinery to all firms in an industry, technology "leaks" allowed small companies to keep pace with cost reductions achieved by the industry leader. According to BCG's critics, a preemptive strategy of slashing prices or building a new factory ahead of demand made little sense, because rapid technology diffusion meant that long-term cost savings would be too narrow to offset short-term losses.[15]

None of BCG's critics questioned the validity of the learning curve itself. Instead, they argued that a simple extrapolation of an industry's curve cannot alone provide enough information to tell the president of Company X what to do next. By predicting cost and price trends, the learning curve furnishes decision-makers with vital insights into future industry conditions, but the subtle nuances of each market niche, the relative strengths of competitors, and the potential for unpredicted technological shifts demand that a comprehensive analysis be completed before a company's strategy is plotted.[16]

In short, the learning curve is a general observation. It cannot provide automatic, detailed prescriptions for every strategic dilemma. Consequently, after a decade in the corporate limelight, the learning curve was downgraded from "ultimate weapon" to "essential tool" in the arsenal of corporate planners.

But even as the curve lost stature among businessmen, it should have gained adherents among economists. In principle at least, the role of the economics profession is to explain the general workings of the economy. Even though the learning curve proved to be too broad a concept to satisfy all the information needs of an executive facing a particular decision at a specific moment, a simple formula that accurately describes historical cost behavior in every known industry would seem to be a perfect candidate for discussion, if not adoption, by economists. But this never happened.

Despite the studies proving its universality, the learning curve has been shunned by most academic economists. The term *learning curve* is not mentioned in *Economics*, the immensely popular introductory college text written by Nobel laureate Paul Samuelson. In the book's most recent edition, the notion that product costs might decrease is buried in an appendix to the chapter on supply and demand. Allocated a page and a half in a 900-page tome, the concept of continuously eroding costs is treated as a possible exception to the laws of supply and demand. Another leading textbook by Edwin Mansfield briefly mentions the learning curve but treats it as a special phenomenon limited to high-technology products such as aircraft, semiconductors, and machine tools. Most other big-selling college texts don't even mention the subject. Neither *learning* nor *experience* appears in the index of the leading history of economic thought.[17]

This conspiracy of silence reveals far more about the sorry state of orthodox economics than it does about the learning curve. Although a smattering of learning-curve articles have appeared in economics journals, the curve has remained a fringe concept, well outside the mainstream of accepted thought. When asked about their profession's treatment of the learning curve, several respected economists, including Nobel winner Kenneth Arrow, agreed, "It's been ignored." No economist denies the curve's existence, and no one criticizes it. It's just that virtually no one writes or talks about it. Since economists build their careers by disputing economic concepts, the lack of discussion is almost eerie.[18]

Perhaps, if the learning curve lent factual support to the core concepts of Western equilibrium economics, a way would have been found to unify fact and theory. But the entire edifice of classical economics rests upon the assumption that technology does not change.[19] Unless "technology is held constant," it is impossible to calculate the "equilibrium prices" at which consumer purchases and supplier outputs magically "clear all markets."

John Stuart Mill, the nineteenth-century philosopher whose ideas undergird modern equilibrium theory, built his economics on the "law" of diminishing returns.[20] *Diminishing returns* means that adding more inputs cannot yield as much incremental output. For example, by doubling the labor expended cultivating a plot of land, the crop will increase, but it will not double. As applied to industry, this logic says that a company's costs will fall at first, as its factory fills up with enough orders to use its physical capacity efficiently. But as output expands, inefficiencies creep in and force up unit costs again. Consequently, there is an optimal level of production for any enterprise. Trying to produce more than that quantity of goods is inherently unprofitable, because—beyond the equilibrium point—extra costs grow faster than extra revenues.[21]

As Mill wrote, "This general law of agricultural industry is the most important proposition in political economy. Were the law different, nearly all the phenomena of the production and distribution of wealth would be other than they are."[22] But the learning curve—discovered by T. P. Wright 80 years after Mill wrote those words—proves indisputably that *all* sectors of the economy, including agriculture, operate according to *increasing* rather than diminishing returns. With the learning that flows from accumulating experience, producers squeeze ever more output from less and less input. Since real costs keep eroding, there is no way to calculate an equilibrium price. No equilibrium prices, no equilibrium economics. It's as simple as that.[23]

Economists should not be singled out for ignoring unpalatable facts. Every academic discipline defends its accepted wisdom until that superstructure is torn apart by new facts. Until recently, evolutionary biologists simply ignored fossils unearthed by paleontologists because those fossils contradicted the reigning dogma of steady, gradual change. Once an elaborate theoretical edifice has been lovingly crafted by generations of respected scholars, it is terribly difficult to admit that it's just plain wrong.

By ignoring the learning curve, orthodox economics negates the very thing that is unique about human economics—the capacity to respond to experience with intelligence and creativity. By steadfastly denying that output grows faster than input, conventional economics abides by

Thomas Malthus's 200-year-old population principle. The precursor to the "law of diminishing returns," Malthus's "iron law," said that population would grow exponentially while food production could only expand linearly. The horrifying but unavoidable consequence was intensifying global poverty, intermittently relieved by population declines stemming from epidemics and wars.[24]

In 1798, when Malthus published his *Essay on Population*, the prediction that the food supply could not expand exponentially was perfectly reasonable. Before James Watt's steam engine kicked off the Industrial Revolution, there wasn't a shred of evidence to suggest the possibility of organizational learning or sustained technological change. Reliable economic statistics did not yet exist. Had Malthus been foolish enough to assert that the human population would quintuple over the following two centuries and that food output, along with all other kinds of production, would outpace that growth, he would have been dismissed as a crackpot.[25]

Hindsight is supposed to be 20/20, but somehow the historical record has failed to impress theorists in either camp of conventional economic thought. On the Left, Karl Marx and his followers accepted Malthus's prediction and dedicated themselves to remedying the inevitable impoverisation of the working class by redistributing output from the rich to the poor. On the Right, J. S. Mill and the equilibrium economists who followed him also accepted Malthus's population principle, but they chose to overlook its long-term implications. Concentrating exclusively on the near term, they constructed mathematical models of a mythical, machinelike economy where the population does not grow and technology never changes.

Compelling evidence of the learning curve's universality has been available for nearly 20 years, but neither the Left nor the Right has recognized the learning curve for what it is—proof that the "law of diminishing returns" is wrong. As Mill himself pointed out, if the "law" of diminishing returns was false, nearly all the rules about the production and distribution of wealth would be different. Instead of a depressing world where the good things in life become ever more expensive and unattainable, where output is crippled by the inevitability of diminishing returns and rising marginal costs, we would see an economy of abundance where real costs continue to decline, so that even the poorest members of society eventually gain access to benefits once reserved for the very rich.[26]

This, of course, is precisely what happens under capitalism. Here is just one trivial but revealing example: In the late 1930s, shortly after television was invented, only the richest families in America could afford TV sets. Today, 98 percent of American households own at least one television. Even in remote villages in China, peasant farmers now own TVs. In one sense, America's poor and China's peasants now have television because their incomes rose during the last 50 years. But, in another sense, they can enjoy their favorite situation comedies because manufacturers learned how to make TVs with far less labor and materials.

By constantly nibbling away at the costs of providing goods and services, organizational learning gradually transforms luxuries into commodities. Organizational learning—encoded as new technology—drives up living standards by driving down real costs. Although capitalism will never produce a Utopia where all the desires of all the people are fully satisfied, worsening poverty is not preordained. As long as there is learning, there will be progress. The truth of the learning curve obliterates the central myth of the "dismal science."[27]

No matter how perfect a particular design seems to be, the mind can improve upon it. Ultimately, it is human creativity that distinguishes learning by organizations from learning by organisms. Once a rat has memorized the layout of a maze, it cannot continue to improve its speed because its body simply cannot move any faster. Without long-term evolutionary change to the genes of the rat's offspring, there is no way to improve rat performance. But a human organization is infinitely flexible. Innovative ideas become the new methods and new equipment that push back the limits of productivity. A firm's efficiency is constrained only by its technology, and its technology is limited only by its members' ability to work together as an intelligent, creative organization.[28]

Perhaps, if learning was caused by the passage of time rather than the accumulation of experience, someone would have discovered the learning curve long before T. P. Wright did so. Time, of course, must elapse in order for experience to be gained. But whether organism or organization, it is the accumulation of experience, not the passage of time, that drives improving performance. Since economists, like everyone else, are in the habit of comparing costs and output levels against those recorded in earlier periods, the learning effect is not obvious.

As in the chicken-egg industry, after millions or billions of units already have been produced, it takes so many years for the industry to achieve another doubling of cumulative output that the learning effect is easily obscured by the veil of inflation. T. P. Wright noticed the learning effect in airplane assembly because the phenomenon is most conspicuous when previous experience is slight and the rate of experience growth is high. Wright's access to sufficiently detailed data and his urgent need to understand the behavior of costs put him in an ideal position to draw the crucial connection between production experience and organizational learning.

Since at any point in time the economy produces a mix of long-established and newly invented products, and since economists study time-related rather than experience-related measures of performance, traditional economic monitors do not reveal clear patterns of change. Depending upon which industries they happen to study, analysts notice widely varying rates of technological change. Consequently, some observers argue that economic progress is caused by sudden bursts of invention, while others stress the steady accumulation of minor innovations.[29]

Oddly enough, this debate is a refrain of the 200-year-old "sudden change vs. gradual change" argument among biologists. In the early 1800s, Baron Cuvier was foremost among those who dismissed gradual change as impossible. Cuvier's followers believed that species changed in sudden, global cataclysms. The catastrophists were opposed by the gradualists, led by Lamarck, who chose to ignore fossil evidence indicating sudden change. Instead, the gradualists pointed to the subtle differences that distinguish closely related species.

Until 1972, when Stephen Jay Gould and Niles Eldredge proposed the theory of punctuated equilibrium, few biologists could imagine how to reconcile the conflicting evidence for sudden and gradual change. Punctuated equilibrium holds that a new species emerges when a small group becomes genetically isolated from the rest of its population. If the offshoot group happens to find a vacant, supportive niche, reduced competitive pressure allows it to reproduce rapidly.

Genetic mutations that would never have been replicated in a normal, intensely competitive population are afforded that opportunity in an isolated, well-nourished group. Once population expansion causes crowding to resume, natural selection begins gradually to shape the offshoot population into a new species tailored to the nuances of its niche. Except for these intermittent pulses of evolution, a species will remain largely unchanged for millions of years.

In the economy, when a new industry buds off from a parent industry, its low base of cumulative experience and the vacancy of its market niche allow it to compress a great deal of technical evolution into a brief period. Even the most startling inventions, when studied in detail, are composed of many subsidiary innovations achieved in quick succession.[30] Just as the population explosion experienced by a new species in a vacant niche compresses an extraordinary amount of genetic trial-and-error into a brief period, a rapid growth in product output gives a new industry's "technological genes" the chance to squeeze a tremendous amount of evolutionary learning into a short pulse.

As in nature, gradual and sudden change are not mutually exclusive. Brief bursts of technological speciation interrupt long periods of gradual refinement. For instance, following a classic learning curve, 60 years of minor modifications steadily reduced the cost per horsepower of Thomas Newcomen's original atmospheric engine. Then, with James Watt's addition of the condenser, the far-more-fuel-efficient steam engine arrived. On a per-horsepower basis, Watt's first engines were more expensive than the refined Newcomen machines, and Watt's firm was unable to compete with companies building Newcomen engines for use at coal mines.

But despite the steam engine's high cost per horsepower, Watt's firm prospered in market niches distant from the coal mines—in copper mines and in urban water-pumping stations—wherever Newcomen's coal-wasting machines were too costly to fuel. As steam-engine production experience accumulated, the per-horsepower cost of Watt's engines declined along a learning curve. Before long, steam engines were cheaper than atmospheric engines in all market niches—including coal mines. Firms making Newcomen engines were driven to extinction.

The cycle of innovation began again in 1860, when Nikolaus Otto invented the internal-combustion engine. Decades later, with the invention of the jet turbine engine, yet another round of experience accumulation and cost reduction began. In the future, another technology undoubtedly will displace the jet engine from many of its uses. Like all of its predecessors, this as-yet-unknown engine technology will decline in cost along the familiar logarithmic pattern of the learning curve. Over the course of nearly three centuries, the pulsating rhythm of sudden and gradual change drove down the real cost of machine power from roughly $6,000 to $3 per horsepower.[31]

Wherever one looks, the same basic pattern of economic progress reappears. In agriculture, innovations ranging from the first Sumerian drainage ditch to the latest genetically engineered rice crop have steadily chipped away at the cost of food. In textiles, incessant tinkering with devices ranging from water-powered spindles to computer-controlled knitting machines has whittled down the cost of clothing. In transportation, a series of linked learning curves stretching from the ox cart to the Boeing 747 has pushed the cost per seat-mile ever lower. Throughout human history, the syncopated rhythm of economic progress reflects a succession of linked learning curves.[32]

CHAPTER
18

JAPAN'S SECRET WEAPON

Since few journalists bother to adjust for inflation when making historical comparisons, the public is thoroughly convinced that real prices keep rising. For example, hardly a month goes by without some television commentator whining about the escalating price of cars. Before castigating the greedy automakers, the commentator fondly recalls the "good old days" of 1912, when Ford's Model T listed for just $600. Neglecting to adjust for the erosion of the dollar's value, he'll inevitably fail to realize that Ford's Escort—the company's current best-seller and an immensely superior vehicle—is actually 20 percent less expensive in real terms than that 1912 Model T.[1]

Although organizational learning cuts costs and prices in every sector of the economy, its effects are extremely uneven. In mature product categories, such as autos, money inflation masks the downward trend in real prices. Only in brand-new industries, where explosive experience growth overwhelms inflation's distorting effects, does the price-cutting power of the learning curve become obvious to the average consumer.[2]

Such a situation occurred in the late 1970s and early 1980s, when it became common practice for American consumers to delay their purchases of Japanese-made digital watches, hand calculators, compact stereos, and VCRs because the prices of these goods were falling so precipitously. Because all of these goods were based on the recently invented microchip, Japanese manufacturers were enjoying the huge cost declines that come in the first phase of new learning curves. In Japan's factories, measured against cumulative output, costs were declining gradually and predictably, but in America's retail showrooms, measured against last season's price tags, the cost of consumer electronics seemed to be in free-fall.

To the extent that anyone thought much about it, Americans seemed to regard the collapsing prices of consumer electronics as little more than an unexpected gift from those clever Japanese. In fact, the sharp price drop marked an economic turning point of great historic significance. By spawning so many new products and so many new learning curves, the invention of the microchip had launched a new economic era. Just as the steam engine had bred the urban factory, the steamship, and the railroad, the microchip created a raft of products that were technically impossible or economically infeasible only a few years earlier.

In other cases, product categories that had gone undisturbed for decades suddenly were thrown into competitive chaos by new microchip-based models. Japanese makers of digital watches decimated much of the traditional Swiss watch industry. At the same time, American producers of bulky electromechanical calculators were wiped out by Japanese firms manufacturing less expensive and more capable electronic calculators. Hundreds of firms in dozens of product categories were crippled or eliminated by a tidal wave of microchip-based designs.

Only Japan was prepared to exploit the incredible economic opportunities presented by the microchip. At a crucial moment in economic history, when the first pulse of microchip innovation reached its peak, only the Japanese pursued policies that took full advantage of the learning curve's central lessons.

Of course, no single formula can explain every aspect of America's economic defeat by Japan. But without an appreciation for the sheer power of organizational learning, Americans have no framework for understanding the inexorable forces that continue to propel their economic descent. By now, the symptoms of America's economic disease are well known, but its root causes—policies, attitudes, and habits that stifle organizational learning—have gone largely unreported. And unless the learning disabilities of America's companies are remedied soon, the prognosis for the American standard of living and America's role in the world will remain bleak.[3]

Tangible proof of America's demise at the hands of Japan surrounds us. In televisions, microwave ovens, cameras, stereo equipment, office copiers, construction equipment, machine tools, and a host of other categories, Japanese firms have demolished one American competitor after another. Eight of the world's ten largest consumer electronics firms are Japanese. The other two are European. In most areas of electronics, with the exception of computers, the Japanese no longer consider the United States a significant factor. The only real threat to Japan's continued dominance in electronics comes from South Korea, Taiwan, Hong Kong, and Singapore.[4]

In ultra-high-tech businesses, where top-notch American firms once held enormous leads, the Japanese caught up and overwhelmed them. In 1986, Intel Corporation—inventor of the computer memory chip— was driven out of the business, along with nearly every other American memory-chip maker. In VCRs and fax machines, the story was much the same. By the late 1980s, all of these high-growth industries were virtually 100 percent controlled by the Japanese.[5]

In 1987, the National Academy of Engineering concluded that Japan already had surpassed the United States in 25 of 34 critical emerging technologies, including artificial intelligence, optoelectronics, and systems engineering and control. That same year, Japan's real GNP per person—the ultimate measure of a society's productivity and income— soared past America's long-stagnant performance. To top it all off, 1987 was also the year the United States became the world's largest debtor nation.[6]

Derided as mere copycats only 20 years ago, the Japanese now are dreaded as unstoppable economic Godzillas. Tensions with the Soviet Union have eased. Polls show that most Americans now view Japan's tremendous commercial might as the greatest single threat to their future well-being.[7] In the last few years, American fears have been heightened by a deluge of books and articles warning about the anemic productivity growth of U.S. workers, the superior quality and lower cost of Japanese goods, the hemorrhaging trade deficit, America's increasing dependence on Japanese loans, and the deepening Japanese financial control over American companies, farms, and real estate.[8]

Explanations offered for Japan's triumph fall under two broad themes that can be conveniently labeled the "tilted playing field" and "nuts and bolts." Americans stress the first view while Japanese emphasize the second. In truth, both explanations are valid. Indeed, they are the two prongs of a coherent competitive strategy based on the learning curve.

According to adherents of the "tilted-playing-field" argument, the blame for America's competitive collapse can be pinned on the machinations of the Japanese government. By this view, Japan's government exploited the bumbling ineptitude of the United States government while it methodically rigged the global economic game to the advantage of its own conglomerates.[9]

During the 1970s and 1980s, while naive American officials prattled on about the virtues of free trade and opened U.S. markets to all comers, American firms were systematically barred from Japan by high tariffs, bureaucratic red tape, and so-called nontariff barriers. At the same time, Japan's government allowed its firms to earn the fat domestic profits needed to subsidize their costly penetration of foreign markets. Guided by Japan's powerful Ministry of International Trade and Industry (MITI), these conglomerates targeted one set of foreign competitors after another. In effect, Japan's interlocked business and political elites marshaled their country's resources for an unremitting economic war for global domination.

The Japanese government assisted its firms further with tax policies that strongly encouraged Japanese families to save rather than consume. This created vast pools of investable funds that were made available to businesses at very low rates. Japan's investment advantage was bolstered further by the fact that the United States kept pouring at least 6 percent of its GNP on defense, while Japan—safe and snug beneath America's nuclear umbrella—wasted less than 1 percent of its national output on the military. While America fended off the Soviets, Japan reinvested that extra 5 percent in the technologies and infrastructure needed to outdistance American firms.

The evidence supporting the "tilted-playing-field" explanation is overwhelming. But even a tilted playing field is not enough to secure victory in virtually every contest. Ultimately, in the competition for customers, Japanese firms had to deliver the goods. MITI's bureaucrats may have drafted brilliant plans for the global automotive and electronics markets, but the flawless road handling of a Honda Accord and the crystal-clear image on a Mitsubishi wide-screen TV required the sustained efforts of workers, managers, and executives toiling on assembly lines and in laboratories and conference rooms.[10]

With these facts in mind, partisans of the "nuts-and-bolts" perspective tend to ignore the intrigues of Washington and Tokyo. Instead, they focus on workaday details of life inside Japanese companies. In their view, the Japanese emphasis on total quality control, just-in-time manufacturing, long-term investment, lifetime employment, workforce education, cooperative labor/management relations, and consensus-style decision-making combine to give Japanese producers an unbeatable edge in product quality and cost. Comparing business practices typical of American producers to those of their Japanese rivals, the "nuts-and-bolts" experts argue that the unmatched rigor of Japan's manufacturers is the ultimate source of Japan's economic might.[11]

In many industries, the evidence strongly supports the "nuts-and-bolts" explanation. The Japanese win not only by exploiting the "unfair" governmental tactics of the "tilted playing field" but also by outclassing their competitors in the "nuts-and-bolts" of day-to-day business management. Although the "tilted-playing-field" and the "nuts-and-bolts" views are distinct, they are not mutually exclusive. Both ring true.

However, both schools of thought fall short. Although they portray accurately the key elements of Japan's success, neither view fully explains *why* this particular combination of government and business tactics proved to be so amazingly effective. To this day, America's academic and political elites have not grasped the fundamental economic logic behind Japan's brilliant strategy. As Naohiro Amaya, former head of MITI, put it, "We did the opposite of what American economists said. We violated all the traditional economic concepts."[12]

Slavishly devoted to the mythology of equilibrium economics, American economists must bear much of the blame for America's competitive collapse. Ignoring the learning curve and its implications, American economists recommended policies that effectively condemned the nation to decline. Unaware of the most basic rules in the evolutionary struggle for economic survival, the United States has become a pitiful giant, stunned and bewildered by its mounting losses. While Japan continues to roll up one victory after another, the United States—crippled by its profound ignorance of real-world economics—has little hope of devising an effective counterstrategy.[13]

Only after the reality of the learning curve is accepted do the two paramount principles of economic competition become obvious. First, gaining an efficiency advantage by accumulating experience faster than competitors is the key to any organization's long-term growth and survival. Therefore, if a firm can somehow accelerate its own experience growth and/or slow down its competitors' experience accumulation, its competitive position will improve. Also, when a firm is very far behind in experience accumulation, it can catch up only by obtaining the proprietary technology of a leading company.

Second, if two firms are accumulating experience at the same pace, the more intelligent firm will prevail in the contest for economic survival. A more intelligent organization, like a more intelligent organism, extracts more learning from each unit of experience. With its steeper learning curve, the more intelligent firm cuts product costs faster than its equally experienced competitor. Highly intelligent organizations, like highly intelligent organisms, respond quickly to shifting environmental conditions. Any technique that bolsters the overall intelligence of an organization enhances its chances of survival.

Only the Japanese fully appreciate these twin principles and their far-reaching implications. Whether categorized under "tilted playing field" or "nuts and bolts," every notable feature of Japan's economic system—from its impenetrable import barriers to its mundane manufacturing practices—helps its firms extract maximum competitive leverage from the learning-curve effect. Taken together, Japan's tactics accelerate learning by Japanese firms while retarding the learning of their non-Japanese competitors.[14]

The crucial role of the learning curve in Japan's triumph and America's defeat is illustrated best by comparing the key economic policies of their governments. First, the Japanese government encourages smaller enterprises to merge and form larger firms. With market demand divvied up among fewer competitors, each surviving organization accumulates production experience faster, driving down costs and prices more rapidly. Substantial corporate size is seen as crucial to survival in marketplaces that now span the globe.

By contrast, the American government traditionally has tried to prevent mergers. According to the conventional economic thinking that underpins American antitrust law, technology does not change and costs do not decline with experience. Since costs are unchangeable, increasing profits can come only through higher prices. By this reasoning, any trend toward fewer competitors in a market poses a threat of consumer exploitation as surviving firms collude to raise their prices.[15]

To prevent this, American antitrust law employs a "divide-and-conquer" strategy, trying to keep industries fragmented, and competitors too small and numerous to coordinate price hikes. A merger is blocked if it would result in a company with an "excessively" large share of the U.S. market. Until recently, the courts have remained blissfully unaware that many markets are global, not national.[16]

Paradoxically, even as American antitrust law attempts to keep producer prices low, it forbids them from falling too low. In antitrust jargon, cutting prices below costs is illegal "predatory pricing." Since orthodox economics teaches that all competitors must have roughly the same costs, unusually low pricing by one firm is viewed as an unfair attempt to monopolize its industry by driving competitors out of business. The idea that competition *should* weed out less efficient firms or that consolidation is a natural consequence of industry evolution plays no role in antitrust law. Because the learning curve is ignored, there is no place in antitrust philosophy for the notion that cutting prices broadens the market, accelerates experience growth, and lowers costs and prices to the benefit of all consumers.[17]

In Japan, "predatory pricing" is not prohibited. In fact, because the Japanese live by the learning curve, they flatly reject the whole idea that "predatory" pricing is harmful. The Japanese realize that the more aggressive the pricing, the faster an industry will consolidate. With the surviving firms accumulating experience faster than before, the erosion of costs and prices will accelerate. Companies that are efficient enough to survive in the viciously competitive Japanese domestic market prove to be formidable competitors when their products reach foreign shores.

Because leading American firms genuinely fear the huge penalties triggered by a court finding of "predatory pricing," they often restrain themselves from competing as vigorously as they could. Instead of slashing prices, driving for maximum market share and the lowest possible costs, they hold back. Consequently, even America's leading firms have often been ill-prepared to keep up with Japanese companies hardened by no-holds-barred domestic competition. Considering their devastating impact on the ability of American firms to accumulate adequate production experience, America's antitrust laws should be called antilearning laws.

In a similar way, a comparison of American and Japanese foreign-trade policies reveals America's complete ignorance of and Japan's strict adherence to the basic teachings of the learning curve. With some notable exceptions, America has held to a "free-trade" philosophy, leaving it wide open to imports. By the conventional logic, if foreign companies happen to outperform American firms, then the consumer benefits from free access to better and cheaper foreign goods. Americans should concentrate on businesses where they have a comparative advantage. As one economist put it, "We'll buy semiconductors from them and sell them rock music."[18] The tactics that put the foreign competitor in a superior competitive position are deemed irrelevant.

According to equilibrium economics, there is no need to worry about trade imbalances. Trade flows will balance themselves automatically once the countries' currencies find their new equilibrium exchange rates.[19] Only after years of widening trade deficits and mounting public outrage over the decimation of American industry did Congress decide to ignore the soothing words of respected economists and pass a trade law whose key section requires retaliation against nations pursuing "unfair" import restrictions.[20]

Without question, Japan was the prime target of America's tough 1988 trade law. Shortly after its passage, the U.S. government formally labeled Japan (as well as India and Brazil) an "unfair" trading nation. Of course, being resource-poor, Japan always has imported plenty of raw materials, but, to the extent possible, it has kept out sophisticated foreign goods. As a portion of their total imports, the United States and the Western European economies import manufactured goods at three times Japan's rate. From American skis that weren't right for Japan's "unique" snow to telecommunications gear that wasn't right for Japan's airwaves to jet fighters that weren't quite adequate for Japan's special defense needs, stories of Japan's obstinate refusal to import manufactured goods are legion.[21]

In the past, Japan's extreme protectionism often was excused as an island nation's peculiar paranoia, an understandable fear of becoming overly dependent on distant foreign suppliers. But the real reason for Japan's strict import control is that it gives an enormous boost to Japanese firms in their quest for accelerated experience growth. Japanese firms accumulate experience by selling in both Japan and the United States, but since American firms rarely can sell their goods in Japan, their experience must be derived from a smaller overall market. Coupled with America's open door to imports, Japan's staunch protectionism has had a dramatic impact on the relative rates of experience growth for Japanese and American firms.

There are, of course, specific instances where American manufacturers have been allowed to sell in Japan, but even these seeming exceptions to the rule reveal Japan's consummate skill at the learning-curve game. For instance, in the early 1970s, when it became clear that microchip technology would define the futures of all electronics industries, the Japanese government targeted the semiconductor business for an all-out effort. At the time, American companies such as Intel, Motorola, and Texas Instruments had commanding leads in all aspects of microchip technology. By every measure—price, quality, and performance—American microchips simply overwhelmed the Japanese products. American firms held more than 55 percent of the worldwide chip market—more than twice Japan's share.[22]

But when these American firms tried to sell their chips in Japan, they were denied import licenses. When they persisted, the Japanese government informed the Americans that they could sell in Japan only if they agreed to license their technologies to Japanese firms. The American government ignored the complaints of its chip firms for fear of upsetting its Japanese ally.

Prevented by U.S. antitrust law from forming a united front, the American firms were skillfully played off against each other. One by one, the American chipmakers handed over technical secrets gained from hard-won experience and gave their Japanese competitors the tools needed to catch up almost overnight. To add insult to injury, the Japanese never followed through on their promises of open-market access. Through the 1980s, Americans never were allowed more than a 10 percent share of the vast Japanese chip market.[23]

Pursuing its learning-curve strategy from every possible angle, the Japanese government successfully implemented three key policies: (1) It impeded the experience accumulation of American chipmakers by blocking access to the Japanese market; (2) it propelled Japanese firms down the industry's learning curve with technology extorted from American chipmakers; and (3) it accelerated the experience growth of Japanese firms by supporting "predatory" export pricing that ultimately drove many U.S. chipmakers out of business.[24]

By 1989, the Japanese had surpassed the Americans in almost every niche of the microchip business. The U.S. share of the worldwide semiconductor business had dropped to about 35 percent and was falling fast. Japan's share was more than 50 percent and rising rapidly.[25] In what someday will come to be regarded as the single most devastating loss of American technological and economic leadership, the Japanese government exploited learning-curve dynamics to the hilt, while American policymakers sat by impassively, secure in the knowledge that they had economic truth on their side.[26]

But despite the supercharged pace of experience growth fostered by Japan's "tilted-playing-field" policy, this was not the only source of Japan's swelling economic power. By the late 1970s and early 1980s, it became painfully obvious to American management experts that even in industries where the playing field was level, Japanese firms simply were doing a much better job of manufacturing than most of their American counterparts.

Throughout the 1980s, progressive American firms faced up to their inadequacies and tried to improve before it was too late. Few topics received more attention in the business press than advice on how to become more like the Japanese. But even as American companies adopted "quality circles" and "consensus-style management," there was little genuine appreciation for why these and other practices had yielded such enormous productivity gains to Japanese firms. All too often, American companies aped Japanese management techniques without grasping the underlying purposes of these practices.

Simply put, the ultimate goal of Japanese management techniques is to create superior learning organizations. Intuitively, if not explicitly, Japanese managers recognize that if two competing firms have the same rate of experience growth, the more intelligent organization will enjoy a steeper learning curve and reduce unit costs faster. Because of its more efficient use of resources, the smarter organization has a better chance of long-term survival in a constantly changing economic environment.[27]

Japan's profound commitment to organizational learning can be summed up in one word—*Kaizen*, a word that has no English equivalent. *Kaizen* means continuous, incremental improvement. One Japanese management expert writes,

> *Kaizen* strategy is the single most important concept in Japanese management—the key to Japanese competitive success. . . . *Kaizen* is one of the most commonly used words in Japan. In the newspapers and on radio and TV, we are bombarded daily with statements by government officials and politicians regarding the *Kaizen* of our trade balance with the United States, the *Kaizen* of diplomatic relations with country X, and the *Kaizen* of the social welfare system. Both labor and management speak of the *Kaizen* of industrial relations. In business, the concept of *Kaizen* is so deeply ingrained in the minds of both managers and workers that they often do not even realize that they are thinking *Kaizen*.[28]

This emphasis on the value of sustained, gradual change contradicts common Western attitudes. Particularly in the United States, where few people are even aware of the learning-curve effect, economic progress usually is equated with dramatic technological breakthroughs such as superconductivity. In American culture, lab-coated scientists are the technology heroes. Progress is their exclusive domain. The gritty details of cost reductions achieved by fine-tuning inventory controls are no match for legends about eccentric inventors and their marvelous creations. In a society that believes in the "home run" and the "quick fix," the modest contributions of average workers—far and away the dominant source of technological learning—are virtually ignored.[29]

While commonly held expectations might not seem important, they are in fact critical to the pace of economic progress. As one early proponent of the learning curve put it,

> If progress is believed possible, it will likely be sought; and if it is looked for, there is some possibility of finding it. . . . The assumption that continual progress can occur may also create an atmosphere which encourages uncovering ideas or recognizing them when stumbled upon. . . . Conversely, if betterment is not believed possible, then the incentive to seek improvement is reduced, and an atmosphere of maintaining the status quo is encouraged.[30]

Although the learning curve proves that the link between accumulating experience and improving performance is highly regular, it is not automatic. By itself, production experience does not reduce unit costs. Experience provides the opportunity for organizational learning, but specific acts of learning require intelligent effort by individual human beings. If the people working in a firm do not believe that small gains are possible or worthwhile, they have no reason to expend the effort needed to turn experience into learning.[31]

In America, a favorite expression is, "If it ain't broke, don't fix it." In Japan, a similarly popular saying is, "Pursue the last grain of rice in the corner of the lunch box." The *Kaizen* philosophy may be a feature of Japan's ancient culture, but its application to the learning-curve economics of high-technology manufacturing has been at the heart of Japan's extraordinary productivity surge.[32]

Kaizen teaches that the first step to improvement is admitting that a problem exists. As long as a problem goes unrecognized, it cannot receive the attention required to eliminate it. Following this self-evident logic, it is not surprising that the two most famous Japanese manufacturing practices—total quality control and just-in-time production—are designed to expose hard-to-detect production problems.[33]

Under the Japanese system of total quality control, every single step in a manufacturing process is monitored for defects. By contrast, traditional American quality control tends to emphasize inspections made at the very end of the line by a quality-control department. In Japan, every worker is his or her own quality inspector. Defects are caught and fixed where they happen. Instead of relying on final checks to catch defective products, Japan builds in quality at every stage by exposing problems as they occur.[34]

In a similar way, Japan's just-in-time production system contradicts traditional American practices. In American factories, each machining station is an island of production. During the work shift, the parts produced at each station are loaded into large containers, which then are carried by forklifts to inventory holding areas. Whenever a worker at the next stage needs more parts, a forklift driver delivers a container drawn from this inventory. When the second worker finds a defective part, he tosses it onto the scrap pile or into the bin for rework. If the machinery at the first location happened to be out of adjustment, hundreds or even thousands of defective parts could be sitting in inventory before the defect is discovered. To keep production flowing and avoid scrapping all those bad parts, the defects may simply be ignored.

The Japanese just-in-time system eliminates this practice by forbidding inventories between work stations. Small batches of parts are passed immediately from one work station to the next. As soon as a defect is detected, the flawed part is sent right back to the previous worker. Where traditional American factories resemble an archipelago of production islands isolated from each other by an ocean of inventory, Japanese plants are tightly integrated, continuously flowing production systems. Submerged obstacles to quality are revealed when the ocean of inventory is drained away.

Of course, without parts inventories to buffer disruptions at individual work stations, the entire production line becomes vulnerable to shutdowns. To prevent the enormous losses that such shutdowns entail, Japanese workers and managers are under tremendous pressure to root out subtle problems before they interrupt the flow of output. In effect, the just-in-time system is an extremely rigorous manufacturing discipline that forces the recognition of problems before they trigger intolerable consequences. Refinement never stops. Thousands of minuscule improvements in procedures and tooling must be made to turn the production of complicated machines into a continuously flowing stream of product.[35]

Without question, just-in-time production and total quality control are at the heart of Japan's manufacturing prowess, but even these twin techniques cannot fully explain the learning superiority of Japanese firms. After a problem has been uncovered, those who found it must be motivated to invent a solution. Identifying a problem is only the first step in the learning process. Without a reward, there is no incentive to exert the effort that the act of learning requires. Even a rat running through a maze must be rewarded with a food pellet before it shows any interest in learning. Unrewarded rats roam around aimlessly, showing no evidence of learning.[36]

Not surprisingly, then, Japan's other most frequently cited management practice is rewarding those who contribute to organizational learning. For instance, while most American employees are paid a straight salary or an hourly wage, the typical Japanese worker takes home about one-third of his or her annual compensation in the form of profit-sharing bonuses. If Japanese workers do not contribute to their organizations by uncovering problems and finding ways to cut costs, reduced corporate profits lead to smaller bonuses.[37]

But the Japanese reward system is much broader and deeper than semiannual bonus checks. While all too many American executives and managers assume that they are the sole source of new ideas, Japanese managers realize that the workers themselves know far more than anyone else about improving their productivity. After all, the workers are closest to the practical problems of production. Consequently, Japanese firms place tremendous emphasis on worker suggestions. In 1984, Mazda's employees submitted 2.8 million specific suggestions—more than 100 per worker—70 percent of which were implemented. Each year throughout Japan, companies stage elaborate awards ceremonies where top officials heap praise and rewards on workers who have made particularly useful suggestions.[38]

Japan's vaunted lifetime employment system can also be seen as part of its elaborate reward structure. An employee who knows that a labor-saving suggestion will not lead to a layoff is far more likely to make the recommendation than one who fears the consequences of improved productivity. In fact, the lifetime employee knows that he will share in the long-term savings derived from any cost reductions, and he sees a close linkage between his well-being and that of the organization. In American firms, where the interests of employees and shareholders often diverge, the incentives for employee-inspired productivity gains are much reduced.

Perhaps the strongest argument for organizational learning's dependence on individual rewards can be made by looking at an economy where rewards have been virtually outlawed. Until quite recently, the Soviet Union has systematically severed the relationship between output and reward. Consequently, the Soviet rate of organizational learning, as reflected by stagnant worker productivity, has been dismal. While the American pace of organizational learning is much faster than that of the Soviet Union, it is in Japan, where elaborate reward systems bind workers to the fate of their firms, that organizational intelligence has reached its highest form.[39]

None of this is to say that Japanese workers are committed to the success of their organizations strictly because of financial incentives. Japanese culture stresses the importance of "the group" to a degree that is incomprehensible to the Western mind. In the modern Japanese economy, that group is the corporation. To Western eyes, a corporation is simply a workplace where individuals come together to make a living. To Western economists, a firm is machinelike, an entity whose only goal is profit maximization. But the Japanese conceive of a corporation as a living organism whose goal is survival.[40]

Because the capitalist economy operates like an evolving ecosystem, this difference in attitudes helps explain why the Japanese have overtaken the Americans. Although Japanese firms may not explicitly recognize the biological analogy, corporations that abide by the rules of economic evolution are far more likely to flourish than those that blindly follow an orthodox mythology that pays no heed to these immutable forces. Instead of trying to jack up short-term profits whatever the consequences, the firm that considers itself a living organism will pursue strategies intended to enhance its chances of long-term survival.[41]

Japanese firms are famous for sacrificing quick profits for the growth that comes from increasing market share. Unlike conventional American firms that try to maintain constant real prices even as their costs decline along a learning curve, Japanese firms always cut their prices in parallel with their falling costs. The steady price erosion of Japanese consumer electronics is just one example of their normal pricing policy. By steadily lowering their real prices, Japanese firms wrest market share from competitors bent on profits above all else.[42]

Intuitively, the Japanese know that gaining market share by forcing other firms out of a market niche is equivalent to driving competing organisms out of an ecological niche. Since greater market share translates into faster experience growth and accelerated organizational learning, which further strengthens the survivability of the organization, the logic behind common Japanese business tactics becomes terribly obvious. In fact, it is only from the perspective of orthodox Western economics that Japanese behavior seems bizarre. From a bionomic perspective, Japanese strategies are perfectly sensible; it is American behavior that is economically suicidal.

Considering the events of the last 20 years, many commentators now believe that the twenty-first century inevitably will witness Japan's ascendance as the world's leading economic and political power. Perhaps they are right. But there is nothing inevitable about it. Although the United States will never regain the global economic dominance it enjoyed at the end of World War II, America's present economic decline need not continue. Self-defeating policies can be changed.

But changing political and business practices enough to reverse America's economic demise must begin with a new understanding of how capitalism really works. If the value of experience growth is overlooked, then indifference to the protectionism of America's trading partners is entirely appropriate. As long as the reality of the learning curve is ignored, the "divide-and-conquer" antitrust system makes sense. If American executives continue to think of their corporations as money-making machines rather than intelligent organisms, then pursuit of short-term profit rather than long-term market share is sound strategy. If the link between learning and reward is denied, then there's no reason for firms to establish comprehensive incentive systems for all employees.[43]

There is no shortage of suggestions for revitalizing American competitiveness. In fact, many progressive American firms already have absorbed Japanese methods and are winning back market share in global competition. But unless all Americans recognize that our traditional beliefs about the workings of the economy are wrong, it will remain politically impossible to implement the reform proposals that offer the greatest potential benefits. Changing one's mind about basic principles is never easy, but without such a reassessment, there is little genuine hope of raising our standard of living or reversing America's diminishing global role. As *Kaizen* teaches, the path to improvement begins by admitting there is a problem.[44]

For America, the nation that dominated the twentieth century, such an admission is excruciatingly painful. Rather than face the future, too many Americans prefer to dwell on the past. For them, America's greatest moment came on September 2, 1945, aboard the USS *Missouri*, when General Douglas MacArthur accepted Japan's unconditional surrender. In all history, no nation had so completely dominated the globe.

But, according to those who attended the surrender ceremony, the most striking event of that historic day occurred when 400 B-29 bombers and 1,500 fighters, flying in close formation, darkened the skies over Tokyo Bay.[45] In the midst of a ceremony celebrating America's greatest military triumph, a display of American industrial strength stole the show. Ironically, none of those awed by the massive overflight knew that every single one of those warplanes was built on an assembly line managed according to T. P. Wright's learning curve. Somehow, the economic lessons riveted into the fuselages of those aircraft were deeply impressed upon the vanquished Japanese, while the victorious Americans failed to grasp the source of their triumph.

PART **V**

STRUGGLE AND COMPETITION

Jack Sprat could eat no fat,
His wife could cat no lcan,
And so between them both, you see,
They licked the platter clean.
—*"Mother Goose"*

CHAPTER
19

ESCAPE THROUGH DIVERSITY

Rising out of the sea, just south of the equator and midway between South America and Africa, is Ascension Island. Far from the major Atlantic shipping lanes and 800 miles north of its closest island neighbor, Ascension is one of the most remote spots on the planet. But unlike the similarly isolated Hawaiian archipelago, whose towering peaks wring moisture from the trade winds, Ascension has a dormant volcano that lies low and squat. What under other geological circumstances would have blossomed into a lush tropical paradise is little more than an arid outcrop in the middle of an endless, deep-blue sea.

Unbothered by the island's deficiencies, several seabird species find that Ascension serves as an ideal perch in the midst of a vast fishing ground. Hundreds of frigate and boatswain birds nest alongside terns, petrels, noddies, and boobies on the narrow ledges carved into the sheer cliffs that rim the island. Many more raise their young atop rock pinnacles that stand just a few feet offshore. Every morning, as they have for millennia, the seabirds of Ascension dive into the wind and head out to sea in search of food.[1]

As is true throughout much of the tropics, the warm waters surrounding Ascension do not retain enough chemical nutrients to support the growth of plankton. Without these microscopic plants—the base of the ocean food chain—microscopic animals have nothing to eat. And without these minute creatures, fish have no food. Consequently, the only fish found in great numbers near Ascension are those passing by as they migrate from one distant plankton bed to another. Ascension's seabirds feed on these migrating schools, relying upon large predatory fish and dolphins to flush their prey to the surface.

The key to any seabird's hunting success is its flying range. Following simple geometry, the longer the radius from the nest, the larger the searchable area. But, for reasons shrouded in evolutionary history, one of Ascension's seabird species, the brown booby, does not fly long distances and fishes only in the waters immediately adjacent to the island. Since several months can pass without any large schools coming near Ascension, the brown boobies often face famine.

The ever-present threat of starvation has, among other things, shaped the brown boobies' rather peculiar breeding practices. Most seabirds breed on a regular annual cycle, but brown-booby pairs maintain permanent nests and copulate whenever the fish supply seems adequate. Two weeks after mating, the female lays a pair of undersize eggs, with the first destined to hatch exactly five days before the second. This modest head start turns out to be crucial, because as soon as the second egg hatches, the first nestling shoves its newborn sibling out of the nest to a certain death.

When this murderous sibling rivalry was first observed, biologists were at a loss to explain why brown boobies always laid two eggs if one was destined to be destroyed. They realized later that the second egg serves as reproductive insurance. If for some reason the older hatchling fails to make it through the first few days of life, the parents have another offspring ready to go. The alternative strategy, producing just one egg, would force the pair to start the breeding cycle all over again, wasting precious weeks when fish are within range.[2]

By producing just one hatchling per nest per cycle, the strategy of two eggs followed by infanticide helps ensure the survival of the species. Brown-booby parents never find themselves hopelessly overburdened by two famished nestlings. Even so, the parents often are unable to gather enough food for even a single offspring. When their prey swim too far from Ascension, brown-booby parents simply abandon their young. On average, only one nestling in ten survives long enough to fend for itself—a rate just high enough to maintain the population.[3]

But the plight of the brown boobies is by no means the most rigorous of nature's struggles. In many species, siblings go beyond murder and engage in outright cannibalism. Among hundreds of species of protozoa, insects, fish, snails, birds, and mammals, cannibalism is a common occurrence. For several hours after hatching, monarch butterfly larvae gorge themselves on unhatched eggs. In fact, for the young of many species, predation by brothers, sisters, and parents represents a far more serious threat than consumption by the more typical predators. And while the very thought of cannibalism is repugnant to civilized human beings, its widespread reality speaks to an undeniable fact of life: Nature's most severe competition takes place among members of the same species, among individuals—such as brown-booby siblings—that need precisely the same resources to survive.[4]

Ever since Charles Darwin first suggested that natural selection was the central force driving evolution, biologists have accepted the fundamental importance of competition.[5] Just as Malthus's "population principle" shaped the thinking of generations of economists, Darwin's emphasis on the "struggle for survival" dominated the ideas of evolutionary biologists. In fact, once Darwin had pointed it out, competition's role seemed so terribly obvious that few biologists bothered to study it in detail.[6] But since the 1950s, with the emergence of ecology as a rigorous branch of biology, scientists have made tremendous strides in untangling the subtleties of natural competition.[7]

Central to the biologist's view of competition is the concept of the "niche." In fact, one prominent ecologist writes, "Ecology might almost be defined as the study of niches."[8] Another leading ecologist defines an organism's niche as its "profession" in the economy of nature. Every species must find a way to make a living in the ecosystem. Each strain of genetic information must sustain itself by transforming a particular mix of chemicals and energy into living, reproducing organisms. By cataloging all the resources that a species consumes, an ecologist can describe its ecological role, its niche in the web of life.

All organisms need two basic resources—living space and food. Only when both are abundant can organisms avoid competition. In cases where two individuals share *exactly* the same niche, with either space or food in short supply, competition is unavoidable. In economic jargon, life becomes a zero-sum game.[9] Whichever one wins, the other must lose. In a brown-booby nest, there is plenty of room for two chicks, but the parents cannot possibly feed both of them. The genetically programmed eviction of the second hatchling heads off a futile struggle for food that neither chick would survive.

Despite examples of murderous brown boobies and cannibalistic monarch butterflies, however, such kill-or-be-killed contests are not the rule. Competition pervades nature, but only occasionally does it take the form of direct confrontation. Despite a limited supply of blossoms, bumblebees do not attack each other or bother to defend nectar-rich flowers. Instead, they race frantically from one to the next. With their tiny food reservoirs widely scattered and many competitors buzzing about—a common situation in nature—it is uneconomic to waste energy or risk injury in battle. The bumblebee's best strategy is to outhustle the competition. The struggle for survival is intense, but there are no bloody battles to show for it.[10]

Even in situations where direct confrontations might make economic sense, potential adversaries often find ways to avoid one another. By partitioning a niche into territories, animals minimize dangerous encounters. For the most part, pitched battles break out only when scarcity forces the starving to trespass established boundaries. Otherwise, peaceful coexistence is the norm.[11]

From the evolutionary perspective, avoiding conflict makes sense because competition imposes costs. Winners as well as losers get injured, and even when competition amounts to nothing more hazardous than a mad scramble for food, the extra effort burns off precious energy. Resources frittered away in competition cannot be reinvested in offspring.[12]

Consequently, individuals able to avoid conflicts with their speciesmates tend to reproduce more successfully. If an individual mutant's physical characteristics allow it to live in another climate or eat a different diet, it escapes some of the costs of conflict. If a group carrying a mutated gene becomes reproductively isolated, it may become the founder of an offshoot species.

Paradoxically, competition works most powerfully when there is scant evidence to show it is even happening. Unrelenting competitive pressure stimulates an evolutionary process that creates differences, reduces direct conflict, and promotes coexistence. Along with brutal battles for food and living space, vigorous competition leads to a proliferation of new species, each specialized for a slightly different niche. Rather than constant combat, the hallmark of intense competition is diversity.[13]

Nowhere is this fact more conspicuous than in the tropical rain forests, where feverish competition drives evolution to its fullest flowering. Biological diversity runs rampant in these dense jungles, home to at least half of all the earth's species. A hundred different tree species exist in just a few acres of Amazonian rain forest, while only a handful of species carpet vast tracts of Siberia. A researcher in Peru's rain forest recently collected from a single tree 43 different ant species—a number equal to all the ant species in Canada.[14]

From the time of Charles Darwin's first collecting expedition in Brazil, naturalists have been awestruck by the variety of life in the rain forests. Not surprisingly, few habitats hold more allure for ecologists: Each day in the jungle brings new discoveries. But, at the same time, the bewildering complexity of the rain forest often has stymied the search for coherent patterns. Ecology is, after all, the attempt to describe recurring patterns in the relationships among organisms and between organisms and their environment. Ecology's ultimate goal is to explain how these hidden patterns allow ecosystems to operate as integrated living systems.[15]

The inherent difficulty of this task is compounded by the fact that ecologists rarely can perform meaningful laboratory experiments. Even if it were practical, a forest or a seashore could not be moved into a lab without destroying the very relationships under study. To decipher life's basic patterns, ecologists must conduct their research inside "natural laboratories," out in the field, in ecosystems that are complex but not so convoluted that nature's fundamental architecture is obscured.

By these criteria, the world's premier natural laboratory is the island of New Guinea. Halfway around the world from Ascension Island, New Guinea could hardly be more different. Located 100 miles off the northernmost tip of Australia, New Guinea teems with tropical life. The world's second-largest island, this minicontinent offers ecologists a full range of equatorial habitats—from coastal mangrove swamps to inland rain forests to snow-capped volcanic peaks.[16]

Like all islands, New Guinea is well protected from invasions by foreign species and contains fewer species than if it were connected to a major continent. But because New Guinea is extraordinarily large, it harbors far more species than most islands. From the ecologist's perspective, New Guinea's size strikes just the right balance, permitting enough species diversity to make it instructive but not so much as to make it incomprehensible.

New Guinea's position along the equator also insulates it from the confusing effects of seasonal migrations. Birds that summer in extreme northern and southern latitudes tend to winter in the subtropics. True equatorial tropics like those in New Guinea are too densely populated with year-round residents to accommodate seasonal migrants. In effect, New Guinea is a 1,500-mile-long terrarium, the perfect place to observe nature's own evolutionary experiments.

Of all the creatures inhabiting this splendid natural laboratory, none have revealed more ecological secrets than New Guinea's birds. Their brilliant plumages, diverse body shapes, and distinctive songs make them much easier to observe than protozoa or spiders or hanging vines. Beyond this, in the villages, are tribesmen who are walking encyclopedias of bird life. From decades of hunting and patient observation, they know the subtlest nuances of bird behavior.[17]

For the last 25 years, Jared Diamond—a leading bird ecologist—has taken full advantage of this native expertise. Accompanied by local hunters, Diamond has spent many months tromping across New Guinea's rugged terrain in search of rare specimens. His research documents the lifeways of New Guinea's 513 bird species and provides compelling evidence of the evolutionary connection between competition and diversity.

For example, Diamond found several bird species, all descended from a common ancestor, that now live in separate altitude zones. In one pair of warblers, the first species inhabits a swath of mountainside stretching from about 500 to precisely 1,643 meters above sea level. At the 1,643-meter mark, regardless of the local vegetation, the second species takes over. Its range extends up to about the 2,500-meter level. Both warbler species are most populous right around the altitude boundary that separates them. And, as odd as this arrangement may seem, Diamond reports that 45 pairs, 13 trios, and 3 quartets divvy up their mountainsides into precise horizontal stripes.[18]

On smaller Pacific islands less densely packed with birds, there is a good deal of overlap in the altitude ranges of related species. But sharp divisions are the norm in species-rich New Guinea. Although the birds of a given species could easily survive above or below their accepted ranges, Diamond believes that younger birds learn to stay within their own species' boundaries. With alien species living above and below, wandering out of bounds diminishes a juvenile's chances of finding a mate. Competition compresses each species into a narrower band than it would inhabit if its uphill or downhill neighbors were not present. In fact, on certain isolated New Guinea mountains where one species happens to be missing from the normal altitude sequence, its neighbors expand into the vacant zone.[19]

Diamond also found that even when two species do not subdivide the available living space, they find other ways to avert head-on competition. In some cases, cohabiting species avoid each other by feeding at different times of the day. In other cases, birds limit competition's costs by specializing in different foods. Diamond's most elegant example of this type of niche differentiation involves the fruit pigeons of New Guinea's lowland rain forest. Eight distinct species of fruit pigeon, all offshoots of related ancestors, live side by side in fruit trees. On any given tree, birds of the larger species concentrate on the sturdier main branches, while the smaller birds forage in the slender twigs.

Observing the adage "The jack of all trades is the master of none," each of the eight pigeon species is specialized for a particular size of fruit.[20] A bird of the smallest species weighs just 50 grams and eats berries about 7mm in diameter. Individuals of the largest species are 16

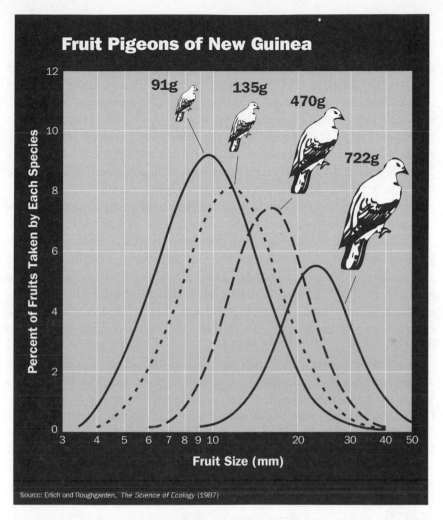

Fruit Pigeons of New Guinea

Percent of Fruits Taken by Each Species

91g   135g   470g   722g

Fruit Size (mm)

Source: Erlich and Roughgarden, *The Science of Ecology* (1987)

Figure 19.1

times that size, or about 800 grams. They feed on fruits averaging 40mm across. Six intermediate species are almost perfectly spaced between these two extremes.

The birds in each fruit-pigeon species weigh about 1.5 times their next smaller relatives. Adjacent species with a lower weight ratio would be too similar to coexist; birds with a higher weight ratio would leave an intermediate niche empty. Protected from the invasions, migrations, and climatic changes that usually distort the results of competition, New Guinea's fruit pigeons evolved into an exquisitely precise sequence of specialized life-forms.[21]

Because the trees yield only so many fruits of each size, competition *within* each species is intense. Survival is won by those individuals more efficient at gathering fruit and converting it into babies. But to a lesser degree, competition also occurs *between* populations of neighboring species. Because of the overlap in fruit sizes taken by adjacent species, each bird's chances of reproducing are diminished by the foraging success of birds in neighboring niches. As the difference between two species' preferred fruit sizes increases, the intensity of their competition declines. Since there is almost no overlap in the fruit sizes consumed by the largest and smallest fruit pigeons, they do not compete.

Outside of New Guinea's laboratorylike conditions, competition has conjured up countless other less ornate examples of niche specialization. Throughout nature, diversity provides a partial escape from direct competition. Along the Scottish seacoast, for instance, two distinct barnacle species live in horizontal bands. The barnacles attached to low-lying rocks are adapted to full-time submersion, while the species living higher up is adapted for living out of water during low tides. In the same way, certain weeds flourish in silica-rich soil, while their cousins do better in limey soil.[22]

In every ecosystem on earth, diversity is the rule. Members of the same species rely on territories and subtle differences in behavior to escape struggles for survival. Closely related species evolve distinct physical characteristics that allow them to exploit subtly different niches. Even the so-called generalist species are specialists of a sort: Their ecologic specialty is flexibility.

Nature's patterns would be far easier to decipher if diversity were the exception rather than the rule. But life did not evolve so that it might be comprehended more easily by its most intelligent product. Life splintered into millions of distinct species so that more genetic information might be squeezed from the planet's finite resources. Seeking refuge from life-threatening competition, genetic information mutated to fit into nature's nooks and crannies. Propelled by its blind urge to reproduce, DNA evolved marvelously efficient ways of turning distinct sets of resources into more life and more DNA. The earth's 30 million species provide living testimony to competition's power to create diversity.[23]

CHAPTER

20

ECONOMY AS ECOSYSTEM

Every organism is defined by the information in its genes, but a living thing also is defined by its relationships to its prey, competitors, and predators. In the same way, an organization is defined by its technology and by its associations with its suppliers, competitors, and customers. From a bionomic perspective, organisms and organizations are nodes in networks of relationships. As time passes and evolution proceeds, some nodes are wiped out and new ones crop up, triggering adjustments that ripple across each network. Constrained by its key relationships, each organism and each organization is held in its niche, pursuing the same goal—the survival of the genetic or technological information it carries.

In the ecosystem, resources flow up the food chain. Sunlight powers the entire system. Energy flows from plants to herbivores to predators. Completing the materials cycle, bacteria break down dead tissues and excrete chemical wastes that become nutrients for plants.

In the economy, resources flow up the value-added chain from mines and farms to fabricators, assemblers, and service firms. Human work powers the system. The economy's end products are used up by individual consumers. And, now that our awareness of environmental destruction finally is maturing, consumer wastes are beginning to be recycled to the bottom of the value-added chain.

Although ecosystems and economies share a basic architecture, several subtle differences distinguish these living networks. To comprehend fully their profound similarity, it is necessary to understand their superficial differences. For instance, ecologists define an organism's "niche"—its profession in the economy of nature—by cataloging the resources it

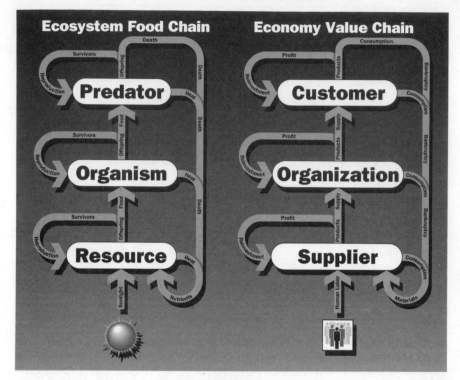

Figure 20.1

consumes from the level *below* it in the food web. By contrast, when businesspeople speak of a company's "niche," they refer to its market position, its links to customers *above* it in the value-added web.

The inverted usages of the term *niche* stem from the basic difference between an ecosystem and an economy. In nature, the population of a species is constrained primarily by the availability of resources. Without sunlight, there are no plankton. Without plankton, there are no fish. The abundance of life at each level in a food web depends upon the "carrying capacity" of the resources immediately below. Ecosystems are "resource-limited" networks. Defining a species' niche—how it copes with scarcity—is the key to understanding its role in the ecosystem.[1]

By contrast, an industry's size is limited by customer demand, not the availability of resources. Under capitalism, firms die for lack of paying customers, not for lack of supplies. Without demand for air travel, airlines cannot survive. Without demand from airlines, aircraft assemblers shut down. Without aircraft makers, avionics makers and engine builders vanish. At each level in a value-added web, organizational survival depends upon the layer of customers just above.

Limited resource supply restrains the growth of a species' population just as limited consumer demand holds back an industry's expansion. In this sense, economies are "consumer-limited" networks. The ecologist's "carrying capacity" is the businessperson's "market size." Describing an industry's niche—how it taps into limited consumer demand—is the key to understanding its role in the economy. Even though their uses of *niche* seem inverted, both ecologists and businesspeople apply the term to the growth-limiting factor.

At a deeper level, the contrast between these "resource-limited" and "consumer-limited" networks stems from a very basic difference between organisms and organizations. Organisms cannot live forever. They must produce offspring that survive long enough to yield their own progeny. When a predator kills a prey organism, it diminishes the survival prospects of the prey species' DNA. A fox cannot eat a rabbit without destroying the rabbit's reproductive capacity. To preserve the genetic code residing in its cells, a rabbit must avoid foxes until it has reproduced. As far as any rabbit is concerned, the world has far too many foxes.

Organizations face exactly the reverse situation. Since firms do not have finite lifespans, they can maintain their technology in perpetuity. Firms need not produce offspring capable of reproducing. Instead of generating baby organizations, companies convert resources into products. A company's technology shapes its product's features just as parents' genes determine their child's characteristics. But unlike offspring, which contain the genes needed to make more organisms, products cannot make more products. Products reflect the technological "genes" that shaped them, but they do not hold the information needed to produce more copies. Products are like the shells abandoned by molting crabs—shaped by the genes, but not alive.[2]

Technology stays within the organization. Aircraft makers sell jetliners, not blueprints, to their airline customers. By applying its special expertise to purchased components, the aircraft maker adds real value to its resources. Under normal conditions, the amount the aircraft maker receives for a jetliner exceeds the cost of the resources used in its production. By reinvesting its profits in more technology, the aircraft builder improves its chances of long-term survival. In short, where a rabbit's survival is threatened by too many potential consumers, an aircraft maker's survival is threatened by too few.[3]

Since the "motivations" of the players in these "resource-limited" and "consumer-limited" networks are inverted, it makes sense for organisms and organizations to practice contrary survival techniques. For instance, many species use camouflage to hide from their consumers. Some butterfly pupae imitate inedible objects, such as leaves and bird droppings. The colorations of moths and lizards often match the bark of the trees they inhabit. First-time visitors to rain forests often complain about an apparent scarcity of animal and insect life. In reality, creatures are abundant, but, given the intensity of rain-forest competition, their camouflage has evolved to such perfection that many species are all but invisible.[4]

Following the opposite strategy, companies devote enormous resources to attracting consumers. Advertising, packaging, public relations, and all other forms of marketing—so often criticized as evidence of capitalism's pointless excess—are natural consequences of a "consumer-limited" system. Just as camouflage is essential to survival in a fiercely competitive ecosystem, grabbing the customers' attention is crucial in a vigorously competitive economy. In major urban centers—the "rain forests" of the global economy—competition is so severe that advertising reaches levels of sophistication not required in less crowded areas.

Instead of camouflage, some species use "reverse psychology," relying on false advertising to protect themselves from predators. For example, monarch butterflies feed on milkweed plants that contain toxic compounds to which they are immune. After a few nauseating experiences, a bird learns to leave monarchs alone. Taking advantage of this, viceroy butterflies, which do not feed on milkweed and are perfectly edible, have evolved color schemes that mimic the distasteful monarchs.

Unscrupulous firms also use deceptive advertising. But they rely on mimicry to attract rather than repel consumers. Many small companies eke out an existence using trade names and logos that are hard to distinguish from those of famous firms. In Taiwan and Hong Kong, back-alley factories take mimicry to its logical conclusion, churning out counterfeit Rolex watches and Apple computers. Like viceroy butterflies, they persist by confusing gullible consumers. Indeed, trademark protection boils down to an effort to squelch deceptive techniques commonly practiced in nature.

While the survival strategies employed by organisms and organizations typically are inverted, some notable exceptions exist. Certain species produce nongenetic products as well as gene-bearing offspring. In the classic example, flowering plants produce nectar as well as gene-bearing pollen. A bumblebee's consumption of nectar does not harm a plant's chances of reproducing. In fact, by carrying pollen to neighboring plants, the bumblebee provides a service that drastically improves the plant's chances of passing on its genetic heritage.[5]

Mistletoe plants and the birds that devour their berries also enjoy a mutually beneficial relationship. The bird digests the fruit's fleshy part but excretes the gene-bearing seed at another location, where it has a better chance of taking root. Whenever a species evolves ways of physically segregating genetic and nongenetic products, it can engage in mutualistic exchanges. As in business, mutually profitable trades require products—goods and services—that do not put genetic information at risk. But since most organisms only produce offspring, the normal food-chain transaction means a meal for the predator and death for the prey.[6]

Surprisingly, despite the differences between predator/prey and customer/supplier transactions, the basic designs of ecosystems and economies are much the same. To overcome the survival threat posed by predators, rabbits produce as many offspring as possible. To capture the survival opportunity offered by customers, aircraft builders produce as many planes as possible. For diametrically opposed reasons, organisms and organizations both maximize output.

To boost production in nature's "resource-limited" network, organisms must compete for shares of limited carrying capacity. Within each species, natural selection weeds out inefficient, unprofitable organisms. Responding to competitive pressure from adjacent species, each species becomes an ecologic specialist, adapted to a particular resource niche. Assuming no environmental shift, a species will survive as long as it enjoys a competitive advantage in producing offspring from its narrow band in a resource spectrum.

In the economy's "consumer-limited" network, firms compete for shares of a limited market. Within each industry, competition weeds out inefficient, unprofitable organizations. Responding to competitive pressure from adjacent industries, each industry becomes an economic specialist, adapted to a particular market niche. An economic species survives as long as it maintains a competitive edge in producing the products demanded by its segment of the market.[7]

Throughout a capitalist economy, competition drives the evolutionary process forward, splintering ancestral economic species into ever more-specialized offshoots. Barely a century ago, the very first horseless carriage rolled onto the streets of Stuttgart, Germany. Today, the world's highways are jammed with an astonishing menagerie of automobiles. Sedans, station wagons, luxury cruisers, subcompacts, minivans, Jeeps, muscle cars, hatchbacks, and sports cars all serve discrete, but overlapping, market niches. Most economists speak of the "auto industry" as if it were a single industry, but car dealers and buyers treat it as a collection of distinct businesses.[8]

Automakers do not build "general-purpose" cars; they try to differentiate their products, tailoring vehicles for specific market segments.

Each product category includes cars made by several competing organizations. The survival of each firm hinges on its product's ability to attract willing buyers. The largest firms, like General Motors and Toyota, comprise many subsidiary organizations, each of which manufactures cars targeted at a particular market segment. Smaller firms, such as Ferrari and BMW, compete in just one or two niches.[9]

Because technology and consumer lifestyles keep changing, the boundaries between market niches constantly move. After the OPEC oil embargo in 1973, the niche for gas-guzzling station wagons shriveled, while demand for subcompacts surged. Occasionally, a company will design a vehicle for a new, unexploited niche. Chrysler's minivan is one recent example. Until its competitors managed to copy this car/truck hybrid, Chrysler's foresight was rewarded with superior profit margins. By spawning a crowd of imitators, this breakthrough product led to a new economic species—the minivan industry. Trying to avoid direct competition while pursuing growth, the "auto industry" has spontaneously fragmented into an array of ever more-specialized industries, each focused on the demands of a specific customer group.[10]

Nowhere is the process of market fragmentation more obvious than in that shrine of consumer choice, the typical American supermarket. A quick tour of a suburban store reveals 15 brands of toilet paper, 8 brands of cat litter, 24 laundry detergents, 26 kinds of pickles, and—the grand champion of product diversity—113 breakfast cereals. Product 19, Special K, Nutri-Grain, All-Bran, Just Right, 40+ Bran Flakes, Cracklin' Oat Bran, and Fiber One slug it out for the dollars of health-conscious adults, while their sugar-addicted kids choose among Cocoa Puffs, Cap'n Crunch, Froot Loops, Frosted Flakes, Rice Krispies, and Fruity Yummy Mummy.

Twenty years after Procter and Gamble introduced the first disposable diaper, competing firms offer versions for boys and girls that are regular or biodegradable, thick or thin, normal or ultraabsorbent, and with or without leak-blocking cuffs. Some toothpastes promise a war on plaque, others fight cavities, and still others guarantee fresh breath, whiter teeth, lower abrasion, or tartar control. Whether your hair is normal, dry, oily, gray, color-treated, or needs moisture, body, fragrance, vitamins, or protein, there's a shampoo just right for you. Infants, dandruff sufferers, and chlorine-afflicted swimmers all have their own special potions.[11]

In one of the most publicized business events of the 1980s, an icon of American culture, Coca-Cola, splintered into Coke, Classic Coke, Caffeine-Free Coke, Diet Coke, Caffeine-Free Diet Coke, Cherry Coke, and Diet Cherry Coke. After years of losing cola market share to Pepsi, the Coca-Cola Company redrew the niche boundaries with drinks designed for cola lovers of varying tastes, degrees of obesity, and states of desired alertness.

The cacophony of choice in America's supermarkets strikes many observers as proof that capitalism has run amok. But, as demonstrated by the Soviets, the result of the alternative approach—where central planning stamps out both competition and diversity—has proved to be far worse—namely, nothing at all on the shelves. Along with incessant and obnoxious advertising, mind-numbing product variety is an inevitable consequence of vigorous competition in an immense consumer market.[12]

Most Americans could probably live just as happily with fewer brands of breakfast cereal. But, obviously, somebody out there is paying good money for the stuff. No one is forcing supermarkets to carry Fruity Yummy Mummy. The products in the nation's supermarkets are the current winners in a never-ending struggle for shelf space and market share. More than 80 percent of all new supermarket products don't even last a year. As in nature, the overwhelming majority of mutants do not find a niche and die a quick death.[13]

Despite the economic efficiency of spontaneous market action, if the prime benefit of a competitive economy comes down to the freedom to choose between waxed and unwaxed dental floss, reasonable people might well question whether it's worth all the effort. But the creation of diverse choices is not merely a matter of fashioning gimmicks to satisfy fickle consumer tastes. The proliferation of options pervades every aspect of economic life, including those of great social significance.

For example, during the 1960s and 1970s, several writers warned of the immense political power being concentrated in the hands of America's three major television networks. By slanting the coverage offered in their nightly news programs, a clique of network executives could make or break politicians and policies. To prevent this, Congress passed the "fairness doctrine," which required television stations to provide equal access to advocates of opposing views.

But with the advent of satellite uplinks and cable TV, the media giants lost their stranglehold over televised information. In recent years, the combined market shares of NBC, CBS, and ABC have plunged as new firms have launched channels specializing in everything from round-the-clock news to classic movies, old sitcoms, public-affairs documentaries, sports, comedy, music videos, adult entertainment, and children's shows. American television has been so radically transformed that industry experts now speak of "narrowcasting" rather than broadcasting. The major networks, though still important, no longer wield the political influence they once had. Recognizing this shift, the Federal Communications Commission abolished the "fairness doctrine" in 1987.[14]

An explosion of new choices also swept through the world of printed information. Just since the late 1970s, the number of regularly published magazines jumped 50 percent to 3,000 titles. Once dominated by *Time*, *Life*, and *TV Guide*, the magazine industry has fragmented into an array of periodicals focused on everything from home computing to windsurfing.[15]

Competition is most intense among magazines inhabiting the same market niche (i.e., *Time*, *Newsweek*, *U.S. News & World Report*), but the battle extends beyond the bounds of any single information-publishing species. Just as a New Guinea fruit pigeon must compete with individuals from adjacent species as well as against other members of its own species, *Time* magazine must compete with television, radio, and newspapers even as it struggles against the other weekly newsmagazines.[16]

As in nature, the intensity of competition among the various information media diminishes as their differences widen. Since radio and television are both instantaneous, they tend to compete quite vigorously. When pictures are important in telling a story, television has a clear edge. But because radio is more portable, it reaches more people more often. Every car and nearly every jogger is radio-equipped, but portable television—even with the advent of the Sony Watchman—is still reserved for those who ride in limousines.

Since newspapers are published daily, they compete more intensively with radio and television than the other print media do. By virtue of their format, newspapers can offer more detail than either radio or television. Since magazines appear less frequently than newspapers, they specialize in less time-sensitive feature articles and in-depth analyses. Newspapers have the space to cover local events, but magazines offer higher-quality photographs. Some products are hybrids, straddling niches. *USA Today*, America's newest national daily newspaper, often is ridiculed as TV masquerading as a newspaper. The niches of the various media species differ and overlap, with no single medium able to satisfy all customer needs equally well.[17]

The media also differ markedly in their production costs. Since costs drive prices in all industries, comparing the resource costs borne by the various media is central to understanding how their niches fit together. Logically, economic species that face similar costs should inhabit neighboring market niches. Because of their proximity on the resource spec-

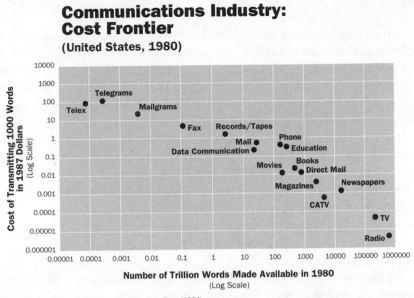

Communications Industry: Cost Frontier

(United States, 1980)

Cost of Transmitting 1000 Words in 1987 Dollars (Log Scale)

- Telegrams
- Telex
- Mailgrams
- Fax
- Records/Tapes
- Mail
- Data Communication
- Phone
- Education
- Movies
- Books
- Direct Mail
- Magazines
- Newspapers
- CATV
- TV
- Radio

Number of Trillion Words Made Available in 1980
(Log Scale)

Source: De Sola Pool, et al., *Communications Flows* (1984)

Figure 20.2

trum, they compete with each other more vigorously than media with radically different cost structures.

This reasoning is borne out by a 1985 study conducted by MIT and the University of Tokyo.[18] The researchers calculated the cost per thousand words produced in 17 different media for the period from 1960 through 1980. They studied production costs for everything from radio and television to books and mailgrams. For example, to estimate the cost of a thousand words transmitted via radio, they multiplied the average number of words spoken per hour by the number of radio stations and the number of programming hours. The total of words broadcast was then divided by radio industry's combined costs as reported by government authorities.

Not surprisingly, the study found that the volume of words transmitted increases as the cost per word falls. Whether its ice cream or information, the cheaper the variety, the greater the quantity produced and consumed. Because of the technology involved, radio is by far the cheapest way to disseminate information to a mass audience. Radio is the bargain basement of the information-publishing sector of the economy, transmitting more words than any other medium. Television, the next cheapest method, is about ten times more costly per word and broadcasts only one-fourth as many words.

The high-cost/high-price end of the information market is populated by firms that transmit telexes and telegrams. These expensive, low-volume methods are used primarily by businesses and governments sending urgent, sensitive information to specific individuals. Because the perceived value of the information carried is so great, these media species are worth the expense even though their per-word transmission cost is roughly ten million times that of radio.

One new mode of information transmission, the overnight air courier, was not reported in the study. Federal Express, the firm that founded the air-courier business in 1973, initially concentrated on shipping lightweight/high-value packages like electronic components. Only later did it become an important player in information transmission as customers began shipping urgent documents as well as packages. In effect, the Federal Express document-delivery service pioneered an unpopulated economic territory.

As the first organization in an entirely new economic species, Federal Express enjoyed extremely rapid growth throughout most of the 1980s. It had no direct competitors. In recent years, however, the firm's growth has been slowed by copycat competitors, and, even more important, by a new generation of low-cost/high-performance facsimile machines. Millions of documents that would have been delivered by air courier now are transmitted by fax. For documents under 20 pages in length—the zone of niche overlap between these technologically unrelated species—fax machines are forcing the air couriers into retreat.[19]

The battle between air couriers and fax machines was not the only major change in the information-transmission business set off by technological advance. During the 1980s, explosive growth in modem-equipped personal computers collapsed the cost of data communications and led to a tremendous surge in its volume. Similarly, a recent massive increase in cable TV programming has moved that medium to a cost/volume position more directly between newspapers and broadcast TV. No position is ever secure. All along the cost curve, firms and industries jockey for position in a never-ending race.

Over time, as the efficiency of each information-transmission species improves, the cost curve shifts down. But cost curves do not glide downward smoothly. Cost/performance breakthroughs are sporadic. Every once in a while, a firm such as Federal Express manages to burst across the then-existing cost frontier and colonize virgin economic territory. New markets are areas where latent demand existed but no previous technology was low enough in cost and high enough in performance to satisfy it profitably. Properly managed, an innovative firm might—at least for a while—become a star, enjoying astounding growth.

Along a cost frontier, some industries accumulate experience faster than others. Each industry is on its own learning curve, pushing down unit costs . A cost curve for an entire economic sector shows the current location of a society's economic capabilities. In 1980, it simply was not technically feasible for any company to transmit a thousand words by mailgram for less than $10. No book publisher knew how to transmit that much information for less than a penny. Given the state of technology in 1980, that's how much it cost to get those jobs done.

As real costs fall, the limits of the economically possible are pushed back and the economy expands. Activities that were impossible or fantastically expensive become routine and cheap. But, of course, not every economic species can keep pace with gains in efficiency. Some information-transmission species—jungle drums, smoke signals, pony express, telegraph, and courier pigeons—that were crucial in earlier times became extinct because their inherent costs could not be brought low enough to stay competitive with new alternatives.

Just as competitively superior species force their predecessors out of ecological niches, new economic species conquer their forerunners, pushing them into retreat if not outright extinction. Word processors have driven typewriters from most modern offices. But one typewriter usually is kept around to handle odd-size labels and envelopes. Telephone calls have displaced letter writing, but love letters probably will always be written. Compact disks have narrowed the niche of vinyl records and video rentals have demolished "adult" cinemas. What ecologists call "invasions," business strategists refer to as "technology substitutions." In every case, a new industry compresses an entrenched industry into a portion of its former domain.[20]

From the earliest days of the industrial era to the present time, patterns of competition familiar to ecologists have propelled human economic history. As the stockpile of scientific knowledge has grown, whole new industries have sprung up to capture its potential benefits. After the usual fits and starts and a short burst of adolescent growth, each industry matures, bumping up against a ceiling of limited market demand. Quite often, industry expansion overshoots real demand. Subsequent periods of extreme competitive pressure—known as "consolidations" or "shakeouts"—then weed out the least efficient organizations. After considerable turmoil, workers and machines from unprofitable, bankrupted firms are reabsorbed by viable organizations.[21]

In each industry, the firms surviving these competitive crunches fall into one of two categories—"cost leaders" and "niche players." Cost leaders compete by being more efficient than their adversaries. Through meticulous attention to the details of the production process, cost leaders find ways to consume less labor and material for each unit produced. During shakeouts, when industry-wide oversupply causes prices to plunge, low-cost leaders manage to squeeze out narrow profits or sustain more modest losses than their rivals.

By contrast, "niche players" survive by avoiding head-to-head price competition. Instead of attracting customers with rock-bottom prices, they custom-craft their products to meet the peculiar requirements of a few customers. Since personalized products are worth more to customers than standard models, buyers are willing to pay a premium.[22]

While the "cost leaders" stress cost reduction, "niche players" survive by providing more added value. Cutting costs and adding value are the twin goals of economic efficiency. Some businesses emphasize one, some the other. Balancing these irreconcilable objectives is the art of strategic management.[23]

Like an amoeba, the economy is bound on all sides by its cost frontiers. Along each frontier, the competitive frenzy never lets up. In information, transportation, food, clothing, housing, health, energy, finance, and all the other economic sectors, firms differentiate their products to avoid head-on confrontation. Competition and innovation keep poking holes in and pushing back the cost frontiers, allowing the economy to extend itself into previously uninhabited regions. This is the source of economic expansion.[24]

The daily events of the struggle are chaotic, messy, and unpredictable. The people involved are haunted by the risks and the unknowns. But beneath the economy's turbulent surface, competition compels an inexorable trend toward higher output at lower cost. By specializing, by concentrating their experience on a narrow set of problems, firms keep learning to squeeze more value from less resource.[25]

In both ecosystem and economy, survival rewards efficiency. Inefficiency is punished by extinction. Attempting to escape scarcity, species as well as industries fragment into ever more-specialized offshoots. By adapting to the peculiarities of their niches, ecologic and economic life forms become more efficient at making offspring and products. Lacking any grand design other than the urge to escape threats to their continued existence, genes and technology spontaneously weave living webs of ever more-intricate filigree. The future details of these stunningly complex systems are unknowable, but their basic architecture and historical direction are quite clear and similar.

Ever since Darwin, the similarity of natural selection and economic competition has been obvious. But, until quite recently, it was impossible to develop a meaningful comparison. After all, the great bulk of thorough ecological research is a product of the last thirty years. Since no one knew the facts of ecologic competition, any attempt to draw a compelling comparison to economic competition was futile.[26]

Beyond this, even if the biological knowledge had existed long ago, the hidden patterns of business competition were not well understood until recently. Prior to the widespread use of computers, precise data on market shares, costs, prices, and other key variables simply was not available. Even in the largest corporations, critical decisions were based on "seat-of-the-pants" intuition rather than rigorous competitive analysis.[27]

Computers not only made analysis possible, they also radically accelerated the pace of business evolution. Industry life cycles and competitive scenarios that once stretched over decades now unfold in months or years. Together, time compression and accessible data revealed the underlying patterns of economic competition. Today, the study of competitive dynamics is standard fare in business schools. But, ironically, the professors never mention that nature has been playing by the same rules for eons.[28]

CHAPTER
21

DIVIDE AND PROSPER

Since 99.99 percent of all the species that ever lived are now extinct, it's absurd to argue that any one species has found the ultimate winning formula in the struggle for survival. No species can live forever on a planet that experiences intermittent environmental catastrophes. The best one can hope for is to make a brief appearance on evolution's stage before shuffling off to fossilized oblivion.[1]

But longevity is not the only measure of biologic success. An ecologic approach calculates the total weight of all the organic material on earth—the biomass—and then estimates the portion accounted for by each major life-form. According to this method, the larger the share of the biomass held in the tissues of a given life-form, the greater its ecological success. For instance, among land animals, mammals outrank all other vertebrates, while ants dominate the invertebrates. In the competition for a fixed quantity of organic resources, the strategies pursued by mammals and ants have proven fabulously effective.[2]

Physically, mammals and ants could hardly be more different. Ants lack both the size and high intelligence so crucial to mammalian success. But ants do have something that all mammals (except one) lack—an extremely elaborate social organization.[3]

Biologists still argue about the origins of ant sociality, but its essential precursor appears to have been the ant's unusual reproductive system. The great majority of an ant queen's offspring are sterile females. The only way these "worker" ants can promote the survival of the genes they carry is by laboring on behalf of their mother and the few fertile siblings she produces. Each worker is an individual animal, but since it cannot reproduce, it is not a complete organism. The organism—or "social organism," as it is called—is the ant colony as a whole. The members of the social organism play the roles of specialized cells just as heart, liver, and lung cells might be considered nonreproductive workers in a human body. For the organism's genes to survive, all components must make their particular contributions.[4]

The great advantage of the social organism's mode of life is an energy-saving division of labor. With various workers groups, or "castes," dedicated to specific duties such as nest excavation, food gathering, and parental care, the social organism is far more energy-efficient than a comparable population of individual insects. Workers do not waste time and energy moving around, switching from task to task. Beyond this, the colony's reproductive chances are enhanced because its critical functions are physically isolated. Dangerous activities like food foraging are handled by expendable workers, while offspring are fed and defended in an underground hideaway. In a resource-limited world, the efficiencies yielded by the division of labor endow an ant colony with a powerful competitive edge.[5]

In a sense, the division of labor is just another example of competition's power to create diversity. Externally, an ant colony must compete for resources against nearby colonies. To the extent that its needs differ from those of its neighbors, it stands a better chance of reproducing. Internally, the colony's efficiency is enhanced by worker diversity. Each worker caste is specialized for a particular "niche" or profession in the economy of the nest. Head-to-head competition among workers is reduced and the colony's food production is increased because worker diversity makes cooperation practical. The peculiar characteristics of an ant colony's worker diversity are shaped by its position among the ecosystem's immense variety of ant species.

For instance, of the roughly 10,000 ant species, the 38 species known as the leafcutters employ the most elaborate division of labor. Found from Patagonia to New Jersey, the leafcutters are the dominant animals in the American tropics. In the rain forests of Central and South America, leafcutters consume more vegetation than any comparable group, including the more abundant forms of caterpillars, grasshoppers, birds, and mammals. In Brazil, which the Portuguese settlers called "The Kingdom of the Ants," farmers still consider leafcutters the number-one agricultural pest. Competitors often view each other as pests.[6]

A leafcutter trail looks like a miniaturized jungle freeway, jammed with tens of thousands of brick-red ants streaming along in twin columns. In one direction, foraging workers head from their nest to a tree being stripped of its leaves. As they arrive at the doomed tree, the foragers use their serrated jaws to scissor sections from the edges of leaves. Then, with their leaf slices held high overhead, the foragers run back down the tree trunk to join the column returning to the colony's nest.[7]

A fully developed nest of *Atta sexdens*, one of the most advanced leafcutter species, houses two to three million ants. A mound several feet across caps an intricate system of tunnels and chambers that may penetrate 15 feet into the ground. The corridor leading from the nest entrance connects to a broad circular thoroughfare lying about two feet below the surface. This traffic circle expedites the flow of incoming and outgoing foragers. Narrower passages connect this major artery to hundreds of subterranean rooms. Fresh air circulates through a separate system of ventilation shafts whose outlets ring the perimeter of the mound.[8]

As the returning foragers approach the nest entrance, they pass through a cordon of soldier ants. The largest workers in the colony, the soldiers do little except eat and self-groom. But when a predator approaches the nest entrance, the closest foragers spray tiny clouds of alarm chemicals, which stimulate the soldiers to attack the intruder with suicidal zeal. A battery of about 20 other chemicals works in a similar fashion. Exuded from various glands on the leafcutters' bodies, these fumes make up a language of odors, a communications system that coordinates the social organism.[9]

Most of the time, the leaf gathering proceeds without disruption. After the returning foragers drop their booty inside the nest, workers somewhat smaller than the foragers pick up the fresh leaf sections and tear them into pieces. When they finish cutting up the vegetation, they turn the bits over to a group of even smaller workers. These workers repeat the process, subdividing the leaf bits into tiny specks. Finally, these thoroughly chewed particles are added to a spongelike clump that fills a room the size of a man's head.

Inside these subterranean chambers, the gardeners—the tiniest ants in the colony—cultivate tufts of snow-white fungus that grow upon the processed vegetation. Before planting immature fungal strands in newly deposited leaf specks, the gardeners prepare the specks by defecating on them. Elsewhere in the darkness, the very smallest gardeners meticulously weed out the spores of alien fungal species. Still others harvest the crop, tiny fungal "cabbage heads" that serve as the colony's food.

The most important consumer of the colony's crop is its queen. As large as a newborn mouse, she lies on the floor of her royal chamber, swallowing fungus and laying eggs. On an average day in a life that may span ten to 20 years, a leafcutter queen will produce several thousand microscopic eggs. Workers carry the eggs to nearby nursery chambers, where they hatch into maggotlike larvae. Incessantly licked and fed fungus by the nurses, the larvae mature into pupae before finally emerging as new adult leafcutters. Each year, a few thousand larvae become the virgin queens and males that fly off to start new colonies, but the vast majority become sterile workers.

Since they are sisters, the colony's workers have almost the same genes. Nonetheless, those that emerge as soldiers are 300 times the size of the gardeners. Apparently, by varying the amount of fungus fed to each larva, the nurses manage to grow the same genes into ants of wildly different dimensions. This bizarre feature of leafcutter existence is made all the more remarkable by the fact that the great majority of ant species have just one size, or "physical caste," of workers. In most ant species, jobs are allocated by a worker's age rather than its size. Young adults perform nest duties like nursing and excavation, while their older sisters risk their lives on foraging expeditions.[10]

In addition to a caste of gigantic soldiers, the most advanced leafcutter species have three physically distinct worker castes (gardeners and nurses; within-nest generalists; and foragers and excavators). For perspective, if the tiniest gardeners were the size of German shepherds, their foraging sisters would be as large as horses. Not surprisingly, the leafcutters' size-based division of labor comes down to a matter of economic efficiency.[11]

The 38 leafcutter species represent just a fraction of the 200 or so fungus-growing ant species, most of which have just one size of worker. These ants cultivate their fungus on decaying vegetation, insect remains, and insect excrement—materials ready-made for fungal growth. Since this simple technique is not accomplished more efficiently by the cooperation of several worker sizes, most fungus-growers never evolved more than one worker caste.[12]

But the leafcutters' unique method of cultivating fungus from fresh vegetation necessitated a division of labor based on worker size. Foragers must be big enough to carry large leaf slices. Edward O. Wilson, Harvard's famous sociobiologist and the world's leading authority on leafcutters, conducted an experiment that demonstrated that leafcutter foragers are just the right size for carrying the greatest quantity of vegetation at the lowest energy cost to the colony. By the same token, the nest workers must be tiny to prepare the minute vegetation particles. If the leaf specks were larger, they would have less surface area and could not support as much fungus. In short, the physical dimensions of the work define the physical dimensions of the workers.[13]

The leafcutters' finely tuned division of labor allowed them to develop an enormously successful way of life. Condemned like all other species to the struggle for resources, they evolved a unique way of prying open one of nature's richest treasure troves—the foliage of the tropical rain forest. By adapting the colony's worker profile to the tasks involved in cultivating fungus from fresh leaves, the leafcutters achieved their preeminent position among the earth's dominant invertebrates.

Then again, the leafcutters do not deserve sole credit for their ecological triumph. After all, they are utterly dependent on the fungus they cultivate. Many tropical plants protect themselves from animal attack by lacing their leaves with poisons. Without the fungus's ability to break down these toxics and digest cellulose, the leafcutters never could have gained such free access to the biomass. Leafcutter genes lack the biochemical technology to convert plant tissues into safe, digestible food. To dominate the tropical landscape, the leafcutters had to rely on the biochemical technology embedded in the genes of their fungus.[14]

At the same time, the fungus's success depends on the leafcutters. Researchers have long been frustrated by the difficulty of growing the fungus in the lab without the assistance of leafcutters.[15] Only leafcutter colonies seem able to prepare the vegetation properly and weed out competing fungal species. The fungus also relies on the ants for dispersion to new locations. Just before a virgin queen leaves the nest to establish her own colony, she bites off a wad of fungus and tucks it under her tongue. If she is lucky enough to survive her nuptial flight, she digs a small burrow, coughs up the fungus, and lays her first brood of eggs in it. As soon as the first workers hatch, they begin the colony's growth process by gathering and preparing leaves for the fungus.[16]

Their ecologic partnership is so intimate that the leafcutters actually stimulate the fungus's growth by the very act of eating it. The "cabbage heads" harvested from mature garden plots are packed with the enzymes the fungus uses to dissolve plant proteins. These enzymes pass right through the leafcutter digestive tract. When the gardeners defecate onto new substrate before planting fungal threads, the enzymes are delivered right where they will do the most good.[17]

Although the finer details of their exquisite interdependence have only recently come to light, the leafcutter/fungus partnership has existed for at least 25 million years.[18] Like every other example of mutualism, it is a product of spontaneous evolution. Successful colonies produce more offspring than the ecosystem can support. In the competition among leafcutter colonies, the most efficient agricultural economies survived. Millions of years of genetic mutation and natural selection honed the leafcutter/fungus partnership. Together, two radically different life-forms evolved a way of tapping the earth's richest lode of plant biomass. In a feverishly competitive ecosystem, this strange partnership turned out to be a big winner.

Not coincidentally, the earth's other leading land-animal species—*Homo sapiens*—also achieved its ecological dominance by forming partnerships with plants. In the hundreds of thousands of years before agriculture began, human beings could hardly have been considered the earth's dominant mammal. Far more of the earth's biomass resided in herds of caribou than in bands of hunter-gatherers. Measured by our ecologic success, we were just another mammalian species eking out a marginal existence.[19]

For millennia, hunter-gatherers had collected seed grains from wild plants, but it was only after the cultivation of wheat and rice began in earnest that our species was able to vastly expand its food supply. In a similar way, the leafcutters' evolutionary predecessors ate whatever fungus happened to sprout on material brought into their nests. But the leafcutter population explosion came after they had taken up active fungus farming. Condemned like all animals to a dependence on plants, both leafcutters and humans found that farm work yields more food than the same effort spent on gathering.[20]

To succeed as agriculturalists, our ancestors arranged their lives to satisfy the needs of the plants that kept them from starving. Just as the organic requirements of fungus defined the leafcutters' tasks, crops determined our forebears' chores. For 9,000 years, season after season, they turned the soil, planted seeds, cleared irrigation ditches, pulled weeds, and harvested their precious grain. As it was for every species, endless labor and bare subsistence seemed to be humanity's unalterable fate.

Population pressure drove the leafcutters to spread northward and southward from their base in the Amazon, and crowding forced our ancestors to bring more land under cultivation. Several thousand years after agriculture began, rich soils in river valleys were fully populated. To increase the food supply further, the efficiency of farm workers had to increase. The leafcutters solved the efficiency problem biologically, by evolving a physical division of labor. But, because the human body lacks the amazing plasticity of the ant's, our ancestors had to take a totally different approach to improving worker efficiency.

Using their brains—the most flexible feature of the human anatomy—they invented farm tools. They designed implements that helped their bodies perform the arduous labor of cultivation. A woman harvesting grain with a scythe works much faster than one ripping up plants with her bare hands. By picking up the appropriate tools—the rake, the hoe, the plow, and the scythe—our ancestors magnified their strength and efficiency. In a sense, the sophisticated division of labor the leafcutters achieved through body-size differentiation was simulated by our fore-bears' use of simple farming tools.

But logically, even this solution to the food-supply problem had its limits. Unless farm tools could be improved infinitely, humanity could never advance beyond subsistence agriculture. Any increases in food output soon would be absorbed by population growth. Even though our species had established a complex division of labor and partnerships with several crop species, the "economy" of the agricultural era was just another fascinating feature of the global food web.

Whether leafcutter/fungus or human/wheat, a purely agricultural economy is nothing more than an intimate ecologic relationship between diverse species of DNA. Such relationships prosper because the partners capture and share the benefits of their biochemical diversity. The wastes of one are food for the other. Crop and cultivator populations expand by joining forces in a hostile natural environment.

But a species's population growth—its success in absorbing an in-creasing share of the earth's biomass—does not imply a rising standard of living. As the leafcutters' natural history demonstrates, even an elab-orate agricultural system promises nothing more than bare subsistence. In and of itself, agriculture offers no escape from the rigors of natural selection. Despite our ancestors' intelligence and tools, their agricultural economy could not shield them from the brutality of nature. Floods, droughts, locusts, and plagues destroyed their lives with horrible regu-larity. Only the strong and the lucky survived.

Without tremendous advances in science and technology, humanity could not possibly distance itself from the fate shared by all other species. But the jump from simple tools to complex machines—from, say, the wooden ox plow to the steel tractor—required more than the mere passage of time. Before the invention of printing, humanity had no reliable method of communicating detailed technical information. And without this capability, it was impossible to accumulate the scientific knowledge required for radically better technologies.

Indeed, printing made all the difference between tools and technology. The crude stone choppers found in East Africa prove that our prehuman ancestors as far back as Homo habilis used tools. Several other animals—including chimps, otters, and certain birds—use objects as tools. None of these tools, however, demand the existence of writing, much less printing. But every piece of complicated machinery is constructed from blueprints, designs, and specifications. Simple tools are handcrafted by imitation, but advanced equipment cannot be built without precise printed instructions.

Obviously, printing's invention did not lead to the immediate dissemination of blueprints for tractors and combines. But, by establishing a medium that could reliably copy and communicate detailed information, Gutenberg accomplished something far more profound. In effect, the invention of printing created an entirely new form of living information. After 3.5 billion years, DNA was no longer the only evolving code on earth. Technological information now existed alongside genetic information. For the first time, the human species had a second realm of evolving information with which to partner.[21]

A purely agricultural economy shows no signs of technological evolution. The leafcutter economy has gone virtually unchanged for the last 25 million years. It is inextricably bound to its fungus. For leafcutter agriculture to change in any appreciable way, the fungus's genes must evolve. A strictly agricultural economy is stable because increased efficiency requires genetic changes in both crop and cultivator, and genetic evolution is terribly slow.

Technology, of course, evolves with blinding speed. Just 200 years after the printing press became commonplace, enough technical knowledge had been accumulated to allow the invention of the machine that ignited the Industrial Revolution—Thomas Newcomen's atmospheric pumping engine. By draining flooded coal mines, the atmospheric engine allowed humans access to energy locked in fossilized plants just as the fungus gave leafcutters access to energy stored in living plants.

But, unlike the leafcutter/fungus partnership, the human/technology partnership allowed humanity to tap an energy supply external to the food web. Cheap coal made possible the age of iron and steel. With these materials, clever designs could be transformed into complex machines. Throughout the nineteenth century, steamboats and railroads opened vast new lands to cultivation. Farm machines poured out of factories, propelling massive increases in agricultural efficiency. When the Industrial Revolution began in 1800, 97 percent of Americans fed themselves by farming. Today, only 3 percent of Americans work on farms. In less than 200 years, techniculture replaced agriculture, forever changing humanity's economic and social life.

Both humans and leafcutters developed agricultural economies. But because only humans can read and write, only our species could move beyond agriculture. Once a reliable mechanism for information copying was in place, we could begin exploring the full potential of human intelligence.

For 9,000 years, we had used our bodies and crude tools to cultivate plants. Our division of labor was simple and physical. But with printing, we could use our minds to cultivate technology. Techniculture allowed a far more elaborate, intellectual division of labor. For the first time, the prime source of human diversity—the mind—could be harnessed for humanity's benefit. With technology as our new partner, the human economy was no longer chained to the sluggish pace of biological evolution.

The epochal shift from agriculture to techniculture did not, however, mean that the evolutionary process had been abandoned. Whether an economy happens to be based on genetic or technical information, the same basic rules apply. Limited resources compel organisms to compete. Limited demand forces organizations to compete. Externally, they evolve specializations to avoid conflicts and boost efficiency. Internally, they evolve divisions of labor in pursuit of the same goals. In both realms and at all levels, competition is evolution's shaping force.[22]

22

ENDING POVERTY

One critical difference between human and ant economies is remarkably easy to overlook. When an uncompetitive leafcutter colony fails, every ant in the nest dies. If the colony collapses before it reproduces, its genes are obliterated. But when an uncompetitive business firm folds, the company's employees do not die. They move on to other jobs. The bankrupt firm's corporate "genes" disappear, but the genes of its employees are unaffected.

Leafcutter workers labor in support of genes they share with their queen. Human workers need no queen. They handle their own reproduction. Genetic independence from the work group means that the organization's downfall will not wipe out its workers' posterity. Of course, in hunter-gatherer and agricultural times, when the human "economy" was still just an exotic feature of the global food web, a failed hunt or crop often led to starvation. Back then, a community's economic ruin meant genetic oblivion for its members.

But the rise of technology shattered this bond. Today, producing enough food no longer poses a serious economic challenge. Several of the most advanced economies are plagued by food surpluses, while their citizens fight a losing war against obesity. In the wake of the 1960s Green Revolution, even India now exports food. Once commonplace, famines now are regarded as inexcusable, freakish tragedies. Hunger and malnutrition are still rife in the Third World, but widespread starvation strikes only where technology has yet to transform human existence.[1]

In a technicultural economy, the penalty for uncompetitiveness is not death, but poverty. And, much as humanity's struggle against mass starvation characterized the agricultural age, the battle against mass poverty shaped the industrial era. From the onset of the Industrial Revolution, bitter political controversy raged over the best way to expunge poverty.[2] Years later, this dispute solidified into the great contest between capitalism and socialism. During the twentieth century, billions of people in many nations served as guinea pigs in a test of these rival economic concepts. In 1989, with the stunning, nearly simultaneous collapse of the world's socialist economies, this colossal experiment came to an end. The results are plain—socialism cannot erase mass poverty.

But, by the same token, any claim that capitalism cures all is undermined by the persistence of widespread poverty amid great affluence. As many as three million homeless Americans sleep on the streets.[3] Another 30 million live below the federal government's "poverty line," their lives deformed by violence, drugs, and despair.[4] In the 25 years since America's War on Poverty began, the number of poor people has *increased*. Nearly 40 percent of America's poor are children.[5]

In America's middle class, many families feel that they are sliding into semipoverty—caught between falling real wages and a rising cost of living. Some writers now suggest that the American middle class is disappearing, ripped apart by the centrifugal economic forces of the Information Age and global competition. Socialism failed. But capitalism, at least as it is practiced in the United States today, has yet to deliver on the promise of a decent life for every citizen. As one bumper sticker puts it, "If you think the system is working, ask someone who isn't."[6]

Regrettably, dispassionate analyses of America's poverty problem are rare. Whether the specific topic is welfare reform, taxes, or health care, the positions taken by political adversaries are reminiscent of those first taken in Great Britain nearly two centuries ago. For the extreme Left, poverty is not so much an economic question as it is a moral outrage. In their view, the poor are poor because they are ravaged systematically by the rich. They see capitalism as a system where "the rich get richer, while the poor get poorer."

Those of more moderate liberal views see poverty as a tragic but inevitable consequence of a highly productive but intrinsically inequitable economic system. To demonstrate the inherent unfairness of American capitalism, they cite some rather appalling statistics. For example, an American family ranked in the ninety-fifth percentile of income distribution earns about $80,000 a year—roughly 15 times as much as the $5,500 earned by a family in the fifth percentile. The top 20 percent of American families take in 44 percent of all family income, while the bottom fifth earns just 5 percent—a 9-to-1 ratio.[7]

This wildly disproportionate income distribution is seen as so unconscionable that it begs to be corrected by government action. To retain the manifest benefits of capitalism while achieving some semblance of economic fairness, traditional American liberals support a policy of income redistribution. In their view, steeply progressive income taxes, coupled with transfer payments, are the only way to narrow the enormous gap between rich and poor that capitalism generates.[8]

On the far Right, the poor are dismissed as victims of their own indolence, not deserving of any government aid. More sober-minded conservatives believe that income redistribution, although well intended, does not achieve the desired effect—that the "social safety net" actually is a web trapping those who fall into it.[9] In their view, the welfare system suffocates the poor, robbing them of the will to help themselves. Since "a rising economic tide lifts all boats," conservatives believe that faster economic growth is the only way to cure poverty. And, since high taxes slow economic expansion by eroding incentives for work and investment, they favor lower taxes and less government spending.[10]

In the United States today, neither Right nor Left commands enough political support to install its own economic program. Bogged down in ideological trench warfare, a series of Right-leaning presidents and Left-leaning Congresses have struck a ruinous compromise—lower taxes *with* higher spending. This hideous fiscal hybrid incorporates the politically palatable half of each program while piling an awesome burden of $200 billion in annual deficits on those too young to vote.[11]

As the cumulative U.S. federal debt soars past $3 trillion, America's economic growth has stalled. Real per capita income—the true measure of economic performance—has risen quite slowly for the last 20 years. During the same period, America's major competitors, Japan and West Germany, have produced stunning increases in average personal incomes. To top it all off, American poverty is not withering away, and mounting interest payments to foreign lenders are beginning to lower the living standards of all Americans, especially the poor.[12]

The longer this misbegotten fiscal policy continues, the bleaker the prospects for American society. Despite recent efforts to reduce the federal deficit, policymakers on both the Right and the Left seem immobilized, wedded to their versions of nineteenth-century economic wisdom, insisting that their way is the *only* way. In fact, because neither side comprehends how capitalism works, neither can hope to devise policies that will harness its forces to cure poverty. Instead of resolving our central economic problems, we continue to compound them.

To grasp the true causes of poverty, it is crucial first to figure out *why* the range of incomes is so great. Since only the top 10 percent of American families draw any appreciable portion of their incomes from investments, differences in wages earned from work account for most of the disparity in income levels.[13] Obviously, wages vary by occupation. Surgeons make far more than pediatricians. Pilots earn more than flight attendants. Pastry chefs earn more than dishwashers. Exceptions can be found, but statistically the influence of occupation on income is overwhelming.

In a market economy, differences in pay rates reflect differences in the amount of value-added per hour worked. Two hours spent by a surgeon saving a child's life after an auto crash is worth more to society than the same time spent by a pastry chef frosting birthday cakes. Reasonable people will disagree over exactly how much more hourly value the surgeon produces. No fixed premium can be mathematically derived.

Wage differentials widen and narrow with shifts in the demand for and supply of surgeons and pastry chefs. In any occupation, an oversupply of qualified workers means more labor hours of a given type are available than are needed. Competition for employment in that specialty pushes wages down. Conversely, a shortage of qualified people reduces competition and drives wages up.[14]

In effect, each occupation is a niche in the market for labor. Just as organisms compete primarily with other individuals in their own species, and firms compete against other companies in their industry, workers compete against other individuals in their occupation. To a lesser degree, workers in one occupation compete against those in related fields. Cardiac surgeons occasionally perform general surgery. Bakers sometimes take over for pastry chefs. But surgeons and pastry chefs never compete. Workers populating adjacent labor-market niches compete, but those in distant occupations do not.

In nature, species escape direct competition by evolving distinctive physical features, but human beings do not have this option. Because all human beings belong to the same species, our physical capabilities are extremely similar. Aside from those who are mentally or physically handicapped, physical features play a small role in determining one's occupation. Of 120 million employed Americans, just a few thousand athletes and entertainers are able to parlay their extraordinary physical attributes into livelihoods.

Superficial differences in skin color, facial features, and body size are trivial compared to what we have in common. Recent research shows that human beings share 99.6 percent of their genes. Of the 0.4 percent genetic diversity that does exist, nearly all occurs *within* racial groups.

The genetic distance *between* races is vanishingly small, just 0.04 percent.[15] Of course, economically relevant genetic differences do exist among *individuals*. Some children are born geniuses, others are slow learners. But despite the most determined efforts, no scientist has proved that substantial differences exist in the innate intellectual capabilities of ethnic or racial *groups*.[16]

Nevertheless, American society is plagued by age-old prejudices. Discrimination against minorities and women continues to play an important role in the poverty problem. Then again, the last three decades have witnessed a remarkable weakening of racism and sexism. Even though the process of human liberation is far from complete, more and more Americans now agree that superficial differences in physical features should have no bearing on a person's opportunities. We can only hope that the next few decades will witness the final realization of a true meritocracy, a system in harmony with the biological facts.[17]

Because our biologic features are so similar, we have long relied on tools to differentiate ourselves and achieve a division of labor. But while the crude farm implements of the past could be used without training, today's technologies demand highly skilled workers. Leafcutter larvae are readied for their diverse economic roles by their nutrition, while young people are prepared by their education.[18]

Of course, these development processes are not identical. Leafcutter larvae passively receive food allocated by the colony's genetic program. A leafcutter's future economic role is predetermined. By contrast, young people must actively study. Where genuinely open access to educational opportunity exists, knowledge is available to anyone who cares to pursue it. Consequently, human economic roles are not predetermined. This is a crucial distinction. But, in both cases, genetically similar individuals are transformed into occupationally diverse specialists appropriate to particular roles in the community's economy. "You are what you eat" may apply to leafcutter workers, but "You are what you know" more accurately describes human workers.[19]

By the 1960s, education's economic importance had become so apparent that several economists began writing about "human capital." They argued that the two traditional forms of wealth—land and capital (machinery)—had been joined by a third—knowledge. In the agricultural era, landowners controlled the economy. In the industrial era, economic power was held by the factory owners. With the onset of the Information Age, economic power began shifting once again—this time to the owners of knowledge. Education, or "investing in human capital"—became the prime source of wealth.[20]

In a high-technology economy, wages are not simply a payment for raw labor. In effect, earnings are a financial return on the worker's past investment in human capital. General surgeons need 13 years of post–high-school education before they are allowed to practice. They earn more per hour than pastry chefs not only because their output is considered more precious but also because a premium is needed to induce students to defer consumption and make such a large investment. Without a stream of future income paying dividends on that educational investment, most people would not bother to acquire advanced skills.[21]

The research is not conclusive, but a variety of studies on the financial returns generated by educational investments show consistent results. Investments in human capital (forgone earnings and education costs) yield about a 15 percent rate of return. Of course, the rate of return varies somewhat by type of education. Investments in certain kinds of human capital, like investments in certain types of machine capital, are more profitable than others. On average, however, even as a person invests in more years of education, the percentage rate of return stays roughly the same.[22]

Paradoxically, then, income redistribution makes dollar earning streams *more* equal by making percentage returns on educational investment *less* equal. Progressive income taxes *lower* the rate of return for well-educated high-earners, while transfer payments *raise* the rate of return for less-educated low-earners. In short, one type of equality is achieved by sacrificing another. In view of the growing importance of human capital, making investment in education less profitable is stupid social policy. And, though unintended, it is a logical consequence of the nineteenth-century economic thinking that ignores human capital.[23]

Two centuries ago—at the dawn of the industrial era—illiterate, unskilled peasants just off the farm were perfectly capable of operating the simple machines used in the first factories. This is why David Ricardo, the first economist of the Industrial Age, saw no economic value in education. But as science advanced and technology grew more sophisticated, the division of labor had to become more elaborate. Techniculture demanded workers with ever more-developed skills. Today, with complex equipment permeating every corner of economic life, the demand for unskilled workers keeps shrinking.[24]

In effect, technicultural production depends upon an intimate relationship between machine capital and human capital. Humanity's efficient cultivation of technology, like the leafcutter's efficient cultivation of crops, requires a finely tuned division of labor. In a leafcutter colony, the fungus's needs determine the workers' sizes. In a business firm, technology's requirements define the workers' skills. As technology evolves, required skills change.[25]

If the bodies of the workers in a leafcutter colony did not match their tasks precisely, the colony would be less efficient, leaving the bionomic organism vulnerable to competitors. When the skills of a company's workers do not correspond precisely to the demands of current technology, the bionomic organization is exposed to competitive attack. The more rapid the pace of technological evolution, the more difficult it is to keep workers' skills in synch with state-of-the-art equipment. Continuous education and training is the only way to transform undifferentiated human beings into an array of extremely diverse, appropriately specialized workers. As in nature, increasing specialization is the only way to minimize conflict, boost efficiency, and raise output.

But, at least on first impression, the notion of highly differentiated workers seems to clash with the most cherished principle of a democratic society: "All men [and women] are created equal." Or, as a bumper sticker on a battered Volkswagen phrased it, "If all men are created equal, where's my Porsche?"

This view seems to hold that American political equality is incompatible with economic inequality. Logically, however, equality of political rights does not imply equality of economic benefits. In a democracy, the surgeon and the pastry chef each get one vote. As political beings, they deserve absolutely equal protection before the law. But, as economic beings, they are as different as the leafcutter soldier is from the fungus gardener. They are political equals, but it is absurd to pretend that they are economic equals.[26]

Indeed, in China and the Soviet Union—the socialist countries that pushed economic egalitarianism to its extreme—all political power became concentrated in the hands of elite cadres. Apparently, political and economic equality *are* incompatible. Nevertheless, critics of America's income diversity believe that since all people have equal rights, they should earn roughly equal incomes. Existing differences are ascribed to genetics and luck, factors for which no one is responsible. In keeping with nineteenth-century economic dogma, education's role in creating meaningful economic differences is overlooked.[27]

Of course, if workers were economic equals, or if economic differences were due solely to genetics or chance, the egalitarian view would be unarguable. Nothing could possibly justify such wide income differences. But workers are not interchangeable. Income diversity is caused primarily by education, not by genetics or luck. Because surgeons own more human capital than pastry chefs, they are able to use more so-

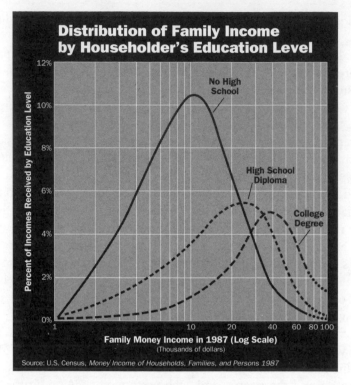

Distribution of Family Income by Householder's Education Level

Source: U.S. Census, *Money Income of Households, Families, and Persons 1987*

Figure 22.1

phisticated technology and are able to produce more value per hour worked. Only by comparing workers of equivalent education can one get an accurate sense of American income diversity.

Indeed, when American income data are recast to show how pay varies with education, the pattern confirms expectations. Workers with less than a high school education tend to earn less than those in any other education group. These low-skilled workers are crowded together at the bottom end of the income spectrum. As the education level increases, average earnings rise. Much as the sizes of the fruits taken by New Guinea's fruit pigeons are related to their body sizes, the incomes earned by American workers are tied to their educational attainment. Each educational group occupies a distinct economic attitude.

Of course, income overlaps exist among these broad education groups just as fruit-size overlaps exist among the fruit pigeons. Everyone knows a story about a Ph.D. candidate who quit graduate school and wound up driving a taxi. Conversely, there are plenty of stories of wealthy businessmen who never graduated from high school. Education is a powerful but by no means perfect predictor of income. In an open labor market, no rule prohibits the uneducated from becoming rich or the well-educated from becoming poor.

But, for the most part, the high degree of overlap reflects the imprecision of categorizing workers simply by their amount of education. Type and quality of human capital are as important as quantity.[28] A bachelor's degree in aeronautical engineering fetches a far higher salary than the same diploma in English. Similarly, a history degree from Yale carries a greater market value than one from Northeast Louisiana University.[29]

To assess American income diversity fairly, the broad curves for the major education groups ought to be replaced by hundreds of curves, each one showing workers' earnings in a particular occupation. Income data gathered in comprehensive national surveys show that earnings by occupation are quite predictable. For example, a typical auto mechanic currently makes between $21,500 and $28,700. Intermediate-level word processors make between $16,000 and $19,800, while industrial designers earn between $25,000 and $34,900. Exceptions exist, but income variation within each job category is limited.[30]

The earnings diversity that does exist within a given occupation is easily explained. Because workers in well-managed firms add more value per hour, these companies can afford to pay premium wages and still be cost-competitive. In regions where living costs are higher, workers earn more than their counterparts in low-cost areas. Experienced workers are paid more than novices.[31] And, of course, even in the same firm, equally qualified workers sharing the same job title rarely show the same talent and ambition. For whatever reasons, some people simply work harder. Individuals are, after all, individuals.[32]

The overall pattern of earnings is unmistakable. Education determines occupation and occupation determines income.[33] Assembly-line workers may not like the fact that the design engineers in their company get paid more, and the engineers may resent the higher salaries of the top executives, but everyone recognizes that a rational system underlies the income differentials. Indeed, firms that overpay become uncompetitive. And companies that underpay find that their employees keep quitting. In an open labor market, workers as well as employers have the freedom to make choices.

Indeed, adjusting to changing circumstances is especially important now that technology is evolving so rapidly. The emergence of each new technology creates completely new job categories. A 1986 update of the U.S. government's *Dictionary of Occupational Titles* added 760 occupations that had not existed ten years earlier. Radioactive materials waste-management engineers, solar-energy systems designers, home-health technicians, integrated-circuit layout designers, and amusement and recreation laserists joined the list of more familiar jobs.[34]

In new and expanding occupations, where the supply of qualified workers has not caught up with demand, pay premiums and vigorous employee recruiting campaigns are the norm. One typically inscrutable newspaper advertisement for computer programmers reads,

> Must have 3-4 years IMS/VS and/or CICS/MVS experience, and know JCL/utilities, ICF, TSO/ISPF and SMPE. Familiarity with IMS utilities, BAL, real time performance/tuning, OMEGAMON and CLIST helpful. Competitive salary and benefits program, opportunities for recognition and advancement.[35]

Persistently unfilled programming jobs reveal a negative unemployment rate in this field. Not surprisingly, the number of newly minted computer-science graduates is rising each year. An expanding labor market niche supports a growing population of specialists.[36]

Simultaneously, new technology eliminates traditional occupations. In the 1950s, when diesel locomotives replaced steam engines, the fireman's position became obsolete. No one was needed to stoke the coal fire or tend the boiler. During the 1980s, 60 percent of all American steelworker jobs disappeared, although total output rebounded to its original level. In an attempt to catch up with lower-cost, higher-quality Japanese competitors, American firms adopted continuous-casting technology, slashing the labor hours in each ton of steel. In the 1990s, computerization will eliminate thousands of jobs for telephone repairers, directory-assistance operators, stock clerks, statistical clerks, and payroll clerks. Shrinking niches support declining populations.[37]

Although technological obsolescence disproportionately affects low-skill jobs, its effects are felt across the occupational spectrum. In the newest jetliners, computers perform tasks that once kept the navigator busy. Cockpit crews are shrinking from three to two members. Even surgeons have been hurt by technical change. With new drugs and non-invasive therapies, the average surgeon performs 25 percent fewer operations than he did just five years ago. Ulcer drugs, for example, have virtually eliminated stomach and upper intestinal surgery. General surgeons have been particularly hard hit, since much of their business has been taken by specialists.[38]

Only a few decades ago, job obsolescence was an insignificant problem. Young people could plan on spending their entire careers in a single occupation. But, in the wake of the microprocessor revolution, a once-stable array of occupations has become quite fluid. As the struggle for economic survival compels firms to cut costs and improve performance, technology is substituted for labor at every level of every industry. Regardless of their income or status, workers who cannot or will not be retrained face lower incomes and long-term unemployment. No one is immune to the effects of evolutionary change.[39]

Such are the facts of life in a technicultural era. The astute observer sees a collection of diverse occupational specialists rather than an imaginary labor force of perfectly interchangeable workers. Each profession has its own educational requirements, performs particular economic functions, and yields earnings that fall within a fairly narrow range. As the sheer amount of knowledge grows, an increasing number of ever more-specialized occupations is required to cultivate technology. But even as new occupations are created, older job categories are wiped out. In each labor niche, the fortunes of individual workers are subject to the unpredictable currents of technological evolution.

None of this should surprise anyone acquainted with modern economic reality, but when it comes to proposing solutions for America's poverty dilemma, neither the Left nor the Right pays much attention to these facts. Blinded by their faith in nineteenth-century economic dogma, both sides cling to beliefs that simply make no sense in a rapidly evolving technicultural economy.

Scratch the surface of any sophisticated argument for income redistribution and one finds a zero-sum mentality. As David Ricardo wrote and his disciple Karl Marx believed, "There is no other way of keeping profits up but by keeping wages down."[40] Principles that accurately described the no-growth agricultural era were wrongly assumed to apply to the emerging technicultural economy. In the mid-1800s, no one—not even Marx—could have imagined the explosive economic growth that techniculture was about to yield. Ironically, zero-sum socialist thought became established just as the constraints of the agricultural age began to fade away.[41]

Among non-Marxists, belief in zero-sum economics was just as strong. John Stuart Mill, the grandfather of modern Western economics, accepted the Malthusian prediction that population increases would outstrip production gains. Like every other major nineteenth-century economist, he dismissed Adam Smith's emphasis on education and the division of labor as critical sources of economic growth. Committed to a no-growth mindset, economists of all stripes thought of the economy as rather like a brown booby's nest, where insufficient resources compelled conflict. The equitable distribution of goods—not their production—was seen as the ultimate economic question.

Logically, redistribution *is* the only remedy for income inequality in a no-growth economy. But the higher an economy's potential rate of growth, the less sense redistribution makes. Assuming that the poor get at least some share of output growth, everyone is better off if the economy expands. But growth requires investment. Only investment can turn new science into new technology. Since an economy produces only a certain total output at any given moment, a trade-off between consumption and investment is unavoidable. To pay for more consumption by the poor, income redistribution must cut investment by the rich.

Simply put, every nation faces an inescapable trade-off between its rate of long-term economic growth and the "fairness" of its income distribution. To raise the "social safety net," taxes rates must be increased. This compresses the naturally generated range of education-based income differences. Income "fairness" is obtained largely by diverting what would have been private investment funds to government-supported consumption. Capital accumulation slows, the pace of technological change slackens, and the average standard of living rises more slowly.

Of course, to recognize the hidden costs of income redistribution is not to argue against the need for a social safety net. It is painfully obvious that many people cannot possibly support themselves. Basic human decency demands that we assist the needy. No rational person disputes this.

But reasonable people often do disagree over the appropriate height of the social safety net. No level of compassion is intrinsically "correct." In a democracy, the height of the social safety net, the fineness of its weave, and the breadth of its coverage emerge as the consensus of the tax-paying public. Every democratic nation designs its safety net in keeping with its political culture and economic position. No two nations need to choose the same spot on the growth/fairness spectrum, but all societies must face the same basic choice.[42]

If the poor always benefitted from economic expansion, few people would want to reduce long-term growth to pay for more generous "entitlements." But, in reality, the poor do not automatically participate in growth: A rising tide does *not* necessarily lift all people. To float on a rising economic tide, a worker must have a boat built of human capital. Those without such vessels are doomed to drown in a swelling sea of affluence. This is the reality of poverty in America.

In a technicultural economy, the root problem is not the maldistribution of consumption but the maldistribution of human capital investment. Of America's poor families, more than half are headed by high-school dropouts. Another third have high-school degrees, but, in view of abysmally low graduation requirements, many of these diplomas are worthless. In fact, some estimates suggest that two-thirds of America's poor adults are functionally illiterate. Imagine trying to function in today's economy without the ability to read.[43]

In a world where the handling of information is the very essence of economic life, illiterates are completely outside the economic system, unable to add value except in menial jobs.[44] With an estimated 30 million adult illiterates, America has the lowest literacy rate of any developed country. Since literacy is so plainly connected to economic capability, America's huge illiteracy problem should excite widespread concern. But, curiously, this fact—or the fact that Japan and Western Europe have achieved virtually complete literacy—is rarely even noted in discussions of America's poverty dilemma or its collapsing competitiveness.

Any mismatch between the skills possessed by the working population and the skills required by current technology opens up an inefficiency gap. The worse the mismatch between human capital and machine capital, the wider the gap and the greater the vulnerability to competitors. Illiteracy is the worst possible case of a skill mismatch—a complete lack of skills. In this sense, America's poor are the tip of an economic iceberg, the most pathetic products of a society that has consistently underinvested in its most precious resource—its own people.

Obviously, many millions of American workers are highly skilled. But over the last two decades, the proportion of those as skilled as their foreign counterparts has fallen. As a percentage of the workforce, the U.S. population of scientists and engineers reached its peak in 1969, the year Americans first walked on the moon. With only half as many people, Japan graduates more engineers—and far fewer lawyers—than the United States.[45]

In both Japan and Western Europe, firms invest far more heavily in worker training than their American counterparts. Consequently, American firms are plagued by shortages of technically skilled workers. Too many American workers simply cannot handle state-of-the-art production technologies. The firms that employ such workers find it increasingly difficult to compete in high-skill, high-wage industries.[46]

During the 1970s and 1980s, as the microprocessor accelerated the integration of the global economy, shifts in America's income distribution reflected the increasing value of human capital. The well-educated, those in high-skill occupations, were able to contribute to the production of goods and services sold on a global market. Typified by the "yuppies," these workers saw their incomes rise rapidly as worldwide economic growth outstripped the supply of highly trained professionals.[47]

At the same time, however, millions of Americans—mostly those with a high-school education or less—saw their jobs lost overseas. This was particularly true in manufacturing, where products are transported easily and where equally qualified foreign workers are willing to work for lower wages. Even in cases where jobs did not actually move offshore, workers were forced to make wage concessions to keep the work in the United States. No longer insulated by distance and trade barriers, America began losing an economic contest that it was unprepared to fight.[48]

Because the role of human capital in economic competition is ignored by conventional economic theory, neither the Left nor the Right comprehends the fundamental forces eroding the living standards of working Americans and crushing the hopes of poor Americans. Both Left and Right continue to overlook the fact that income is an effect, not a cause, and that the only sustainable way of raising a worker's earnings is by increasing his or her productivity. Instead of stressing better education and job training, too many politicians blame racism or seek economic salvation in protectionism and redistribution.[49]

In essence, both liberals and conservatives have come to accept widespread poverty as a fixture of American society.[50] Having conceded defeat in the War on Poverty, the political debate is focused not on the eradication of poverty but on the level of food, housing, and medical subsidies needed to sustain what has come to be called "the permanent underclass." Because widespread poverty is regarded as inevitable, we devote virtually all our social-welfare resources to consumption redistribution and ignore investment redistribution. In a typical recent year, 95 percent of the federal money directed to the poor went for Medicaid, food stamps, housing assistance, and the like. Less than 5 percent went to education.[51]

In short, America has been losing the War on Poverty because we have been attacking the wrong enemy. We use redistribution to redress the unfairness of a zero-sum agricultural economy even as accelerating technological evolution is creating previously unimagined opportunities for economic growth. In a technicultural economy, the only remedy for poverty is aggressive investment, especially in human capital. Genuine progress requires truly open access to quality education for every single American who is willing to put forth the effort to learn.

It is no accident that millions of those in each new generation of

America's poor are products of the country's most horrendous schools. Without question, radical reform of the public schools should be the first step toward solving America's poverty problem.[52] Providing every American child access to a high-quality education would be the single most powerful antipoverty program ever launched. If this were supplemented with a comprehensive, lifelong system of government-backed loans for higher education, vocational training, and job retraining, America's weakening competitive position surely would be resurrected.

In a world where technology is pulverizing the barriers that once isolated nations, the United States must fashion a coherent economic strategy, one that bolsters the competitiveness of its firms and its workers. We must recognize that the poverty that is destroying the lives of so many millions of our fellow citizens is just a warning, a foretaste of life in a hopelessly uncompetitive America.

But a future of society-wide poverty is by no means inevitable. Given an understanding of the evolutionary nature of economic change, the major features of an effective American competitive strategy become obvious. Overhauling a tax system that causes excessive consumption and inadequate investment is the first step. Slashing federal income-tax rates and replacing the lost revenues with a national sales tax would be the fastest, fairest way of motivating a profound change in the consumption/savings decisions of the American people.

Beyond this, the recognition that experience and learning drive down real costs should lead American companies to appreciate the value of modest, incremental improvements. Like their Japanese competitors, American firms must learn to stress long-term market share more than short-term profit. The U.S. government should continue to pry open closed markets that allow foreign firms to accumulate insurmountable leads in production experience. Antitrust laws that prevent technological cooperation among American firms should be repealed.

Government programs based on the notion that redistributing income solves poverty must be replaced by policies that emphasize investment in human capital. To accomplish this, a complete transformation of America's public-school system is essential. Without universal access to quality education, widespread illiteracy and general incompetence will eliminate any hope for an American economic revival.

Of course, some might argue that implementing such changes in America's public policies cannot rescue our fast-eroding competitive position. Things might improve a bit, but it is not enough to copy Japan's strategy of high-investment, learning-curve economics, and aggressive technical education. After all, America cannot out–Japanese the Japanese.

Such a criticism is partly correct. We must implement these basic policy changes just to get back into the global economic race. But doing so will not be enough to ensure American competitiveness. To regain economic parity with Japan, the American people must come to grips with the most fundamental rule of competition—that coexistence demands diversity. We must absorb whatever valuable lessons we can from the Japanese, but in the end, America will prosper by competing in a different way. Capitalism's processes are universal, but within any economic ecosystem there is room for diverse competitive styles. We must build our competitive strategy upon the features of American society that make us profoundly different from Japan.[53]

First and foremost, the Japanese are a homogeneous people. They are terribly polite about it, but they abhor foreigners. They adamantly refuse to integrate non-Japanese peoples into their society. Koreans who have lived in Japan for generations are still treated as noncitizens. Japan has accepted far fewer Southeast Asian refugees than its population or economy could absorb. Proposals to import more foreign workers for a labor-short economy set off howls of protest. The Japanese genuinely believe that their "racial purity" is the source of their economic and social success. They show no indication of abandoning these views.[54]

Unfortunately, too many Americans seem to agree with the Japanese that racial purity creates competitive advantage. Without doubt, millions of Americans silently agreed with Japan's former prime minister Yasuhiro Nakasone when he laid the blame for America's economic troubles on its "intellectually inferior" black and Hispanic populations. Too few Americans seem to grasp that it is our very heterogeneity that makes America such an incredibly vibrant society. America's astonishing creativity is unquestionably derived from its racial, ethnic, and cultural diversity. Creative sparks fly when people of different backgrounds approach the same problem. Particularly when it comes to competing with Japan, the diversity of our immigrant society must be the foundation of our competitive strategy.[55]

While race hate still warps the minds of many Americans, there has been an undeniably massive shift in popular attitudes since the civil-rights movement. More and more, people are accepted not for who they are but for what they can contribute. As technology continues to shrink the world, this willingness to accept each person as a fully human being will prove vital to America's economic turnaround.

After all, of the five billion people on the planet, only 120 million are Japanese. Already, Japanese-only hiring policies at the higher echelons of Japan's multinational corporations have sparked substantial resentment. Non-Japanese investors are beginning to demand equal treatment in Japan's corporate boardrooms. Foreign cultural influences are beginning to erode traditional values among young Japanese. In short, Japanese society is just beginning to adjust to life in a racially integrated global village. In stark contrast, America is well prepared for this new world.[56]

Although the Japanese have in the past shown themselves to be remarkably adaptable, it remains to be seen whether or not they can transform themselves into a nonracist society. Such a change threatens the very essence of what it means to be Japanese. If they resist change, mounting global resentment will threaten their access to markets. But if they welcome change, allowing full participation by immigrants and foreigners, their society will be utterly transformed. Either way, the coming of the global village will place incredible strains on Japan.

If, in the decade ahead, the American people come to recognize the evolutionary nature of economic life, they will demand that their government jettison its self-defeating economic policies. Through the democratic process, a new economic strategy will emerge. This strategy will stress investment over consumption, long-term organizational learning rather than short-term profit-taking, and access to quality education instead of income redistribution. Together, these policies can revive America's competitiveness, rekindle real economic growth, and eradicate widespread poverty. All these problems are symptoms of the same disease. Their solution demands a coherent strategy.

With the cold war ending, the United States will gain an enormous boost in its economic contest with Japan. If the "peace dividend" is not squandered in yet another consumption binge, the United States will be able to pursue a reinvestment strategy much more aggressively than would otherwise be politically possible. By the same token, since Japan spends relatively little on defense, the Japanese will derive less economic benefit from the cold war's conclusion.

But even if the cold war does not quickly fade away, the United States still can get back into the race with Japan. If we recognize that being different from Japan should be the starting point of America's competitive strategy, we can begin to exploit the full potential of our cultural diversity. And, as the world continues to shrink, Japan's great "strength"—homogeneity—will come to be seen as a weakness. America's great "weakness"—diversity—will be recognized as its strength.

PART **VI**

FEEDBACK LOOPS AND FREE MARKETS

The art of progress is to preserve order amid change
and to preserve change amid order.
—*Alfred North Whitehead*[1]

SPONTANEOUS ORDER

O
f the species now being annihilated by the torching of the tropical rain forests, the cellular slime molds undoubtedly are the least conspicuous. The first link in the rain-forest food chain, they recycle to the living the nutrients recovered from the dead. Few if any species are more crucial to rain-forest ecology.[2]

As it turns out, slime molds are neither molds nor slimy. In fact, they aren't even a distinct animal group. A slime mold is just one phase in the remarkable life cycle of certain amoeba species. For most of their four-day lifespans, these amoebas live as single-celled animals, like all other amoebas. In the moist detritus covering the forest floor, they prey upon the bacteria that digest the tissues of dead organisms. When a prosperous amoeba has grown too large, it splits itself down the middle, leaving two daughter cells to carry on the bacteria hunt.[3]

An amoeba's major problem is its limited mobility. It oozes through the soil at a pace that makes a snail seem like a Kentucky Thoroughbred. At full speed, the microbe covers about half an inch in 24 hours. Consequently, as soon as the creature has engulfed all the bacteria within immediate reach, it begins to starve. But instead of curling up to die, the amoeba reacts by excreting a hormonelike substance called cyclic AMP. Pulses of the chemical spread through the soil in concentric waves, like those emanating from a pebble tossed into a pond. Roughly once every eight minutes, the starving amoeba pumps out another pulse of its chemical distress call.[4]

Nearby amoebas sense the cyclic AMP molecules with special receptors that stud the outer surface of their cell membranes. They respond by moving toward the source of the chemical wave and by emitting their own pulses of cyclic AMP. As more and more neighboring amoebas join the chemical chorus, the synchronized pulses grow stronger. Drawn like microscopic zombies to the chemical's densest concentration, as many as 100,000 amoebas stream toward each other until their minute bodies merge into a single gelatinous mass—the slime mold.[5]

Barely visible to the naked eye, this cigar-shaped collection of cells wriggles across the dank forest floor in search of light and heat. Upon finding a suitable spot, some of the cells extend downward, becoming a rootlike anchor. Other cells then flow upward, forming a hollow shaft. Most of the amoebas then flow up through the shaft, coming to rest inside a bulbous tip called the fruiting body. Inside this tiny bud, each amoeba encases itself in a tough cellulose spore. When the fruiting body is eaten by a worm or bird, its spores are carried off to places far beyond the oozing range of a single amoeba.

Despite the organism's role as the rain forest's chief recycler, few of the world's slime-mold experts concern themselves with the ecology of the species. Most of those devoting their careers to slime molds have done so because these organisms represent the simplest-known example of independent cells organizing into a single organism. Laboratory researchers are trying to discover exactly how slime molds get organized. Many scientists believe that similar principles must explain one of biology's great mysteries—how a few identical cells in an embryo spontaneously order themselves into a complex creature such as a human being.[6]

Anyone who has ever cradled a newborn in his arms knows the sense of awe driving those who study slime-mold development. On its face, it seems impossible that a sophisticated life-form could simply emerge from a clump of identical components without someone or something in charge, barking out orders. How could a house be built without a general contractor to oversee the work, to make sure that all the pieces conform to the plans? Can it really be that a living thing has no centerpoint, no one cell that directs all the others? Is life's marvelous complexity the collective behavior of simple components?[7]

The slime mold fascinates because, by its very existence, it challenges our deepest intuition about consciousness and control. The slime mold also blurs the line between the individual and society. Which is the organism, the amoeba or the slime mold? And, at a higher plane, the slime mold's self-organization compels us to face the ultimate question raised by evolution. Putting aside the details of genetic variation and natural selection, is it really possible that an unconscious, spontaneous phenomenon could have brought forth a natural world of such awesome diversity, beauty, and balance? We know it is true. We can see it. But it still boggles the mind.[8]

Oddly enough, the same sense of incredulity underlies the widespread mistrust of free markets. Anyone who thinks carefully about capitalism must ask, How could such a vast and complex system emerge without the benefit of some grand design? Somewhere, somebody *must* be in charge. How else could simple, self-interested components coalesce into an immensely complicated, well-coordinated economy? The notion that no one is in control—that economic order spontaneously emerges from the chaotic interaction of millions of individuals and firms—is, quite simply, hard to swallow.

For the Soviets, the implausibility of free markets is revealed in an anecdote told by Arkady Shevchenko, a high-ranking foreign-ministry official before his defection to the United States. Writing of the era just before Mikhail Gorbachev came to power, Shevchenko reported that top Kremlin officials

> are simply baffled by the American system. It puzzles them how a complex and little-regulated society can maintain such a high level of production, efficiency, and technological innovation. Many are inclined toward the fantastic notion that there must be a secret control center somewhere in the United States. They themselves, after all, are used to a system ruled by a small group working in secrecy in one place.[9]

Lacking experience with capitalism, it is little wonder that Soviet leaders doubt the power of markets. But the Kremlin authorities are not alone. A great many Americans—particularly those isolated from the business community—are enormously skeptical of market potency. In fact, markets are widely regarded as necessary evils—messy, erratic affairs that fool everyone. We rely on markets only because they seem to work, not because we like them.

Indeed, several important social ills—pollution, traffic congestion, and unemployment—are cited regularly by conventional economists as prime examples of "market failure." The usual prescription for "market failure" is the one employed so indiscriminately in the Soviet Union: government planning and control. But the standard solution for "market failure" overlooks a rather crucial point: If we do not understand how markets work, we can hardly claim to understand why they fail, or how to fix them.

The sad truth is that two centuries after Adam Smith launched the study of economics, we still cannot explain how markets work. Trading and exchange—the most persistent features of the human economy—remain an enigma. Perhaps this is why Smith's celebrated phrase, "invisible hand," retains its broad appeal. Frustrated by our profound ignorance, we find such an expression soothing, even though it sheds no light.

Stalled for decades at a theoretical dead end, economics has no respectable alternative but to set off again in a new direction. And, if free markets are the economy's version of spontaneous self-organizing behavior, then the path to understanding may begin with the lowly slime mold. Fortunately, biologists have figured out the basic principles of slime-mold development. Complete understanding will take several more decades, but at least the fundamentals are clear.

In essence, a starving amoeba is the central element in an information feedback loop. The chemical signal that emanates from its body is picked up by sensors on a nearby amoeba. In addition to causing the second amoeba to move toward the signal's source, the stimulation of its surface receptors triggers two other responses—one internal, one external. Internally, activated receptors turn on certain genes that control the cell's shape and activity. Externally, receipt of the signal causes the amoeba to respond with its own pulse of cyclic AMP.

When this chemical echo gets back to the first amoeba, it completes an information feedback loop. With its own receptors now stimulated, the first amoeba moves, activates dormant genetic programs, and puts out another pulse of cyclic AMP. In effect, the first amoeba's original distress call has circled back and stimulated it to produce a second signal. Output feeds back as input that stimulates more output, and so on. Cause becomes indistinguishable from effect. As the cycles accumulate, more amoebas are caught up in the pulsating waves. The initial signal is amplified until thousands of cells communicating chemically begin behaving as a coordinated whole.

There is, of course, nothing new in the feedback-loop concept. Anyone who has ever been subjected to the high-pitched shriek of a public-address system knows what happens when a microphone feeds back on the signal coming from its own loudspeakers. But, until quite recently, scientists trying to understand feedback mechanisms faced an insurmountable obstacle. They could not build mathematical models capable of depicting feedback-loop behavior.

Feedback-loop formulas are fundamentally different from the "linear" equations that generate the smooth curves of Newtonian physics and equilibrium economics. "Linear" equations are continuous, producing a family of lovely, regular curves when the equations are plotted on graphs. The position of any point along such a curve can be calculated easily by merely plugging the appropriate values into the equation. Very little computation is required to obtain an answer.

Fortunately, a great many scientific problems yield to linear math. For studying the relationship between two objects not linked by a feedback loop—the sun and earth, a proton and an electron, or a speeding car and a brick wall—Newton's calculus is the perfect tool. With just paper and pencil, any linear phenomenon can be modeled and predicted readily.

But feedback-loop equations are "nonlinear," and even though nonlinear equations are terribly simple, they can produce amazingly complex results. Instead of steady curves, nonlinear formulas generate wildly erratic, zigzagging lines. From one cycle of a feedback loop to the next, output values jump around without any apparent rhyme or reason. Consequently, the only way to figure out how much chemical is produced on the slime mold's hundredth cycle is to iterate through the calculation 100 times. In the past, few bothered to crunch these numbers because the unpredictability of nonlinear equations makes the effort pointless. Why build models of phenomena if they are inherently unpredictable?

The great tragedy in this is that most natural phenomena are nonlinear. Only a tiny portion of nature's processes meet the rigid criteria of linear math. If a feedback process is involved, or if more than two objects are interacting, linear equations are useless. Much of physics, most of chemistry, and all of biology falls outside the domain of classical linear science.[10]

Shapes of clouds, paths of lightning, oscillations of species populations, turbulence in a flowing stream, and the collective acrobatics of a bird flock, as well as the pulses of cyclic AMP organizing a mass of amoebas into a slime mold—all these natural phenomena are nonlinear.[11] Indeed, it has been said that the term *nonlinear science* is misleading, because it's like calling the bulk of zoology the study of nonelephant animals. With most natural phenomena written off as inherently unpredictable, science has been like a tiny rowboat restricted to the safe harbor of classical linearity while nature's vast oceans of complex nonlinearity lay unexplored.[12]

Not long ago, all this began to change. After the microprocessor's invention in 1971, cheap computing power began to become widely available. Physicists, chemists, mathematicians, and ecologists intrigued by nonlinear problems no longer had to crunch numbers manually. With a personal computer, it was easy to run a set of related nonlinear equations through thousands or millions of cycles.

In place of painstakingly plotted paper graphs, moving three-dimensional graphics sprang to life on computer screens. Just as the printing press made widely available the astronomical observations from which Newton derived his laws, the microprocessor is allowing today's scientists to visualize previously unseen patterns. Almost overnight, the computer has turned the rowboat of Newtonian science into a sailing ship ready for nonlinear seas.[13]

Because this great scientific revolution has barely begun, our comprehension of nonlinear phenomena is still primitive. But a few things are clear. First and foremost, nonlinear phenomena are not totally unpredictable. The nonlinear world occupies a middle ground between perfect Newtonian predictability and utter randomness. Although the terminology is still somewhat fluid, most scientists refer to this nonlinear middle ground as "chaos." For nonscientists, this is an unfortunate choice of words, because chaotic phenomena are not "chaotic" in the vernacular sense of total disorder. As Alan Garfinkel of UCLA puts it, "Chaos is not disorder; it is a higher form of order."[14]

In its narrow scientific sense, "chaos" covers natural phenomena that seem to be disorderly but in fact adhere to underlying patterns. The weather is a perfect example of this blend of disorder and order. Nonlinear equations describe the feedback interactions of temperature, humidity, and barometric pressure that make weather. In computer simulations, these equations yield results that follow the familiar, repetitive pattern we call climate. At this macro level, the weather is predictable. We know that it will not be sweltering hot in Minneapolis on New Year's Day.

But the results generated by nonlinear equations happen to be incredibly sensitive to slight deviations in initial conditions. This makes accurate forecasts impossible at the micro level. For example, if a computerized weather model starts off at noon on June 1 with a temperature of 72.0°F instead of 71.99999°F, its prediction for New Year's Day six months later will be dramatically different. In linear systems, tiny variations in inputs yield proportionately small differences in results, but chaotic systems are absurdly sensitive to slight deviations. Since neither the temperature nor any other variable can be measured with infinite precision, no computer model will ever accurately predict the temperature in Minneapolis on New Year's Day. All that can be said is

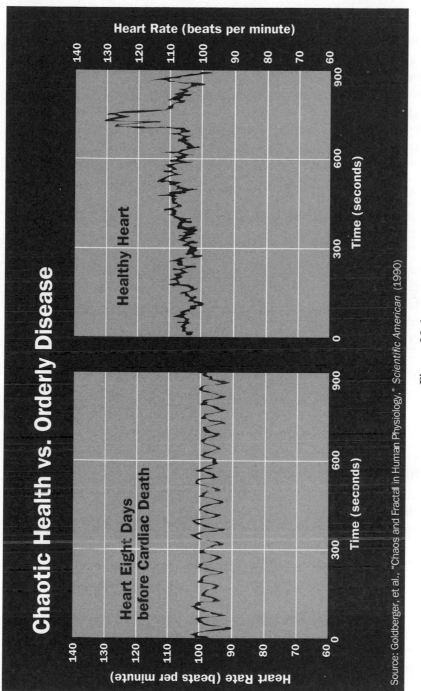

Figure 23.1

Source: Goldberger, et al., "Chaos and Fractal in Human Physiology," *Scientific American* (1990)

that the weather will not go outside the limits defined by its underlying chaotic pattern.[15]

Fortunately, precise forecasting is not necessary for most purposes. Just knowing there is chaos can be quite valuable. For example, a recent Harvard Medical School study of the human heart showed that although the pulse of a person at rest seems regular, it is not. Exact measurements of the times between beats reveal that the pulse rate of a healthy heart fluctuates erratically. Instead of beating periodically—say, once a second—a healthy heart keeps speeding up and slowing down—not randomly but chaotically. A completely random, spasmodic pulse occurs only during a heart attack.[16]

The discovery of chaos in the healthy heart is turning cardiology on its head. It has long been believed that a healthy heart is a perfectly regular metronome, returning to its normal, periodic pulse soon after being disturbed by some external stress. An irregular pulse was thought to be a symptom of a diseased heart, one unable to maintain a steady pace. But sophisticated computer analysis shows that it's just the opposite. A diseased heart beats with extreme regularity in the hours prior to a heart attack. It is the healthy heart that beats chaotically.[17]

In light of this new knowledge, the emerging view is that chaos is healthy because it keeps the heart flexible, ready to respond to changing physical demands. When a chaotic system is perturbed by an external shock, it eventually wobbles back to its starting point. But when a linear system is bumped, it tends to remain slightly off kilter. Perhaps a heart that is too regular loses its adaptability and becomes more vulnerable. No one knows.[18]

As in many other fields, research on chaos in medicine has just started. But several examples of chaos in the human body have been detected. Brain waves of the mentally healthy are chaotic, while those of an epileptic during a seizure are regular. Hormone levels rise and fall chaotically in healthy people. White-blood-cell counts fluctuate chaotically in healthy individuals but vary periodically in those stricken with leukemia.[19]

These findings are leading some researchers to think about the body in a new way. Instead of viewing it as a remarkably complex machine controlled by the brain, these scientists see a collection of 10,000 billion cells incessantly conversing via chemical messages. Dozens of so-called informational substances, produced by various cell types, flow through the body triggering responses in distant cells. One of these informational compounds is cyclic AMP, the molecule that orchestrates slime-mold organization. In this new view, the human organism is a community of cells coordinated by interlocking chaotic feedback loops.[20]

Apparently the organizing power of feedback loops is not limited to the interaction of cells within an organism. A few ecologists have dusted off old population histories of certain species and found ample evidence of chaos. Three hundred years of data on the Canadian lynx population recorded by the Hudson's Bay Company and decades of data on measles outbreaks kept by the New York City Department of Health show chaotic processes at work. The traditional equilibrium view—that a population is stable unless disturbed by some external shock—is still dominant among ecologists, but a small and growing number are challenging that perspective.[21]

These ecologists see gyrating species populations as perfectly healthy. For them, the notion of stable populations in a "balance of nature" is a myth. And if the ecosystem is thought of as a living organism, the population swings of a species may be seen as an organizing signal for the ecosystem. After all, every species is a link in a food web connected by physical feedback loops to its resources, competitors, and predators.

A sudden population spurt in a plankton species may trigger a population boom among certain fish that in turn ignites a population explosion among predatory seabirds. In effect, the plankton bloom is communicated to the seabirds by the fish. One change sets off another, with populations endlessly reverberating inside an immensely complex system. All the species jockey for survival under the constraints imposed by the feedback loops that tie them together. As in a single organism, an ever-changing order emerges spontaneously from the chaos.[22]

Of course, even if future research proves that every living system—from slime molds to ecosystems—emerges naturally from the chaotic communication of simpler components, this would not necessarily mean that free markets represent the same process in the economy. After all, human beings are not just a bunch of cells gelling into a slime mold on a dank forest floor. We have technology. We have consciousness. We are rational. Chaos may be the organizing force in natural systems, but in our gleaming, computerized economy, we employ our intelligence to plan and control events.

Then again, one could hardly claim that the pandemonium in the trading pits of Chicago's Mercantile Exchange is planned and controlled. Each individual transaction may be a rational act. No cosmic force takes over a trader's mind, forcing her to buy winter-wheat futures. But a market is something more than a sequence of independent trades. A market represents the collective behavior of its traders.[23]

Strangely enough, the ultimate example of market chaos is found not on the floor of a stock exchange but in a computer lab in Palo Alto, California. Here, the Xerox Corporation maintains the Palo Alto Research Center (PARC) for the purpose of pushing information-processing technology beyond its present limits. Among other things, PARC's researchers have been responsible for the innovations that led to the personal computer and graphic desktop interface that made Apple's Macintosh computer so popular.[24]

Quite recently, a team of Xerox's computer scientists, led by Argentine-born physicist Bernardo Huberman, has been trying to make PARC's high-power computer network run more efficiently. Computer networks first appeared in the mid-1980s, soon after personal computers became commonplace business appliances. At first, the idea was to wire computers together so that a user at one machine could retrieve data stored in another one on the network.[25]

But some computer users don't need access to remote files. Instead, they want lots of raw compute power. Crunching through the billions of calculations needed to run a weather model can keep even a high-speed computer's central processor busy for hours. Since the scientists in Huberman's team all specialize in modeling chaotic systems, they often found themselves waiting for their computers to finish up.

As in most offices, only a few people at Xerox's research center keep their machines fully occupied at any given moment. Most central processors sit idle, while others are only partially engaged in such light-duty tasks as word processing. Huberman's team figured they could eliminate their waiting time if they could harness the wasted number-crunching capacity of the network's idle computers. The five-man team spent the better part of 1988 trying to make their idea work.

The obvious solution was to write a piece of software that would manage the network. This control program would slice up big computational tasks and dispatch the pieces to idle machines. When the calculations were done, partial answers would be reassembled into final results. In essence, the control program was an ultrasophisticated scheduler.

This "command-and-control" approach had been tried a few years earlier at MIT, but it had never worked. There was no fair and simple way of assigning work priorities. Sometimes idle machines became busy again when their own users started a project. At other times, machines sat idle, waiting for results from calculations delegated to other computers.

Because the workload on the network kept changing, the most efficient

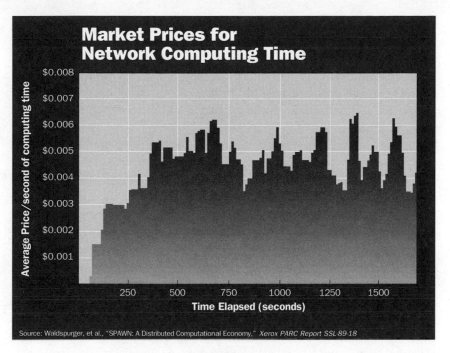

Market Prices for Network Computing Time

Average Price/second of computing time

$0.008
$0.007
$0.006
$0.005
$0.004
$0.003
$0.002
$0.001

250   500   750   1000   1250   1500

Time Elapsed (seconds)

Source: Waldspurger, et al., "SPAWN: A Distributed Computational Economy," *Xerox PARC Report SSL-89-18*

Figure 23.2

allocation of computing power could not be figured out in advance. Worst of all, the computers were spending more of their precious processing time communicating with the central controller than doing real work. In short, the "command-and-control" solution became hopelessly bogged down by the costs of coordination.[26]

To solve these problems, Huberman's team did what all true innovators do. They turned the problem upside down. Instead of building a system with an even more sophisticated control program, they designed one without any central control. In its place, they created an internal market for computing time.

This synthetic market was built atop a path-breaking software program called SPAWN. In essence, SPAWN is a useful computer virus— or, in light of its helpful properties, what programmers call a "worm." Copies of SPAWN code replicate themselves across the computer network under prescribed conditions.[27]

Before launching a new computational problem, the user assigns it a "dollar" budget. Then SPAWN subdivides the problem and its budget into smaller pieces. In effect, each problem component rides through the network piggybacking atop a copy of SPAWN. Problem modules offer to "buy" slices of computing time with their "dollars" by broadcasting their bids on the network.

Under SPAWN's open-auction system, idle computers respond by "deciding" individually whether to accept a particular bid. When a bid is accepted, the problem module moves over to that computer for the agreed amount of time. Both the problems and the computers constantly monitor "market prices." Problems must purchase enough time to get themselves completed, but they cannot overspend their budgets. The computers are programmed to maximize their revenues.

SPAWN works. Less than 10 percent of each machine's time is wasted in the bidding process. Without a central controller, a flexible and efficient use of resources spontaneously emerges from buying and selling among independent agents.[28] In this self-organizing system, "dollars"— rather than hormones or cyclic AMP—are the signaling medium. Auction prices fluctuate chaotically. When new machines are added to the network or more problems are run simultaneously, market prices respond appropriately. An increased supply of computing time lowers prices; a demand surge raises them. But the precise future path of prices cannot be predicted, because a healthy free market is intrinsically chaotic.[29]

CHAPTER
24

RULES VS. PRICES

To create their free market, Xerox's scientists had to build an eco-system. In fact, the authors of SPAWN refer to their brainchild as a "computational ecosystem." On its face, it seems impossible that the same piece of software could be both a market and an ecosystem. But then again, market economies and natural ecosystems are versions of the same fundamental phenomenon.

Sets of information—whether carried by organizations, organisms, or copies of the SPAWN code—interact for their individual benefit. These exchanges, though unplanned, spontaneously weave immensely complex, efficient, and adaptable information webs. In nature, genetic information and energy flow through the feedback loops of the food web. In the economy, technological information and value flow through the feedback loops of the value web. Both living systems display the erratic pulses characteristic of chaotic, evolutionary change.

Although important differences distinguish economy from ecosystem, these are differences among cosmic cousins. Both genetic and techno-logical information live by resisting entropy. Both grow by becoming more efficient. Both squeeze more life from fixed resources through the trials and errors of evolutionary learning.

No one set up the ecosystem. No one set up the market economy. No one needed to. Like any self-organizing system, capitalism just happened. The printing press allowed capitalism to get going. The microprocessor kicked it into high gear. And, by revealing patterns long obscured by the superficial disorder of chaos, computers have demonstrated the pro-found similarity of ecology and economics.

News of Xerox's computational ecosystem piqued the interest of two groups not traditionally thought to have much in common—ecologists and economists. Innovators in both disciplines were quick to realize that SPAWN makes possible a new era of experimentation. For the first time, researchers can test their theories in a fairly realistic, yet controlled environment. Together, high-speed computer networks and nonlinear math will provide future researchers with an immensely powerful scientific workbench.[1]

Already, the study of chaos is becoming an across-the-board scientific enterprise. Barriers that have long isolated the disciplines are beginning to erode. In economics, equilibrium orthodoxy is just starting to give way to the ecological view. In late 1987, the first conference dedicated to "the economy as an evolving complex system" attracted economists, biologists, and physicists. In 1989, a journal entitled *Ecological Economics* started up. In the coming years, as computers and chaos offer new insights, much of ecology and economics will blend into a field that might well be called bionomics.[2]

Several decades will pass before this paradigm shift completes itself. But it is possible to anticipate at least one insight to be gained from this new perspective: Just as nonlinear science is now showing physicians that unpredictable fluctuations are normal and healthy for the human body, chaos will prove to economists that erratic oscillations are normal and healthy for the economy. The classical ideal of predictable, equilibrium prices will be abandoned. Instead of regarding erratic price swings and unpredictable business cycles as indicators of economic weakness, the chaos of the marketplace will be seen for what it is—a sign of vitality.

Of course, knowing that chaos is healthy for the overall economy is small solace to someone who has just lost a bundle in a deal turned sour. If markets were "fair," a farm family's years of struggle could not be wiped out by an inexplicable plunge in the price of soybeans. In the abstract, we may applaud the concept of erratically fluctuating prices, but in our personal affairs, we seek order and security. Everyone wants the prosperity that free markets yield, but no one wants to bear the risks implicit in market chaos.

At bottom, this is why popular support for free markets is so weak. The tiny efficiency gains achieved by learning organizations seep into the markets in the form of price cuts and product improvements. These gains are diffuse, however, spread far and wide by billions of transactions. Everyone in society benefits in incremental, unnoticed ways. But the losses experienced by those on the wrong end of a market swing are obvious and often quite painful. No constituency exists for widespread, invisible gains, but plenty of influential groups demand government protection from the vagaries of free markets.

In its most extreme form, the suppression of market chaos creates a black market. Of course, banning markets never seems to achieve the desired effect. Several analysts now argue that America's illegal drug market is so enormous largely because the illegality of drugs drives their prices far above production costs. High prices create fantastic profit margins in the illicit distribution network.[3]

In effect, banning cocaine is like setting its price at infinity. No amount of money is enough to permit a legal transaction. Operating beneath the government's "price umbrella," black marketeers willing to bear the risks of the drug trade enjoy profit margins unmatched by any free-market activity. High profits draw in more sellers, who in turn work hard to expand their base of addicted customers. By setting a drug's price at infinity, government policy achieves precisely the opposite of its intended effect.

Whenever a society bans a product, it must be prepared to expend whatever resources are necessary to stifle the black market made so profitable by its rules. But experience shows that even under the harshest penalties, black markets persist. A seller is drawn to the smell of money much as an amoeba is lured by the taste of cyclic AMP. Profit-seeking is a self-organizing phenomenon, impossible to eradicate. This is as true on the streets of Moscow as it is in Washington.[4]

Although black markets are rare in the capitalist West, "gray" markets are quite common. In "gray" markets, the products are not illegal, but their prices are not allowed to fluctuate. Instead, a law prescribes a fixed price. Throughout the West, the politically powerful use such laws to insulate themselves from the discipline of free prices. Domestic manufacturers demand tariffs to make imports more expensive. Farmers demand guaranteed price floors for their crops. City dwellers demand rent control for their apartments. Credit-card borrowers demand interest-rate ceilings. Every special interest has its own bone to pick with free prices.

Nevertheless, for the most part, the Western capitalist economies are comprised of "white" markets, where prices are free to find their own levels. Regulations may control the circumstances of a trade, but non-price rules do not inhibit free markets. Only when a price formula is written into the law does a "white" market go "gray." Many nonprice rules, such as safety regulations and information-disclosure requirements, actually improve market function.

For example, the law defines what a company must disclose about its finances before it can sell its stock to the public. But securities regulations do not set the stock's price. Similarly, government regulations restrict farmers' use of toxic pesticides, but the price of tomatoes gyrates with shifts in supply and demand. In the United States, airline safety is tightly regulated, but airfares are market-driven. Under modern capitalism, virtually every product is regulated in some way, but nearly all products are exchanged in "white" markets where prices float freely.

Whether a market is black, gray, or white is a matter of politics, not economics. In deciding where to draw the lines separating these market types, every society faces the same basic questions: When should rules replace prices? Who should hold decision-making power—buyers and sellers or government officials? Where should economics end and politics begin?[5]

For most of the twentieth century, governments took control of an increasing share of economic activity. In many countries, government bureaus set prices for all kinds of things. The gold price was fixed. Airfares were fixed. Long-distance phone rates were fixed. Interest rates were fixed. Not long ago, the French government was still setting prices for bicycle-tire repairs. In thousands of cases, white markets had become gray markets. Fluctuating market prices were replaced by inflexible government rules.

But, in the late 1970s, this historic trend was reversed. China's abandonment of farm price controls, and the subsequent doubling of its food output, was the single most dramatic instance of this shift. The West also experienced a revival of free-market policies. In the United States, prices were deregulated throughout the transportation, energy, and financial sectors. In Western Europe, the privatization of nationalized firms returned large chunks of the economy to the market sector. And throughout the Third World, governments began abandoning "command-and-control" methods. As political control of the economy receded, gray markets began turning white again.[6]

Oddly enough, this worldwide trend did not spring from any impassioned popular outcry for free markets. Instead, the shift simply reflected the public's frustration with the massive waste caused by the "command-and-control" approach. To provide farmers with guaranteed prices, taxpayers found themselves erecting huge storage facilities and paying massive subsidies for crops no one wanted. In rent-controlled cities, apartment construction slowed and the housing stock deteriorated. Protected industries failed to invest in new technology or reduce costs. Again and again, those protected by "gray"-market price rules extracted their gains by causing damage elsewhere in the system.[7]

Responding to the distortions caused by a fixed price, the adjacent feedback loops spontaneously adjust the economic network to its next most efficient solution. But the adjustment—millions of pounds of U.S. government cheese stacked in warehouses, or apartment buildings abandoned by their owners—never yields a net economic gain. Rules cannot create value. Value is simply transferred from taxpayers to dairy farmers or from the owners of rent-controlled buildings to their tenants.

Of course, if the economy were machinelike, social engineers could write laws that always achieved desired results. Unwanted side effects would be unknown. But because an economy is a fabulously complex web of feedback loops, simpleminded "solutions" ricochet through the network in unpredictable ways.

In a sense, an economy where fixed prices replace fluctuating prices is like a river valley "improved" by the construction of a dam. Downstream residents may be spared occasional flooding, but only by the destruction of the watershed ecosystem above the dam. What had been a living network of pulsating information channels is sterilized by the imposition of a hard-and-fast barrier. In their zeal to "improve" a system that they do not comprehend, the dam-builders do irreparable harm to nature. Rule-makers do similar damage to the economy.

By contrast, free markets work because they allow society to communicate honestly with itself. Market prices emerge democratically. They express a tentative, collective view of relative values. No product has an intrinsic or fixed value. No one "knows" what something is "really" worth.

As auctions demonstrate, a single item can simultaneously have different values to different buyers. Or, one buyer's perception of an object's value may shift radically in an instant. Shortages and gluts appear and disappear spontaneously, as buyers and sellers react to fluctuating price signals by changing their rates of consumption and production.[8]

In most cases, trades happen because a positive gap exists between an item's value to its buyer and its cost to its seller. The transaction price lies somewhere within this value/cost gap. Trading allows buyers and sellers to divvy up these differentials. Tiny slivers of value get created and redistributed by millions of firms and individuals. Repeated additions to and transfers of value are like the repeated handoffs of leaf bits from large, foraging leafcutters to their smallest sisters, the fungus gardeners. At each step along the line of social production—from raw materials to consumption—specialized workers add and redistribute economic energy.

Even the simple act of trading adds value. In and of itself, producing products is useless. Unless a product reaches the ultimate consumer, there is no point to all the effort. Traders are the links between producers and consumers. They add value by bearing the risks of price volatility. By arranging mutually beneficial exchanges among others, a trader helps potential value become realized. Price differentials tell traders where mutually beneficial exchanges can and cannot be made.

Spontaneous mass communication through prices does not work for governments. Governments communicate through written rules. The rule-making body, be it a legislature or a dictator, exerts power by writing rules that get passed down through a hierarchy of officials. The last fellow in line is charged with applying these rules to the real world. More often than not, this presents genuine difficulties.

Although the world is diverse, society's rules must be applied consistently, as if every situation were identical. Indeed, the entire judicial system is dedicated to applying society's general rules to specific cases. Moreover, since laws do not adjust spontaneously to changed circumstances, rules that are sensible when written often lead to idiotic results at a later time. Rule-makers can, of course, revise the rules or write exceptions. But even exceptions are written rules. Unless held in check by some larger constraint, a "command-and-control" system grows on itself, becoming ever more ornate and inefficient.

As the experiments at Xerox's research center demonstrated, the productivity of even a small network of resources cannot be optimized by a "command-and-control" approach. Appropriate rules simply cannot be written for every contingency. No matter how sophisticated a rule-based system becomes, by its very nature it cannot organize resources efficiently. The more complex and fast-changing a system becomes, the worse the rule-making approach performs. Only decentralized, self-organizing evolutionary systems manage to make the most of scarce resources.

If this fact were more widely known, it would have profound implications for public policy. Rather than attempting to rid itself of problems by legislating them away, society could set up markets to pursue agreed-upon goals. Today, for example, markets could be created to relieve the threat of global environmental devastation, a monstrously complex problem that has been made far worse by several decades of "command-and-control" futility.

Of course, many environmentalists would argue that the only way to halt the destruction of the environment is by toughening antipollution rules. They believe sincerely that only government rules can compel the changes in economic behavior needed to rescue the ecosystem before it collapses. But since ecosystems and free markets are so profoundly alike, a truly ecological view of the pollution problem leads to precisely the opposite conclusion.

Our ecosystem is being ravaged not because antipollution rules are too few or too weak but because they are too many and too strong. Wherever a rule substitutes for a price, inefficiency is guaranteed. Indeed, if the problem is complex enough, a rule-based approach promises that there will be no solution at all. Massively complex problems can be solved only by the self-organizing interaction of independent, self-interested actors.

But even if one accepts this reasoning, a free-market approach to the global pollution crisis seems inherently impossible. No one owns the air or the water. The environment is a public "commons." We all "own" it together. With no private property to buy or sell, market prices are impossible. And with prices impossible, society has no alternative but to establish a system of rules to control our access to the environmental commons.

However, this logic assumes that the air and water *must* be treated as a commons. This is not so. The way a society treats a gram of cocaine, a loaf of bread, or a cubic foot of fresh air is a matter of politics, not economics. In a sense, a nonmarket commons is the exact opposite of a black market. In a black market, the price of the outlawed item is fixed at infinity. In a nonmarket commons, the price of the resource is set at zero. But oddly enough, whether government regulations set prices at infinity or at zero, the economic consequences are equally disastrous.

An example seemingly unrelated to the pollution problem illustrates this point. The greatest financial scandal of all times—America's savings and loan fiasco—is usually blamed on weak regulation and inadequate enforcement of the regulations that do exist. To these critics, the plundering of America's savings institutions during the 1980s is yet another example of "market failure," of capitalist greed run amok.

But such commentators ignore the crucial fact that led to this $500 billion rape of the public purse. In 1980, Congress quietly removed the limits on the 50-year-old federal deposit insurance program. Federal guarantees on savings accounts went from $40,000 per depositor to $100,000 per account on an unlimited number of accounts per depositor. This change was not required by the deregulation interest rates. With the federal government now guaranteeing virtually all deposits, the savings banks were no longer ultimately responsible for paying back their depositors' funds. With their legal liability all but eliminated, several thousand savings and loan executives promptly squandered an ocean of free taxpayers' money on high-risk, supposedly high-return, investment schemes.

What had long been a tightly regulated private market for loanable funds was suddenly transformed into a vast, deregulated public commons. With a stroke of the legislative pen, the penalty for making a mistake with depositors' money had been reset to zero. Once Congress gave an unlimited "credit card," backed by the United States Treasury, to any outfit calling itself a savings and loan, no army of regulators could have controlled the subsequent orgy of waste and fraud. Only the self-regulation of the market—where individuals directly bear the costs of their bad judgment—can discipline greed. Whenever the cost of a valuable resource is fixed artificially at zero, that resource will inevitably be abused.[9]

In the environment, as in the savings and loan disaster, where the political system sets the cost of air and water at zero, economic players are virtually begged to abuse the commons of nature.[10] This problem is by no means new. Much the same dilemma plagued our forebears. In England, prior to the sixteenth century, farm land was usually held in common. Private landownership did not make much sense. With the population so small, there was far more land than there were people to work it. For all intents and purposes, land was free.

But, as the population increased, land became relatively scarce. What once seemed limitless began to feel terribly finite. Despite the need for higher farm output, the elaborate rules governing the use of commons fields frustrated the introduction of new farming methods. Over the centuries, the higher productivity of private lands led to the complete privatization of England's commons lands, a historical episode known as the enclosure movement.[11]

Today, after two centuries of industrial life and phenomenal population growth, what were once limitless quantities of fresh air and water are now in short supply. What were once free resources are now quite valuable. And even though new antipollution technology could dramatically improve air and water quality, the world's polluters have no economic incentive to invest in improvements that will benefit everyone else.

Tragically, as long as the political system insists on a zero price for resources that have real value, the pollution crisis will become worse. A black market stimulates abusive private behavior by setting prices at infinity. A nonmarket commons does the same thing by setting prices at zero. At either extreme, when markets are not allowed to work, the normal self-organizing processes of the economy are straitjacketed. No efficient solution can emerge. The "greenhouse effect" and other looming calamities are inevitable consequences of the insistence on free air and water.

Simply by revoking this outmoded rule, our headlong rush to ecologic oblivion would be halted. By allowing the costs of air and water resources to find their own level, the economics of pollution would be transformed radically. And, thankfully, setting up a free market to cope with the pollution problem would be simple and inexpensive.

One way would have the United States Congress set up a new environmental trust fund called the "EcoTrust." The EcoTrust would be authorized to auction off EcoTrust pollution permits. Ownership of a permit would grant its holder the legal right to emit a given quantity of a certain pollutant. For instance, a "one-ton sulfur-dioxide" permit would allow a company to discharge one ton of that chemical each year. If an enforcement agency caught a firm releasing an amount in excess of the quantity authorized by its EcoTrust permits, the firm would be subject to heavy penalties.

EcoTrust permits would be issued just once. Like pieces of real estate, the permits could be resold an indefinite number of times, but no additional EcoTrust permits could be authorized after the initial offering. Like a tract of land, an original EcoTrust permit could be subdivided into smaller units. But the total quantity of pollution authorized in the initial offering would remain fixed.

To determine what pollution levels would be authorized in the initial EcoTrust offering, Congress would set specific amounts for each pollutant. The fairest method would authorize the amounts of pollutants actually released in a recent "base year." For example, if Congress selected 1988 as the base year and the Environmental Protection Agency (EPA) report for that year showed 15 million tons of sulfur dioxide dumped into America's air, the EcoTrust would be allowed to sell permits covering 15 million tons of sulfur dioxide.[12]

EcoTrust permits would be sold at public auction as is done with government bonds. Of course, prior to the EcoTrust auction, no one would know the market price of a "one-ton sulfur-dioxide" certificate. But thousands of firms, each in need of certificates, would bid against each other to secure these limited property rights.

During the auction, a flexible consensus price would emerge for each permit type. Chemical makers would bid for various hydrocarbon permits. Electric utilities would bid for sulfur-dioxide permits. And auto manufacturers would bid for "auto emission" permits, since each vehicle sold would be required to carry a permit adequate to cover its annual emissions. Private or public, large or small, every organization and individual polluting the air or water would have to possess EcoTrust permits sufficient to cover their uses of formerly free resources.

One might think that the polluter no longer has any incentive to reduce emissions once he has purchased a permit, but this view ignores the fact that nobody wants to sink money into a piece of paper issued by the EcoTrust. For example, if an electric utility is required to buy $30 million worth of sulfur-dioxide permits, that's $30 million it cannot use for other purposes. At an interest rate of 10 percent, $30 million tied up in EcoTrust permits would cost the utility $3 million per year. For the first time, pollution's costs will show up where they belong, as a line item on the polluter's annual profit-and-loss statement.

Implementing a "white" market in pollution permits would be a radical departure from the existing "nonmarket," rule-based system. Under the present scheme, the government orders polluters to change their behavior and tells them how to change it. In the United States, state and federal regulators tell each polluter how much to cut back and specifically which pieces of antipollution equipment to use. All the while, the air and water remain free. The rules send one message; price signals send another. Consequently, despite all the congressional hearings held, laws passed, regulations drafted, and court battles fought, environmental quality keeps deteriorating.[13]

Under the present "nonmarket" system, it makes powerful economic sense for a polluter to drag its feet by lobbying and litigating with state and federal agencies. The longer a polluter can put off installing antipollution equipment or switching to more-expensive, less-polluting fuel, the more money it saves. Stiff resistance to government antipollution regulations is economically rational. Delay, in and of itself, is profitable.

But a free-market system would reverse this logic. For the first time, it would cost polluters money *not* to reduce emissions. Any change in a firm's operations or technology that cuts emissions for less than the cost of a permit is economically sensible. With use of the ecosystem no longer free, it would no longer be profitable for polluters to dump so much filth into it.

In fact, establishing a market price for a particular pollutant is like putting a price on its head. If the market prices sulfur-dioxide permits at $1,000 per ton, then any new technology that can scrub out a ton for significantly less than that will get a trial. As in every other sector of the economy, cost-reducing techniques will emerge and be improved along learning curves. The full innovative powers of capitalism will be harnessed in the service of environmental conservation.

By contrast, under the existing "command-and-control" system, innovation by pollution-cleanup firms has been sluggish. Firms selling antipollution gear have no way to cost-justify their equipment to potential customers. No matter how cheap an antipollution technology gets, it can't beat the alternative—free dumping. With the law fixing pollution's cost at zero, the normal capitalist process of cost reduction and performance improvement cannot get rolling. In short, the rule-based system prevents environmental recovery by broadcasting all the wrong economic signals to those with the practical ability to reduce pollution.[14]

But if a "pollution market" existed, society would use the signaling device that economic actors understand—money. By placing a fluctuating dollar value on clean air and water, the market will instantaneously stimulate desired changes in our collective economic behavior. Creating a new market in pollution rights will establish a set of information-feedback loops linking economy to ecosystem. Free markets will bring chaotic order to a problem far too complex to solve through "command-and-control" rules.

A free market solution also avoids the pitfalls of pollution taxes, a method often proposed as an alternative to the "command-and-control" system. Taxing pollution is a "gray"-market approach. Tax rates on each type of pollutant would have to be set by law. But no one knows what those tax rates should be. Which should be assigned a higher tax? A pound of ozone or or a pound of nitrogen oxide?

As in every other "gray" market, special interests would exert all the leverage they command to extract favored treatment from lawmakers. By its very nature, the "gray"-market approach creates the fetid conditions that lead to political corruption. No such problems pertain to a "white" market in pollution permits. There is no one to bribe. The market, not politicians, would set the relative costs of various pollutants.

With a pollution market in place, policymakers would be free to focus on larger strategic questions of environmental policy, leaving the minutiae of implementation to self-interested private parties. For example, society may decide that the amount of pollution authorized by the initial sale of EcoTrust permits exceeds the level acceptable for the long term. To reduce ozone emissions 10 percent, the government could use tax money to buy up and retire 10 percent of all ozone permits, just as it purchases land for parks.

As public purchases shrink the supply of pollution permits and ratchets their prices higher, the cost of owning permits would climb. Incentives for further pollution cutbacks and the development of new antipollution technologies would become even more powerful. Private citizens and conservation groups, such as the Sierra Club and the Nature Conservancy, could further accelerate this process by buying permits and destroying them. A positive, self-reinforcing process would replace the hopeless bureaucratic morass that now exists.

Pursuing the market approach to the pollution crisis would also raise vast sums for environmental recovery projects. The initial auction of EcoTrust permits would likely raise tens of billions of dollars. EcoTrust funds could be used to buy up development rights in the Amazonian rain forest. EcoTrust investments might subsidize reforestation projects or support research in solar technology. "Save the Rain Forest" bumper stickers are fine, but achieving meaningful ecological recovery will take money—huge amounts of money.[15]

A market system has the added benefit of being easy to set up anywhere in the world. Any country can sell permits for its existing pollution levels. In keeping with the practices of international commodities exchanges, carbon-monoxide and ozone permits could be traded just like tin and cocoa futures. A global problem demands a pragmatic solution that can be scaled up quickly to global proportions.

Despite its powerful advantages, the free-market approach to pollution control has been largely ignored. In the 20 years since the market technique first was proposed, it has been tried just a few times. Indeed, the market has been used only in situations where strict adherence to standard regulations would have triggered intolerable economic disruptions. In one case—the rapid phaseout of leaded gasoline—a special EPA program allowed refineries to trade lead permits among themselves as they worked through the transition period.[16]

In the other major example, an EPA administrator in Los Angeles set up an experimental program called "emissions trading." Under this program, firms were allowed to start up new sources of industrial air pollution only if they bought "emission-reduction credits" from established companies that were shutting down or reducing their emissions. By this method, the overall level of industrial pollution was contained without choking off all new industry. Despite the program's complicated restrictions, and the fact that only a few hundred trades have occurred, it worked. Estimates of the cost savings run into the billions.[17]

More recently, the EPA's successful experience with "emissions trading" led to a section of the 1990 Clean Air Act that allows electric utilities to trade "acid-rain" permits. Although it may ultimately become law, the plan met stiff resistance in Congress, where the "command-and-control" approach is still much preferred. Taking their cue from anti-market forces within the environmental movement, many lawmakers view the market approach with deep distrust.[18]

Of course, a certain skepticism is warranted. It is counterintuitive to think that selling permits *to pollute* will lead to *less pollution*. To appreciate how powerful an antipollution weapon a market would be, one must first understand how an economy incessantly reorganizes itself in response to market-feedback signals. Spontaneous, self-organizing behavior is hard to explain and hard to accept, especially for those who have spent their careers as rule-makers.

Indeed, although advocates of market solutions often see environmentalists as their primary adversaries, one prominent environmentalist claims that this view is unfair. Carl Pope, Conservation Director of the Sierra Club, contends that serious environmentalists have no problem with genuine market mechanisms. Instead, according to Pope, resistance to market-oriented policies comes from (1) businessmen who realize delay tactics would no longer save them money, and (2) members of the "governmental culture" (congressmen, legislative staffers, EPA bureaucrats, and Washington lobbyists and lawyers) who fear losing their rule-making power.

Much like the Soviet Union's economic planning bureaucrats, America's environmental "eco-crats" vigorously resist any threat that would decentralize their control. In Carl Pope's words, "The environmental movement is now powerful enough to overwhelm the business forces that don't want to face the costs of cleaning up. But we cannot beat the alliance of business interests and government bureaucrats that opposes market solutions."[19]

Interestingly, few of those who attack market proposals argue that markets will not work. Instead, most market opponents claim to object on moral grounds. According to one congressman, trading in pollution permits is tantamount to "trafficking in a morally objectionable commodity." In other words, a pollutant is not a legitimate item of commerce. By this logic, pollutants—like black market goods—ought to be stamped out by the full force of the law.[20]

Obviously, when it comes to plainly hazardous chemicals, a market solution will not work. Strict regulations are appropriate. As is the case with airline safety, regulation is the only practical means of protecting the public's health. We must rely on the vigilance of experts to protect us from technology's unseen dangers.

But the world's most worrisome pollutants are not inherently toxic. Carbon dioxide, the leading cause of the "greenhouse effect," is no poison. We exhale carbon dioxide with every breath. Carbon dioxide is a pollutant only because there is too much of it. Excessive production of a harmless substance is an economic problem, not a public-safety problem.

Back in 1712, when Thomas Newcomen's first coal-fired engine began belching clouds of smoke and carbon dioxide into England's air, global warming posed no threat. The earth was immense and human technology was puny. Only in recent decades, after we began choking on the wastes generated by our machines, did we conclude that polluting is, in and of itself, an immoral act. But wildly excessive production of otherwise-harmless substances is a technical and economic problem, not a moral and political one.

Nonetheless, for many self-proclaimed "radical environmentalists," opposition to the concept of pollution markets runs much deeper than a misguided objection to the "immorality" of carbon dioxide or ozone. In the final analysis, many outspoken environmentalists see the free-market system itself as the primary cause of environmental degradation. They see industry, technology, and economic development as the arch-enemies of nature. For them, the continuing betterment of humanity's economic condition means the inevitable destruction of the global eco-system.[21]

Ignorant of technological history, they do not realize that modern machines are incomparably more efficient and less polluting than their predecessors. They do not comprehend that a high-growth, low-environmental-impact economy is attainable, if only the prices of precious environmental resources were allowed to reflect their value. Seeing nothing ahead but catastrophe, these radical environmentalists offer the public a refurbished version of Thomas Malthus's dire predictions. Once again, humanity finds itself running up against the "iron laws" of nature. These modern-day Malthusians do not realize that the capitalist system, like the ecosystem itself, spontaneously reduces its dependence on scarce and expensive resources.

Ironically, those who claim to care most deeply about the earth's future insist on government policies that condemn the planet to the very catastrophe they seek to avoid. The longer the "command-and-control" outlook dominates thinking in the environmental movement, the closer the world will come to ecosystem breakdown. As urban smog thickens and the rain forests vanish, as global temperatures climb and economies stagnate, the demands for still tougher regulations and even harsher sanctions will grow more shrill.

In a futile attempt to pull back from the brink of ecological oblivion, we will cede ever more power to society's rule-makers. Even now, the most radical elements of Europe's Green Movement are demanding vastly enhanced government control over the economy. The so-called Red-Greens see capitalism as the real enemy. Under the morally unimpeachable banner of environmental protection, they intend to succeed where old-fashioned socialists failed. But as Eastern European environmentalists are quick to point out, the Red-Greens are demanding precisely the kind of unlimited state power that has already inflicted such massive economic and ecologic devastation in Eastern Europe and the Soviet Union.[22]

Today, no one knows which path—rules or prices—the environmental movement ultimately will take. In all likelihood, the industrialized nations will intensify their pursuit of the traditional approach—stricter rules and larger, more powerful bureaucracies. Unfortunately, the longer the "command-and-control" approach is followed, the more the ecosystem and the economy will suffer. As the situation deteriorates over the next few decades, the radical totalitarian program of today's Red-Greens will seem more necessary and will attract wider support from a desperate public. Extremists always gain power from crises.

On the other hand, if pollution markets are given a chance, they will prove their effectiveness quickly. Already several nonideological environmentalists, those who care more about the environment than about political power, have begun speaking out in favor of a remedy that works. As the list of pollutants and countries covered by the market approach expands, improvements in environmental quality will become obvious.

In pursuit of still cleaner air and water, governments and private groups will raise funds to retire pollution permits. Polluters will discover thousands of tiny ways to trim their emissions levels and permit costs. At a tiny fraction of current costs, the capabilities of robust new antipollution technologies will startle the world. Worldwide economic growth, unrestrained by the threat of ecological devastation, will allow people in even the poorest Third World nations to raise themselves far above their current misery. In the twenty-first century, the warnings of today's environmental Malthusians will seem just as ludicrous as Malthus's original predictions are to us.

But for now, the rape of the environment continues. Regulations grow more convoluted, costly, and unworkable with every passing year. Irresponsible businesses support the existing system to avoid recognizing the costs of their pollution. Legislators, lawyers, and bureaucrats resist market reforms that would erode their power and their incomes. An unholy alliance crushes any hope of significant progress against ecological devastation.

Fair-minded environmentalists know that traditional "command-and-control" methods have failed, yet too few are willing to abandon their faith in rule-making and trust the spontaneous power of free prices. Confused "moral" arguments keep a solvable economic problem imprisoned by politics. To this day, most environmental activists remain blind to the fact that the chaotic, self-organizing system known as capitalism is the only tool we have to rescue the chaotic, self-organizing system called nature.

Throughout history, the forces of central control and decentralized self-organization have been locked in perpetual struggle. Since civilization began, societies have had to draw boundaries between state power and personal freedom, between politics and economics, between fixed rules and fluctuating prices. In the final analysis, despite its momentous consequences, the battle over the future of environmental policy is just another skirmish in a centuries-old war for the power to decide.

PART VII

■

PARASITISM AND EXPLOITATION

■

The Vermin only teaze and pinch
Their Foes superior by an Inch.
So Nat'ralists observe, a Flea
Hath smaller Fleas that on him prey,
And these have smaller Fleas to bite 'em,
And so proceed *ad infinitum:*
—*Jonathan Swift (1733)*[1]

CHAPTER

25

THE HOOK

J ust a few years ago, the word *epidemic* seemed a bit outdated. With the enormous strides made in medicine over the last century, deadly epidemics no longer seemed possible. Outbreaks of typhus, cholera, polio, rabies, and plague, which intermittently had decimated humanity, were all but eliminated in industrial nations. Smallpox, a scourge for millennia, was eradicated from the planet in 1977. But as smallpox departed, AIDS arrived, and for millions accustomed to the protection afforded by medical science, "epidemic" resonated with dread once more.

By far the most infamous epidemic is the Black Plague, which killed off at least one-third of the European population in the mid-fourteenth century. Nonetheless, in terms of the total number of deaths, the worst epidemic of all time occurred in our own century. Just as World War I was ending, in the ten months from September 1918 through June 1919, somewhere between 20 and 50 million lives were blotted out by a worldwide epidemic of influenza. The death toll dwarfed even the unprecedented slaughter of five million people during the four years of trench warfare. In the United States, at least 550,000 perished from the flu, five times the number of America's World War I combat losses.[2]

Because the flu is not regarded as a serious disease, the story of the killer influenza epidemic is hard to comprehend. Every year or so, nearly everyone comes down with the cough, shivers, headache, and muscle pain of the flu. The flu may be a nuisance, but it rarely is a threat to life. Only infants and the elderly—whose immune systems are either too immature or too decrepit to combat infection—are susceptible to death.[3]

Influenza is caused by a virus. Biologically, viruses are a life-form entirely distinct from bacteria and other microorganisms. An influenza particle is far too tiny to be seen under a light microscope—being only about one-twentieth the size of a typical bacterium. There are several viral types, but most viruses are little more than a short segment of genetic code (DNA or RNA) wrapped inside a protein coat. For decades, scientists debated whether a virus could be considered a living thing, because on its own, a virus is inert. To come alive, a viral particle must invade a living cell.[4]

Influenza starts with a sneeze. Microscopic droplets packed with virus particles are breathed in and land on the cells lining the nose and throat. The spherical coat of the influenza virus is dotted with minute "hooks" that attach to the surface membranes of these cells. After a virus has latched onto a cell, its genetic code is injected into the cell's interior through a pore in the membrane. Once inside, the viral genes travel to the nucleus, where the cell's own DNA is stored. By a mechanism that still is not fully understood, the viral genes slip into the nucleus and take control of the cell's DNA. Instead of using its resources to produce normal proteins, the hijacked cell begins to manufacture copies of the virus. Eventually, hundreds of offspring viral particles make their way out of the cell to be sneezed onto the next involuntary host.[5]

Many biologists describe viruses as the ultimate parasites. Definitions of parasites vary, but the meaning of the original Greek *parasitos* is close enough—"one who eats at another's table," or "one who lives at another's expense." Parasites cannot live on their own. They must drain life-giving energy and materials from their hosts. Unlike the two-way flow of mutually beneficial relationships, the benefits of a parasitic relationship flow in one direction only—from host to parasite. The host gains nothing. In fact, the host is injured by the loss of resources siphoned off to support the reproduction of the parasite. Because viruses are little more than fragments of genetic information bent on their own reproduction, they represent parasitism refined to its highest form. Viruses are the purest and simplest form of life—information copying itself.[6]

The parasitic lifestyle is commonplace in nature. No precise figures are available, but of the estimated 30 million species, a substantial portion are parasites. Parasitic species of bacteria, protozoa, fungi, worms, mollusks, insects, fish, plants, and birds abound. Virtually all of the diseases afflicting humans, plants, and animals are caused by parasites of one type or another. Some parasites specialize in living off other parasites. Living at a host's expense apparently is a perfectly viable evolutionary strategy.[7]

Since reproduction is genetic information's primary objective, every other life function plays a subsidiary role. And, since the host provides these support services for free, the parasite can concentrate virtually all its resources on the fabrication of more gene copies. The parasitic plant *Rafflesia*, for instance, produces the largest flower in the world—five feet in diameter—but has no leaves, stem, or roots.[8]

Only one common exception exists to the parasite's concentration of resources on its reproductive apparatus. Every parasite has a "hook." Regardless of its size or way of life, a parasite must be able to physically attach itself to its host.[9] For example, the tapeworm, a common parasite of mammals, has a head covered with hooks that attach to the intestinal wall of its host. Of the 25 tapeworm species that infect humans, only a few—the fish, pork, and beef tapeworms—are found with much frequency. And although the beef tapeworm (*Taenia saginata*) has been largely eliminated by sanitation practices in modern countries, a recent estimate concluded that 60 million people still carry it around in their bellies.[10]

Cattle swallow tapeworm eggs while grazing in fields fertilized with human "nightsoil." The eggs hatch into tiny tapeworm larvae that burrow into the muscles of the cattle. People then are infected by eating contaminated beef that is raw or inadequately cooked. While passing through a person's digestive system, the larval worm latches onto the wall of the small intestine.

Its tiny head, called a scolex, has four muscular, cup-shaped suckers that grip the intestinal surface. Just behind the scolex, the tapeworm's neck continually generates new segments. Each segment is a full-blown reproductive system complete with male and female organs. As the scolex produces additional segments, forming a lengthening chain, the tapeworm grows into a long ribbonlike shape, yellowish or white in color. As new segments are generated, older segments move farther down the intestinal tract. A mature worm may have several thousand segments. Once established in its new home, a beef tapeworm may live inside its human host for decades. Indeed, it may live as long as its host.[11]

Beef tapeworms as long as 75 feet (three times the length of the small intestine) have been removed from humans, but the normal length is about 15 feet. Three months after the scolex first implants itself, the oldest segments, packed with ripened eggs, begin detaching themselves from the rest of the worm at the rate of about six per day. They ride the feces for the trip to the outside world. Tapeworm segments are firm and very active. They often creep out of the anus and crawl away like caterpillars, spilling their eggs as they go.

To us, the beef tapeworm leads a particularly revolting existence, but to the tapeworm, it's simply a matter of trying to survive in a tough world. The likelihood of any one egg successfully completing its life cycle is infinitesimally small. A beef tapeworm produces more than 720,000 eggs a day, but, on average, only one of its many millions of offspring will survive long enough to reproduce.[12] In classic parasite style, the tapeworm is a superb gene-copying machine anchored to its host by a specially adapted hook, and little else. The tapeworm is about 100 million times larger than an influenza virus, but its mode of existence is essentially the same: latch onto a host, drain its resources, and convert those resources into offspring.

To cure a tapeworm infection, its hook must be purged from the intestine. Removing segments is useless. As long as the parasite remains hooked to its host, it will recover, producing more segments and more eggs. Fortunately, physicians can prescribe tablets containing chemicals that cause the suckers on the scolex to relax. If the dosage is inadequate, and the suckers don't let go of the intestinal wall, the cure won't take. Only by examining the patient's stools for segments in the weeks following treatment can a physician be certain the parasite has been expelled.[13]

Since tapeworm infections are now cured easily, this parasite no longer attracts the interest of medical researchers. But one aspect of tapeworm biology remains incompletely understood. Mammals enjoy a sophisticated, multilayered internal-defense system able to distinguish "self" from "nonself" proteins. Why doesn't the human immune system detect this foreign invader and then wage an all-out war on it? How can a tapeworm, totally alien tissue, be accepted by the body when a transplanted organ from an immediate relative often is rejected? One guess is that tapeworms have evolved a form of biological stealth technology over the last several hundred million years. But no one really knows.

Because tapeworms are unnoticed by their victims, millions of cases go untreated. Clinical studies report that beef tapeworms rarely cause obvious physical harm to their hosts. Some victims complain of abdominal pain, excessive appetite, weakness, and weight loss. For most people, however, the symptoms are "subclinical," or not serious enough for concern. In fact, of those seeking treatment for tapeworms, the only universal complaint stems from the discomfort and embarrassment of involuntarily excreting segments from the anus.[14]

Were it not for this problem, the beef tapeworm might be the perfect parasite—a hook and a well-nourished reproduction system unnoticed by its host. Although many parasites cause symptoms that wind up destroying their hosts, it's not in a parasite's interest to kill. After all, a dead host cannot support the parasite's reproduction. A well-adapted parasite weakens but does not kill. By this measure, the mutant strain of influenza that swept away so many lives in 1918–19 was a very imperfectly evolved parasite.[15]

By contrast, the tapeworm displays its evolutionary sophistication by remaining virtually invisible. Even though the tapeworm has drained life's energy from people for millions of years, it has done so in such an inconspicuous manner that it manages to survive even after humans have acquired the knowledge needed to eradicate it. Because tapeworms cause no catastrophic epidemics, they don't stimulate the kind of concerted retribution that wiped out smallpox. Tapeworms employ a strategy of unobtrusive persistence. And it works.[16]

The influenza virus and the beef tapeworm could hardly be more dissimilar in size and structure. Nonetheless, biologists have no trouble categorizing both as parasites. Each one is such a clear example of the core features of parasitic behavior that there is no controversy over whether these organisms are parasites. There is, however, a great deal of disagreement among ecologists as to the precise definition of *parasitism*. Most definitions require that an organism, to be considered a proper parasite, live in intimate physical contact with its host and draw life-giving energy without contributing any benefit back to the host. But there is no string of words that all the experts accept. No crisp line divides what *is* from what *is not* a parasite.

Nature defies our desire to categorize neatly the convoluted results of evolution. For example, many plant species have roots covered with fungus. In optimal soil conditions, where the mineral concentrations are just right for the plant, the fungus is a parasite, drawing food from the root cells to which it is attached. But in poorer soils, at least one class of fungi actually enhances the plant's growth. Apparently the fungus has a particular aptitude for extracting phosphate from soil that possesses scarce amounts of the chemical. A mutually beneficial relationship—in which the fungus absorbs and processes phosphates in exchange for sugars shipped down from the plant—aids both plant and fungus. Is the fungus an exploitive parasite or a cooperative mutualist? It depends on environmental conditions.[17]

From the human perspective, cooperation is worthier than exploitation. In nature, however, a parasite is not a "bad" organism any more than a mutualist is a "good" organism. In the ecosystem, being a parasite carries no moral stigma. As lethal as the AIDS virus is to humans, it is no more or less "moral" in its behavior than a lovable St. Bernard puppy. No natural code of ethics condemns the exploitive lifestyles of viruses, tapeworms, and fungi. Parasitic species, or intermittently parasitic species, like all other forms of life, are merely strands of genetic information that happen to have evolved ways of surviving by exploitive techniques. Human ethical standards are simply irrelevant in the attempt to understand nature's ways.

But in economics, grasping the ecological characteristics of a relationship can help us understand why we intuitively regard it as ethical or unethical. Without exception, exploitive economic relationships look like parasitic relationships. On the other hand, "fair deals" look like mutualistic relationships. In society, the impulse for fair dealing represents a general desire to eliminate parasitic behavior and encourage mutualistic behavior. Discerning "right" from "wrong" in economics is a matter of distinguishing mutualistic from parasitic relationships.

The history of civilization chronicles the gradual erection of a system of laws banning parasitic economic behavior. From long before one of the Ten Commandments stipulated, "Thou shalt not steal," economic parasitism has been under attack. Slavery, the most obscene form of economic parasitism, has been virtually eradicated. And, while feudal elites still exploit the poor in much of the Third World, we can hope that South Africa's apartheid will be history's last example of a society expressly based on the intentional economic parasitism of one group of human beings by another.[18]

Hosts are victims. No victim ever chooses to be robbed, enslaved, or denied basic human rights. Economic parasites use secrecy, deception, brute force, and legal authority as their "hooks." By latching onto their unwilling hosts, they are able to extort profits that no mutually voluntary relationship would provide.

In certain cases, it's easy to identify a parasitic transaction. When a mugger robs a victim at knifepoint, the economic benefits of the mugger's hurried relationship with his victim flow in just one direction. The imminent threat to the victim's life serves as a particularly effective "hook," temporarily attaching the parasite to his unwilling host.

Because traditional crimes are such extreme forms of parasitism, elaborate measures are taken to control them. Nonetheless, every year in the United States, more than 12 million acts of robbery, burglary, larceny, and auto theft siphon about $12.5 billion from those who earn their goods through mutually beneficial exchange.[19] Even so, as severe as America's crime problem is, property losses account for less than 0.3 percent of the economy's $5,000 billion annual output. Far more economic parasitism takes place, but most of it goes unreported.

For example, when an unscrupulous taxi driver takes a naive passenger on a long detour from New York's Kennedy Airport to the American Museum of Natural History, is a crime reported? Probably not. But if the driver gets $40 for what normally is a $30 trip, he is stealing. At least for that trip, he is behaving like an economic parasite. Once inside the cab, the "host" is hooked. Trying to escape from a taxi speeding across the Triborough Bridge entails obvious risks. The cabbie is well-positioned to drain economic energy from his "host."

But the taxi driver/passenger relationship is not entirely parasitic. After all, by getting to the museum, the passenger receives a benefit. On the passenger's behalf, the taxi company and the driver expended gasoline, vehicle wear and tear, and labor. So, to be precise, only the excess portion of the fare, $10, represents the ill-gotten gains of parasitic behavior. The normal $30 fare represents the fair exchange of a mutualistic transaction. As in the plant/fungus example, mutualism and parasitism sometimes coexist. Their relative significance depends on the circumstances.

As technology changes, some economic parasites become extinct while others emerge to take advantage of new, unoccupied niches. Holding up stagecoaches at gunpoint doesn't provide anyone with much of a living anymore, but tapping into the banking system's electronic funds-transfer network supports the economic descendants of Jesse James in a grand style.

Economic parasitism, of course, is by no means confined to the actions of lone bandits and small gangs. In fact, the larger the parasitic organization, the more devastating its acts become. Some organizations, such as the Mafia, are dedicated parasites. Other organizations that usually behave as market mutualists occasionally are called to account for specific acts of parasitism. Kodak not long ago was convicted of stealing instant-film technology invented and patented by Polaroid. In effect, Kodak had commandeered Polaroid's "corporate genes" and siphoned off Polaroid's profits and growth.

No one ever argues that computer fraud, extortion, or patent infringement should not be considered crimes. Incentives for hard work, innovation, and investment are undermined in a society that condones economic parasitism. From long experience, society fully accepts the notion that one-way transactions made covertly or under duress are inherently wrong. Healthy economic relationships are open and voluntary. When either party feels that the relationship is no longer profitable, it must be able to disengage and find other trading partners. The risk of losing profitable relationships keeps mutualistic organizations efficient.

Aside from the moral repugnance of exploitive behavior, an unspoken

economic rationale underpins society's insistence that its members behave as mutualists. In open-market transactions, "free-living" organizations voluntarily engage in mutually profitable exchanges. But in
imposed transactions, a host organization cannot escape its parasite,
because it is hooked.

When the hooks of economic parasites are outlawed, individuals and
companies have no alternative but to act as productive mutualists. If
they do not add value, no one trades with them and they go bankrupt.
Of course, no society ever has or ever will completely stamp out exploitation, but to the extent that parasitic behavior is curtailed, society
benefits. A healthy capitalist economy is a community of interdependent
mutualists.

To create an environment where cooperation flourishes, the elimi-
nation of exploitation in all its forms should be the chief objective of a
society's economic laws. But keeping antiparasite laws in step with a
rapidly evolving economy isn't simple. Identifying the economy's true
parasites and writing laws that destroy their hooks requires a bionomic
perspective.

CHAPTER
26

PRIVATE CORPOCRACY

In business, the groups that join together to form an enterprise—investors, managers, and employees—must all benefit from their relationships if the organization is to remain healthy and competitive in its market. Unfair, exploitive relationships among the parties weaken the organization. Managers who exploit workers with below-market wages and dangerous working conditions cause high employee turnover, shoddy workmanship, absenteeism, and strikes. Workers who exploit management through restrictive work rules and job featherbedding cause high costs, defective products, and poor customer service.

Exploitive labor/management relationships afflict many firms. And, generally speaking, firms that fail to remedy exploitive internal relationships eventually are forced out of business by competitors who enjoy predominantly mutualistic relationships. Poor labor/management relations inside American steel and auto firms accelerated their loss of market share to Japanese firms, which carefully cultivate mutualistic corporate cultures. Whether they wear the hat of management or of labor, unchecked internal parasites can kill off their host organizations.

In fact, although exploitive worker/manager relationships traditionally have received the most attention, the real problem area in the United States today is the relationship between a company's owners—its shareholders—and its management. Parasitism tends to afflict the very largest companies far more often than it affects smaller firms. Corporate behemoths, like elephants that harbor huge tapeworms, are so immense that they can endure decades of parasitic damage. Smaller firms, struggling for survival in hotly competitive niches, tend to die off quickly when weakened by parasitism.

A corporation's shareholders depend on management to organize the company's people and equipment. Ideally, a mutualistic relationship exists. Executives are paid high salaries and benefits in exchange for delivering sufficient profits on the capital invested by the shareholders. If the shareholders fail to compensate the executives well enough, they jump ship to other firms where the shareholders are more appreciative. By the same token, if the executives fail to manage the company's resources effectively, the shareholders fire them and bring in new managers. Excessive demands by either shareholders or executives are kept in check by the alternatives available in the marketplaces for investment capital and executive talent.

While this system works pretty well in small and medium-size corporations, it often breaks down in extremely large companies. As a firm grows into a giant, the original investors, who monitored management carefully, sell off their shares to thousands of small shareholders. Effective ownership power dissipates. A "commons problem" emerges because no single shareholder has a strong proprietary interest.

The small shareholder realizes that she owns far too little of the firm to be influential in its affairs. Consequently, most small shareholders pay no attention to what's going on inside the companies whose shares they own. As long as the company's stock price keeps rising, the small shareholder is happy. If the price falls, she usually becomes disenchanted, sells her shares, and puts the money into another firm's stock. By selling out, she avoids further losses. But the problems that caused the stock price to decline often go unremedied. One of the fundamental tenets of capitalism breaks down. Owners do not attempt to nurture the growth of their capital.

Under corporate law, a company's board of directors is obligated to protect the financial interests of the shareholders. But where no shareholder is wealthy enough to own more than a sliver of the company, board members usually are nominated by the company's top manager, the chief executive officer (CEO). So-called "inside" board members are senior executives who work for the CEO. "Outside" directors typically are attorneys, bankers, and consultants who do not work directly for the CEO but whose firms depend in part on the CEO's willingness to do business with them. Quite often, outside board members are simply old friends and supporters of the CEO.[1]

The market-feedback loop that keeps management responsive to shareholders breaks down. A two-way mutualistic relationship—high pay, "perks," and power for executives in exchange for excellent returns on investment for shareholders—is transformed into a one-sided, parasitic relationship. In the absence of effective shareholder power, all real authority is ceded to top management. Rather than playing the role of managers hired to perform a job, subject to dismissal for poor results, executives atop large companies gain de facto control over the shareholders. The balance of power between owners and managers shifts decisively and allows the top executive group—sometimes called a "corpocracy"—to sink a hook into the shareholders. Like a tapeworm, a corpocracy can feed undetected for decades on the wealth of a great corporation.

Among the many American firms infected with this silent, parasitic disease was Walt Disney Productions, the multibillion-dollar business empire built by Mickey Mouse, Donald Duck, Snow White, and the other well-loved denizens of the Magic Kingdom. The roots of the company's corpocracy problem can be traced back to Walt Disney's unexpected death in 1966. Disney, a story-telling wizard and marketing genius, was one of those rare entrepreneurial personalities who, by virtue of talent, drive, and ambition, constructed a fabulously successful enterprise almost single-handedly. His untimely death left his company without its prime creative force and business visionary.

His death also left the company with a power vacuum at the top. Because Walt and his family members held the controlling interest in the firm, Walt wielded all power. His decisions were law. The board of directors was a rubber stamp. When Walt died, the board did not even attempt to search for a CEO talented enough to replace him. Instead, Card Walker, Disney's senior marketing executive, a man with no film-making experience, grabbed the top spot and the board of directors went along.

The financial momentum built up while Disney was still at the helm obscured the impact of his death and carried the company through the 1970s. Walt Disney World, the enormous theme park in Florida that Walt conceived and designed, was opened to the public in 1971. Its constantly climbing attendance levels, along with the continuing growth of Disneyland in southern California, drove the company's revenues and profits higher year after year.

But the Disney movie studio, the heart and soul of the company, had become the laughingstock of Hollywood. By 1984, the studio had gone 15 years since its last live-action hit—*The Love Bug*. Throughout the 1970s, the studio churned out insipid formula films like *The Boatniks*, *The Shaggy D.A.*, and *The Unidentified Flying Oddball*. A flourishing center of filmmaking ingenuity under Walt's leadership, the studio had become hopelessly outdated, producing "fresh-scrubbed, wholesome family entertainment" for a society that had changed dramatically since the 1960s. While George Lucas and Steven Spielberg produced such immensely profitable movies as *Star Wars* and *E.T.*—films that the Disney studio should have made—Card Walker kept asking himself, "What would Walt have done?" The public's tastes had changed, but Disney's corpocrats could do no better than crank out mindless imitations of products the market no longer wanted.

The studio had accounted for more than half of total company revenues before Walt Disney World opened, but by 1979 it generated less than 20 percent of sales. And half of that came from regular reissues of the great Disney animated classics like *Snow White, Bambi, Pinocchio*, and *Fantasia*. Stifled by management's aversion to innovation, talented young animators quit the studio for places where they were allowed to do challenging work. With each passing year, Disney made fewer films and its share of the movie market dwindled, but the costs of maintaining the studio did not. Consequently, the profits of the film division slipped from $35 million in 1981 to $20 million in 1982, and 1983 saw a loss of $33 million.[2]

Despite rising attendance at the theme parks, the studio's loss caused a drop in overall profits, and falling profits finally awakened Wall Street to the company's profound troubles. Many investors feared that without successful films keeping the Disney magic alive, attendance at the theme parks eventually would decline. As pessimism about Disney's long-term viability took hold, many investors dumped their shares, and the price of Disney stock headed south. In one year, the stock's price slumped from $80 to $50.

At the annual shareholders' meeting in February 1984, one man stood up and pleaded to the top executives assembled on the dais:

> My mother asked me what stocks to invest in and I advised her to buy Disney when it was at $85. It started going down, and she keeps calling me and asking me why, and I say, "Don't worry, Mother. It will come back up; it's a great company." I'm tired of answering her questions now, so if I give you her number, will you call her and explain what's going on so she will get off my back?[3]

This shareholder's dismay was nothing compared to that of Walt's nephew, Roy E. Disney, the company's single largest shareholder. With more than a million Disney shares in his portfolio, the drop from $80 to $50 a share had cost him a paper loss of more than $30 million. Yet, with nearly 35 million shares of stock on the market, Roy's shares accounted for only 3 percent of total ownership. Ousting top management would require the support of 51 percent of the shares. With share ownership so widely dispersed among thousands of investors, Roy was powerless.

Card Walker consistently had ignored Roy's advice to reinvigorate the studio. Ron Miller, Walt's son-in-law and the number-two man in the company hierarchy, was more sympathetic, but he did little to improve the studio. "Card would listen but not hear; Ron would listen but not act," said one former executive.[4] Roy Disney knew that his chances of rescuing the Magic Kingdom from its corpocracy were practically nil.

As is typically the case, the parasitism of the Disney corpocracy was not overt. Disney executives did not pay themselves outrageous salaries or provide perks out of line with normal practices. In fact, salaries were modest by Hollywood standards. Card Walker and Ron Miller were not evil or malicious people. By all accounts, they were fine human beings trying to do the very best job they could.

The problem was that their best wasn't good enough. Top managers, like professionals in any field, must be measured against the best talent available. Card Walker and Ron Miller just didn't have "the right stuff." Being born without the talents of Walt Disney is no sin, but clinging to powerful positions that demand extraordinary ability becomes a parasitic act once the organization's financial results show that performance consistently falls short of reasonable investor expectations.

The steep drop in Disney's stock price attracted the attention of several corporate raiders, the top predators in the corporate jungle. Always on the lookout for weakened prey, they target firms that cannot keep pace with the herd. Not always, but quite often, these financial stragglers are organizations whose profits are being drained away by a parasitic corpocracy. In an environment where large companies frequently are parasitized by incompetent managements, there are hundreds of diseased firms from which to choose. The rational raider—and they all are remorselessly rational—targets the firm he believes will yield the richest profits for the risks involved in the takeover chase.[5]

Saul Steinberg, a Wall Street raider known for getting rid of the managements in the companies he takes over, decided to take a close look at the Disney situation. He began by having his staff prepare an exhaustive evaluation of the company's assets. Essentially, Disney was comprised of three parts. The first was the library of hundreds of cartoons, movies, and TV shows that had been produced since the company began in 1923. The second piece consisted of the two theme parks—Disneyland and Walt Disney World. The third was 17,000 acres of undeveloped land in Florida surrounding Walt Disney World.

While the stock-market consensus of buyers and sellers valued the ongoing operations of the company at $50 a share, or roughly $1.75 billion ($50 a share times 35 million shares), Steinberg's appraisal of the three pieces totaled about $3.5 billion, or $100 a share. Instead of the whole company being worth more than the sum of its parts—the economic rationale for any organization—because of mismanagement, the business was worth less than its physical assets. In short, the Disney corporation was worth twice as much dead as alive.

But knowing that a property is a fantastic bargain does not necessarily mean you have the wherewithal to acquire it. Even the very wealthiest investors do not have the cash to buy up a 51 percent controlling interest in a firm that, even at a depressed stock price, was still worth nearly $2 billion. For this reason, the sheer enormity of companies such as Disney protected them from raiders even when, economically speaking, they deserved to die. The fiercest lion is still too puny to bring down the most parasitized bull elephant. By infesting organizations too huge to be attacked by predators, the corpocracies kept safe and snug, beyond the reach of predators eager to dismember their hosts—and them.

Only a major economic innovation could upset these bionomic relationships and make these lumbering giants vulnerable to corporate predators. In 1977, just such an economic mutation took place when the "junk bond" was invented by Michael Milken of the Wall Street firm Drexel Burnham Lambert. Although Milken and Drexel Burnham later would be convicted and bankrupted for violating U.S. securities laws, the invention of junk bonds took place well before those transgressions and is regarded by experts as a major contribution to the field of corporate finance.

Simply put, a bond is a loan agreement. Like a mortgage or a promissory note, a bond is an IOU, a piece of paper signed by a borrower that promises to repay the loan with interest. A "junk" bond is nothing more than a bond that promises to pay the lender an unusually high rate of interest—say, 15 percent when U.S. government bonds are paying 10 percent. There's nothing magical about junk bonds—it's just that in the hidebound world of high finance, no one had ever arranged such financings before Milken began doing it.

Wall Street tradition said that bonds could be issued only at normal interest rates by blue-chip companies. But Milken realized that hundreds of smaller corporations—companies snubbed by Wall Street as "junk," too risky to lend to—were perfectly sound and legitimately needed to borrow money to finance expansion. Milken believed that if high-interest loans were made to enough of these up-and-coming firms, the investors—wealthy individuals, banks, pension funds, corporations, and mutual funds—could be protected from the risk of default. A few of these small companies would go bankrupt and not pay back their loans, but the great majority would pay back, and the extra interest earned on a diversified portfolio of junk bonds would more than offset the incremental risk to investors.

It took some time for junk bonds to catch on, but by 1983, they had grown to represent about 5 percent of the $400 billion American corporate bond market.[6] As the middleman between borrowers who needed cash and investors who wanted high interest rates, Milken and his firm collected a fee of 3 to 4 percent of the bonds they sold. Milken and his firm grew fabulously rich in this previously unoccupied niche of the market for capital.

With investors clamoring for more high-yield bonds, Milken began to search for other kinds of borrowers, people who needed billions and whose projects could tolerate the hefty fees and interest charges. In an adjacent niche of the corporate finance market—a niche populated by smart but puny predators and parasitized corporate behemoths—Milken found his new borrowers.

Corporate raiders, such as Saul Steinberg, were perfect borrowers for the capital source that Milken had tapped. Milken's junk bonds worked like an instantaneous supergrowth hormone, turning individuals into economic giants able to devour the largest corporate prey. Almost overnight, the availability of junk-bond financing set off the feeding frenzy of hostile takeovers that reshaped much of corporate America in the 1980s.[7]

Steinberg's plan to buy up 51 percent of Disney's shares on the open stock market would absorb more than $1 billion of borrowed money. After gaining control of Disney, Steinberg planned to sell off enough of the company's assets to pay off the junk bonds. Steinberg and the shareholders who chose to hold onto their shares would wind up owning a down-sized Disney. Steinberg's plan for the company is the plan behind most hostile takeovers.

In accordance with federal law, Steinberg publicly announced that he had purchased several million shares of Disney. He then offered to buy all the additional shares he needed at a premium over the stock-market price. The premium represented an immediate profit for shareholders willing to sell. A board of directors looking out for the interests of shareholders at least might have considered the offer. After all, it would have benefited the shareholders, whose interests the board was legally bound to protect.

But Disney's executives didn't want to lose control of "their" company. They rejected Steinberg's offer and, with the board's support, began a series of antitakeover maneuvers. After decades of inaction, management suddenly decided that the time was right to buy a Florida land-development company—the Arvida Corporation. They paid for Arvida by issuing new shares of Disney stock to the Bass brothers, the owners of Arvida. With more Disney shares outstanding, Steinberg's recently purchased 12 percent position shrank to 11 percent.

Through intermediaries, Disney executives made it clear to Steinberg that they would use every legal technique to keep him from snatching control of the company. They announced plans for another major acquisition—Gibson Greeting Cards. If this deal went through, Steinberg's ownership position would be diluted further. But Steinberg knew before he started his attack that a vigorous defense was likely. Like any shrewd businessman, he had a fallback position.

Steinberg continued buying up Disney shares while simultaneously offering to sell his shares back to the company at a premium over the market price. In essence, Steinberg offered to abandon the chase and leave the company alone if the corpocracy paid him off. After much pious soul-searching, Disney's board of directors, at the urging of top management, did exactly that. Using company funds—the property of the shareholders—Disney's management bought back Steinberg's stock, leaving him with a $32 million "greenmail" profit.[8]

"It's an outrage. They have raped the shareholders," fumed one livid Wall Street trader.[9] In a torrent of articles, speeches, and editorials, the investment community and the press pilloried Disney's management and Saul Steinberg. Shareholders launched lawsuits. Congress held hearings. But it was all perfectly legal. Under corporate law, a company can buy back shares owned by one shareholder at a price not offered to all shareholders. Without a shareholder vote, the board of directors has the power to use company money—again, shareholders' money—to pay a threatening shareholder to go away.

But Steinberg's profitable retreat did not end the Disney takeover battle. In fact, his attack set the stage for a takeover campaign led by Roy Disney, who had been waiting in the wings. In a complex series of moves and countermoves, the Roy Disney forces assembled a coalition of major shareholders. The most important among them were the Bass brothers, formerly the owners of Arvida, who now owned a large chunk of Disney. Together, these shareholding allies had the concentrated ownership power needed to overthrow Disney's executives. With effective shareholder power restored, the days of Disney's corpocracy were numbered. Realizing the game was lost, Card Walker and Ron Miller quit, and the Roy Disney/Bass brothers coalition replaced them with a team led by Michael Eisner and Frank Wells. Eisner had been president of Paramount Pictures, and Wells had been president of Warner Brothers. Both had outstanding track records in Hollywood.

Within months of their ascension to top spots at Disney, Eisner and Wells revitalized the company, attracting new talent to the long-neglected studio. In 1988, Disney became the leader in box-office receipts among all Hollywood studios, with hits such as *Who Framed Roger Rabbit?*; *Good Morning, Vietnam*; and *Three Men and a Baby*. Only four years earlier, Disney had finished last at the box office. The video-cassette of *Pinocchio* became one of the best-selling videos ever released. Disney's network television show, "The Wonderful World of Disney," which had been canceled in 1983 after 29 years on the air, reappeared as "The Disney Sunday Movie." George Lucas, Francis Ford Coppola, and Michael Jackson were brought in to create a new Disneyland and Epcot attraction called *Captain EO*.[10]

Revenues and profits soared. Investors expressed their renewed confidence in the company's future by bidding its stock up to $145 in March 1986, just two years after Saul Steinberg began buying up shares at $50. Riding a wave of enthusiasm about Disney's long-term prospects, the company whose stock the market thought was worth $1.75 billion had nearly tripled to $5 billion in just 24 months.

Despite the storybook ending that saved the Magic Kingdom from demolition, the Disney takeover battle left the general public and law-makers with a distorted perception of the problems that had set off the battle in the first place. Most media attention focused on the $32 million that Saul Steinberg had reaped from 90 days of jousting with Disney's management. Many were outraged by Steinberg's plan to break up "a national treasure." A *Los Angeles Times* columnist wrote, "Breaking up Disney to cash in on its assets would be on the order of smashing a Tiffany vase to get at a penny that fell inside."[11] No one acknowledged that a silent, parasitic disease had been devouring this national treasure from within for two decades.

The sudden, bloody acts of predators—from a lion's dismemberment of a parasitized water buffalo to a corporate raider's breakup of a familiar-yet-diseased company—affront our sensibilities. But, like top predators in an ecosystem, corporate predators serve a vital economic role. They weed out weak firms that mismanage people and resources. Predators kill for their own profit, but, in so doing, they begin the process of recycling scarce skills and equipment back into healthy and productive organizations. It is parasitism by corpocracies, not predation by takeover artists, that weakens an economy. The real enemy of efficiency, growth, and innovation is inept and shortsighted management.

Saul Steinberg was not a parasite because he had no "hook." After risking $265 million to buy 11 percent of the Disney shares, he had to go ahead and purchase another 40 percent or sit around and hope that something would boost the value of his holdings. He never had the power to extract a quick profit. Only the Disney board of directors had that legal power. A capable and confident board, acting in the interests of the shareholders instead of the corpocrats, would have welcomed Steinberg as a savvy shareholder with worthwhile ideas. But Steinberg knew that Disney's corpocrats would use their "hook" into the shareholders' purse to extract a bribe.[12]

Steinberg's fast $32 million is the kind of number that draws attention. Few realize that the long-term ineptitude of Disney's top management cost the shareholders far more. The difference between the $50 share price under the Card Walker/Ron Miller regime and the $145 stock price under Michael Eisner/Frank Wells amounted to about $3.3 billion. Compared to the $32 million "greenmail" crumb tossed to Steinberg, two decades of unobtrusive, persistent parasitism by an entrenched corpocracy had cost Disney's shareholders more than 100 times as much.

Because Disney is such a well-known company, its takeover saga sparked a surge of interest in "reforming" corporate takeover law. In 1985 alone, more than 50 bills were introduced in Congress to deal with the sudden surge in takeover activity. More than 20 hearings were held by nine committees. The testimony of the experts was divided over whether hostile takeovers are good or bad for the economy, and not one piece of legislation came close to passing. America's lawmakers were baffled. Should society limit the ability of corporate raiders to buy stock in public companies and wrest control away from their current managements?[13]

Legislative confusion stemmed from the fact that attention was focused on the symptoms rather than the cause of the disease. Many lawmakers wanted to stamp out the "epidemic of takeovers," but few understood the conditions that had spawned them. At the state level, several legislatures wrote laws dealing with takeover tactics that had created a whole new business vocabulary—"greenmail," "poison pill," "shark repellent," "golden parachute," "Pac-Man defense," and "crown

jewels lockup." For the most part, changes in state laws further entrenched management power. Not one addressed the erosion in shareholder power that had created corpocracies, weakened companies, and
caused hostile takeovers to become economically sensible.[14]

Difficult public-policy questions arise whenever the parasitic/mutu-
alistic qualities of an economic activity are unclear. To keep the law in
step with a fast-evolving economy, lawmakers need to understand precisely which new economic phenomena are parasitic and which are not.
In the search for a parasite, the only reliable clue is finding its economic
"hook." Legislators who ignore the hook and focus on takeover tactics
are like doctors who treat the stomach pains of a tapeworm victim by
prescribing an antacid. No cure is possible unless the parasite's hook is
purged from the host.

In America's corporate world, the hook is the nearly invulnerable
power of the corpocracies. At present, company managements nominate
new directors and draft the resolutions mailed to shareholders. Dissident
shareholders must overcome several legal hurdles to get their views
printed on proxy statements. Managements control shareholder mailing
lists. Managements even count shareholder votes. Voting does indeed
take place, but the result is a foregone conclusion in all except the rarest
of situations.

In the United States, the laws governing the relationships between
shareholders and managements are written at the state level. Since choosing the state of incorporation seems like a technical legal matter, shareholders rarely object to the state selected by management. But the choice
of a corporation's state of legal residence makes an enormous difference
in the balance of power between shareholders and management. The
favorite state of corpocracies is Delaware. To attract such lucrative legal
business, the Delaware legislature has doubled over backward to make
the rules absurdly favorable to management. More than half of the
Fortune 500 firms are registered in tiny Delaware. Shareholders trying
to block an unfair action by the management of a "Delaware" corporation are out of luck.[15]

But Delaware is not the only state that abuses shareholder rights.
Across the country, under the guise of protecting workers' jobs, state
legislatures have passed laws that further strengthen the powers of top
management. Legislators understandably are anxious to help constitu-
ents threatened with the loss of jobs in takeovers led by "rapacious Wall
Street predators." With little hesitation, they pass laws authorizing new
antitakeover defenses. These lawmakers fail to recognize that the only
true protection for jobs is companies that are consistently well managed

and intensely competitive. Only independent boards of directors that aggressively represent the interests of shareholders can force managements to work to their fullest potential.[16]

Political realism suggests that the managements running America's largest firms will be able to thwart the reforms that would strengthen the independence of corporate boards. Unlike worker/management battles, this isn't the kind of issue that excites the passions of voters. Consequently, many of America's largest companies, weakened by inept managements, will continue losing contests with foreign competitors, while lawmakers remain oblivious to the fact that existing corporate laws condemn the nation's largest firms, and the millions who depend on them, to slow death by parasitism.

The only bright spot in this otherwise-dismal picture is the growing power of pension funds, which manage the retirement savings of millions of American workers. Today, the funds own about one-third of the stock of all public companies—nearly twice as much as they held in 1970. The professional money managers who vote the stocks owned by these funds are strictly regulated by federal pension law and are obliged to earn the highest possible return for their worker-owners. In the last few years, fund managers have begun to assert themselves, demanding that managements and directors act in the best interests of shareholders.[17]

Pension funds are now opposing management proposals that would further erode corporate democracy and shareholder rights. They are voting against the plans of some corpocracies that want to entrench themselves further by issuing new stock that carries no voting rights. In this pivotal but virtually unreported battle for economic power, pension funds are insisting that the "one share, one vote" principle be maintained.[18]

Now that working people are on the verge of accumulating the dominant ownership position in America's largest corporations, executives in these companies want to abolish the fundamental link between the ownership of and power over capital. Ironically, it is America's workers who, through their pension funds, are fighting to protect the most basic property rights of the capitalist system. Genuine corporate democracy— where shareholders have the power to hire and fire the managers running their companies—seems cruelly unfair to a corpocratic clique grown accustomed to the perquisites of the parasitic life.[19]

No one can accurately calculate the damage done to the American economy by corpocracies. One guess puts the total cost of corpocracy at more than $800 billion per year.[20] At 16 percent of America's GNP, this estimate probably is way too high. But whatever the invisible cost of corpocracy, it certainly dwarfs the annual $13 billion damage done by all the highly publicized parasitic acts of robbery, burglary, larceny, and auto theft.

How much more efficient and internationally competitive would America's corporations be if all executives were held to reasonable performance standards? Would America have lost the automobile industry to Japan if Detroit's Big Three had not been so hopelessly paralyzed by corporate bureaucracy? Just a 5 percent increase in the sales of America's 500 largest firms would yield a $150 billion rise in GNP and several hundred thousand new jobs.[21]

Without question, our standard of living would rise significantly if the corpocracies were purged from corporate America. In all likelihood, however, the required reforms will not be implemented. Like enormous tapeworms, these persistent, unobtrusive parasites will be sapping our economic strength for a very long time to come.

CHAPTER
27

PUBLIC BUREAUCRACY

t's hard to believe that America might be infected by an even more devastating form of economic parasitism than corpocracy. But, sadly, large-scale exploitation is not limited to the domain of private enterprise. Economic parasitism exists wherever an organization has the power to attach itself to a host. Whether the parasite and host happen to be in the private or the public sector is irrelevant.

Without question, the most debilitating case of public-sector parasitism involves America's public schools. Few interpret the demise of these schools as an example of economic parasitism, but all the usual symptoms of this organizational disease are readily apparent. The sole objective of a public-school system is to produce a well-educated citizenry. But, as exhaustive studies have shown and the personal experiences of millions of Americans can attest, the U.S. public-school system is a catastrophic failure. For the last three decades, the organization charged by American society with responsibility for preparing literate, economically competent adults has been in an appalling tailspin.[1]

For a democratic society seriously challenged by powerful foreign economic competitors, the litany of public-school failures is ominous. More than 25 percent of American high-school students drop out before graduation. Of those who remain in school, only one in five eleventh graders is able to write a note applying for a summer job at a swimming pool. Only one in five young adults is able to read a schedule well enough to figure out when a bus will arrive at a terminal. Less than 40 percent of Americans in the twenty-one-to-twenty-five-year-old bracket are able to read well enough to interpret an article by a newspaper columnist. Among blacks, the ratios fall to just one in ten.[2]

Less than one-third of high-school seniors know in which half-century the Civil War occurred, what the Magna Carta was, what the Reformation was, or that the Declaration of Independence is the document that marked the separation of the American colonies from Great Britain, or that Lincoln wrote the Emancipation Proclamation.

Even the performance of America's very best students has collapsed. In international rankings of top high-school students, America's advanced science students were near the bottom in chemistry and physics. In biology, they came in dead last, behind such nations as Singapore and Thailand.[3]

Just half the nation's 17-year-olds can solve math problems at the junior-high level, and fewer than one in 15 can cope with problems at the high-school level that require several steps or involve algebra or geometry. In a calculus and algebra test comparing the best students in 11 industrial countries, the top 5 percent of U.S. high-school seniors came in last. In fact, America's *top* math students scored below Japan's *average* 17-year-olds. Among fifth graders, the situation is even worse. The *lowest* math and science test scores in Japan are higher than the *highest* scores in comparable American schools.[4]

While Japanese kids spend about 1,100 hours each year in actual study time at school (240 days a year at 4.7 hours a day), American kids put in only about 500 hours per year (180 days a year at 2.8 hours a day). After the typical Japanese student gets home, he puts in at least two hours a day on homework, while his American counterpart exerts no more than 30 minutes of effort. One education expert comments, "People often say that our best and brightest can compare with Japan's best and brightest, who only memorize. But it's simply not true."[5] One need look no farther than the nearest classroom to explain America's accelerating decline and Japan's emerging dominance.

Americans worry that too many new jobs are low-pay and low-skill, but our schools simply are not turning out enough graduates capable of performing in high skill occupations. Recently, more than 80 percent of the applicants taking a simple test for entry-level jobs at New York Telephone flunked. While the newspapers are filled with listings for high-skill jobs that go begging for qualified applicants, the flood of dropouts and functional illiterates disgorged by the public-school system swells a pool of 30 million illiterate adults already trapped in menial jobs.[6]

Without question, student performance has been hurt by the social ills of shattered families, violence, and drugs. But these plagues cannot account for the whole problem. After years of intense publicity, Americans have concluded that the public-school system desperately needs fixing. Democracy is imperiled in a nation that has forgotten its heritage. With intensifying global economic competition and advancing technological complexity, good jobs will not go to near-illiterates just because they happen to be *American* near-illiterates. But the problem, as always, is to figure out what pragmatic steps can reverse the decline. The advice of the education establishment—teachers' unions, school boards, superintendents, and colleges of education—is not surprising. In short, their response to the crisis is, "Give us more money and we'll do a better job."

But, contrary to common perceptions, the resources devoted to public education have climbed rapidly during the 30 years of the system's performance collapse. In 1950, public schools consumed 2 percent of America's GNP to educate its school-age population. By 1986, it took 3.5 percent for the same portion of the population. If private and public colleges are included, America now spends more on education than it spends on its other grotesquely bloated system—defense.

On a per-student basis, the United States spends more on its public schools than any nation except Switzerland.[7] Adjusted for inflation, one year of public school for one student cost $1,200 in 1952; by 1989, it cost $4,400. During the same period, average scores on Scholastic Aptitude Tests collapsed. In short, while the quality of American education disintegrated, the price society paid to the public-school system to produce one student-year nearly *quadrupled*. The claim that inadequate spending is the problem simply does not hold water.[8]

Clearly, something is profoundly wrong with an organization that consumes ever more resources to produce an ever more-pitiful product. Indeed, the record of the American public-school system shows a negative "learning curve"—ever higher costs for deteriorating performance. One clue to the cause of this disease can be seen in the shift in the mix of spending by public schools. In 1955, nearly 55 percent of school operating budgets went to teacher salaries. By 1985, just 40 percent went to pay teachers. This shift was not caused by fewer teachers. In fact, since 1965, as the number of students fell 8 percent, the number of teachers grew 29 percent. An expanding teacher population absorbed a declining portion of public-school budgets, because the number of administrators and other nonteaching staffers grew even faster—jumping to 102 percent.[9]

Of course, every sizable organization needs people in administrative jobs. There is nothing "wrong" with administration per se. Rules and procedures must be established and maintained if an organization is to run smoothly. Policies need to be decided and communicated. But every

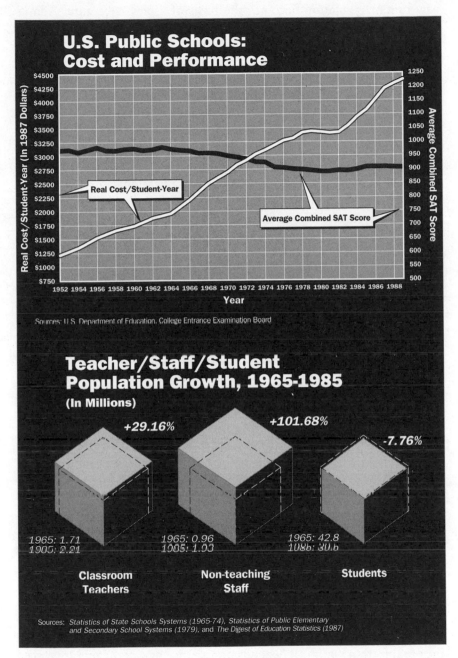

U.S. Public Schools: Cost and Performance

Sources: U.S. Department of Education, College Entrance Examination Board

Teacher/Staff/Student Population Growth, 1965-1985

(In Millions)

+29.16%   +101.68%   -7.76%

1965: 1.71   1965: 0.96   1965: 42.8
1985: 2.21   1985: 1.93   1985: 39.5

Classroom Teachers   Non-teaching Staff   Students

Sources: *Statistics of State Schools Systems (1965-74), Statistics of Public Elementary and Secondary School Systems (1979)*, and *The Digest of Education Statistics (1987)*

Figure 27.1

new rule or regulation becomes the basis of a new exception. Administrative edicts, like all other forms of information, have an inherent tendency to evolve to greater complexity.

Because the number of rules tends to grow, the number of rule-makers must grow with it. The only force powerful enough to counter the inherent tendency of organizations to add administrative overhead is the pressure of competition. Only organizations whose very survival is threatened by high costs have the fortitude to slash unnecessary administrative expenses. Organizations that have no competitors—monopolies—grow immensely inefficient and bureaucratic, because their waste of resources carries with it no threat to organizational survival.

By virtually every measure, the bureaucracy running the Chicago Public Schools system is among the worst in America. Student performance is consistently at the bottom in nationwide rankings. School buildings are in shambles, classes lack funds for basic supplies, and money for teacher raises is unavailable. But the 3,000 bureaucrats who work in the Chicago Board of Education's newly renovated headquarters listen to piped-in music, walk on plush carpets, and enjoy a panoramic view of the city from their well-appointed offices.

Prior to a recent reorganization, Chicago's 514 school principals reported up through a chain of command that included layer after layer of assistant superintendents, associate superintendents, directors, coordinators, and facilitators. Deputy and associate superintendents are still paid $70,000 to $80,000 a year, yet no one is quite sure what they do. Chicago School Superintendent Manford Byrd was paid $110,000 a year but admitted that he didn't know what to do about the city's chronically ailing school system, or why the system's children didn't perform better on standardized tests. When asked about leaking roofs and lacking supplies, he responded, "Money is hard to come by."[10]

Like all other parasites, a bureaucracy lacks the capacity to do anything but grow and reproduce itself. A bureaucracy—that portion of an administrative apparatus that exceeds what is necessary for essential coordinating functions—does not contribute to its host organization. Indeed, a bureaucracy's drain on resources and its excessive rule-making cripples the efficiency of its host. The only way to prevent an administrative group from growing into a bureaucracy is by denying it the money to hire more "administrators." In a market environment, where the organization's survival depends on its efficiency, managers are forced to pare expenses and contain the growth of bureaucracy.

But wherever organizations, private or public, are insulated from competition, there is little to stop the growth of bureaucracy. The bureaucracy becomes the noncompeting organization's tapeworm, consuming scarce resources and giving nothing back in return. Just as it is impossible for the human immune system to detect a tapeworm ensconced in the intestines, it seems impossible for organization leaders to distinguish clearly between necessary administration and damaging bureaucracy. When it comes to America's public schools, the wildly disproportionate growth in "administrative" spending over the last 30 years shows that the education bureaucracy has mushroomed into a massive parasite. It has absorbed immense quantities of public money, frustrated dedicated teachers, and destroyed the futures of millions of Americans.

Because America's public-education bureaucracy is so deeply entrenched and politically potent, the education reform campaign of the last few years has not directly challenged it. Until recently, reformers have limited themselves to changes that the bureaucracy can tolerate— more spending and more new programs to be administered. Teachers' salaries have been increased. Teacher competency exams have been instituted to weed out the very worst teachers. More money has been granted to establish computerized learning centers and "magnet" schools. Reading and mathematics remedial programs have been launched. Students are being tested more frequently and thoroughly to determine what they have learned. In many states, students now must demonstrate competence in basic skills before being granted a high-school diploma. All these reforms are helpful, but they do not strike the schools' disease at its source.[11]

For all the additional spending and new programs, improvement since the early 1980s has been slight. College-entrance-exam scores are up a bit, but they appear to be flattening out again. Dropout rates are higher than ever. Unmistakable signs of a dramatic recovery, indicators of the rapid progress so urgently needed, are nowhere to be found. Such a turnaround will remain elusive, because school reforms, like antitakeover laws, have addressed the symptoms of parasitism instead of the cause. If the parasitic bureaucracy that has infested America's public schools is to be expelled, its hook must be purged.[12]

The hook is the legal monopoly of America's public-school bureaucracies. Except for the 11 percent of children whose parents are wealthy enough to send them to private schools, American kids are subject to the monopoly power of their local school districts. Almost without exception, state laws grant each local school district an exclusive right to provide educational services to the children living within its geographic boundaries. Under penalty of law, children must attend the schools in their district. They must swallow the product their local school district dishes out, however unpalatable. For most, the only real option is dropping out—an arguably rational act for the hundreds of thousands condemned to the nation's worst schools.

Because state laws grant monopolies to each of America's 16,000 local school districts, these organizations do not compete with each other. Regardless of how badly it performs, no district faces the prospect of being put out of business. And even though hundreds of well-run school districts do exist, the problem is that high-quality school districts are exceptional. If the system were competitive rather than monopolistic, high-quality schools would be the norm.[13]

The only way to cure the parasitic infestation of the American public-school system is to sever the parasite from the student body at its point of attachment. Despite all the claims made for other remedies, no other reform can revive American public education. Students and parents, like shareholders, must be granted the power of choice. They must be transformed from captives into consumers. School districts, like all other efficient providers of service, must be forced to compete with each other for customers. The parasitic, involuntary relationship between school district and student must be converted into a mutualistic, voluntary relationship. If, and only if, this reform takes place will radical improvement in education quality occur.[14]

Remarkably, there is hope for real reform. One state, Minnesota, already has recognized that consumer choice and school-district competition are the keys to progress.[15] In May 1988, after a few years of experimentation, Minnesota's legislature passed a bill that stripped school districts of their monopoly power. Under the law, students are permitted to leave the school districts in which they live and apply for admission to another. The law does not *force* school districts to admit these "foreign" students, but once a school board decides that its schools have seats available for a given number of students, it cannot pick and choose among applicants. If too many students want too few spaces, a lottery determines which students "immigrate" into the district.

Traditionally, the state of Minnesota, like the other 49 states, automatically paid $3,600 directly to the resident school district of every child attending school. Now, the state's money travels with the student. The state funnels the money to whichever school district the student decides to attend. Simply by allowing students to emigrate and backing up their choices with state funds, Minnesota has utterly transformed the relationship between education producers and consumers.

In the new market environment, educational quality, as measured by the performance of students, ultimately will determine the survival of the organization running a school district. If a district fails to deliver a quality education, it will lose $3,600 each time a student transfers out. If the district's schools fail to improve, continuing emigration will force the district to close more and more of its facilities. Ineffective administrators and teachers will lose their jobs. On the other hand, school districts that produce a quality educational product will gain $3,600 with each new customer. If a district has classroom space available, the state's $3,600 is profitable revenue, since each extra student generates only a few hundred dollars in direct costs for books and supplies.

Districts that attract students can reinvest their "profits" however they see fit. Some will use the funds to create programs tailored to the special needs of student-customers. Others may boost salaries to recruit outstanding teachers. Whatever decisions are made, they will be driven by the desire to improve performance, because for the first time, job security and organizational survival will be linked directly to student performance. The incentive system that propels the responsiveness of private firms will be replicated in the public domain. Customer satisfaction will become the key to school-district survival.

In a society built on freedom of choice, the idea of school choice seems radical only because Americans have grown used to having no choice over their children's schools. But Dr. Ruth Randall, until recently Minnesota's Commissioner of Education, asks:

> Why shouldn't we be able to choose? We can choose our spouse, our church or synagogue or wherever we get our values from. We can choose where we live, our car, the food we eat. We can choose our preschool up to age five. We can choose our college after age 18. Why, between the ages of five and 18, should we not be allowed choice?[16]

In hearings before the Minnesota legislature, school administrators opposed choice largely on the grounds that it would harm minority students. They claimed that some minority students would get left behind in crumbling schools as others headed off to the best suburban districts. But, much to the administrators' embarrassment, black parents vigorously supported the idea of choice. They argued that while middle-class parents can afford to rescue their children by moving to tolerable suburban districts, they are left behind to endure the disastrous schools foisted on them by urban school-district bureaucracies. Without the power of consumer choice, they have no leverage over their local schools.

Because the implementation of Minnesota's "open-enrollment" plan is so recent, fully documented results will not be available for several years. But a few years earlier, Minnesota launched a trial program—the Secondary Options Program—which allows eleventh- and twelfth-grade high-school students to attend any public or private college in the state. Within months, Minnesota's Secondary Options Program unleashed all the evolutionary phenomena common to market environments—competition, cooperation, innovation, cost reduction, and specialization. Now, with choice becoming available at all grade levels in all public schools, these organic processes will take hold and utterly transform Minnesota's schools during the 1990s.[17]

When introduced in the state legislature, the Secondary Options Program was opposed vigorously by the most powerful groups in the state's education establishment—the Minnesota Education Association (the largest teachers' union), the Minnesota Association of School Administrators, and the Minnesota School Board Association. At first, they argued that thousands of kids would abandon their high schools for college. But only a small number of the eligible students actually shifted to colleges. The opposition then contended that the brightest kids would desert the high schools, leaving behind only the poor students.

But analysis showed that the top high-school students didn't move to the colleges. These kids were content where they were. Most transfers were among average students who weren't happy with their education. Opponents then argued that average kids should not be allowed to leave, because they would do terribly in college. But, despite the tendency of these students to select rigorous courses, they outperformed average Minnesota college freshmen. In fact, several hundred of the participating students were former dropouts who decided to return to school once they were given some control over their lives.

Threatened for the first time by competition from colleges, Minnesota's high schools didn't sit around waiting for students to desert them. Like organizations trying to survive in any market, the schools began offering what their customers had long said they wanted—more challenging courses. In just two years, the number of college-credit advanced-placement courses offered by Minnesota high schools quadrupled.[18] Several districts established new cooperative relationships with nearby universities to offer college-level courses inside the high schools.

Encouraged by these early signs of success, Minnesota Governor Rudy Perpich, the leader of the school-choice movement, set up an advisory panel to recommend legislation that would spread choice to every grade level and public school in the state. After a year and a half of negotiations, the advisory group hammered out draft legislation that sailed through both houses of the state legislature in early 1987. Under this law, school districts could, but did not have to, allow their students to emigrate. One year later, the legislature changed the law to mandate open enrollment for every school district by 1991.

The impact of the legislation was immediate. Ken Zastrow, former director of the Open Enrollment Program for Minnesota's Department of Education, recalled a conversation with the superintendent of a district in northern Minnesota just one month into the program. "Already I notice a difference at the school board meetings, and in our meetings with principals and teachers," the superintendent said. "For a long time, the board opposed spending any money on new programs. Now they say things like, 'Maybe we should get involved with that new early-childhood, family-education program [where mothers come to school with their babies for special classes]. Otherwise someone else is going to do it, and the kids are going to leave and go over to the other district. If we can get the parents involved early on, they'll be supportive of us.' " "You know," the superintendent commented, "those kinds of discussions weren't happening before."

As in the private market, Minnesota school districts are pursuing a strategy of specialization to minimize the impact of head-to-head competition. The "one-size-fits-all" school is beginning to be replaced by an array of alternatives. Some schools focus on "fundamentals," where basic skills are taught in a highly structured classroom setting. Others position themselves as "continuous-progress" schools, where students learn at their own pace using computers and programmed-learning texts. Certain schools emphasize strong math/science curricula, others specialize in classes for those "gifted and talented" in music and arts, and still others are built around the "open-classroom" concept. Individual students learn in different ways. Some teachers are more effective in one setting than in others. Choice stimulates variety and allows students and teachers to work in classrooms suited to their individual needs. The "take-it-or-leave-it" style of education-by-monopoly is vanishing in Minnesota.[19]

Fearing the loss of students to urban schools large enough to offer a variety of special courses, small rural districts are beginning to cooperate. In one case, two districts have agreed that one district will manage all the elementary schools while the other handles the junior highs. By combining student populations, they will be large enough to offer a broad range of courses. Like small companies that merge to achieve competitive size, school districts are finding ways to make better use of limited resources. Over time, they will move people out of redundant administrative jobs and devote the savings to programs that improve student performance.

Open enrollment is also beginning to reshape Minnesota's housing market. Before choice, the purchase of a home was linked to the selection of a school system. Now the housing and school decisions are unbundled. Price differentials are disappearing between identical homes on opposite sides of a school-district boundary. A family that likes a neighborhood, but doesn't like the local schools, isn't forced to move to a high-price neighborhood for the well-being of the children. The implications for neighborhood and school desegregation are far-reaching.

"White flight" is the result of both racism and the fear of poor urban schools. School choice empowers minority parents to demand real improvements. Unless the worst urban school districts reform, their students will abandon them. As urban school quality improves, there will be less motivation for whites to transfer to suburban districts. White families may decide not to flee the cities, and neighborhoods will not become as segregated. Perhaps the historical lack of school choice has been an unrecognized factor in the vicious cycle of white flight and forced school busing. If so, school choice may well do more to encourage the voluntary reintegration of America's cities than any other conceivable program.

Ironically, the Minnesota teachers' union, which strenuously fought against choice, now sees possible benefits in what is taking place. A lobbyist for the Minnesota Education Association said, "We are starting to see it as a teacher empowerment bill. You can't really talk about improving schools if it doesn't matter what the labor force does. Now, the superintendent and principal are the most threatened if a large number of students opt to leave a district or a school. Teacher input will be much greater to avert or stem such a flow." Just as competition forces firms to listen to their skilled employees, choice is causing power to shift from the bureaucrats to the teachers.[20]

Now that most of those who opposed choice are busy adjusting to the realities of the market, a new and unexpected source of opposition is springing up. Some wealthy parents who have been sending their kids to expensive private schools are pulling them out and registering them in public schools. In some cases, these kids take the demanding courses now available in the public high schools. In others, they transfer into colleges. Either way, it's free.

Minnesota's Roman Catholic schools also are witnessing a decline in enrollments as neighboring public schools boost their quality. In effect, the monopoly that created awful public schools simultaneously enlarged the market for high-quality private and parochial schools. Now that the public schools have lost their monopoly power and are turning into effective competitors, the private/parochial-school market is shrinking. Not long ago, the archbishop of Minneapolis telephoned Governor Perpich and complained, "This is not good. Can't you find some way to make our schools eligible for open enrollment?"

These dynamics show that the conflict between public and private, which plagues so much of America's political discourse, is entirely misplaced. The issue isn't public versus private; it's choice versus lack of choice. It's a struggle between economic relationships founded on voluntary association and relationships based upon legal coercion. As soon as the power of consumer choice is injected into the domain of publicly provided goods, public solutions to social problems acquire the best characteristics of the private market.[21]

Lacking a "hook," an organization—public or private—must behave as an efficient mutualist. It must control the inexorable tendency of necessary administration to turn into parasitic bureaucracy. Conversely, any organization that has a hook inevitably will be infected by the bureaucracy parasite, wasting scarce economic resources. Parasitic private corpocracies and public bureaucracies flourish wherever effective choice is denied to their hosts, whether those hosts are shareholders attempting to grow financial capital or students trying to acquire human capital.

The concept of public-school choice is just beginning to catch on.[22] But Dan Loritz, Governor Perpich's aide, says that although the concept is incredibly simple, it's difficult to get across:

> The rest of the country doesn't yet understand what we've done. They think choice is always private. They have it confused with magnet schools or vouchers or whatever. They don't understand that the districts are sovereign on the way in. Districts can choose to accept nobody, or take a hundred. But they can't discriminate among those trying to get into their district. We don't promise students they can get in anywhere. But the districts can't stop them from leaving.

Governor Perpich compares the traditional American school-district monopoly to the emigration policies of the Soviet Union—it's forbidden. The people simply have to accept the situation as it is, like it or not. Dan Loritz says,

We don't expect a lot of students to switch districts. Just because the boundaries of the United States are open, we don't expect everyone to leave. They just feel better knowing that they can. And there's a reason for people who want to provide services to them to do a good job so they won't leave, instead of relying on a law so they can't get out.

By surgically removing the monopoly's hook, Minnesota has taken the crucial reform step. Follow-on measures already underway will enhance the ability of students and parents to use their consumer power intelligently. The Minnesota Department of Education plans to publish school-by-school, grade-by-grade statistics reporting student performance levels. Parents and students will be able to judge from these "consumer reports" which schools merit their patronage.

Minnesota's schools will not be revolutionized overnight. Thoroughgoing institutional reform takes time. But, by establishing a marketlike environment, profound change at the grass roots becomes inevitable. Freed from the bureaucracy's hook, the state's education consumers will demand and get a radical improvement in the quality and variety of public-school offerings.

Progress will cost money, but most of it won't come from higher spending. As in other well-managed, intelligent organizations, the learning curve will allow more to be accomplished with the same resources. Consolidations, reorganizations, school closures, and new cooperatives will hack away at previously impervious layers of bureaucracy. Savings recovered through reduced waste will fund quality improvements. As they struggle to protect their jobs in an environment that permits organization death, capable teachers and administrators will gain the upper hand against their inept colleagues. School-by-school and classroom-by-classroom, the able will force out the incompetent. As the results of thousands of microscopic decisions accumulate, true reform will unfold.

If only one system in American society can be rescued from the depredations of bureaucratic parasitism, it must be the public-education system. Unless America's 16,000 public-school districts are forced to rid themselves of their bloated bureaucratic parasites, Americans will not be able to compete for decent jobs in the twenty-first century's global economy.

The damage already done by the education bureaucracy must run into the trillions of dollars in forgone economic growth. Because this parasite has so grievously damaged America's most vital resource, its costs dwarf even those caused by corpocracy. Revamping the public schools must be America's number-one economic and social priority. Unless this monopoly is eradicated, the nation will not rebound from its slide into economic and political oblivion.

As dismal as America's public-school situation is at present, there is hope. Our democracy works. In their 1989 conference on school reform, the president and the governors declared school choice to be one of their key objectives. Minnesota has shown the way and its success will inspire others. Massachusetts, Colorado, Wisconsin, and California already are in the process of switching to schools-by-choice.[23]

From their daily experience with the cornucopia of quality goods and services provided by the private sector, the American people know the power of choice and competition. It may well prove impossible to build public support for the reforms needed to purge the corpocracies infesting our largest corporations. Few voters can be rallied to demand arcane amendments to corporate governance procedures. But the American people are more than ready for meaningful school reform. Recent polls show that 60 percent of Americans support the concept of school choice. Despite its awesome political clout, the education bureaucracy soon will be overwhelmed by an exasperated public.[24]

PART VIII

■

MUTUALISM AND COOPERATION

■

All men are interdependent. Every nation
is an heir to a vast treasury of ideas and labor
to which both the living and the dead
of all nations have contributed.
—*Martin Luther King, Jr. (1967)*[1]

PART VIII

MUTUALISM AND COOPERATION

28

SOVIET CAPITALISM

merica's private corpocracies and public-school bureaucracies have leeched away so much potential wealth and blighted the futures of so many children that the full cost to society is incalculable. But, as massive as the losses to these organizational parasites have been, imagine a society where all economic activities are controlled by monopolies, a society where each monopoly is part of one gargantuan "ultramonopoly." Imagine the staggering waste of human potential and natural resources, the stagnation and lack of technological innovation. And, finally, imagine a society where the absence of political choice forecloses even the possibility of purging the ultramonopoly's hook.

Ironically, the Soviet Union's thoroughly parasitic economy is the inevitable consequence of an economic theory intended to eradicate economic parasitism. In essence, Marxism was based on the principle that profit is evil because it can be made only by exploiting workers. In keeping with the zero-sum mentality of the preindustrial era, Marx believed that every gain must come from someone else's loss.[2]

Entrepreneurs, owners, and inventors (all "capitalists") contribute nothing; they simply steal the "surplus value" created by laborers. For Marx, those not actually engaged in physical labor were society's parasites. This contradicts the bionomic view of capitalism, which sees value created through the voluntary collaboration of efficient, specialized mutualists—a system where parasites persist only when monopoly power blocks competition and market choice.

By branding profit—the North Star of capitalism—as inherently evil, Marx captured the "moral high ground" in what became a century-long struggle between socialism and capitalism. Marx's belief that all profit was "expropriated" from laborers became socialism's moral touchstone. To this day, even for millions who have never regarded themselves as socialists, profit remains a dirty word. No decent human being can condone an economic system based on extortion.

In the first decades of the Industrial Revolution, when Karl Marx made his observations, excessive profit was squeezed from powerless workers and peasants. Marx's great error was to assume that such exploitation was the *only* way to make profits. Given the "zero-sum" outlook of his era, this was a logical conclusion. Marx never imagined the existence of a "positive-sum" process, where the whole is worth more than the sum of its parts—a phenomenon where value is created by the cooperation of diverse economic specialists. The biological concept of mutualism—also called "symbiosis"—was unknown in Marx's day.[3]

Marx could not have described profit as a flow of surplus economic energy whose reinvestment creates new information. He could not have explained profit as the reward for organizational learning. He could not have imagined profit as a positive-feedback signal transmitted to a firm through its network of ecological relationships. Biology had yet to construct this vocabulary of ideas.

By defining profit as the result of unconscionable behavior, Marx turned his economic analysis into a moral crusade. The problem with crusades, of course, is that when they triumph, their principles must be carried out. A society founded on the notion that profit is evil must redesign itself to expunge the possibility of profit. Anything less would be reprehensible.

In practical terms, the only way to eliminate profit-making is by forbidding market transactions altogether. Otherwise, buyers and sellers will spontaneously seek each other out to make mutually profitable exchanges. To implement Marxist thought, buying and selling must be made criminal acts.

This is precisely what the Communists did after the 1917 Russian Revolution. They abolished private property and outlawed private transactions. By decree, they turned all markets into black markets. But, of course, the production and distribution of food, clothing, housing, and machinery still had to take place. So the Soviets vested their economic planners with the legal power to decide the price of every single item— from baby shoes to steel mills.

Since "fair" transfer prices were set by state decree, production quantities also had to be mandated by the planners. Otherwise, shortages would appear whenever prices were mistakenly set below actual costs.

By centralizing decision-making over all prices and production, the state consolidated virtually all economic power.

A market economy is democratic. Economic power resides in no single place. Decision-making authority is diffuse. Individuals and firms react to news of the latest prices at which other buyers and sellers have made similar trades. Economic power is atomized. No one controls; everyone responds.

By choking off the thousands of natural feedback loops that markets represent, Lenin and Stalin vested awesome power in the state. They fashioned the single most powerful parasitic "hook" in the history of the human economy. Once this hook was embedded in the Soviet people, the growth of a massive bureaucracy was a foregone conclusion. The Soviet people became the host of a parasitic organization more devastating than the worst exploitation experienced under capitalism.

For nearly seven decades, this bureaucracy has run the Soviet Union from top to bottom. Its powers are so pervasive, its control over daily life so total, that even in a period of great change, few Soviets can even imagine life without it. The bureaucracy is so central to Soviet society that a special term applies to its top officials—the *nomenklatura*. In biology, the nomenclature is the list of Latin species names. In the Soviet Union, the *nomenklatura* is the list of all the key jobs in the bureaucracy. Of the Soviet Unions 17 million administrators (15 percent of the workforce), the top 750,000 positions are considered part of the *nomenklatura*.[4] Of these, the highest-ranking 250,000 officials wield all-important power. The next 500,000 exercise limited authority in specific fields. These people are the factory directors, scientists, and regional authorities who wield day-to-day control over Soviet life. Virtually all of them are members of the Communist party. Together, these 750,000 officials and their families comprise the three million members of the Soviet elite, slightly more than 1 percent of the population.

Members of the *nomenklatura* are paid handsomely to do what markets do for free. They enjoy the highest salaries, the best apartments, free vacation homes, chauffeur-driven government cars, and special railcars, as well as VIP treatment at airports, resorts, and hospitals that are off-limits to average Soviets. Their children attend elite schools. Top bureaucrats collect "invisible earnings"—fees from books, articles, and lectures—and enjoy access to fine foods and foreign goods in special shops, restaurants, and bars closed to the Soviet public.[5]

While the *nomenklatura* luxuriate, average Soviet citizens cannot find meat, butter, or sugar in the shops. In the world's only "classless" society, the *nomenklatura* is the ultimate parasitic class. During the cold war, the Soviets cloned their bureaucracy throughout Eastern Europe, where information about the opulent lifestyles of top officials was kept secret. In the days after the Berlin Wall fell, reports of the hunting lodges and lavish homes enjoyed by top bureaucrats stunned and enraged the people. Referring to the Communist creed of strict egalitarianism, one East German worker said, "They were preaching water and drinking wine."[6]

The *nomenklatura*'s stranglehold was not consolidated until years after the Russian Revolution. In the mid-1920s, when the economy faltered, Lenin backed away from blind pursuit of Marxist ideology, but when Stalin took power, he crushed these market-oriented reforms and perfected the modern Soviet system of centralized economic control. But Stalin's handiwork was disrupted by the devastation of World War II, so it wasn't until the 1950s that the *nomenklatura* tightened its grip on the Soviet economy.

For a time, it looked as if the Soviet's centralized system worked rather well. The *nomenklatura* organized the postwar reconstruction of the Soviet Union, launched Sputnik, and put the first man into orbit. In 1959, when Nikita Khrushchev vowed to overtake the United States economically, his threat was taken seriously. Many Western economists believed that a centrally planned economy was inherently more efficient than the chaos of capitalism.[7]

But, on reflection, the achievements of the Soviet *nomenklatura* should not have been so surprising. Despite their flaws, gigantic monopolies are capable of getting some things done. The U.S. Department of Defense— perhaps America's single most wasteful bureaucracy—builds aircraft that fly and ships that float. The Postal Service almost always delivers mail to correct addresses. It's just that these organizations are woefully inefficient. They consume far more of society's scarce resources than they return in value produced.[8]

The Achilles heel of a bureaucratically controlled economy was not exposed until the 1970s microelectronics revolution kicked the pace of technological evolution into overdrive. Change and innovation undermine the stability that bureaucrats crave. Instead of rewarding innovators, bureaucrats strangle them with rules, regulations, and red tape. Any shift in established procedures threatens the "turf" of the bureaucrat involved. Consequently, bureaucrats actively resist any modification to existing methods. This is why—despite an enormous pool of talented scientists and engineers—the Soviet economic monolith has been so pitifully incompetent at developing high-technology goods and services.

By its very nature, economic evolution—particularly in the Information Age—is incompatible with the top-down "command-and-control" system erected by Stalin. Once the microprocessor demolished the cost of information processing, the hierarchical organizations erected in the first decades of the twentieth century became ponderous economic dinosaurs. An organization's agility and intelligence became more important to its economic survival than did its size and strength.[9]

Learning from experience—constantly tinkering with existing processes—is stymied when an organization's most powerful officials try to prevent change at all costs. An economy dominated by a vast parasitic organization simply cannot keep pace with an economic ecosystem composed of fiercely competitive, highly specialized mutualists. It was this objective reality—the *nomenklatura*'s utter inability to cope with the demands of a rapidly evolving Information Age economy—that gave Mikhail Gorbachev's reformist faction the chance to take power from the Kremlin's far-Left conservative ideologues.[10]

Glasnost and *perestroika*, Gorbachev's twin campaigns for political reform and economic restructuring, were intended to reinvigorate Soviet society. Under *glasnost*, press freedom was broadened and most political prisoners were released. In 1989, the first partially democratic elections were held. And in 1990, the Communist party's Central Committee renounced its constitutional monopoly on political power. By any measure, this period witnessed a stunning political transformation.

But, tragically, the first five years of Gorbachev's economic reforms were wasted. The remedies offered under *perestroika* were all too reminiscent of the ill-conceived, superficial "reforms" of America's corporations and schools. Spotty, partial measures confused an increasingly desperate economic situation. By Gorbachev's own admission, the Soviet economy was in much worse shape in 1990 than when he came to power.

Five years of *perestroika* attacked symptoms of the economy's disease but left the parasite's "hook" unmolested. At first, Gorbachev tried to fix the economy by replacing "bad" old bureaucrats with "good" new bureaucrats. But, of course, the real problem was monopoly power itself the corrupting influence of unchallengeable authority—not the quality of the people who filled slots in that system.

In fact, as individuals, the highest-ranking members of the Soviet *nomenklatura* are among the most talented and well-educated people in the world. In a society where all opportunity for personal advancement has been centralized for 70 years, a great many gifted people naturally decided to spend their careers climbing society's only power structure. It was the only game in town.[11]

Had these individuals grown up in a competitive, capitalist society, many would have risen to the top of their professions. They would have

MUTUALISM AND COOPERATION

acquired the skills demanded by profit-making enterprises. But the *no-menklatura* was not shaped by such a professional experience. And, regardless of their native abilities, once these people became functionaries inside the parasitic apparatus, they did what all rational bureaucrats do—they protected their personal positions by defending their power, the power of the *nomenklatura*.[12]

Again and again, Gorbachev condemned the bureaucracy, calling it the single greatest threat to economic reform. For a while, he even tried to cut the size of the *nomenklatura*.[13] But, as anyone who has ever worked in a bureaucracy could have predicted, new people soon were hired to replace those purged. Any bureaucrat worth his salt can come up with a persuasive justification for increasing his "overworked staff." After all, bureaucrats gauge their power by the number of bodies and budget authority they command. High cost, not high output, is the barometer of success.

In a civilized world, normal human beings seek security for themselves and their families by accumulating power and wealth. It is the survival instinct in action. Capitalism implicitly recognizes this fact of human nature and compels businesspeople to choose between these immutable goals. The corporate manager who increases his personal power by building a bureaucratic empire is likely to demolish his organization's profits and lose his job. The entrepreneur who fritters away resources on self-glorification will lose her investment. In effect, capitalism relies on greed to counterbalance megalomania.

Without the lure of profits and the fear of losses, there is no disciplinary force to restrain bureaucratic growth. In a hotly competitive environment, where cost reduction is the only sure route to profits and survival, staff growth is considered an evil. Organizations that face no competitors or need not at least balance their budgets have no compelling reason to contain the growth of internal organizational parasites. Without natural selection, organizations weakened by parasitic infections are not weeded out. Without the requirement that "value produced" exceed "resources consumed," all economic self-control breaks down.

If the *nomenklatura*'s monopoly hook were excised, with managers and workers suddenly finding themselves in a market system, the impenetrable Soviet bureaucracy would begin to wither away. For example, if the Soviet steel ministry were sliced into a half-dozen competitive steel firms and employees were allowed to earn cheap stock in their new firms, previously impossible improvements in cost, quality, and productivity suddenly would materialize. Fearing bankruptcy but drawn by the promise of wealth, the competent and hard-working people in each firm would evict the incompetent and lazy. Under new ecological conditions, a vast parasite impervious to mandates from above would spontaneously transform itself into a population of efficient mutualists.[14]

But, so far, the Soviets have made none of the essential reforms. As it enters the 1990s, the Soviet economy—bled dry by the *nomenklatura*—staggers toward collapse. With the parasite's hook still firmly embedded, the world's most powerful economic tapeworm persists. Unless its hook is purged, *perestroika* will go nowhere. And, having failed to revive the Soviet economy, Gorbachev and his reform-minded allies will be forced to give the Marxist conservatives another chance to fix things their way—through more central planning.

Such a turnabout already may have occurred. In December 1989, the Soviet leadership announced economic policies that undercut *perestroika*'s superficial reforms. The new "five-year plan" called for tighter economic control by Moscow's ministries and postponed tentative plans for price decontrol. In short, the prescription was another dose of the same disease.[15]

Clamping down may defer the inevitable, but sooner or later, the Soviet economy will grind to a standstill. The *nomenklatura* will have made the classic parasite error—killing off the host. Extreme shortages of food and fuel will set the stage for a popular revolution.

From Beijing to Berlin, the stunning events of 1989 showed that the unimaginable can happen. But even an optimist must conclude that the prospects are poor for a peaceful Soviet transition to democratic capitalism. Gorbachev repeatedly has rejected all suggestions that Marxism be jettisoned. His avowed goal is to reform socialism, not destroy it. He wants "market socialism," not capitalism.[16]

But "market socialism" is a contradiction in terms. There is no "third way" between socialism and capitalism. Socialism is an ideology. Capitalism is a natural phenomenon. The closest thing to a hybrid—a market economy equipped with a social safety net—is still capitalism. Indeed, the "market" is the epitome of capitalism. Karl Marx never could have imagined the words *market* and *socialism* next to each other on a printed page.[17]

Parasitic state socialism and mutualistic market capitalism cannot coexist in the same society. Laws that compel organizations to fend for themselves as productive mutualists cannot be reconciled with laws that create parasitic hooks. In the end, a society must choose.[18]

Stripped of all the brave talk and empty gestures, this is the crux of the Soviet dilemma. Going ahead with genuine economic reform—free prices and private property—means the end of the *nomenklatura* and of Marxism. For Gorbachev, who derives his power not from the people but from supporters in the *nomenklatura*, this is political suicide. But failing to carry out true economic reforms ultimately will lead to a revolutionary situation. In a popular uprising, the people will violently purge their parasite.

Should the Soviet Union slip into the vortex of social disorder, a desperate faction within the *nomenklatura* might well use the military to lash out at the West. "Foreign devils" always have served as convenient targets for leaders trying to divert attention from internal crises. In the worst possible scenario, even "mutually assured destruction" might not be enough to prevent a rogue attack from somewhere within a disintegrating Soviet military command structure.[19]

Although outsiders can do little to affect the outcome, the whole world's fate hinges on the success of peaceful reform inside the Soviet Union. And, in view of the potential for disaster if Soviet reforms fail, the United States and its allies must do whatever they can to improve the odds, however slightly, in favor of a peaceful transition. But, as always, the question for policy-makers is How?

Above all, we must make clear our ultimate objective—that the Soviet Union should join the other major world powers as a prosperous capitalist democracy. We must explain why free elections, free prices, and private property are essential to all peaceful, progressive societies. We must explain why mutualistic capitalism works and why parasitic socialism unavoidably grows from state monopoly power.

Second, the West should strike a new bargain with the Soviets. If the Soviets commit themselves to truly free elections, free prices, and private property, the West must commit itself to an unprecedented package of economic assistance. In short, we should commit ourselves to a post–cold war Marshall Plan even before strategic disarmament is completed.

Western economic aid for the Soviet Union must focus on two primary goals: (1) Buffer the initial shocks of change; (2) help private enterprise reconstruct the Soviet economy. In the days immediately after price decontrol, the Soviets' most severe problem will be hyperinflation. Since Soviet shops have stocked nothing worth buying, Soviet consumers have socked away a massive hoard of paper money. When prices are allowed to find their own level, the "ruble overhang" will be chasing an extremely limited pool of consumer goods. Prices will skyrocket.[20]

But if the West inundated the Soviet Union with food and consumer goods just before price controls were lifted, the first surge of inflation could be muffled. The psychology of runaway inflation could be broken before it built momentum. For four or five years—roughly the time it would take before domestic Soviet factories and farms could come on line with reasonable quantities of consumer goods—Western producers could easily fill the demand gap. Soviet consumers should not be protected indefinitely from the reality of market prices. But, during the wildest phase of the transition, the prices of consumer necessities—meat, butter, oranges, coffee, soap, razor blades, winter boots, and the like— could be suppressed artificially by a massive flood of imports.

For the United States to take the lead in such a policy would require a dramatic reversal of traditional American political attitudes. For the tide of American exports to reach the Soviet people fast enough, U.S. banks would have to extend credit to private businesses in the Soviet Union. Direct loans to the Soviet government would only strengthen the *nomenklatura*. But for American banks to make loans to upstart Soviet capitalists, a portion of the inherent risk must be borne by the U.S. government. In effect, American taxpayers would be cosigning part of a consumer loan to the Soviet people.

Such a guarantee would not require a budgetary expenditure. Like "Ginnie Mae" and "Sallie Mae"—the federally backed guarantee programs for home mortgages and student loans—an "Ivan Mae" would be an off-budget item. In a time of severe budget constraints, no other type of significant U.S. commitment is feasible.

If the Soviets repay their loans, the cost to American taxpayers would be zero. If, on the other hand, some Soviets default, the American people pick up the tab for a Soviet buying spree. In view of the shaky financial condition of the American government, it may seem crazy to take on a potentially massive debt so citizens of an adversary power can buy butter and blue jeans. But the United States has no more important goal than bringing the cold war to a quick, nonviolent conclusion. Achieving this result, in the face of imminent social revolution in the Soviet Union, demands that America rapidly shift its strategy from reliance on its military might to the deployment of its economic power.

The pundits will undoubtedly agree with each other that such strategic agility is impossible, but then again, none of them predicted 1989's collapse of communism. The breaching of the Berlin Wall symbolized a fundamental shift in the world's strategic situation, but it did not eliminate the risk of war. The threat of nuclear annihilation will not disappear until the Soviets have turned to democratic capitalism. The "peace dividend" cannot become a reality until most Americans are absolutely convinced that the Soviet threat has been eradicated permanently. Only genuine peace will allow the U.S. government to balance its budget and begin long-neglected reinvestments in America's future.

Financially, if for no other reason, this logic supports the idea of federally backed loans to private Soviet businesses. The losses on bad loans would be more than offset by the prospect of an accelerated reduction in U.S. defense spending. Each year, the U.S. spends $300 billion, or 6 percent of its GNP, on the military. Approximately $150 billion of that is spent just keeping American forces in Western Europe. If the Soviet threat vanished, roughly $200 billion a year could be saved. In five years, the United States could save $1 trillion, one-third of the total federal debt. With such potentially gargantuan savings, it would be folly *not* to extend credit to a Soviet Union converting to democratic capitalism.

Over five years, if the Soviets borrowed as much as $300 billion—half of it federally guaranteed—they could buy more than $1,000 worth of goods for every man, woman, and child. For Soviet consumers, the infusion of $1,000 of Western goods would mean a major step up in their standard of living. Western economists often argue that the Soviet people must endure rigorous austerity before they can get to the promised land of capitalist prosperity. But the last thing the Soviet people need right now is more hardship. They need a taste of "the good life" to whet their appetites and win their support for what will be wrenching changes in their way of life.

With few exceptions, the Soviet leadership has opposed buying consumer goods on credit. Other than their vast purchases of wheat, they have used their hard currency to purchase machines for factories. But much of this equipment is said to be sitting in storage, waiting to be installed. As usual, the *nomenklatura* has proved itself incapable of utilizing scarce resources. To get through the period before market forces begin to generate huge jumps in output, the Soviet government must buy time by making consumer goods available.

Fortunately, the Soviet Union carries one of the lowest per-capita debt burdens in the world. With the rapid economic growth that would follow genuine reform, the Soviets could easily handle the payments. But they must make it through the turmoil of radical change. Eventually, they must become world-class economic competitors. Even though the United States already faces intense competition from Japan, East Asia, and a unifying Europe, America will be far better off with the Soviets as serious economic rivals than as aggressive military adversaries.[21]

Less than five years after the Soviets legalize capitalism, their economy would be back on its feet and growing fast. In ten years, it would be utterly transformed. Within 20 years, the Soviet standard of living could approach current Western levels. Along with fabulous natural resources, the Soviets have legions of well-educated people. Their scientists are world leaders in many fields. If the Soviet people are given a genuine opportunity to improve their lives, their long-suppressed ambitions will sustain productivity increases undreamed-of by Moscow's economic planners.

By eliminating trade restrictions; welcoming the Soviets to international trade and banking organizations; and providing technical assistance in setting up stock markets, business schools, and the other features of a modern capitalist system, the United States could make a major contribution to the long-term progress of the Soviet economy. But none of these long-term measures will be of any use if the Soviets keep putting off the switch to free prices and private property.[22]

Unless the true nature of the Soviets' economic disease is understood, we will fail to deploy our vast wealth in ways that encourage meaningful economic reform. Unless we commit ourselves to helping the Soviets through the turmoil that will accompany such radical change, they will most certainly slip into the abyss of anarchy. To be honest, it probably already is too late to avert such a catastrophe. But it would be unforgivably irresponsible not to try.

CHAPTER
29

GLOBAL COEVOLUTION

S ocial scientists often grumble about the impossibility of conducting experiments. But the cold war's nuclear standoff allowed history's grandest economic experiment to run virtually undisturbed for five decades. Isolated by the "Iron Curtain," capitalism and socialism ran side by side. The West was the "control group," a natural, unplanned economy that went on pretty much as before. The East was the "experimental group," where Marxist economic theory was imposed by law. By the mid-1980s, the results were clear even to the most fervent socialists.

From an experiment of such staggering cost, one would hope that knowledge of even greater value was extracted. But, to this day, not one expert seems able to explain precisely why socialism collapsed and capitalism flourished. For hardheaded pragmatists, knowing *why* isn't important. That capitalism "won" is good enough.

But unless we understand why capitalism works, we will never be able to make the most of it. We will continue to pursue public policies that fly in the face of immutable economic processes. Prosperity that would lift burdens and brighten lives will be delayed needlessly. Worst of all, unless we can explain the hidden patterns of economic life, the zealots of some future generation will feel compelled to run society through this dreadful exercise yet again.

Simply put, capitalism has been impossible to comprehend because we have continued to stare at it from the wrong angle. Two centuries of economic thought, both capitalist and socialist, conditioned us to accept blindly the notion of "economy as machine." Long after physicists jettisoned Isaac Newton's conception of the universe, orthodox econ-

334 ·

omists still envision the economy as a predictable clockwork mechanism where historical change is irrelevant because all movement is cyclical.

But even the most casual observer knows that the economy is a system where history matters. Spectacularly complex and often swept by turbulent change, the human economy could hardly be more different than the stately model Newton created to predict planetary orbits. But, for lack of a convincing alternative, economists stuck to the familiar.[1]

It wasn't until the middle of the twentieth century—after DNA was discovered and its code was cracked—that biology attained the status of a science worth emulating. Bolstered by stunning breakthroughs in cellular biology, molecular biology, paleontology, and ecology, biology moved to the front rank of science by the 1970s. For the first time, it was possible to completely rethink economics, using the new discoveries of biology as a guide. The paradigm of the "economy as a cyclical machine" at last could be discarded. In its place, one could imagine the "economy as an evolving ecosystem."

Bionomics is the branch of ecology that examines the economic relations between organisms and their environment. As such, bionomics provides the best starting point for a new way of thinking about the human economy. Cutting through the mind-boggling complexity of the ecosystem, the bionomic perspective illuminates the interplay of forces that maintain stability while spawning change. Problems beyond the reach of orthodox economics are readily understood from the bionomic perspective.

For example, although the advance of knowledge propels economic change, the equilibrium models of conventional economics ignore this process. But, as the study of biology makes clear, understanding how information changes is the key to understanding life itself. Consequently, explaining how technological information evolves is central to the bionomic view of economics. What is extraneous to orthodox economics is the very essence of bionomics.

Bionomics describes the ecosystem and the economy as separate, parallel domains of evolving information. Genetic information, recorded in the DNA molecule, is the basis of all organic life. Technical information, captured in books, blueprints, scientific journals, databases, and the know-how of millions of individuals, is the source of all economic life. Over time, genetic variation and natural selection—phenomena similar to technical innovation and market competition—yield the pulsating rhythm of evolutionary change. In both biology and economics, long periods of information stability are punctuated by bursts of change.

As mankind's ability to copy and communicate information improved—first with Gutenberg's invention of the printing press and more recently with the creation of the computer—the accumulation of scientific knowledge quickened and then accelerated again. Today, a staggering profusion of organizations—from supermarkets to microchip makers to chicken-egg farms—use discrete pieces of this vast body of technical knowledge to turn raw materials into products that satisfy human needs.

Since these organizations cannot dictate their competitors' prices, they must cut costs to achieve a reliable margin of profit. As an organization accumulates production experience, it uncovers subtle new ways of avoiding waste and trimming costs. Profits—the savings achieved through learning—are reinvested to turn these new methods into productive technology. Over time, organizational learning expands the stockpile of technology, reduces real costs, and raises living standards. In a world of fixed resources, learning allows the economic pie to keep growing. Economic growth is limited only by human creativity.

Unrelenting competition for limited resources compels every life-form to become more specialized, to develop a particular way of getting by that only a few direct competitors can match. The attempt to escape head-on competition—in the wild and in the marketplace—leads to diversity, which, in turn, leads to interdependence. Mutualistic relationships—like that between the bumblebee hive and the flowering plant—also are commonplace in the economy, where the vast majority of affiliations are based upon mutual gain. Together, the twin phenomena of competition and cooperation have produced the diversity and abundance of the earth's ecosystem as well as the variety and productivity of the global market economy.

Remarkably, neither the global ecosystem nor the global economy needs a conscious force to keep it organized. A spontaneous order emerges from the interactions of each system's component parts. From the interplay of hormones in the human body to the expansions and contractions of the great arctic caribou herds, nature's intricately linked feedback loops automatically maintain a delicate yet robust balance. Free markets perform the same function in the economy. Without central planning, self-interested buyers and sellers adjust constantly to shifting prices for commodities, capital, and labor.

Whenever these natural feedback loops are blocked, inefficiencies inevitably result. For example, if a firm is granted a monopoly, it no longer faces the harsh discipline of the market. The firm's costs can exceed the value it produces without threatening its survival. Instead of adding value, a protected firm siphons value from the rest of the economy to subsidize its inefficiencies. Whether public or private, such parasitic organizations resume efficient, mutualistic behavior only if market feedback loops are restored.

As the twentieth century unfolded, the evolution of technology did more than just transform the original parasitic relationship between capital and labor. In the 1980s, we were stunned by the quickening pace of change. In short order, the VCR, microwave oven, satellite TV, cellular phone, and personal computer—all offspring of the microchip—wove themselves into our daily routines. Major industries lost center stage to newcomers that seemed to spring from thin air. Satellites, jumbo jets, faxes, container ships, and fiber optics transfigured the distant trading partners of the 1950s into the inextricably interdependent neighbors of the 1980s. For the first time, the "global village" began to feel real.[2]

Every day, three million people flit across continents and oceans by air. Bitter enemies find themselves linked by satellite for televised debates held for the amusement and education of the public. Japanese car dealers in the United States now use satellite dishes to transmit daily sales data to the factory back in Tokyo. Wired into a global nervous system by phones, data lines, and computer screens, traders in Tokyo, New York, London, and Frankfurt monitor capitalism's chaotic pulses in a never-ending vigil for profit.[3]

Soon the nations of Europe will form a single trade zone. Day by day, joint ventures, partnerships, and technology licensing agreements are weaving American, European, and Asian firms into ever more-intimate interdependence. Today's cutting-edge products are "world products," embodying the skills of people throughout the global village. Like the organisms and species that make up the global ecosystem, the world's firms and industries have spontaneously coevolved to form a vast living system.[4]

However, none of this is to say that the citizens of every capitalist nation are equally prepared for life in the global economy. Although the Western economies melded into a single economic entity during the cold-war era, these countries did not pursue identical economic policies. In Western Europe and to a lesser extent in the United States, heavy regulation, confiscatory income taxes, and nationalization of key industries significantly slowed growth. But even where socialist parties held power, capitalism never was rooted out. Throughout the West, private property and free prices remained the rule rather than the exception.

And, after experiencing the stagnation brought on by excessive government intervention, voters changed their minds and began electing pro-market candidates. In the 1980s, deregulation, lower tax rates, and privatization helped revive growth. The United States, Canada, Great Britain, France, Spain, and most recently Sweden—the archetypal welfare state—began to reverse long-standing policies. Well before state socialism imploded in Eastern Europe, most Western nations had turned back from their detours through diluted socialism.[5]

Crucial to this basic redirection was the explosive growth of Japan, South Korea, Taiwan, Hong Kong, and Singapore. For the United States and Western Europe, the threat of being overtaken by a more potent form of capitalism replaced that of being surpassed by socialism. During the first gigantic growth pulse of the microelectronics revolution, Japan employed a brilliant learning-curve strategy to catapult itself to global economic leadership. Today, only in sheer size does America's economy still lead the world. By virtually every other vital measure—income per person, education, savings, investment, nondefense R&D, and technically skilled population—Japan outdistances the United States and is pulling away.[6]

While some analysts still point to the Japanese government's industrial planning as the key to the country's dramatic upsurge, such conclusions miss the mark. The real story is simpler. Karl Marx's anticapitalist dogma never was absorbed by the Japanese. Government officials never saw their business counterparts as "enemies of the people." The bitterness so typical of government/business relations in the United States and Western Europe was unknown. Instead, Japan's government took responsibility for creating a supportive business environment.

Japan's government tried—and often failed—to manage the development of specific industries. In some cases, such as semiconductors, it succeeded brilliantly. But overall, the Japanese government's stimulation of broad social investments was far more effective than its narrow industry interventions. By redoubling investment in education and information technologies just as the microprocessor kicked the Information Age into fast-forward, Japan rocketed past every other major economy.

For Americans, the contrast to the incoherent and self-defeating "industrial policy" of the United States is chilling. The federal government taxes earnings and savings, but not consumption. In the economy's single most crucial sector—public education—state governments grant geographic monopolies to the nation's 16,000 school districts. Untouched by the discipline of consumer choice, the majority of America's school districts have performed disastrously. Despite the second highest per-pupil expenditure in the world (just behind Switzerland's), the products of America's monstrous education bureaucracy rank dead last in the developed world.[7]

In the 1960s, as government spending rose to pay for the Vietnam War and the War on Poverty, America began reducing its savings and investment to avoid cutbacks in personal consumption. In the 1970s, the nation's physical infrastructure was allowed to deteriorate. Without sufficient reinvestment in plant and equipment, the nation's productivity growth could not keep pace with Japan's. Despite several fluctuations, average real output per person—the ultimate measure of every economy—grew sluggishly through the 1970s and 1980s. Along with the slowdown in real growth went the promise of a rising standard of living.[8]

But to avoid this truth, Americans became ever more creative in finding ways to raise their consumption, despite flat production. In the 1970s, inflation induced Americans to convert their savings into consumption. As the inflationary spiral intensified, people purchased items they didn't want just to avoid having their savings melted away by inflation. For a decade, high inflation produced the illusion of rising incomes by papering over a transfer of wealth from past savings to current consumption.

In the 1980s, when inflation's corrosive effects could no longer be tolerated politically, alternative ways were found to prop up consumption. Tens of millions of American women reluctantly joined the labor force to help sustain their families' lifestyles. Trade deficits mounted as Japan and other nations shipped consumer goods to America on credit. With the voters' tacit approval, the federal government began spending far more than it taxed, using deficit financing to issue promissory notes against America's future output. Having burned through the capital passed down by previous generations, today's Americans began plundering their children's birthright.[9]

Perhaps if our children were being well educated, the mounting debt load would not pose much of a burden. But in the global village's division of labor, the real wages of America's future workers will erode as they find themselves unable to compete for the highest-skill, highest-wage jobs. The poverty that now subdues America's least-educated workers will creep up through the social strata. With millions of jobs already lost to comparably skilled but less costly foreign workers, America's highly skilled workers will be the next to feel the heat. Having failed to invest in world-class human capital, America will find that even her high-ability workers will not possess state-of-the-art skills.[10]

For the last quarter-century, America has pursued policies that have unwittingly yet systematically undermined the natural processes of economic development. The same arrogance, the same sense of invincibility that led us into the quagmire of Vietnam also led us to believe that America would always be rich beyond measure, that we could legislate away our social ills without tending to the economy's fundamental needs. Blissfully unaware that an economy is a delicate ecosystem, we starved it of the nutrients required for its health and renewal.

Indeed, in the midst of the greatest spurt in information evolution since the invention of the printing press—when investment in technology and education are paying extraordinary returns—America has been pathologically anti-investment and antieducation. Under these conditions, it is not difficult to fathom the demise of the United States. The Japanese took advantage of our mistakes, but they did not defeat us. We have no one to blame but ourselves.

Reversing America's economic decline demands a reversal of these basic policies. This is by no means impossible, but to change course in a democracy, there must be widespread agreement as to the nature of the problem. And, tragically, a political consensus strongly supportive of a revival for American capitalism is most unlikely. Far too many of America's most influential figures—in government, the media, and academia—still believe Marx's core message that profit comes only from coercive exploitation.

In intellectual circles, socialism is still synonymous with social consciousness. Except for the caricature of a guilt-burdened philanthropist, the notion of a socially conscious capitalist seems silly. To be antiwar, one must be against capitalism. To be proenvironment, one must be against capitalism. To care about the poor, one must be against capitalism. On all vital political questions, the morally correct position demands strict allegiance to anticapitalism.

In this regard, Karl Marx was smashingly successful. Even though his economics never made sense—and failed when put to the test—his demonization of capitalism still carries enormous weight. To this day, *profit* and *capitalism* remain highly charged words. Even as China's socialist dictatorship tottered and those in Eastern Europe came crashing down, virtually everyone involved—from dissidents in the streets to newscasters in New York TV studios—described these stunning events in purely political terms—as the triumph of democracy. The word *capitalism* rarely came up. Even Eastern Europe's new promarket political parties insist on calling themselves "democratic socialist" rather than "democratic capitalist."[11]

But one must ask, Would China's democracy movement have started if the Chinese had not experienced a decade of exposure to free markets?

Would Eastern Europe's dictatorships have been overthrown if socialism had outperformed capitalism? Which way would the traffic be flowing through the Berlin Wall if Eastern shops were well-stocked and Western shelves were bare? Would millions of East Germans have swarmed into West Germany for political freedom alone? Would the great mass of people in *any* society reject dictatorship if it provided a far superior standard of living?

We will never know. Fortunately, political freedom and economic progress are natural partners. Despite capitalism's lingering reputation as the source of all the world's evils, the fact remains that every single democracy is a capitalist country. Half a century of economic experimentation proved beyond doubt that tyranny cannot yield prosperity.

If one accepts the bionomic viewpoint, the result of the great cold-war economic experiment is hardly surprising. Socialism collapsed because it is a policy of unrestrained intervention. It tries to fix what is "wrong" with the spontaneous, self-organizing phenomenon called capitalism. But, of course, a natural process cannot be "fixed." A natural process cannot be right or wrong. A natural process has no moral character. Like it or not, nature just happens. No one argues whether leaves *should* be green. Leaves *are* green. We accept this fact and make the best of it.

For some, the bionomic perspective may be disturbing because it chips away at our species' sense of uniqueness. Having only recently reconciled ourselves to the fact that we are descended from apes, we now must consider that even in our technological and economic lives—the aspect of human culture that so sharply distinguishes us from all other species— we are part of a larger evolutionary unfolding. Because our brains happened to evolve the capacity to read and write, to deal with coded information, we became the living bridge between genetic and technological information. Rather than the be-all, end-all of evolution, humanity is merely the link between two independent, parallel realms of evolving information.

Regardless of how one reacts emotionally to the bionomic outlook, if it portrays economic reality accurately, the future's basic course is clear. If the Soviets make it peacefully through their great transformation and manage to avoid dragging the world into a final catastrophe, the global economy will become ever more tightly integrated. New technologies will keep raising living standards around the globe. Even Latin America and Africa, both long oppressed by their own peculiar forms of feudal parasitism, will be drawn inexorably into the democratic capitalist community.

With or without a competitive United States, the global economy will continue to evolve. And eventually, as the full meaning of the great cold-war economic experiment sinks in, America's elites will abandon their anticapitalist stance. Even now, there are signs of a tentative shift. Proposals for stimulating savings and investment are getting a fair hearing. Market mechanisms for pollution control are being considered seriously. The "school-choice" movement offers hope of genuine reform of the public schools. And, after the traumatic restructuring of the 1980s, many thousands of American firms have recommitted themselves to excellence and learning.

But it is still far from clear whether the United States will reverse course soon enough to give future generations the opportunity to enjoy the full blessings of freedom and progress. Orthodoxy still dominates in an era of dizzying change. In a different context, Martin Luther King, Jr., eloquently captured America's present dilemma when he wrote:

> One of the great liabilities of history is that all too many people fail to remain awake through great periods of social change. Every society has its protectors of the status quo and its fraternities of the indifferent who are notorious for sleeping through revolutions. But today our very survival depends on our ability to stay awake, to adjust to new ideas, to remain vigilant and to face the challenge of change.[12]

Today, the challenge of change is greater than it has been in five centuries. In 1492, shortly after Gutenberg's invention of printing, our ancestors had no inkling that evolving technological information would utterly transform the human experience. Exactly 500 years later, with the invention of the computer just behind us, we now stand where they stood. Like them, we have only the vaguest notion of the frontiers that lay ahead. But if we dare to look, even now we can catch the first glimmerings of scientific and economic revolutions that will dwarf the experiences of history.

POSTSCRIPT:BIONOMICS VS. SOCIAL DARWINISM

> The key instrument of the creative imagination is analogy.
> —*Edward O. Wilson* (1984)[1]

In closing, it is important to distinguish bionomics from social Darwinism, a hodgepodge of social theories popular in the late 1800s and early 1900s, and from human sociobiology, the current form of biological determinism.

Social Darwinism was a crude attempt to apply biology's lessons to human social questions. Ultimately, it contributed to some of the greatest tragedies of all time, including the Nazi Holocaust. Because of its horrifying consequences, biology became a taboo subject for economic thinkers. Consequently, many still close their minds to the idea that an understanding of modern biology might reveal beneficial insights into the workings of the economy.

By historical coincidence, Charles Darwin's *The Origin of Species* reached its readers while Europe and America were in the throes of a cathartic transformation. In the later decades of the 1800s, vast railroad networks were built across Western Europe and post–Civil War America. New factories sprouted at an astonishing pace. Millions of peasants and farmers abandoned life on the land for industrial jobs in the cities. Technologically dominant, these societies established far-flung colonial empires. The century that opened with James Watt's invention of the steam engine closed with an economy and society radically transformed by machine power.

The onset of the Industrial Revolution triggered massive social problems. Some businessmen built staggering fortunes, while the great mass of urban workers endured appalling conditions in overcrowded, filthy slums. With Darwin's new theory of evolution then towering over the intellectual landscape, political writers of all persuasions tried to reinforce their arguments by claiming to have found proof for their ideas in Darwin's treatise. *The Origin* was about nature and didn't even mention human society. But this did not deter the quacks who claimed Darwin's support. Sadly, the name of one of the greatest men in the history of science was besmirched by involuntary association with every half-baked nineteenth-century ideologue seeking to justify his notions as "scientifically correct."

The common point of departure for this grab bag of conflicting social-Darwinist ideologies was *The Origin*'s subtitle—*The Preservation of Favoured Races in the Struggle for Life*. Depending upon the writer's personal prejudices, Darwin's phrase *favoured races* could be interpreted in any of several ways. Around the globe, white European colonialists seized on Darwin's idea of natural selection to justify their exploitation of dark-skinned natives. They had no trouble convincing themselves that "survival of the fittest" meant it was the white man's duty to subdue the "inferior" races.

German philosophers believed nature's brutal struggle for species survival meant an inevitable battle for supremacy among nations. They urged the establishment of a strong central government to build the military machine required for future wars. To a large degree, the German militarism that preceded World War I can be traced to a "scientific" logic that perverted the meaning of Darwin's work. Decades later, the Nazis slaughtered millions of Jews, gypsies, and other "subhumans" in their campaign to eradicate threats to Aryan racial purity. Having witnessed the horrifying consequences of these racist, colonialist, nationalist, and militaristic ideologies, modern thinkers have repudiated all these strains of social Darwinism.[2]

But the most familiar form of social Darwinism is an economic philosophy. Politically, a social Darwinist is a denizen of the far Right—a hard-core, laissez-faire capitalist who believes that in the struggle for prosperity, the capable succeed and the incompetent fail. Economic social Darwinists believe that the struggle for biological survival that preceded the rise of civilization extended itself into the economic realm after organized society came into being.

Simply put, this philosophy holds that the rich are genetically superior and deserve their wealth. Those crushed underfoot in the scramble for riches are inherently inferior and deserve their hard fate. In the 1830s debate over the reform of England's welfare laws, extreme economic social Darwinists argued that the poor ought to be allowed to starve to death. In their view, society could improve only if the rich reproduced while the poor withered away.

Despite their differences, one common thread runs through all forms of social Darwinism—the notion that all important human characteristics are predetermined genetically. True to the prejudices of their day, British colonialists believed that Africans and Asians deserved to be exploited because they were genetically inferior. By the logic of social Darwinism, the backwardness of their nontechnological cultures was proof positive that the black and yellow races were genetically incapable of erecting sophisticated societies. To German social Darwinists, the French, British, and Slavic "races" were inferior forms of humanity. Economic social Darwinists never doubted that the poor and their offspring were condemned to poverty by inborn deficiencies of ability and intellect.[3]

Since "superiority" and "inferiority" were inherited, the only way to hasten the progress of mankind was to subdue and eliminate these genetically weaker forms. Nothing less than the cause of human progress obliged the strong to obliterate the weak. If an inferior group wasn't killed or at least allowed to starve, they would reproduce, leaving more hopeless degenerates to cope with in the future. Confirmed Nazis believed that, as unpleasant as it all might be in the short term, the laws of heredity demanded ruthlessness if society was to continue its upward course. The alternative was survival of the "unfittest," leading to the inevitable decline of civilization.[4]

Today, we know that the central claim of racial social Darwinists is utterly false. Important genetic differences do exist among *individuals*. But, despite the most determined efforts, no scientist has ever found statistically important differences in the intelligence of ethnic, racial, or social *groups*. As anyone who has had the privilege of living in an integrated community knows, intellect and talent know no color. Our superficial physical characteristics bear no connection to our crucial human faculties.[5]

The logic of economic social Darwinism is even more flawed than that of racial social Darwinism. Before the invention of the first tools, when prehumans lived much like other animals, there was a direct linkage between genes and "economic" success. Those able to find food lived and reproduced. Those who didn't, died off. But as human knowledge accumulated, the link between genetic and economic success weakened and ultimately snapped. Today, even the world's most wretched poor—

those who eke out their lives in the garbage dumps of Manila, Rio, and Cairo—are not disappearing. As abysmal as their poverty is, it does not prevent them from reproducing.

In fact, quite the opposite is true. Reproduction rates are highest among the world's poorest peoples. Abject failure in the economic arena simply does not translate into genetic oblivion. It is among the world's rich that reproduction rates are the lowest. Ironically, poverty correlates with "genetic success," and prosperity goes hand in hand with "genetic failure."[6]

Considering the mountain of evidence piled up against the various forms of social Darwinism, one might reasonably assume that all attempts to link human genes and social behavior have been abandoned. But in 1975, Harvard biologist Edward O. Wilson, one of the world's leading authorities on ants, published a massive text entitled *Sociobiology*. In what is widely regarded as a tremendous contribution to biological science, *Sociobiology* showed how the often-puzzling behaviors displayed by members of social species—such as termites, baboons, and hyenas—can be explained in terms of genetic survival.[7]

For example, worker bees are sterile, but by working in support of their fertile siblings, they help ensure the survival of genes they carry in common. Similarly, the instinctive "altruistic" act of a guard ant that puts up a suicidal defense at the nest entrance makes genetic sense, because her genes are carried by siblings saved by her sacrifice. Elaborating on Darwin's principle of natural selection, Wilson demonstrated that, among social animals, seemingly illogical individual behaviors actually enhance the prospects of that individual's genes.[8]

Wilson concluded his 575-page treatise with a 30-page chapter entitled "Man: From Sociobiology to Sociology." This chapter ignited a bitter academic controversy that rages to this day.[9] Essentially, Wilson argues that several universally observed human behaviors are programmed genetically. For example, the incest taboo—which in all human cultures prohibits close blood relatives from having sexual relations—is said to be a genetically determined behavior that prevents the genetic problems caused by inbreeding. By a similar logic, the altruism of a soldier who knowingly lays down his life in battle makes genetic sense because, by doing so, he raises the survival chances of close relatives back home who carry his genes.

Few would argue that there are no genetically programmed human behaviors. In fact, it would be shocking if certain common behaviors such as the fear of snakes were not embedded in our genetic code. Recently, researchers found that a genetic defect causes some forms of schizophrenia. Future studies may prove that the incest taboo is pre-determined genetically. As we learn more about genetic mechanisms, we almost certainly will find that a whole host of basic behaviors are controlled by our genes.[10]

But in the last several years, Wilson and his followers have pushed their argument one crucial step too far.[11] They now claim that there is an interaction between cultural practices and genes. According to Wilson, cultures that fail to evolve in ways that promote the genetic survival of their members are eliminated in competition with other, more fit cultures. The fact that our species has been virtually unchanged biologically for at least 100,000 years, a period of phenomenal cultural change, does not seem to impress these sociobiologists.

Human sociobiologists employ more sophisticated language than old-fashioned social Darwinists, but the core allegation is the same—people are born to behave the way they do. Human sociobiology is biological determinism of a decidedly modern style. The diversity of human cultures is seen as rooted in differences within the human gene pool. To them, culture emanates not from the mind, but from DNA.

The theories of these sociobiologists, like those of their social Darwinist predecessors, eventually will collapse because the most human of human behaviors never will be traced to sequences of genetic code. Creativity, rational thought, and inventiveness set humanity apart from all other creatures precisely because they are products of our conscious minds, not results of our genetic programs. Thinking is instinctive; *what* one thinks is not.[12]

The singular biologic success of the human species was a direct result of accumulating knowledge, not the incest taboo or any other instinctive behavior. The three major spurts in human population coincided with the invention of stone tools, agriculture, and machine power. Each of these epochal breakthroughs was a consequence of creative thought. And creative, inventive thought is the most complex—and least genetically subservient—of all human activities. The truly remarkable aspects of our species' history lie well beyond the scope of sociobiology.[13]

The intellectual bankruptcy of social Darwinism and the confusion created by human sociobiology does not, however, mean that students of society have nothing to learn from biology. A profound relationship does exist, but it is far more subtle than imagined by proponents of these flawed ideologies.

The bionomic perspective holds that the human species' uniqueness flows from the mind's ability to reduce the laws of nature into sequences of written symbols—information. Isaac Newton did not invent the laws of gravity; he reported them. By analyzing written records of celestial observations, Newton's mind grasped relationships that had eluded all earlier human beings. By encoding these relationships in mathematical equations, Newton radically enlarged humanity's stockpile of knowledge about nature.

If our descendants have the good fortune of communicating with extraterrestrial beings, they will find that these creatures are fully familiar with laws of gravity, without ever having heard of Newton. Except for the use of different symbols, their gravitational equations will be identical to ours. To which species will the laws of gravity belong? The laws of nature are distinct and separate from the biological organisms who become aware of them.

Once a natural law has been reduced to a sequence of written symbols, its discoverer becomes dispensable. Like a cell that dies after passing along a crucial mutation to its offspring, the creative mind dies after leaving a legacy of immortal knowledge. Newton died nearly three centuries ago, but that doesn't matter. His thoughts are recorded. The laws of gravity are now woven into the corpus of human knowledge—the extragenetic inheritance of the human species.

Except for the few scraps of this vast body of human knowledge that we each happen to memorize, all knowledge exists outside of human bodies. Technical information—the distilled knowledge of all past generations—is recorded in documents and databases, not in DNA. Since our technological information is isolated physically from the genetic information in our cells, these two realms are best understood as entirely separate, parallel domains. Each realm of information is alive and evolves independently.

This conception of a parallel relationship between an ecosystem based on genetic information and an economy derived from technical information is fundamentally different from that proposed by social Darwinists and human sociobiologists. In their view, human culture is not parallel to, but rather is an extension of, human genetic information. For them, the tree of cultural evolution grows from genetic roots.

By contrast, the bionomic argument holds that economic development—and the social change that flows from it—is shaped not by a society's genes but by its technical knowledge. In this century, wherever advanced technologies have been adopted, cultural chasms once thought to be insurmountable are narrowing to the vanishing point. Europe's current unification is just one example of this process. Throughout human history, profound cultural change has been driven by the evolution of technology, not by the evolution of genes.

In biological parlance, the social-Darwinist/human-sociobiologist view amounts to a claim of "homology," while the argument presented here asserts an "analogy." Homology and analogy describe two distinct types of similarity. A *homology* is the kind of similarity based on direct descent. For example, the bones in a human arm and a bat wing are similar because people and bats, both being mammals, share a common evolutionary ancestor that possessed five-"finger" limbs. The structural similarity of the human arm and the bat wing is meaningful because the likeness was determined by common ancestry.[14]

Following this kind of logic, social Darwinists and human sociobiologists believe that all human cultures, like human arms and bat wings, are similar because all human beings share common ancestors. Their homology also tries to explain the differences among cultures as consequences of genetic changes that occurred since these ethnic groups became dispersed around the globe.[15]

In contrast, an *analogy* is the type of similarity that emerges from like circumstances. Wings of bats and birds also are similar, but their common ancestor did not have wings. Bat wings and bird wings evolved independently. Two completely separate rounds of evolution came up with comparable solutions to the problems of flight. According to the bionomic view, genetic information and technical information independently evolved into an ecosystem and an economy of striking similarity because both realms of information confronted the problems of survival in environments with limited resources.[16]

When an analogy is purely coincidental and superficial, nothing can be learned from it. But if an analogy is close and detailed and has a logical foundation, it may reveal a great deal about the hidden nature of things. The more precise the parallels, the more convincing the analogy becomes. For the analogy between ecosystem and economy to be useful, it need not be perfect. Street maps, for example, are not exact replicas of cities, but they are quite useful in helping us find our way in unfamiliar territory. Then again, maps occasionally have flaws that cause us to become lost. The analogy between genetic and technologic evolution is powerful, but it is not perfect.[17]

One obvious distinction between the two is the pace at which change unfolds. The ecosystem has been evolving for at least 3.5 billion years, the economy for no more than 35,000 years. The randomness of mutations and the incredibly sluggish pace of geological change cause biological information to change very slowly. By contrast, technical information is rearranged consciously in the minds of thinkers. The powered flight made possible by the evolution of the bird's wing took many thousands of years to mutate into existence. But in just a few years, the Wright Brothers juggled scraps of knowledge about aerodynamics and gasoline engines into the design of the first airplane.

Genetic information can only flow vertically through time, following lines of descent from parent to offspring. But in economic evolution, techniques developed in one field often are moved horizontally to recombine with methods used in entirely separate disciplines.[18] The Wright Brothers grafted together aerodynamics and piston and cylinder power—two previously unrelated strains of knowledge—to establish a new lineage of technology. In every field, inventors borrow ideas and tinker with their designs until they work. Intentional evolutionary change is more like Lamarck's willful transformation than like the random variation that propels Darwinian evolution.

Nonetheless, despite these and other differences, an illuminating analogy between biology and economics still holds. As every child knows, when water crystallizes into snow, no two flakes have identical branching patterns. Even so, all snowflakes belong to the same class of self-organizing phenomena. Genetic and technologic information, despite manifest differences in the branching patterns of their evolutionary histories, are nonetheless members of the same class of natural phenomena. Both are living, evolving information systems.

NOTES

PREFACE

1. "Market Civilization," *Wall Street Journal* (June 11, 1990), p. A10.
   Wilson, Edward O., *Biophilia* (Cambridge: Harvard University Press, 1984), p. 66.
2. Holland, John H., Keith Holyoak, Richard Nisbett, and Paul R. Thargard, *Induction: Processes of Inference, Learning, and Discovery* (Cambridge: MIT Press, 1986).
   Hesse, Mary B., *Models and Analogies in Science* (London: Sheed & Ward, 1963), p. 5. Quoting the English physicist N. R. Campbell in *Physics, the Elements* (1920): "[A]nalogies are not 'aids' to the establishment of theories; they are an utterly essential part of theories, without which theories would be completely valueless and unworthy of the name. It is often suggested that the analogy leads to the formulation of the theory, but that once the theory is formulated the analogy has served its purpose and may be removed or forgotten. Such a suggestion is absolutely false and perniciously misleading."

INTRODUCTION, GENES AND KNOWLEDGE

1. Clark, Ronald W., *The Survival of Charles Darwin: A Biography of a Man and an Idea* (New York: Random House, 1984), p. 217.
2. Scott, Andrew, *Pirates of the Cell: The Story of Viruses from Molecule to Microbe* (New York: Basil Blackwell, 1987), p. 14. Some viruses use single-stranded DNA, while some store their genetic information in double or single strands of the closely related nucleic acid RNA.
   See also Fields, B. N. and D. M. Krige, *Fundamental Virology* (New York: Raven Press, 1986), p. 240.
3. Cairns-Smith, A. G., *Seven Clues to the Origin of Life: A Scientific Detective Story* (Cambridge: Cambridge University Press, 1985).
4. Von Neumann, John, "The General and Logical Theory of Automata," in *Cerebral Mechanisms in Behavior: The Hixon Symposium*, Lloyd A. Jeffress, ed. (New York: John Wiley, 1951), pp. 288–315.
   Von Neumann, John, *Collective Works: General and Logical Theory of Automata* (Oxford: Pergamon Press, 1961), pp. 315–18.
5. Cairns-Smith, *Seven Clues*, p. 14.
6. Pittendrigh, Colin S., "Adaptation, Natural Selection, and Behavior," in *Behavior and Evolution*, Roe, A. and G. G. Simpson, eds. (New Haven: Yale University Press, 1958), p. 395. "[O]rganization is nonrandomness; it is the converse of disorder or randomness. An organization is an improbable state in a contingent—a Gibbsian—universe; and as

such it cannot be merely accepted, it must be explained. Organization implies, in modern terms, an information content.

The concept of information as negative entropy . . . promises to be a useful addition to the biologist's language permitting a new and potentially quantitative way of discussing all the so-far vague and ill-defined notions of *complexity, organization, and adaptation that are, in the last analysis, recognized by virtue of their nonrandomness* [italics in original]."

7. Harold, Franklin M., *The Vital Force: A Study of Bioenergetics* (San Francisco: W.H. Freeman, 1986), p. 24. "[L]iving things (unlike nonliving ones) are clearly endowed with purpose, directed toward survival and the reproduction of their own kind. This property, called teleonomy (Pittendrigh, 1958; Monod, 1971), distinguishes living things (and their artifacts, such as our machines) from all other objects and systems in the universe and tells us plainly that we must look beyond physics and chemistry for understanding."

Bonner, John Tyler, *The Evolution of Culture in Animals* (Princeton: Princeton University Press, 1980), p. 14. "It is the gene, the components of the DNA wrapped in the nucleus of the fertilized egg, that is the important object as far as natural selection is concerned. The other materials in the egg, all the other chemicals and structures, both nuclear and cytoplasmic, are there to nurture the genes, to give them an environment in which they can flourish and in which they can be persuaded to initiate the synthesis of certain proteins that become part of the construction of the body."

8. See Dawkins, Richard, *The Selfish Gene* (Oxford: Oxford University Press, 1976).

9. Marshack, Alexander, *The Roots of Civilization* (New York: McGraw-Hill, 1972), pp. 44–49.

Marshack, Alexander, "Lunar Notation on Upper Paleolithic Remains," *Science* (November 6, 1964), p. 744.

Marshack, Alexander, "Upper Paleolithic Notation and Symbol," *Science* (November 24, 1972), pp. 817–28.

But see White, Randall, "Visual Thinking in the Ice Age," *Scientific American* (July 1989), p. 98.

Also see Gaur, Albertine, *A History of Writing* (London: The British Library, 1984), p. 35. "We should re-examine the concept of writing, not from the standpoint of how effectively it can store language, but how effectively it can store information essential to the economic and political survival of a society."

10. There is still debate among paleoanthropologists over the timing and circumstances of the emergence of anatomically modern man (*Homo sapiens sapiens*). Recent fossil findings in an Israeli cave show that modern-looking people lived there 92,000 years ago. Studies of the genetic differences among the world's ethnic groups suggests an origin of modern humans between 140,000 and 290,000 years ago. Relying on these genetic studies—and splitting the difference in these date limits—this book uses 200,000 years as an admittedly rough estimate of when our species first evolved.

But whenever anatomically modern humans actually appeared, there was no sustained improvement in stone-tool technology, no art, no extensive trade, no boats, and no writing—nothing to suggest that continuous innovation began until about 35,000 years ago.

See chapter 6: Brains and Tools.

11. Pfeiffer, John E., *The Creative Explosion: An Inquiry into the Origins of Art and Religion* (New York: Harper & Row, 1982), p.123.

12. Roux, Georges, *Ancient Iraq* (Middlesex: Penguin Books, 1966), p. 77.

13. Moorehouse, A. C., *Writing and the Alphabet* (London: Corbett Press, 1946), p. 78. "Man was passing from the age when each household produced the manifold goods needed by itself, and was introducing the age of specialization. When the supply of goods became more abundant, writing became the means to facilitate their disposal and exchange thus making possible a more complex economic system."

Goody, Jack, *The Logic of Writing and the Organization of Society* (Cambridge: Cambridge University Press, 1986), p. 48.

14. Deevey, Edward S., "The Human Population," *Scientific American* (September 1960), pp. 195–204.

15. Suro, Robert, "New Theories on Early Europe Cite Migration, not Conquest," *New York Times* (May 10, 1988), p. B10.

16. Diamond, Jared, "The Worst Mistake in the History of the Human Race," *Discover* (May 1987), p. 65.
17. Lewin, Roger, *Human Evolution* (New York: W.H. Freeman, 1984), p. 96.
18. Stevens, William K., "Life in the Stone Age: New Findings Point to Complex Societies," *New York Times* (December 20, 1988), p. B5.
19. Cavalli-Sforza, L. L., "The Impact of Farming on Expansion of Human Populations," in *The Origin and Domestication of Cultivated Plants: Symposium*, C. Barigozzi, ed. (*Developments in Agricultural and Managed-Forest Ecology* 16: New York: Elsevier Science Publishing, 1986), p. 71. The human population at the onset of agriculture was between 3 and 15 million, roughly 1/1000th of today's population. "Even with primitive agricultural techniques, population densities could easily become an average 10–50 times higher than for foragers."
    Cohen, M. N., *The Food Crisis in Prehistory: Overpopulation and the Origins of Agriculture* (New Haven: Yale University Press, 1977), p. 279.
    Christenson, A. L., *Change in the Human Niche in Response to Population Growth* (New York: Academic Press, 1980), p. 31.
20. Pianka, Eric P., *Evolutionary Ecology*, 3d ed. (New York: Harper & Row, 1983), p. 82. "Large home ranges or territories usually result in low densities, which in turn markedly limit possibilities for the evolution of sociality."
21. Schmandt-Besserat, Denise, "The Earliest Precursor of Writing," *Scientific American* (June 1978), pp. 50–59.
    Schmandt-Besserat, Denise, "The Precursors to Numerals and Writing," *Archaeology* (November–December, 1986), pp. 32–39.
22. Teitelman, Robert, "Sumericalc," *Forbes* (November 5, 1984), p. 229.
23. Gaur, Albertine, *A History of Writing* (London: The British Museum, 1984), pp. 37–48.
24. Grun, Bernard, *The Timetables of History: A Horizontal Linkage of People and Events* (New York: Simon and Schuster, 1982), p. 3.
25. Boorstin, Daniel, *The Discoverers* (New York: Vintage Books, 1985), p. 526.
26. For accounts of the printing of the Gutenberg Bible, see Fontana, John, *Mankind's Greatest Invention and the Story of the First Printed Bible* (New York: John Fontana, 1964).
    Fuhrmann, Otto, *The 500th Anniversary of the Invention of Printing* (New York: Philip C. Duschines, 1937).
    Thorpe, James, *The Gutenberg Bible: Landmark in Learning* (San Marino, CA: Huntington Library, 1975).
27. Einstein, E., *The Printing Press as an Agent of Change: A Communications and Cultural Transformation in Early Modern Europe* (Cambridge: Cambridge University Press, 1979), p. 11.
    Steinberg, S. H., *Five Hundred Years of Printing* (Baltimore: Penguin Books, 1974), p. 140. "The average edition of a book printed in the fifteenth century was probably not more than about 200—which, however, was a 200-fold increase upon the scribes' work."
    Chappell, Warren, *A Short History of the Printed Word* (New York: Alfred A. Knopf, 1970), p. 60. "Vespasiano, with fifty-five writers working for him, needed almost two years to finish 200 books. Fraben was able to print 24,000 copies of Erasmus' Colloquies in a few months."
28. Asimov, Isaac, Foreword to Goldstein, Thomas, *Dawn of Modern Science* (Boston: Houghton Mifflin, 1988), p. vi. "Neither Copernicus nor Vesalius could possibly have exerted the influence they did on their contemporaries and their successors if their books had been handwritten, with scrawled diagrams and illustrations. Both books would have been too revolutionary to attract many copyists. Too few readers would have found them.
    The books, however, were *printed*. The initial edition might have been limited by our present-day standards, but they reached the scholars and, as their reputations grew, new editions appeared. Since printing made the scientific community possible by spreading new views and discoveries rapidly and efficiently, one should date modern science back not merely to two men and their books, but to the techniques that made these books something more than what had, until then, been considered books [italics in original]."
    Boas, Marie, *The Scientific Renaissance, 1450–1630* (New York: Harper & Row, 1966), pp. 29–30.

29. Steinberg, S. H., *Five Hundred Years of Printing* (Baltimore, MD: Penguin Books, 1974), pp. 44–46. "Printing, instead of just spreading out from Mainz went to the places that offered the brightest prospects: flourishing centers of international trade. Centers of trading, banking, shipping and seats of secular and ecclesiastical courts."
   Clair, Colin, *A History of European Printing* (New York: Academic Press, 1976), p. 120. By 1500, there were presses in 250 towns in western Europe.
30. Smith, Alan G. R., *Science and Society in the Sixteenth and Seventeenth Centuries* (New York: Science History Publications, 1972), p. 62.
31. Hall, Rupert A., *The Revolution in Science, 1500–1750* (London: Longman Group Limited, 1983), p. 22.
32. Grun, *Timetables of History*, pp. 229–37; Boorstin, *The Discoverers*, p. 352.
33. Hall, *Revolution in Science*, pp. 22–36.
34. Boorstin, *Discoverers*, p. 391.
35. Smith, *Science and Society*, p. 62; Einstein, *The Printing Press*, p. 18.
36. Schopf, J. William, "The Evolution of the Earliest Cells," *Scientific American* (September 1978) pp. 110–39.
37. Gould, Stephen Jay, *Ever Since Darwin: Reflections in Natural History* (New York: W.W. Norton, 1977), p. 116.
   Brownlee, Shannon and Gina Maranto, "Why Sex?" *Discover* (February 1984), p. 24.
   Erlich, Paul R. and Jonathan Roughgarden, *The Science of Ecology* (New York: Macmillan, 1987), pp. 182–86.
38. Friday, Adrian and David S. Ingram, eds., *The Cambridge Encyclopedia of Life Sciences* (Cambridge: Cambridge University Press, 1985), p. 321.
39. Mincer, Jacob, "Human Capital and Economic Growth," *Economics of Education Review*, Vol. 3, No. 3 (1984), p. 201. "In a fundamental sense, modern economic growth is a result of the scientific revolution, that is, of the growth of systemized scientific knowledge. The geographic origin and spread of the industrial revolution since the 18th century supports this view and pivotal role of human capital in generating and facilitating it. The industrial revolution started with the scientific revolution in the northwest of Europe and spread most rapidly to those areas where educational development has made the transfer of technology most feasible."
   Ashton, T. S., *An Economic History of England: The 18th Century* (London: Methuen and Company, 1955), p. 103.

PART I, EVOLUTION AND INNOVATION/CHAPTER 1, HINTS OF CHANGE

1. Bowen, Catherine Drinker, *Miracle at Philadelphia: The Story of the Constitutional Convention, May to September, 1787* (Boston: Little, Brown, 1966), p. 94.
2. Sellers, Charles C., *Charles Willson Peale* (Philadelphia: American Philosophical Society, 1947), p. 130.
3. Green, John C., *The Death of Adam: Evolution and Its Impact on Western Thought* (Ames: Iowa State University Press, 1959), p. 112.
4. Sellers, *Charles Willson Peale*, p. 144.
5. Green, *Death of Adam*, p. 88.
6. Rudwick, Martin J. S., *The Meaning of Fossils: Episodes in the History of Paleontology* (Chicago: University of Chicago Press, 1985), p. 7.
7. Trager, Louis, "The Convenience Decade: New Products Gave Us More Time to Enjoy Life," *San Francisco Examiner* (December 24, 1989), p. D1.
8. Asimov, Isaac, "Isaac Asimov, Part I," *Bill Moyers' World of Ideas* (New York: Public Affairs Television, 1988): "The fact is that society is always changing, but the rate of change has been accelerating all through history. It was only with the coming of the industrial revolution that the rate of change became fast enough to be visible in a single lifetime."
9. Raymond, Robert, and Michael Charlton, *Out of the Fiery Furnace: The Story of Metals and Man* (Sydney, Australia: Opus Films, 1983).
10. See Harrison, J. F. C., *The Common People of Great Britain: A History from the Norman Conquest to the Present* (Bloomington: Indiana University Press, 1985).

11. Chandler, Tertius and Gerald Fox, *3000 Years of Urban Growth* (New York: Academic Press, 1974). Constantinople, Peking, and Isfahan were larger than London.
12. Braudel, Fernand, *The Perspective of the World: Civilization and Capitalism, 15th–18th Century, Vol. III* (New York: Harper & Row, 1984), pp. 280, 559.
13. Green, *Death of Adam*, p. 12.
14. Cohen, I. Bernard, *Revolution in Science* (Cambridge: Harvard University Press, 1985), p. 174.
    See also Ernst Mayr, "How Biology Differs from the Physical Sciences," in David J. Depew, and Bruce H. Weber, eds., *Evolution at a Crossroads: The New Biology and the New Philosophy of Science* (Cambridge: MIT Press, 1985), pp. 43–63.
15. Boorstin, Daniel, *The Discoverers* (New York: Vintage Books, 1985), p. 394.
16. Reynolds, Terry S., *Stronger Than a Hundred Men: A History of the Vertical Water Wheel* (Baltimore: Johns Hopkins University Press, 1983), p. 77.
17. Briggs, Asa, *The Power of Steam: An Illustrated History of the World's Steam Age* (Chicago: University of Chicago Press, 1982), p. 21.
18. Dickinson, H. W., *A Short History of the Steam Engine* (London: Cambridge University Press, 1939), p. 26.
19. Pacey, Arnold, *The Maze of Ingenuity: Ideas and Idealism in the Development of Technology* (London: Allen Lane Publishers, 1974), p. 127.
    White, Jr., Lynn and Vern L. Bullough, *Technological Developments and the Emergence of Modern Science: The Scientific Revolution* (New York: Holt, Rinehart and Winston, 1970), p. 88.
20. Rolt, L. T. C., *Thomas Newcomen: The Prehistory of the Steam Engine* (Dawlish, England: David & Charles, 1963), p. 56.
21. Rolt, *Thomas Newcomen*, p. 61.
22. Dickinson, *Short History*, p. 34.
    Rolt, L. T. C., and J. S. Allen, *The Steam Engine of Thomas Newcomen* (New York: Science History Publications, 1977), p. 37.
23. Rolt and Allen, *Steam Engine*, p. 144.
24. Von Tunzelman, G. N., *Steam Power and British Industrialization to 1860* (Oxford: Oxford University Press, 1978), p. 49.
    Method of converting 1724 British pounds to 1987 U.S. dollars: According to the Rousseaux Price Indices in the *Abstract of British Historical Statistics*, where 1885 prices were set to equal 100, the 1724 price index was 78 and the 1913 British price index was 106. The dollar/pound exchange rate in 1913 was about $4.80 per pound. Using the U.S. GNP Deflator with 1982 set at 100, 1913's index was 9.4 and 1987's index was 117.7. Calculation: £1200 (1724) x (106/78) = £1631 (1913). £1631 x $4.8/£ = $7,828 (1913). $7,828 x (117.7/9.4) = $98,013 (1987). See Mitchell, B. R., *Abstract of British Historical Statistics* (Cambridge: Cambridge University Press, 1962).
    Patiky, Mark, "Ceramic Turbines for Cars Could Wind Up on Planes," *High Technology* (April 1987), pp. 56–58. Three dollars per horsepower is a good rule of thumb for gasoline automobile engines today. At $98,000 for 16 horsepower, the 1724 Newcomen engine cost roughly $6,125 per horsepower, or about 2,000 times as much.
25. Dickinson, *Short History*, p. 57.
26. McMullen, John A., "How to Help the Biotech Business," *High Technology* (September 1986), p. 110.
    "IBM's Top Scientist," *New York Times* (July 9, 1989), p. F5. The life cycle on memory-chip technology is now about 30 months.
27. Rolt and Allen, *Steam Engine*, pp. 45, 143.
28. Von Tunzelman, *Steam Power*, p. 67.
29. Dickinson, *Short History*, p. 29.
30. Briggs, *Power of Steam*, p. 48.
31. Dickinson, H.W., and Rhys Jenkens, *James Watt and the Steam Engine—The Memorial Volume Prepared for the Committee of the Watt Centenary* (Oxford: Oxford University Press, 1927).
    Usher, Abbott Payson, *A History of Mechanical Inventions, Rev. Ed.* (New York: Dover, 1954), p. 71.
32. Dickinson, *Short History*, pp. 67–74.

33. Von Tunzelman, *Steam Power*, p. 28.
34. Dickinson and Jenkens, *James Watt*, p. 141.
35. Von Tunzelman, *Steam Power*, p. 248.
36. Briggs, *Power of Steam*, pp. 60–61.

CHAPTER 2, THEORIES OF CHANGE

1. Packard, Alpheus S., *Lamarck—The Founder of Evolution, His Life and Work* (New York: Longmans, Green, 1901), p. 57.
2. Burkhardt, Jr., Richard W., *The Spirit of System: Lamarck and Evolutionary Biology* (Cambridge: Harvard University Press, 1977).
   Packard, *Lamarck*, p. 232.
3. Nordenskiold, Erik, *The History of Biology: A Survey* (New York: Alfred A. Knopf, 1928), p. 322.
4. See Coleman, William, *Georges Cuvier Zoologist: A Study in the History of Evolutionary Theory* (Cambridge: Harvard University Press, 1964).
5. Burkhardt, *Spirit of System*, p. 194.
   Greene, John C., *Science, Ideology, and World View: Essays in the History of Evolutionary Ideas* (Berkeley: University of California Press, 1981), pp. 30–59.
6. Jordanova, L. J., *Lamarck* (Oxford: Oxford University Press, 1984), p. 112.
7. Mayr, Ernst, *The Growth of Biological Thought* (Cambridge: Harvard University Press, 1982), p. 349.
8. Berg, Maxine, *The Machinery Question and the Making of Political Economy, 1815– 1848* (Cambridge: Cambridge University Press, 1980), p. 17.
9. Overton, Mark, "Agricultural Productivity in 18th Century England: Some Further Speculations," *Economic History Review* 37 (1984), pp. 244–51.
   Braudel, Fernand, *The Structures of Everyday Life—Civilization and Capitalism, 15th– 18th Century, Vol. I* (New York: Harper & Row, 1981), p. 123.
10. Gras, Norman Scott Brien, *Industrial Evolution* (London: Oxford University Press, 1930), pp. 90–103.
11. See Hyde, Charles K., *Technological Change and the British Iron Industry 1700–1870* (Princeton: Princeton University Press, 1977).
    Usher, Abbott Payson, *A History of Mechanical Inventions, Rev. Ed.* (New York: Dover, 1954), p. 14. "In England at the close of the seventeenth century the new technology centered around increased use of coal in industry, culminating in the development of techniques for the use of coal as a source of power and as a metallurgic fuel."
12. Heilbroner, Robert L., *The Worldly Philosophers* (New York: Simon & Schuster, 1967), p. 36.
13. Boulding, Kenneth E., *Evolutionary Economics* (Beverly Hills, London: Sage Publications, 1981), p. 17.
14. Smith, Adam, *The Wealth of Nations* (New York: Random House, 1937 ed.), p. 14.
15. Smith, *Wealth*, p. 15.
16. Smith, *Wealth*, p. 508.
17. Blaug, Mark, *Economic Theory in Retrospect* (Cambridge: Cambridge University Press, 1985), p. 36.
18. Smith, *Wealth*, p. 243.
19. Maurice, Charles and Charles W. Smithson, *The Doomsday Myth: 10,000 Years of Economic Crisis* (Palo Alto: Hoover Institution Press, 1984), p. 23.
20. Heilbroner, *Worldly Philosopher*, p. 71.
21. Himmelfarb, Gertrude, *The Idea of Poverty—England in the Early Industrial Age* (New York: Vintage Books, 1985), p. 108.
22. See Lekachman, Robert, *A History of Economic Ideas* (New York: McGraw-Hill, 1959), p. 125.
23. Overton, "Agricultural Productivity," p. 246.
    Braudel, Fernand, *The Perspective of the World—Civilization and Capitalism, 15th–18th Century, Vol. 3* (New York: Harper & Row, 1984), p. 564.
24. Hutchins, B. L. and A. Harrison, *A History of Factory Legislation, 3d Ed.* (London: Frank Cass & Co., 1926), pp. 27–29.

25. Report from the Committee on the "Bill to Regulate the Labour of Children in the Mills and Factories of the United Kingdom" (August 8, 1832).

26. Hutchins and Harrison, *History of Factory Legislation*, pp. 41–49.

CHAPTER 3, DARWIN'S VISION

1. Stanley, Steven M., *The New Evolutionary Timetable: Fossils, Genes, and the Origin of Species* (New York: Basic Books, 1981), p. 29.

2. Mayr, Ernst, *The Growth of Biological Thought* (Cambridge: Harvard University Press, 1982), p. 380.

3. Bowler, Peter J., *Evolution: The History of an Idea* (Berkeley: University of California Press, 1984), p. 154.

4. Mayr, *Growth of Biological Thought*, p. 492.

5. Mayr, *Growth of Biological Thought*, pp. 477–78.

6. Hodge, M. J. S., "The Structure and Strategy of Darwin's 'Long Argument,' " *British Journal of Historical Science* 10 (1977), pp. 237–46.

7. Clark, Ronald W., *The Survival of Charles Darwin* (New York: Random House, 1984), p. 197.

8. Mayr, Ernst, "How Biology Differs from the Physical Sciences," in *Evolution at a Crossroads: The New Biology and the New Philosophy of Science*, David J. Depew and Bruce H. Weber, eds. (Cambridge: MIT Press, 1985), pp. 43–63.

9. Sober, Elliot, ed., *Conceptual Issues in Evolutionary Biology—An Anthology* (Cambridge: MIT Press, 1984), p. 639. "People are dismayed to discover that evolutionists can make no specific predictions about the future of humankind *qua* humankind. Since that's all they are interested in, they conclude that evolutionary theory is not good for much. But dismissing evolutionary theory because it cannot be used to predict the percentage of people who will have blue eyes in the year 2000 is as misbegotten as dismissing celestial mechanics because it cannot be used to predict the physical make-up of Mars. Neither theory is designed to make such predictions."

10. Mayr, Ernst, *Current Controversies in Evolutionary Biology*, Public Lecture, University of California at Berkeley (October 23, 1987): "Biology did not come to life as a science until the 1830s and 40s. And decades later, the great English physicist Ernest Rutherford still referred to biology as nothing more than postage stamp collecting."

11. Mayr, *Current Controversies*, p. 7. "It took almost one hundred years for natural selection to gain the full support of biologists. But Darwinism has stood the test of time with flying colors."

12. Shell, Ellen Ruppel, "Mix 'n' Match DNA," *Science 84* (July 1, 1984), p. 88.
King, Mary-Claire and A. C. Wilson, "Evolution at Two Levels in Humans and Chimpanzees," *Science* 188 (April 11, 1975), pp. 107–10.
Pfeiffer, John E., *The Emergence of Humankind* (New York: Harper & Row, 1985), p. 38.

CHAPTER 4, THE MYTHICAL MACHINE

1. Rosenberg, Nathan and L. E. Birdzell, Jr., *How the West Grew Rich: The Economic Transformation of the Industrial World* (New York: Basic Books, 1986), p. vi. "Perhaps we need to take a hint from the experience of biologists, who, in the last century-and-a-half, have learned that evolutionary processes in nature can generate systems, ranging from protein molecules to the ecology of a swamp, whose subtle and even devious complexities overtax human powers of understanding. There is an analogous absence of overall human design, as well as an analogous presence of accident, experiment, and survival standards, in the evolution of the West's system for generating economic growth."
Ghiselin, Michael, "The Economy of the Body," *American Economic Review* 68 (May 1978), p. 236.

2. Bell, Daniel, "Models and Reality in Economic Discourse," in *The Crisis in Economic Theory*, Daniel Bell and Irving Kristol, eds. (New York: Basic Books, 1981), pp. 76–77.

3. Keynes, John Maynard, *The General Theory of Employment, Interest, and Money* (San Diego: Harcourt Brace Jovanovich, 1964 ed.), p. 383.

4. But see Himmelfarb, Gertrude, *The Idea of Poverty—England in the Early Industrial Age* (New York: Vintage Books, 1985), p. 157. Summarizes Nassau Senior's argument.
5. Himmelfarb, *Idea of Poverty*, p. 230. Quoting Edward Bulwer Lytton from *England and the English*, 1833.
6. Engels, Friedrich, "Preface to *The Communist Manifesto*," in *Aspen Institute Readings*, Martin Krasney, ed. (New York: Aspen Institute for Humanistic Studies, 1977), p. 237.
7. Blaug, Mark, *Economic Theory in Retrospect* (Cambridge: Cambridge University Press, 1985), pp. 257, 291.
   Perelman, Michael, "Marx, Malthus, and the Organic Composition of Capital," *History of Political Economy* 17 (March 1985), pp. 461–90.
8. Marx, Karl, *Capital, Vol. 1* (New York: International Publishers, 1967), pp. 341, 372.
   Kamenka, Eugene, ed., *The Portable Karl Marx* (New York: Penguin Books, 1983), pp. lxxviii, lxxx. The first draft of *Das Kapital—Grundrisse der Kritik der politischen Okonomie* (Outlines of the Critique of the Political Economy) was finished in 1858. Marx read *The Origin* in December 1860 and wrote Engels that it provided the foundation in natural history for their theory of class struggle.
   See also Enrique, M., "A Note on Marx and Darwin," *History of Political Economy* 13 (April 1981), p. 772.
9. Bowler, Peter J., *Evolution: The History of an Idea* (Berkeley: University of California Press, 1984), p. 102.
10. Engels, "Preface," p. 253.
11. Blaug, *Economic Theory*, p. 179.
12. Lekachman, Robert, *A History of Economic Ideas* (New York: McGraw-Hill, 1959), pp. 177–80.
   Stigler, George J., *Essays in the History of Economics* (Chicago: University of Chicago Press, 1965), p. 166.
   Blaug, Mark, *Great Economists Before Keynes: An Introduction to the Lives & Works of One Hundred Great Economists of the Past* (Cambridge: Cambridge University Press, 1986), p. 201.
13. Mill, John Stuart, *Principles of Political Economy*, W. J. Ashley, ed. (London: Longmans, Green, 1909), p. 177.
14. Blaug, *Economic Theory*, p. 220.
15. Heilbroner, Robert L., *The Worldly Philosophers*, 3d ed. (New York: Simon & Schuster, 1967), p. 120.
   Blaug, *Economic Theory*, pp. 211–13.
16. Heilbroner, *Worldly Philosophers*, pp. 187–88.
17. Blaug, *Economic Theory*, p. 296.
18. Blaug, *Economic Theory*, p. 420.
   "Ostensibly, the *Principles* is a study of static microeconomic theory but time after time the reader is told that the conclusions of static analysis are unreliable and that microeconomics fails to come to grips with the vital issues of economic policy."
19. See Heilbroner, *Worldly Philosophers*, p. 188.
20. Blaug, *Economic Theory*, pp. 295–97.
21. Kuttner, Robert, "The Poverty of Economics," *Atlantic Monthly* (February 1, 1985), p. 76. Quoting John Eatwell.
22. Schumpeter, Joseph A., *Capitalism, Socialism and Democracy* (New York: Harper & Row, 1950), p. 81. "If we economists were given less to wishful thinking and more to the observation of facts, doubts would immediately arise as to the realistic virtues of a theory that would have led us to expect a very different result."
23. Rashid, Salim, "Political Economy and Geology in the Early Nineteenth Century: Similarities and Contrasts," *History of Political Economy* 13 (April 1981), pp. 726–44.
24. Flinn, M. W., "English Workers' Living Standards During the Industrial Revolution: A Comment," *Economic History Review* (1984), pp. 88–92.
25. Parker, William N., "Historiography of American Economic History," *Encyclopedia of American Economic History, Vol. 1*, Glenn Porter, ed. (New York: Scribner's, 1980), pp. 3–16.
26. Kuttner, "Poverty of Economics," p. 78.
   Bell, *Crisis in Economic Theory*, p. 58.

27. Cesarano, Filippo, "On the Role of the History of Economic Analysis," *History of Political Economy* 15 (January 1983), pp. 63–82.
28. Bell, *Crisis in Economic Theory*, pp. 69–70.
29. Galbraith, J. K., "A Visit to Russia," *New Yorker* (September 3, 1984), p. 55.
30. Blaug, *Economic Theory*, pp. 224, 711.
31. Kuttner, "Poverty of Economics," p. 79.
32. Nelson, Richard R., and Sidney G. Winter, *An Evolutionary Theory of Economic Change* (Cambridge: Harvard University Press, 1982), p. 10. "[M]uch of contemporary economic theory appears faintly anachronistic, its harmonious equilibria a reminder of an age that was at least more optimistic, if not actually more tranquil. It is as if economics has never really transcended the experiences of its childhood, when Newtonian physics was the only science worth imitating and celestial mechanics its most notable achievement."
33. Blaug, *Economic Theory*, p. 708. "Bad theory is still better than no theory at all and, for the most part, critics of orthodoxy had no alternative construction to offer."

CHAPTER 5, LIFE'S PULSE

1. Eldredge, Niles, *Life Pulse: Episodes from the Story of the Fossil Record* (New York: Facts on File, 1987), p. 148.
2. Stanley, Steven M., *The New Evolutionary Timetable: Fossils, Genes, and the Origin of Species* (New York: Basic Books, 1981), p. 6.
3. Eldredge, Niles, *Time Frames—The Rethinking of Darwinian Evolution and the Theory of Punctuated Equilibria* (New York: Simon & Schuster, 1985), p. 50.
   Eldredge, Niles, "A Trilobite Odyssey," *Natural History* 81 (1972), pp. 53–59.
4. Huxley, T. H., "Paleontology and the Doctrine of Evolution," in *Discourses Biological and Geological Collected Essays*, Vol. 8 (New York: Appleton and Co., 1897), pp. 354–55.
5. Darwin, Charles, *The Origin of Species By Means of Natural Selection or The Preservation of Favoured Races in the Struggle for Life* (New York: Avenel Books, 1979 ed.), p. 444.
6. Rudwick, Martin J. S., *The Meaning of Fossils: Episodes in the History of Paleontology* (Chicago: University of Chicago Press, 1985), p. 264.
7. Goldschmidt, Richard, *The Material Basis of Evolution* (New Haven: Yale University Press, 1982).
   See Hapgood, Fred, "The Importance of Being Ernst: Setting Out to Discredit Another Scientist," *Science* 84 (June 1, 1984).
8. Bowler, Peter J., *Evolution: The History of an Idea* (Berkeley: University of California Press, 1984), p. 322.
9. Darwin, *Origin of Species*, p. 316.
10. Mayr, Ernst, *Systematics and the Origin of Species* (New York: Columbia University Press, 1942), pp. 225–47.
    Mayr, Ernst, *The Growth of Biological Thought* (Cambridge: Harvard University Press, 1982), pp. 600–606.
11. Eldredge, Niles, and Stephen Jay Gould, "Punctuated Equilibria: An Alternative to Phyletic Gradualism," in *Models in Paleobiology*, T. J. M. Schopf, ed. (San Francisco: Freeman Cooper, 1972), pp. 82–115.
12. Eldredge, *Time Frames*, p. 139.
13. Mayr, Ernst, *Current Controversies in Evolutionary Biology*, Public Lecture, University of California at Berkeley (October 23, 1987). "The debate over punctuated equilibrium is still in full swing, but the following conclusions can be drawn: No real saltations occur; they take place over several generations. Periods of long continued stasis are real. Changes in size and proportion are gradual. Large, widespread species are evolutionarily inert."
14. Raup, D. M. and J. J. Sepkoski, Jr., "Periodicity of Extinctions in the Geologic Past," *Proceedings of the National Academy of Sciences* 81 (1984), pp. 801–5.
15. Eldredge, *Life Pulse*, p. 168.
16. Arthur, Wallace, *The Niche in Competition and Evolution* (Chichester [West Sussex]; New York: John Wiley, 1987), p. 139.

Coupled with the idea that lack of interspecific competition tends to be associated with evolutionary shifts goes the idea that occurrence of competition is associated with evolutionary stasis. That is, in a species-rich system, the sort of selection stemming from interspecific competition may most often be stabilizing. This hypothesis (and that is all that it is) seems to run contrary to the idea of competition being an agent of directional selection, as encountered in the process of character displacement. However, the two ideas are not mutually exclusive. One satisfying picture which combines the two is that of a gradual increase in the species-richness of a group as its adaptive radiation proceeds, involving sequentially: (1) Major evolutionary shifts in the absence of competition; (2) coevolutionary fine tuning as pairs of species come into competitive contact; (3) stabilizing selection predominating as each species becomes sandwiched either between two others or between one other and the end of a resource spectrum.

17. Gould, Stephen Jay, "Life's Little Joke: The Evolutionary Histories of Horses and Humans Share a Dubious Distinction," *Natural History* (April 1, 1987), p. 16.
18. Brown, James H. and Arthur C. Gibson, *Biogeography* (St. Louis: C.V. Mosby, 1983), p. 182.

CHAPTER 6, BRAINS AND TOOLS

1. White, Robert and Dan McKenzie, "Volcanism at Rifts," *Scientific American* (July 1989), pp. 62–71.
2. Stager, Curt, "Africa's Great Rift," *National Geographic* (May 1990), pp. 2–41.
3. The author is indebted to William Kimbel of the Institute of Human Origins, Berkeley, California, for reviewing an early draft of this chapter.
4. Allman, William F., "The First Humans," *U.S. News & World Report* (February 27, 1989), pp. 52–59.
   Tierney, John, "The Search for Adam and Eve," *Newsweek* (January 11, 1988), pp. 46–52.
5. Hay, Richard L. and Mary D. Leakey, "The Fossil Footprints of Laetoli," in *Prehistoric Times: Readings from Scientific American* (San Francisco: W.H. Freeman, 1983), pp. 48–55. In 1978, an expedition led by Mary Leakey uncovered a trail of beautifully preserved footprints that proved that our forebears began walking upright at least 3.75 million years ago.
6. Lovejoy, C. Owen, "The Origin of Man," *Science* (January 23, 1981), pp. 341–50.
   Lovejoy, C. Owen, "The Natural Detective: An anthropologist probes the mysterious origin of human bipediality," *Natural History* (October 1984), pp. 24–28.
7. Blumenberg, Bennett, "The Evolution of the Advanced Hominid Brain," *Current Anthropology* (December 1983), p. 612.
   Isaac, Glynn, *Early Stages in the Evolution of Human Behavior: The Adaptive Significance of Stone Tools* (Amsterdam: Stichting Nederlands Museum, 1983), pp. 20–21.
8. Isaac, Glynn, "Early Stone Tools—An Adaptive Threshold?" in *Problems in Economic and Social Anthropology*, G. de G. Sieveking, I. H. Longworth, and K. E. Wilson, eds. (London: Gerald Duckworth, 1976), pp. 39–47.
9. Binford, Lewis R., *Debating Archaeology* (San Diego: Academic Press, 1989), p. 288.
   Binford, Lewis R., "Human Ancestors: Changing Views of Their Behavior," *Journal of Anthropological Archaeology* (1985), p. 292.
   Binford, Lewis R., "Searching for Camps and Missing the Evidence? Another Look at the Lower Paleolithic," in *The Pleistocene Old World: Regional Perspectives*, Olga Soffer, ed. (New York: Plenum Press, 1987), p. 20.
   Potts, Richard, "Home Bases and Early Hominids," *American Scientist* (July–August 1984), pp. 338–47.
   Toth, Nicholas, "The First Technology," *Scientific American* (April 1987), pp. 112–21.
   Johanson, Donald C. and Maitland A. Edey, *Lucy: The Beginnings of Humankind* (New York: Warner Books, 1981), p. 231.
10. Stevens, William K., "Evidence Dates Fire's Use a Million Years Ago," *New York Times* (December 1, 1988), p. A4.

11. Shreeve, James, "Argument Over a Woman," *Discover* (August 1990), pp. 52–59.
Stringer, C. B. and P. Andrews, "Genetic and Fossil Evidence for the Origin of Modern Humans," *Science* (March 11, 1988), pp. 1263–68.
Wilford, John Noble, "Findings Fan Debate on Human Origins," *New York Times* (February 14, 1989), p. B5.
Bower, B., "Modern Humans May Need Redefining," *Science News* (April 14, 1990), p. 228.
12. Gould, Stephen Jay, "A Novel Notion of Neanderthal," *Natural History* (June 1988), pp. 16–21.
13. Diamond, Jared, "The Great Leap Forward," *Discover* (May 1989), pp. 50–60.
Begley, Sharon, "My Granddad, Neanderthal?" *Newsweek* (October 16, 1989), pp. 68–71.
14. White, Randall, "Visual Thinking in the Ice Age," *Scientific American* (July 1989), p. 99. "Although certain types of neural 'hardware' were no doubt a prerequisite for these innovations, the inception of image-based representation should not be seen as the crossing of a neurological threshold. On the contrary, it was more probably a cultural transition based on the establishment of shared conventions of representation."
15. Lewin, Roger, *Human Evolution: An Illustrated Introduction* (San Francisco: W.H. Freeman, 1984), pp. 64–70.
Isaac, Glynn L., "Chronology and the Tempo of Cultural Change During the Pleistocene," in *Calibration of Hominid Evolution*, W. W. Bishop and J. A. Miller, eds. (Edinburgh: Scottish Academic Press, 1972), pp. 392–99.
16. Toth, "First Technology," p. 119.
Isaac, *Early Stages*, pp. 22–23.
17. Lovejoy, "Origin of Man," p. 341. "There is little doubt that material culture has played a role in the evolution of *Homo sapiens* and *H. erectus*, but this does not require it to have been a significant factor in the origin of hominids [*H. habilis*]."
Binford, *Debating Archaeology*, p. 326.
Vrba, E. S., "Environment and Evolution: Alternative Causes of the Temporal Distribution of Evolutionary Events," *South African Journal of Science* (1985), pp. 229–36.
18. Vrba, E. S., "Ecological and Adaptive Changes Associated with Early Hominid Evolution," in *Ancestors: The Hard Evidence*, E. Delson, ed. (New York: Alan R. Liss, 1985), pp. 63–71.
Vrba, E. S., "Ecology in Relation to Speciation Rates: Some Case Histories of Miocene-Recent Mammal Clades," *Evolutionary Ecology* (1987), pp. 283–300.
Vrba, Elisabeth S., "Late Pliocene Climatic Events and Hominid Evolution," in *Evolutionary History of the "Robust" Australopithecines*, F. E. Grine, ed. (New York: Aldine de Gruyter, 1988), pp. 405–26.
19. Professor Vrba offered these "purely speculative comments" at a University of California at Berkeley seminar entitled *Human Ancestors: New Discoveries, New Interpretations* (October 22, 1989).
20. Gould, Stephen Jay, *Ontogeny and Philogeny* (Cambridge: Harvard University Press, 1977), p. 4. "Evolution occurs when ontogeny [development] is altered in one of two ways: when new characters are introduced at any stage of development with varying effects upon subsequent stages, or when characters already present undergo changes in developmental timing."
21. Blumenberg, "Evolution of the Advanced Hominid Brain," p. 614.
22. Riska, Bruce and William R. Atchley, "Genetics of Growth Predict Patterns of Brain-Size Evolution," *Science* (August 16, 1985), pp. 668–71.
23. Gould, *Ontogeny*, pp. 354, 352–404.
24. Lorenz, Konrad, *Studies in Animal Behaviour*, Vol. II, trans. by Robert Martin (Cambridge: Harvard University Press, 1971), pp. 234–35. "When Benjamin Franklin drew sparks from the leash of his kite, he thought no more about the possibilities of a lightning conductor than Hertz thought about the possibilities of radio when investigating electric waves. Anybody who has seen in his own activities the smooth transition from inquisitive childhood play to the life-work of a scientist could never doubt the fundamental identity of play and research. Nietzsche states that the inquisitive child (completely departed from the nature of a full-grown, completely animal chimpanzee) 'is *hidden* within the "true human being;" but in fact it completely *dominates* him [italics in original]!' "

25. Mayr, Ernst, *The Growth of Biological Thought* (Cambridge: Harvard University Press, 1982), p. 50. "There is [not] and never was a program on the basis of which either cosmic or biological evolution has occurred. If there is a seeming aspect of progression in biological evolution, from the prokaryotes of two or three billion years ago to the higher animals and plants, this can be explained entirely as the result of selection forces generated by competition among individuals and species and by the colonization of new adaptive zones."

26. Mayr, Ernst, *Evolution and the Diversity of Life* (Cambridge: Harvard University Press, 1976), pp. 389–93. "*A teleonomic process or behavior is one that owes its goal directedness to the operation of a program....*'[P]rogram' might be defined as *coded or prearranged information that controls a process (or behavior) leading it toward a given end....* The origin of a program is quite irrelevant for the definition. It can be the product of evolution, as are all genetic programs, or it can be the acquired information [learning] of an open program, or it can be a manmade device. Anything that does *not* lead to what is at least in principle a predictable goal does not qualify as a program [italics in original]."
Pittendrigh, Colin S., "Adaptation, Natural Selection, and Behavior," in *Behavior and Evolution*, A. Roe and G. G. Simpson, eds. (New Haven: Yale University Press, 1958), pp. 390–416.
See chapter 9, note 4.

CHAPTER 7, TECHNOLOGY'S RHYTHM

1. See Wolpoff, Milford, *Paleoanthropology* (New York: Alfred A. Knopf, 1980), p. 355. Citing C. L. Brace.

2. Wilford, John Noble, "Excavations Show Fast Culture Change," *New York Times* (June 2, 1985), p. 14.

3. See Frazzetta, Thomas H., *Complex Adaptations in Evolving Populations* (Sunderland, MA: Sinauer Associates, 1975), p. 141.

4. Daumas, Maurice, *A History of Technology and Invention: Progress Through the Ages*, Vol. 3 (New York: Crown, 1979), pp. 49–50, 183–84.
Ferguson, Eugene S. in *The Technology of Western Civilization*, Vol. 1 (New York: Oxford University Press, 1967), p. 257.

5. Meindl, James D., "Chips for Advanced Computing," *Scientific American* (October 1987), p. 86. "Indeed, an inspiring feature of the history of technology is the appearance of discontinuities: points where the established limits are violated and new vistas suddenly open up. Discontinuities are caused by discoveries or inventions that fundamentally change future prospects."

6. Rosenberg, Nathan, *Inside the Black Box: Technology and Economics* (Cambridge: Cambridge University Press, 1982), pp. 5–7.

7. Schumpeter, Joseph A., *Capitalism, Socialism and Democracy* (New York: Harper & Row, 1950), p. 84.

8. Usher, Abbott Payson, *A History of Mechanical Inventions*, rev. ed. (New York: Dover, 1954), p. 10.

9. Usher, *History of Mechanical Inventions*, p. 68. "The history of the reciprocal steam engine involves at least five strategic inventions: the atmospheric engine of Newcomen; the low-pressure engine of Watt; the high-pressure engine of Trevithick and Evans; the steam locomotive of Hackworth and Robert Stephenson; the compound engines. In many instances, it is not possible to cite a single inventor even for a particular stage in this long development."

10. Bryant, Lynwood, "The Beginnings of the Internal-Combustion Engine," in *Technology in Western Civilization*, Vol. 1 (Oxford: Oxford University Press, 1967), p. 664.

11. Bryant, "The Beginnings," pp. 648–50.

12. Schneidawind, John and Don Clark, "Many Technical Forecasts Have Been Big Flubs," *San Francisco Examiner* (November 27, 1989), p. D1.

13. Nelson, Richard R. and Sidney G. Winter, *An Evolutionary Theory of Economic Change* (Cambridge: Harvard University Press, 1982).
Boulding, Kenneth E., *Evolutionary Economics* (Beverly Hills: Sage Publications, 1981).

14. Yew, Lee Kuan, "Abandon a Contest America Has Nearly Won?" *Wall Street Journal* (October 11, 1985).

PART II, ORGANISM AND ORGANIZATION/CHAPTER 8, FORM AND FUNCTION

1. Usher, Abbott Payson, *A History of Mechanical Inventions*, rev. ed. (New York: Dover, 1954), p. 17.
2. McMahon, Thomas A. and John Tyler Bonner, *On Size and Life* (New York: Scientific American Library, 1983).
3. Bradbury, S., "The Quality of the Image Produced by the Compound Microscope: 1700–1840," in *Historical Aspects of Microscopy*, S. Bradbury and G. L'e. Turner, eds. (Cambridge: W. Heffer & Sons, 1967), pp. 151–72.
   Turner, G. L'e., "The Microscope as a Technical Frontier in Science," in Bradbury and Turner, *Historical Aspects*, p. 191.
   Darnell, James and David Lodish, *Molecular Cell Biology* (New York: Scientific American Books, 1986), p. 140.
   Mulvey, T., "The History of the Electron Microscope," in Bradbury and Turner, *Historical Aspects*, pp. 201–27.
4. Wolfe, Stephen L., *Cell Ultrastructure* (Belmont, CA: Wadsworth, 1985), p. 27.
5. Steer, Martin W., *Understanding Cell Structure* (Cambridge: Cambridge University Press, 1981), p. 4.
   Bonner, John Tyler, *The Evolution of Complexity by Means of Natural Selection* (Princeton: Princeton University Press, 1988), p. 145.
   Edwards, N. A. and K. A. Hassal, *Biochemistry and Physiology of the Cell: An Introductory Text*, 2d ed. (London: McGraw-Hill, 1980), p. 3. "Construction processes in biology, as in human technology, are energy consuming and include operations which demand special organization. Left to itself, London Bridge will tend to fall down. To construct objects such as bridges, numerous smaller parts have to be assembled by human endeavor. In one small part of the Universe, and for a short period of its history, local order has increased and energy-consuming operations have been possible. It is the same for a living cell; for the brief time of its living existence, energy, ultimately derived from *sunlight*, is used to provide energy for anabolic processes and for creating a greater local orderliness. Increasing the level of orderliness is known to chemists as *decreasing entropy* [italics in original]."
6. de Duve, Christian, *A Guided Tour of the Living Cell* (New York: Scientific American Books, 1984), p. 64. By means that are not yet understood, the inner lining of a lysosome is constructed in a way that resists the powerful digestive action of the enzymes it contains.
7. Vogel, Shawna, "The Shape of Proteins to Come," *Discover* (October 1, 1988), p. 43.
8. de Duve, *Guided Tour*, p. 86.
9. Rothman, James E., "The Compartmental Organization of the Golgi Appartus," *Scientific American* (September 1985), pp. 74–89.
10. Wolfe, *Cell Ultrastructure*, p. 46.
11. Friday, Adrian and David S. Ingram, eds., *The Cambridge Encyclopedia of Life Sciences* (Cambridge: Cambridge University Press, 1985), p. 10. "ATP molecules are the common unit of energy exchange in the cell. . . . ATP is often thought of metaphorically as the energy currency of the cell."
    Wolfe, *Cell Ultrastructure*, p. 30. "ATP, the molecule that serves as the dollar of the cell's energy economy."
12. Bulger, Ruth Ellen and Judy May Strum, *The Functioning Cytoplasm* (New York: Plenum Press, 1974), p. 2.
    Wolfe, *Cell Ultrastructure*, p. 34.
13. McMahon, Thomas A. and John Tyler Bonner, *On Size and Life* (New York: Scientific American Library, 1983), p. 22.
    Bonner, *Evolution of Complexity*, pp. 122–23, 191.
    Ptashne, Mark, "How Gene Activators Work," *Scientific American* (January 1989), pp. 41–47.
14. Sheeler, Phillip and Donald E. Bianchi, *Cell and Molecular Biology*, 3d ed. (New York: John Wiley, 1987), p. 29.
15. Lentz, Thomas L., *Cell Fine Structure: An Atlas of Drawings of Whole-Cell Structure* (Philadelphia: W.B. Saunders, 1971), p. 194.
16. Lentz, *Cell Fine Structure*, p. 94.
17. Wolfe, *Cell Ultrastructure*, pp. 32–44.

Reid, Robert A. and Rachel M. Leech, *Biochemistry and Structure of Cell Organelles* (New York: John Wiley, 1980), pp. 1–10.

18. See Toong, Hoo-Min D., "Microprocessors," *Scientific American* (September 1977), p. 146.
19. Terman, Lewis M., "The Role of Microelectronics in Data Processing," *Scientific American* (September 1977), p. 163. "Moreover, with the development of the microprocessor there has been an almost Darwinian speciation of computers into machines of different sizes and organizations, each tailored to a different range of functions."
20. Rogers, Everett M. and Judith K. Larsen, *Silicon Valley Fever: Growth of High-Technology Culture* (New York: Basic Books, 1984), pp. 103–11.
21. The author is indebted to Howard High, Greg Spirakis, Scot Ruska, Pat Gelsinger, John Crawford, and Riaz Haq of Intel Corporation for their cooperation in a series of interviews.

CHAPTER 9, DESIGN BY COMPROMISE

1. Avers, Charlotte J., *Molecular Cell Biology* (Reading, MA: Addison-Wesley, 1986), p. 10.
   Hawley, Gessner G., *Seeing the Invisible: The Story of the Electron Microscope* (New York: Alfred A. Knopf, 1945), p. 11.
   Darnell, James and David Lodish, *Molecular Cell Biology* (New York: Scientific American Books, 1986), p. 133.
2. Schopf, J. William, "The Evolution of the Earliest Cells," *Scientific American* (September 1978), p. 114.
   Van Iterson, Woutera, ed., *Inner Structures of Bacteria* (New York: Van Nostrand Reinhold, 1984), p. 11.
3. Reid, Robert A. and Rachel M. Leech, *Biochemistry and Structure of Cell Organelles* (New York: John Wiley, 1980), p. 155. "Once nutritional dependency is established between an endosymbiont and its host, selection might be expected in favour of processes that link them further, so that their individual growth rates and metabolisms are more closely integrated."
4. Staddon, J. E. R., *Adaptive Behavior and Learning* (Cambridge: Cambridge University Press, 1983), p. 6. "Functional explanations can, in principle, be reduced to mechanistic ones: Given perfect understanding of the principles of genetics and development, and complete information about evolutionary history, we can, in principle, reconstruct the process by which the shark achieved its efficient form. For this reason the biologist Pittendrigh (1958) suggested the label *teleonomic* (as opposed to *teleological*) for such accounts. Teleological explanations are not acceptable because they imply final causation— the shark's streamlining is teleologically explained by Mother Nature's hydrodynamic foresight. Teleonomic accounts relate form and hydrodynamics through the mechanisms of variation and natural selection. Teleonomic functional accounts are philosophically respectable; teleological ones are not. In practice, of course, the necessary detailed information about mechanisms is often lacking so that we must settle for functional accounts and hope that they are teleonomic ones."
   See chapter 6, note 26.
5. Like any structure, the design of the eukaryotic cell is the result of trade-offs. An even broader array of more specialized organelles might boost cellular efficiency. But constructing more narrowly specialized organelles might consume more resources than could be saved through enhanced effficiency. See Reid and Leech, *Biochemistry and Structure*, p. 1.
6. Steer, Martin W., *Understanding Cell Structure* (Cambridge: Cambridge University Press, 1981), p. 4.
7. Reid and Leech, *Biochemistry and Structure*, p. 6.
8. Wolfe, Stephen L., *Cell Ultrastructure* (Belmont, CA: Wadsworth, 1985), p. 16.
   Srere, Paul A. and Ronald W. Estabrook, *Microenvironments and Metabolic Compartmentation* (New York: Academic Press, 1978), p. xiii.
9. Margulis, Lynn, *Symbiosis in Cell Evolution* (San Francisco: W.H. Freeman, 1981), p. 162.

Margulis, Lynn and Dorion Sagan, *Microcosmos: Four Billion Years of Evolution from Our Microbial Ancestors* (New York: Summit Books, 1986), pp. 115–19.

Wolfe, *Cell Ultrastructure*, pp. 30–34.

Ahmadjian, Vernon and Surindar Paracer, *Symbiosis: An Introduction to Biological Associations* (Hanover, NH: University Press of New England, 1986), p. 60.

10. Arthur, Wallace, *The Niche in Competition and Evolution* (Chichester [West Sussex]; New York: John Wiley, 1987), pp. 91, 142. "Community structure has no single dominant organizing force, but interspecific competition is one of the group of organizing forces that we find. In the long term, major evolutionary shifts seem to be associated, in a variety of ways, with empty niche space and a *lack* of competition. . . . [L]ack of competition is important for major evolutionary change. Given some empty niche space *and sufficient evolutionary time*, something will evolve to utilize it."

11. Bonner, John Tyler, *The Evolution of Complexity by Means of Natural Selection* (Princeton: Princeton University Press, 1988), pp. 59, 114–17.

12. Bonner, *Evolution of Complexity*, p. 164.

13. Sudd, John H. and Nigel R. Franks, *The Behavioural Ecology of Ants* (New York: Chapman and Hall, 1987), pp. 40–41. "One of the most striking analogies between human factories and ant colonies concerns economies of scale. Ant colonies of intermediate size, just like firms of medium capacity, often grow faster and are more efficient per capita than both smaller colonies (or companies that are especially prone to bankruptcy), and very large colonies (or firms), where inefficiencies arise from stretched and broken lines of communication which cause slow responses to changing environments."

14. Birch, David L., *Job Creation in America* (New York: Free Press, 1987), p. 21.

Birch, David L., "The Hidden Economy: While Big Companies Languish, Little Ones Are Creating Jobs and Fueling Demand," *Wall Street Journal* (June 10, 1988), p. 23R.

CHAPTER 10, AMERICAN *PERESTROIKA*

1. Clark, Don and John Schneidawind, "90's Hold High Tech Promise," *San Francisco Chronicle* (December 27, 1989), p. D1.

2. Shurkin, Joel, *Engines of the Mind: A History of the Computer* (New York: W.W. Norton, 1984), pp. 166, 197.

Noyce, Robert N., "Microelectronics," *Scientific American* (September 1977), p. 650. "Today's [1977] microcomputer, at a cost of perhaps $300, has more computing power than the first large electronic computer, ENIAC. It is 20 times faster, has a larger memory, is thousands of times more reliable, consumes the power of a light bulb rather than that of a locomotive, occupies 1/30,000th the volume and costs 1/10,000th as much."

3. Holton, William C., "The Large-Scale Integration of Microelectronic Circuits," *Scientific American* (September 1977), p. 82.

4. Meindl, James D., "Microelectronic Circuit Elements," *Scientific American* (September 1977), p. 70.

Sutherland, Ivan E. and Carver A. Mead, "Microelectronics and Computer Science," *Scientific American* (September 1977), p. 210.

Terman, Lewis M., "The Role of Microelectronics in Data Processing," *Scientific American* (September 1977), p. 162.

5. Usher, Abbott Payson, *A History of Mechanical Inventions*, rev. ed. (New York: Dover, 1954), pp. 238–57.

6. Noyce, "Microelectronics," p. 63. "[T]here has also been a true revolution: a qualitative change in technology, the integrated microelectronic circuit, has given rise to a qualitative change in human capabilities. . . . And we are only slowly perceiving the intellectual and social implications of the personal computer, which will give the individual access to vast stores of information and the ability to learn from it, add to it and communicate with others concerning it."

See Gilder, George, *Microcosm* (New York: Simon & Schuster, 1989).

7. See Hanson, Dirk, *The New Alchemists: Silicon Valley and the Microelectronics Revolution* (Boston: Little, Brown, 1982), pp. 93–98. In February 1959, Jack Kilby of Texas Instruments filed a patent for a device called a "miniaturized electronic circuit." In July 1959, Noyce of Fairchild Semiconductor filed a patent for a semiconductor integrated

circuit based on the more efficient planar process. Noyce's approach perfected the integrated circuit and made it a commercial reality.
Clark, Don, "New Computer Revolution Looming," *San Francisco Chronicle* (November 27, 1989), p. D8.
8. Birch, *Job Creation,* p. 21.
"The Rise and Rise of America's Small Firms," *The Economist* (January 21, 1989), p. 67.
Winter, Ralph E., "Small Machining Firms Get Boost from Computers," *Wall Street Journal* (April 17, 1989), p. B2.
9. Birch, *Job Creation,* p. 1.
10. Horvath, Francis W., "The Pulse of Economic Change: Displaced Workers of 1981–85," *Monthly Labor Review* (Washington, DC: Bureau of Labor Statistics, June 1987), Table B9.
11. U.S. Department of Labor, estimate per Yvonne Twilliger, April 1989, personal communication.
12. Horvath, "Pulse of Economic Change," Table B3.
13. Bureau of Labor Statistics, "Labor Market Success Continues to Be Linked to Education" (Washington, DC: U.S. Department of Labor, September 28, 1987), Table 1. College-graduate unemployment rate—2.3 percent, less than four years of high school rate—11.1 percent.
14. Horvath, "Pulse of Economic Change," p. 7.
15. Horvath, "Pulse of Economic Change," p. 1.
16. Ansberry, Claire, "Ohio's Steel Towns, Long Laid to Rust, Begin to Resurrect," *Wall Street Journal* (December 27, 1988), p. 1.
17. Hanson, *New Alchemists,* p. 127. Quoting Marshall McLuhan: "[A]ll electronic forms whatsoever have a decentralizing effect, cutting across the older mechanical patterns like a bagpipe in a symphony."
18. Managing America's Business," *The Economist* (December 22, 1984), p. 96.
19. Peters, Tom, "New Products, New Markets, New Competition, New Thinking," *The Economist* (March 4, 1989), p. 19.
20. Gilder, George, "The Revitalization of Everything: The Law of the Microcosm," *Harvard Business Review* (March–April 1988), p. 57.
21. Hanson, *New Alchemists,* p. xiii. Quoting Neil Postman of New York University: "Just as the physical environment determines what the source of food and exertions of labor shall be, the information environment gives specific direction to the kinds of ideas, social attitudes, definitions of knowledge and intellectual capacities that will emerge. . . . [W]hen there occurs a radical shift in the structure of that environment, this must be followed by changes in social organization, intellectual predispositions and a sense of what is real and valuable. . . . We might say that the most potent revolutionaries are those people who invent new media of communication, although typically they are not aware of what they are doing."

CHAPTER 11, A COMMONS FALLACY

1. Hough, Jerry F., *Opening Up the Soviet Economy* (Washington, DC: Brookings Institution, 1988), p. 24.
2. See Brzezinski, Zbigniew, *The Grand Failure: The Birth and Death of Communism* (New York: Scribner's, 1989), p. 34.
3. Goldman, Marshall I., *Gorbachev's Challenge: Economic Reform in the Age of High Technology* (New York: W.W. Norton, 1987), p. 116.
4. Hewett, Ed A., *Reforming the Soviet Economy: Equality vs. Efficiency* (Washington, DC: Brookings Institution, 1988), pp. 31–93.
5. Aganbegyan, Abel, *The Economic Challenge of Perestroika* (Bloomington: Indiana University Press, 1988), p. 6.
6. Abrams, Garry, "How U.S. Marxists Explain Europe," *San Francisco Chronicle* [Los Angeles Times News Service] (December 13, 1989), p. Briefing 3.
7. See Riding, Alan, "Communist Parties in West Are Shaken and Squabbling," *New York Times* (January 9, 1990), p. 1: " 'Communism has not yet existed anywhere,' argued Anicet Le Pors, who is campaigning for change in the French Communist Party. 'In my

view, it remains a high ideal. What's being condemned today is the perversion of socialism in the form of Stalinism, and not socialism itself.' "

8. See Kamenka, Eugene, ed., "The Manifesto of the Communist Party," in *The Portable Karl Marx* (New York: Penguin Books, 1983).

9. Bonner, John Tyler, *The Evolution of Complexity by Means of Natural Selection* (Princeton: Princeton University Press, 1988), pp. 61–62.

10. Hardin, Garrett, "The Tragedy of the Commons," *Science* 162 (December 1, 1968), p. 1243.

11. Wilford, John Noble, "Space Rockets vs. Butter Is the Talk of Russia," *New York Times* (April 17, 1989), p. A13.

12. Keatley, Robert, "Needing Overhaul, Soviet Economy Gets a Patch Job," *Wall Street Journal* (June 5, 1989), p. A19.

13. Pouschine, Tatiana, "Star Wars Isn't Dead Yet," *Forbes* (May 1, 1989), p. 82. Quoting Dennis Kloske, U.S. Deputy Undersecretary of Defense: "The Soviets fully understood the development of an SDI and a technology demonstrator program would create the critical core of new, advanced or even revolutionary technologies for conventional defense."

14. Lewis, Flora, "The Red-Eye Disease," *New York Times* (April 16, 1989), p. E25.

15. D'Anastasio, Mark, "Soviet Health System, Despite Early Claims, Is Riddled by Failures," *Wall Street Journal* (August 18, 1987), p. 1.
Fein, Esther B., "In Soviet Asia Backwater, Infancy's a Rite of Survival," *New York Times* (August 14, 1989), p. 1.

16. Keller, Bill, "For Grim Soviet Consumers, The New Year of Discontent," *New York Times* (January 1, 1989), p. 1.

17. Passell, Peter, "Where Communist Economies Fell Short," *New York Times* (December 17, 1989), p. E3. "Soviet economists once thought they could use computer models to simulate the decentralized workings of markets, but that idea has proved far beyond the capacities of the speediest supercomputer."
Aganbegyan, *Economic Challenge*, p. xvii.

18. Brimelow, Peter, "Why Liberalism Is Now Obsolete: An Interview with Nobel Laureate Milton Friedman," *Forbes* (December 12, 1988), p. 161.

> You have to distinguish between a static economy and a dynamic economy. I think it is perfectly possible that you could handle a static economy better by computer than by the price system. But the problems are twofold. First, there is no conceivable political system which would lead to the correct programs for the computer. And second, the computer is not capable of initiating improvement by itself. You can't innovate by computer. Is there a computer that could have invented the supermarket? People don't realize what are the great inventions of the 20th century. The supermarket is one of them.

19. Aganbegyan, *Economic Challenge*, pp. 25–30.

20. Gumbel, Peter, "Soviet Union Plans to Let Entrepreneurs Fill Gap Left by the Creaky State Sector," *Wall Street Journal* (May 26, 1988), p. 20.

21. Keller, Bill, "Sharp Turn for Russians: Autonomy in Industry to Challenge Worker," *New York Times* (January 2, 1988), p. 1.
Keller, Bill, "Going Co-op: At the Soviet Economic Frontier," *New York Times* (March 26, 1988), p. 1.

22. Keller, Bill, "Private Soviet Entrepreneurs Under Fire Try Closing Ranks," *New York Times* (November 14, 1988), p. 1.

23. Shogren, Elizabeth, "Soviets Weary of Perestroika That's All Talk, No Action," *San Francisco Chronicle* (December 13, 1989), p. A25. Quoting Valerian Odvadze, a lawmaker from Tbilisi.

24. Lewis, "Red-Eye Disease," p. E25.

25. Aganbegyan, *Economic Challenge*, pp. 109–23.

26. "Glasnost and Unemployment: The Labour Pains of Perestroika," *The Economist* (December 26, 1987), p. 15.

27. Keller, Bill, "Soviet Change vs. the Worker's Security: Gorbachev's People, Changing a Reluctant Nation," *New York Times* (May 10, 1988), p. 1.

28. Aganbegyan, *Economic Challenge*, p. xxvii.
    Hough, *Opening Up*, p. 47.

PART III, ENERGY AND VALUE/CHAPTER 12, SURPLUS AND GENES

1. *The Macmillan Book of Business and Economic Quotations* (New York: Macmillan, 1984), p. 157.
2. Childress, James J., Horst Felbeck, and George N. Somero, "Symbiosis in the Deep Sea," *Scientific American* 256 (May 1987), p. 115.
3. Brownlee, Shannon, "Bizarre Beasts of the Abyss," *Discover* (July 1, 1984), p. 73.
   Grassle, J. Frederick, "Hydrothermal Vent Animals: Distribution and Biology," *Science* 229 (August 23, 1985), p. 713.
4. Ballard, Robert D. and J. Frederick Grassle, "Return to Oases of the Deep," *National Geographic* 156 (November 1979), p. 698.
5. "Oasis of Sulphurous Smoke," *The Economist* (December 20, 1986), p. 118.
   Anderson, Roger N., "Sulphur-eating Tubeworms Take to the Oregon Breach," *Nature* (March 7, 1985), p. 18.
6. Meier, Barry, "Clues to Food, Minerals Gains May Lie at Bottom of the Sea," *Wall Street Journal* (September 12, 1986), p. 27. Clams recently discovered in the sewers of Los Angeles, another hydrogen-sulfide–rich environment, appear to rely on the same biochemistry.
7. Childress, et al., "Symbiosis," p. 117.
8. Sullivan, Walter, "Sea Floor Discoveries Pose New Evolutionary Questions," *New York Times* (August 26, 1985), p. 1.
9. Jordan, William, "The Bee Complex," *Science* (May 1, 1984), p. 58.
10. Heinrich, Bernd, *Bumblebee Economics* (Cambridge: Harvard University Press, 1979), pp. 8–10. This chapter draws extensively on Heinrich's work.
11. Heinrich, Bernd, "Bumblebee Foraging and the Economics of Sociality," *American Scientist* 64 (July 1, 1976), p. 386.
12. Grimaldi, David A., "Still Life with Flowers," *Natural History* (September 1988), p. 89.
13. Heinrich, "Bumblebee Foraging," p. 394.
14. Pianka, Eric R., *Evolutionary Ecology* (New York: Harper & Row, 1983), pp. 270–80.
15. Jordan, "Bumblebee Complex," p. 58, and personal correspondence with Heinrich.
16. Heinrich, Bernd, "The Foraging Specializations of Individual Bumblebees," *Ecological Monographs* (Spring 1976), pp. 105–28.
    Heinrich, Bernd, "Bee Flowers: A Hypothesis on Flower Variety and Blooming Times," *Evolution* (June 30, 1975), pp. 325–34.
17. Heinrich, *Bumblebee Economics*, p. 134.
18. Heinrich, "Bumblebee Foraging," pp. 387–92.
    Heinrich, Bernd, "The Invisible Hand Loses Its Grip," *Business and Society Review* (Winter 1974–75), p. 30.
    Heinrich, *Bumblebee Economics*, pp. 142–44.
19. See Kamil, Alan C. and Theodore D. Sargent, eds., *Foraging Behavior: Ecological, Ethological, and Psychological Approaches* (New York: Garland Press, 1981).
20. The author is indebted to Professor Bernd Heinrich for reviewing the author's estimates and calculations in the "Estimated Annual Energy Income Statement for a Typical Hive of *Bombus terricola*."

Revenues and Gross Profit per Foraging Minute

Heinrich, Bernd, "Energetics of Temperature Regulation and Foraging in a Bumblebee, *Bombus terricola Kirby*," *J. Comparative Physiology* 77:1 (1972), p. 55, table 2.

Returning to nest	25.87 avg mg sugar
Leaving nest	-3.50 avg mg sugar
Sugar profit/trip	22.37 avg mg sugar
Average minutes/trip	60

Sugar profit/minute   0.37
Calories/sugar mg   4
Calorie gross profit/min   1.49
Calorie cost/foraging minute   0.28 (Heinrich [1979], p. 100)
Total cal. revenue/min   1.77

Revenue per foraging minute is roughly the same in cold and warm weather. In cold weather, fewer individuals can operate so there is less competition for nectar. In warm weather there is more competition, but there are more flowers.

Direct Costs per Foraging Minute—Heinrich, *Bumblebee Economics*, p. 100, fig. 7.3

Warming up costs about 0.15 calories/minute at about 10°C
  Flying costs about 0.28 calories per minute regardless of temperature
  = 0.43 calories/minute at 10°C
  = 0.28 calories/minute at 23°C or higher

Minutes per Average Foraging Trip—Heinrich, *Bumblebee Economics*, p.35, figure 2.6, and personal communication

60 minutes per average trip

Average Number of Daily Forager Trips—Heinrich, *Bumblebee Economics*, p.36

9 trips per day on warm days
  8 trips per day on cold days (because of later starts and shorter days)

Average Number of Foragers—Heinrich personal communication

45 foragers (90 percent of maximum *B. terricola* worker population of 50)
  In the month of May (and ten rainy summer days) average total population is about 20 (17 foragers)

Number of Cold or Warm Days

40 cold days—May plus 10 rainy summer days
  75 warm days—June, July, and three weeks in August less 10 rainy summer days

Feeding the Queen—Heinrich personal communication

13 cal/hour resting rate at 30°C typical nest temperature × 8 hours/day × 110 days/season = 11,440 calories/season at rest
  13 cal/hour × 2 estimated doubling of metabolic rate during egg production × 16 hours/day × 110 days/season = 45,760 calories/season during egg production
  = 57,200 total calories/season to feed the queen

Feeding the Worker Larvae—Author's estimate

110 days per season/14-day worker lifespan = 7.86 sets of workers/season × 42.5 workers (Population of 20 in May, 50 in June, July, August) = 334 total workers produced during one season × 22,680 calories required for each new queen (see below) × 20% because workers are only about 20% of queen size = 1,515,024 calories to feed all the worker larvae for one season

Incubating the Worker Larvae—Author's estimate

0.10 cal/minute (about one-third the energy of flying) × five nurse workers on an average day (10 percent of 50 population) × 14 hours/day (assumes daytime temps require little incubating) × 60 minutes/hour × 80 days (no workers produced during hive's last 30 days) = 33,600 calories/season

In-Hive Worker Heat Losses (not elsewhere counted)—Author's estimate

0.10 cal/minute × 60 minutes/hour × 14 hours/day (nighttime occupation and low temperatures) × 50 workers × 90 days = 378,000 calories/season

Worker Death (Retained in workers at time of death)—Author's estimate

334 workers (see above) × 30 calories/worker (estimate) = 10,020 calories/season

Net Profit Available for Reinvestment

Feeding the Queen/Drone Larvae—Heinrich, *Bumblebee Economics*, p. 160

New Queens
    B. vosnesenskii queens consume 6.3 g honey from egg-to-readiness
    6.3 g honey × 90% sugar = 5.67 g sugar × 4 calories/mg = 22,680
    calories/new queen × 25 new queens = 567,000 calories
Drones
    22,680 calories/new queen/three Drones are about one-third the size of new queens × 3
    about 3 times as many drones produced as queens × 25 new queens = 567,000 calories
    = 1,134,000 calories for all reproductives

Incubating Queen/Drone Larvae—Author's estimate

0.10 calories per minute × 5 nursery workers × 30 days (estimate to raise *B. terricola* reproductives from eggs) × 18 hours (cool hours on average August day) × 60 minutes = 16,200 calories

Profit Not Reinvested—Heinrich personal communication

8,000 unused calories/4 cal per mg sugar = 2.0 grams sugar

21. Sudd, John H. and Nigel R. Franks, *The Behavioural Ecology of Ants* (New York: Chapman and Hall, 1987), p. 40: "Ant colonies are in many respects closely analogous to human factories; a division of labor is organized so as to maximize profits, portions of which are reinvested to maintain the production machinery, sustain further growth or set up new factories. An ant colony producing more sexual offspring than its neighbors is effectively increasing its market share, just as a profitable company might do." Pianka, *Evolutionary Ecology*, pp. 132–33.
22. Heinrich, *Bumblebee Economics*, p. 95.
23. Heinrich, Bernd, *In a Patch of Fireweed* (Cambridge: Harvard University Press, 1984), p. 79. "A biological view of the world is in many ways an economic one, but with important differences from what an economist might see. An ecologist sees the world in terms of a much larger community—one including other organisms with energy flow or economic transactions involving costs and payoffs at different points along the spectrum. The economist, in contrast, is more apt to isolate man out of the community of which he is a part."

CHAPTER 13, PROFITS AND TECHNOLOGY

1. Hicks, Jonathan, "New Materials Altering the Aircraft Industry," *New York Times* (December 20, 1989), p. C5.

2. Harris, Jr., Roy J., "Technology: Aerospace Firms Are Relying on Unlikely Sources for Help," *Wall Street Journal* (July 27, 1984), p. 21.
3. The author is indebted to Rita Simmer of Super Valu Stores, Inc., Jack Hooley and Cub Davis of Cub Foods, Inc., and to Jerry Golub and Lewis Golub of the Golub Corporation, for their cooperation in interviews. The author would also like to thank Ian Raferty of Willard Bishop Consulting Economists, Ltd., for providing access to its supermarket-industry studies.
4. Breen, Sarah, Jerry Golub, and Jim Chadderdon, *A Competitive Analysis of Cub Foods* (Boston: Boston University; unpublished thesis, June 4, 1985), p. 5.
5. Morris, Betsy and Steve Weiner, "Bigger, Shrewder and Cheaper Cub Leads Food Stores into the Future," *Wall Street Journal* (August 26, 1985), p. 1.
6. Hobart, Carol, "A Big Hit: Indianapolis Shaken Up by Cub," *Supermarket News* (December 21, 1987), p. 30.
7. "The Competitive Positioning of the Super Warehouse Store" (Barrington, IL: Willard Bishop Consulting Economists, Ltd., 1984).

8.	Conventional	Super-Warehouse	Warehouse
Avg. Purchase	$26.67	$35.92	$50.18
GM(%)	24%	15%	11%
GM($)	$6.40	$5.39	$5.52
Savings(%)	0%	15%	20%
Savings ($/Trip)	$0.00	$6.34	$12.55
Roundtrip Min.	40	70	100
Extra Minutes	0	30	60
$ Saved/Minute	$ 0.00	$ 0.21	$ 0.21
$ Saved/Hour	$ 0.00	$12.68	$12.55
Imputed Tax(%)		21%	21%
Gross Shopping Wage		$16.05	$15.88

Please see chart following on pp. 372–73.

9. *Competitive Edge Insight Report*, Vol. X, No. 2 (Barrington, IL: Willard Bishop Consulting Economists, Ltd., October, 1988), p. 2.
10. "Characteristics of Seven American Grocery Store Species, 1987–88." Courtesy of Willard Bishop Consulting Economists, Ltd.

CHAPTER 14, SAVINGS AND TAXES

1. See Part VII: Parasitism and Exploitation
2. Pechman, Joseph A., *Federal Tax Policy*, 5th ed. (Washington, DC: Brookings Institution, 1987), p. 84. If the $13,000 was wage or salary income, the earner would still have to pay Social Security taxes.
3. *The United States Tax System, A Brief History* (Washington, DC: U.S. Government Printing Office, 1960).
   Webber, Carolyn and Aaron Wildavsky, *A History of Taxation in the Western World* (New York: Simon & Schuster, 1986), p. 419.
4. Congressional Budget Office, *Reducing the Deficit: Spending and Revenue Options* (Washington, DC: U.S. Government Printing Office, March, 1988), table 1, p. 3.
5. Summers, Lawrence, "Stimulating American Personal Saving," *The U.S. Savings Challenge: Policy Options for the Future*, Charls E. Walker, Mark A. Bloomfield, and Margo Thorning, eds. (Boulder, CO: Westview Press, 1990).
6. Some might say that home building is investing in the future. This is a common misconception. When you buy a car, you are buying what economists call a "consumer durable"— a long-lasting consumer good. You consume a car gradually, as it wears out. You repair and service it to help maintain its value.
   The same is true of houses, except that houses last longer and are more expensive. Houses last long enough to have their values strongly affected by inflation. Also, because

houses are attached to land, population pressure often drives up land values and prices of houses in a certain area. In other cases, the local population declines and house prices tumble.

Even if you are fortunate enough to sell an old car or an old house at a profit, it is not an "investment" in the economist's sense of the word. Investment means spending on productive facilities, on capabilities that will produce more future output. Cars and homes do not produce anything. They are slowly consumed by their occupants.

7. Bradford, David F., "What is National Saving?" in *The U.S. Savings Challenge*.
8. Summers, "Stimulating American Personal Saving."
9. Pechman, *Federal Tax Policy*, p. 190. "[C]onsumption taxes are less important here [the U.S.] than anywhere else in the world. In 1985 consumption taxes accounted for 14 percent of total federal, state, and local tax revenues."
   Nash, Nathaniel C., "Japan's Banks: Top 10 in Deposits," *New York Times* (July 20, 1988), p. C1.

Store Species	Convenience	Limited Assortment	Conventional
Description/Characteristics	24 hr. Limited Items	Barebones, Low Price	Original Supermarket
	Some Takeout Items	Few Items and	Often with Deli and
	Often with Gasoline	No Perishables	Bakery
Relative Price Index			
(Conventional = 100)	125	85	100
Size (Total Square Feet)	2,600	10,000	24,500
Total Investment ($ Million)	0.3	0.6	2.2
$ Sales/Week	$8,500	$75,000	$130,000
Number of Items	3,500	900	12,000
Percent Nonfood Sales	10.0%	3.0%	8.0%
Gross Margin %	31.0%	12.0%	22.7%
Customer Visits/Week	3,500	3,700	9,600
$ Sales/Customer Visit	$2.50	$20.00	$13.50
Number of Checkstands	1	2	8
Trade Area Population	6,000	65,000	40,000
Est. Market Radius (Miles)	0.5	4.0	2.0
Est. Mins/Shopping Roundtr	10	30	40
Annual inventory Turns	12	40	19
Net Profit Before Tax %	3.8%	2.5%	1.5%

Chira, Susan, "Japan's Lower House Approves Big Tax Overhaul," *New York Times* (November 17, 1988), p. A3. In November, 1988, Japan's lower house approved a sweeping tax overhaul that would cut income taxes and introduce a 3 percent sales tax.
Balassa and Noland, *Japan in the World Economy* (Washington, DC: Institute for International Economics, 1988). The high rate of personal saving in Japan is the major contributor to the country's high national saving rate. The high personal saving rate is attributed to the high price of housing in Japan and to government tax policy. Overall, the tax system is biased toward saving—income from saving is taxed at a relatively low rate and interest payments on debt are not deductible from taxable income.
"Whatever Happened to Saving?" *The Economist* (February 3, 1990), p. 13.
Johnson, Manuel H., "Saving: The Challenges for Economic Policy," in *The U.S. Savings Challenge*.
10. Drucker, Peter F., "Japan's Not-So-Secret Weapon," *Wall Street Journal* (January 9, 1990), p. A14.

Volcker, Paul A., "Speech to the ACCF Conference on Saving," in *The U.S. Savings Challenge.*

"America and Japan: The Unhappy Alliance," *The Economist* (February 17, 1990), pp. 21–24.

Kinsley, Michael, "A Capitalist's Guide to Capital Gains," *Time* (November 6, 1989), p. 108.

11. See Buchanan, James M. and Richard E. Wagner, *Democracy in Deficit* (New York: Academic Press, 1977).

12. Walker, Charls E. and Mark A. Bloomfield, eds., *The Consumption Tax: A Better Alternative?* (Cambridge, MA: Ballinger Publishing, 1987).

Makin, John H., ed., *Real Tax Reform: Replacing the Income Tax* (Washington, DC: American Enterprise Institute, 1985).

Langley, Monica and Alan Murray, "Planning Ahead: Expecting a Tax Rise Next Year, Lobbyists Try to Protect Clients," *Wall Street Journal* (October 12, 1988), p. 1.

Superstore	Food/Drug Combo	Warehouse	Super-Warehouse
Large Supermarket	Superstore plus	Barebones, Low Price	Superstore/Warehouse
Deli, Bakery, and	Drugstore	Limited Selection	24 hr. Wide Selection
Seafood		No Specialty Depts.	Low Prices, Services
105	105	85	90
39,000	48,000	32,000	60,000
4.2	5.0	2.4	5.9
$250,000	$315,000	$210,000	$525,000
17,500	25,000	10,500	16,000
11.0%	16.0%	6.0%	5.0%
24.0%	25.5%	16.0%	15.5%
16,500	18,000	9,500	16,500
$16.00	$17.50	$22.25	$32.00
15	20	25	25
55,000	65,000	75,000	125,000
2.5	2.5	5–10	5–10
45	46	110	70
26	22	24	30
1.7%	1.9%	1.8%	1.6%

Shoven, John B., "Consumption Taxes vs. Income Taxes for Deficit Reduction and Tax Restructuring," in *The U.S. Savings Challenge.*

13. Pechman, *Federal Tax Policy*, pp. 190–213.

14. Bradford, "What is National Saving?" p. 390.

15. Kotlikoff, Laurence J., "The Case for the Value-Added Tax," *Tax Notes* (April 11, 1988), p. 241.

Bradford, David F., "What are Consumption Taxes and Who Pays Them?" *Tax Notes* (April 18, 1988), p. 389.

16. McClure, Charles E., "State and Local Implications of a Federal Value-Added Tax," *Tax Notes* (March 28, 1988).

17. Clark, Jr., Lindley H., "A Consumption Tax Is Better—But Highly Unlikely," *Wall Street Journal* (September 30, 1986).

Birnbaum, Jeffrey H., "Senate Finance Panel Members Begin Talking About Consumption Tax to Raise New Revenue," *Wall Street Journal* (June 26, 1985), p. 52.

Kilborn, Peter T., "Two Tax System Changes Favored by Greenspan," *New York Times* (March 4, 1988), p. D5.

PART IV, LEARNING AND PROGRESS/CHAPTER 15, SURVIVAL TRAINING

1. Jerison, Harry J., "Issues in Brain Evolution," in *Oxford Surveys in Evolutionary Biology, Vol. 2* (1985), pp. 102–34. "From Aristotle to Darwin to our own time, naturalists have identified intelligence with the capacity to learn and to adapt to new situations."
2. Tartar, Vance, *The Biology of Stentor* (New York: Pergamon Press, 1961), p. 8.
3. Jennings, H. S., *Behavior of the Lower Organisms* (Bloomington: Indiana University Press, 1962), pp. 174–75.
   Jennings, H. S., "Studies on reactions to stimuli in unicellar oranisms: IX—On the behavior of fixed infusoria (Stentor and Vorticella), with special reference to the modifiability of protozoan reactions," *American Journal of Physiology* 8:1 (October 1, 1902).
   See Bonner, John Tyler, *The Evolution of Complexity by Means of Natural Selection* (Princeton: Princeton University Press, 1988), p. 203.
4. Mackintosh, N. J., B. Wilson, and R. A. Boakes, "Differences in Mechanisms of Intelligence Among Vertebrates," in *Animal Intelligence*, L. Weiskrantz, F. R. S., ed. (Oxford: Clarendon Press, 1985), p. 53.
5. Staddon, J. E. R., *Adaptive Behavior and Learning* (Cambridge: Cambridge University Press, 1983), p. 2. "[W]e do not really know what learning is. Indeed, there is probably no single process that underlies it. Experience can change behavior in many ways that manifestly do not involve learning, as well as in other ways where we are not sure. In other words, there is no hard-and-fast line separating learning from other kinds of behavioral change."
   Corning, W. C., J. A. Dyal, and A. O. D. Willows, eds., *Invertebrate Learning, Vol. 1, Protozoans Through Annelids* (New York: Plenum Press, 1973), p. 117.
   Macphail, E. M., *Brain and Intelligence in Vertebrates* (Oxford: Clarendon Press, 1982), pp. 9–15.
6. But see Corning et al., *Invertebrate Learning*, pp. 67–71.
   Levandowdsky, M. and S. H. Huntner, eds., *Biochemistry and Physiology of Protozoa*, 2d Ed., Vol. 1 (New York: Academic Press, 1979), pp. 341–52.
7. Tolman, E. C., "The Inheritance of Maze Learning in Rats," *Journal of Comparative Psychology* 4 (1924), pp. 1–18.
8. Honzik, C. H. and E. C. Tolman, "Degrees of Hunger, Reward and Non-Reward, and Maze Learning in Rats," *University of California Publications in Psychology* 4:16 (December 19, 1930), pp. 241–56.
9. Marler, P. and H. S. Terrace, eds., *The Biology of Learning* (Berlin: Springer-Verlag, 1983), p. 157.
10. Jerison, "Issues in Brain Evolution," p. 104.
11. Macphail, *Brain and Intelligence*, p. 7.
12. Jerison, Harry J., *Evolution of the Brain and Intelligence* (New York: Academic Press, 1973).
13. Jerison, Harry J., "Animal Intelligence as Encephalization," in *Animal Intelligence*, L. Weiskrantz, F.R.S., ed. (Oxford: Clarendon Press, 1985), p. 22.
14. Macphail, *Brain and Intelligence*, p. 30.
15. Jerison, "Animal Intelligence," p. 29.
16. Jerison, "Animal Intelligence," p. 27.
17. Macphail, E. M., "Vertebrate Intelligence: The Null Hypothesis," in *Animal Intelligence*, L. Weiskrantz, F.R.S., ed. (Oxford: Clarendon Press, 1985), p. 48.
18. Herman, Louis M., Douglas G. Richards, and James P. Wolz, "Comprehension of Sentences by Bottlenosed Dolphins," *Cognition* (March 1984), pp. 129–219.
19. White, Randall, "Visual Thinking in the Ice Age," *Scientific American* (July 1989), pp. 98–99.
20. Shipman, Pat, "The Gripping Story of Paranthropus," *Discovery* (April 1989), p. 66.
    Diamond, Jared, "How to Speak Neanderthal," *Discovery* (January 1990), p. 52.
    Humphrey, N. K. "The Social Function of Intellect," in *Growing Points in Ethology*,

P. P. G. Bateson and R. A. Hind, eds. (Cambridge: Cambridge University Press, 1976), pp. 303–17.

CHAPTER 16, ORGANIZATIONAL LEARNING

1. Arrow, Kenneth J., "The Economic Implications of Learning by Doing," *Review of Economic Studies* (June 1962), p. 155: "I do not think that the picture of technical change as a vast and prolonged process of learning about the environment in which we operate is in any way a far-fetched analogy; exactly the same phenomenon of improvement in performance over time is involved."
   Hirschmann, Winfred B., "Profit from the Learning Curve," *Harvard Business Review* (January–February 1964), p. 139: "Learning is a property of all living organisms. They can trace improvement patterns characteristic of themselves. Since organized groups can be looked upon as living entities, they can be expected to exhibit learning and to trace such patterns."
2. *Historical Statistics of the U.S., Colonial Times to 1970* (Washington, DC: U.S. Department of Commerce, 1975), p. 524.
3. But see "Cholesterol Lower in California Eggs," *New York Times* (October 20, 1988), p. B15.
4. Pringle, J. W. S., "On the Parallel Between Learning and Evolution," *Behavior* 3 (1951), p. 174–215.
   Conniff, Richard, "Superchicken: Whose Life Is It Anyway?" *Discover* (June 1988), pp. 33–40.
5. The author is indebted to Darwin Lewis and Greg Lewis for agreeing to be interviewed at Darwin Farms.
   Willoughby, Jack, "Eggshells Everywhere," *Forbes* (May 29, 1989), pp. 254–62.
6. Conniff, "Superchicken," p. 33.
7. After researching this chapter, the author invested in Animalens, Inc. and joined its board of directors.
   Posner, Bruce G., "Anatomy of a Start-Up: Seeing Red," *Inc.* (May 1989), pp. 48–59.

CHAPTER 17, THE UNIVERSAL CURVE

1. Ghemawat, Pankaj, "Building Strategy on the Experience Curve," *Harvard Business Review* (March–April 1985), p. 143. The learning curve's formula is: $c(x) = ax^b$, where $c(x)$ is the marginal cost, a is the cost of the first unit, x is the cumulative output, and b is the learning "elasticity," which defines the slope of the learning curve.
   Hirschmann, Winfred B., "Profit from the Learning Curve," *Harvard Business Review* (January–February 1964), pp. 125–39. "Learning is a property of all living organisms. They can trace improvement patterns characteristic of themselves. Since organized groups can be looked upon as living entities, they can be expected to exhibit learning and to trace such patterns."
2. Andress, Frank J., "The Learning Curve as a Production Tool," *Harvard Business Review* (January–February 1954).
   See Weiner, Eric, "Innovative Plane Making its Debut," *New York Times* (June 5, 1989), p. C1.
3. Wright, T. P., "Factors Affecting the Cost of Airplanes," *Journal of the Aeronautical Sciences* (February 1936), pp. 122–28.
4. Yelle, Louis E., "The Learning Curve: Historical Review and Comprehensive Survey," *Decision Sciences* (April 1979), pp. 302–28.
5. Asher, H., "Cost-Quantity Relationships in the Airframe Industry" (Santa Monica, CA: RAND Corporation, July 1956), Report 291.
   Reguero, Miguel A., *An Economic Study of the Military Airframe Industry* (Wright-Patterson Air Force Base, OH: Department of the Air Force, October 1957).
   Alchian, Armen, "Reliability of Progress Curves in Airframe Production," *Econometrica* (October 1963), pp. 679–93.
   Hirschmann, "Profit," p. 127.
6. Hirsch, Werner Z., "Firm Progress Ratios," *Econometrica* 24:2 (April 1956), pp. 136–43.

Rapping, Leonard, "Learning and World War II Production Functions," *Review of Economics and Statistics* XLVII:1 (February 1965), pp. 81–86.

Preston, L. E. and E. C. Keachie, "Cost Functions and Progress Functions: An Integration," *American Economic Review* (March 1964), pp. 100–107.

Barloff, Nicholas, "The Learning Curve—Some Controversial Issues," *Journal of Industrial Economics* 14:3 (July 1966), pp. 275–82.

7. Andress, "The Learning Curve," p. 96.

8. Conley, Patrick, *Experience Curves as a Planning Tool: A Special Commentary* (Boston: Boston Consulting Group, 1970), p. 8.

Henderson, Bruce D., *The Experience Curve—Reviewed II: History* (Boston: Boston Consulting Group, 1973), p. 1.

Henderson, Bruce D., *The Experience Curve Revisited* (Boston: Boston Consulting Group, 1980), p. 2. "The cost characteristics of experience curves can be observed in all elements of cost whether labor costs, advertising costs, overhead costs, marketing costs, development costs or manufacturing costs. It seems to be immaterial whether the value added is labor or capital intensive."

Wright, T. P., "Factors Affecting the Cost," p. 125. Wright reported the same finding in his 1936 article. He found that as labor costs fell on an 80 percent curve, the costs of raw materials and "purchased" materials were on 95 percent and 88 percent curves, respectively. In effect, the term *the experience curve* was a marketing gambit by BCG to attribute recency to the old but obscure discovery of the "learning curve."

9. Dutton, John M. and Anne Thomas, "Treating Progress Functions as a Managerial Opportunity," *Academy of Management Review* (1984), p. 238.

10. Learning curves have been published for steel, soft contact lenses, life insurance policies, automobiles, bottle caps, gas ranges, refrigerators, gasoline refining, room air-conditioners, TV picture tubes, aluminum, optical fibers, vacuum cleaners, motorcycles, steam turbine generators, ethyl alcohol, beer, facial tissues, transistors, microprocessors, float glass, long-distance telephone calls, knit fabric, lawn mowers, air travel, crude-oil production, typesetting, oil-refinery construction, factory maintenance, and hydroelectric power.

11. Thompson, Donald N., "The Experience Curve Effect on Costs and Prices: Implications for Public Policy," in *Regulation of Marketing and the Public Interest*, Balderston, Frederick E., James M. Carman, and Francesco M. Nicosia, eds. (New York: Pergamon Press, 1981), p. 62.

12. Henderson, Bruce D., *Cross-Sectional Experience Curves* (Boston: Boston Consulting Group, 1978), p. 3.

Henderson, *The Experience Curve—Reviewed II*, p. 4.

Henderson, Bruce D., *The Experience Curve—Reviewed III: Why Does It Work?* (Boston: Boston Consulting Group, 1974), p. 4.

Henderson, *Experience Curve Revisited*, p. 2.

13. See Gilder, George, *The Spirit of Enterprise* (New York: Simon & Schuster, 1984), p. 158.

Yelle, "The Learning Curve," p. 309.

14. The author was a consultant with the Boston Consulting Group from 1977 to 1980.

15. Lieberman, Marvin B., "The Learning Curve, Diffusion, and Competitive Strategy," *Strategic Management Journal* (1987), pp. 441–52. "Only rarely is it in firms' interests to pursue 'pre-emptive' strategies. And although often overlooked, information diffusion plays a key role in the competitive process."

Ghemawat, Pankaj and A. Michael Spence, "Learning Curve Spillovers and Market Performance," *Quarterly Journal of Economics* (Supplement, 1985), p. 839.

16. Kiechel III, Walter, "The Decline of the Experience Curve," *Fortune* (October 5, 1981), p. 139. "The news for the 1980s isn't that the EC has been proved wrong. Indeed, its logic has been refined, its implications plumbed for new ideas such as shared costs and the life cycles of technologies. What's happening now, though, is that the curve is being consigned to a much reduced place in the firmament of strategic concepts. With it is a good bit of the importance originally attached to market share."

17. Preston and Keachie, "Cost Functions," p. 105. "Judging from current textbooks and casual observation, the 'learning' phenomenon receives almost no mention in the standard treatments of production costs in economics or industrial engineering courses."

Mansfield, Edwin, *Microeconomics: Theory and Applications, 6th ed.* (New York: W.W. Norton, 1988), pp. 550–56.
Blaug, Mark, *Economic Theory in Retrospect, 4th ed.* (Cambridge: Cambridge University Press, 1985).
18. But see Arrow, Kenneth J., "The Economic Implications of Learning by Doing," *Review of Economic Studies* (June 1962), p. 156. "The role of experience in increasing productivity has not gone unobserved, though the relation has yet to be absorbed into the main corpus of economic theory."
Hirsch, "Firm Progress Ratios."
Preston and Keachie, "Cost Functions."
Ghemawat and Spence, "Learning Curve Spillovers."
Ross, David R., "Learning to Dominate," *Journal of Industrial Economics* (June 1986), pp. 337–53.
Spence, A. Michael, "The Learning Curve and Competition," *Bell Journal of Economics* (Spring 1981).
Barloff, "The Learning Curve."
Fudenberg, Drew and Jean Tirole, "Learning-by-Doing and Market Performance," *Bell Journal of Economics* (Autumn 1983).

Regarding the relationship between the learning curve and conventional economic theory, the following comments are drawn from telephone interviews with three Stanford University faculty members:
Kenneth Arrow (May 3, 1989): "It's kind of ignored."
Nathan Rosenberg (January 16, 1989): "There is a huge literature on the learning curve, but it is very formalistic and it is within a static framework. Most of the literature is from the mid-1960s to the mid-1970s. It is no longer at the forefront of economic thinking."
Marvin Lieberman (April 25, 1989): "The learning curve is outside the mainstream. You can't derive it from a theoretical model. It's not a theory, and it's the theories that get published. It's a topic at the fringe. The learning curve is not explainable within the normal confines of economics, so it's ignored."
But see Ross, David R., "Policy Implications of the Learning Curve," (Chicago: Northwestern University, Ph.D. dissertation, 1984), University Microfilms #8411184.

19. Hirsch, "Firm Progress Ratios," pp. 136–37. "Most economic theory so far assumes the state of the arts as given and no allowance is made for changes in it. Progress functions can be considered to reflect temporal changes of irreversible technical knowledge. They are dynamic cost functions and are distinctly different from conventional long-run cost functions which are timeless or assume stability in technical knowledge. A conventional long-run cost function is related to points on a number of production functions, each point being associated with a different plant, but all plants using the same general technical knowledge."
20. See chapter 4 for a more complete treatment of this point.
21. Blaug, *Economic Theory*, p. 402. "Marshall at last generalizes the law of diminishing returns to all the agents of production, making it applicable to manufacture as well as to agriculture."
Wooley, Kenneth Musser, *Experience Curves and Their Use In Planning* (Palo Alto: Stanford University, Ph.D. dissertation, May 1972), University Microfilms #7230723.
Lieberman, Marvin B., "The Learning Curve, Diffusion, and Competitive Strategy," *Strategic Management Journal* (1987), p. 443. "Using optimal control theory, these studies demonstrate that the standard MR = C condition for profit maximization given by static economic theory fails to be valid in a dynamic environment."
Arthur, W. Brian, "Positive Feedbacks in the Economy," *Scientific American* (February 1990), p. 92. "Conventional economic theory is built on the assumption of diminishing returns. Economic actions engender a negative feedback that leads to a predictable equilibrium for prices and market shares. Such feedback tends to stabilize the economy because any major changes will be offset by the very reactions they generate. . . .
"Such an agreeable picture often does violence to reality. In many parts of the economy, stabilizing forces appear not to operate. Instead positive feedback magnifies the effects of small economic shifts; the economic models that describe such effects differ vastly from

the conventional ones. Diminishing returns imply a single equilibrium point for the economy, but positive feedback—increasing returns—makes for many possible equilibrium points."

22. Mill, John Stuart, *Principles of Political Economy*, W. J. Ashley, ed. (London: Longmans, Green, 1909), p. 177.

23. Blaug, *Economic Theory*, p. 380: "*Competitive equilibrium is incompatible with downward-sloping long-run supply curves* [italics in original]."
Blaug, *Economic Theory*, p. 412. On the difficulties presented by decreasing-cost industries, Alfred Marshall admitted that the problem is one of "organic growth" not "statical equilibrium."
Arthur, W. Brian, Comment in *Bulletin of the Santa Fe Institute*, Vol. 4, No. 1 (Santa Fe: Santa Fe Institute, Winter–Spring 1989), p. 5.
Henderson, *The Experience Curve—Reviewed II*, p. 3. "The experience curve is a contradiction of some of the most basic assumptions of classical economic theory. All economics assumes that there is a finite minimum cost which is a function of scale. . . . The whole concept of a free enterprise competitive equilibrium assumes that all competitors can achieve comparable costs at volumes much less than pro rata shares of the market. That is not true either. Our entire concept of competition, anti-trust, and non-monopolistic free enterprise is based on a fallacy if the experience curve effect is true."

24. See Bailey, Ronald, "Dr. Doom," *Forbes* (October 16, 1989), p. 44.
Arthur, "Positive Feedbacks," p. 93. "Orthodox economists avoided increasing returns for deeper reasons. . . . Some economists found the existence of more than one solution to the same problem distasteful—unscientific. . . . Other economists could see that theories incorporating increasing returns would destroy their familiar world of unique, predictable equilibria and the notion that the market's choice is always best. . . . Economists restricted themselves to diminishing returns, which presented no anomalies and could be analyzed completely."

25. King, Seth S., "Worldwide Food Production Levels Show a Big Rise," *New York Times* (December 2, 1984), p. 12. Worldwide, food production has increased by 30 percent in the last ten years. It has been increasing annually by about 3.2 percent, while the population worldwide has grown about 2.1 percent.

26. Rosenberg, Nathan, "Technological Interdependence in the American Economy," *Technology and Culture* (January 1979) pp. 49–50. "Although electricity was introduced into the household in its early years almost entirely for purposes of illumination, it soon provided the basis for much else, which eventually transformed the operation of domestic households: refrigerators, electric ranges, water heaters, vacuum cleaners, dishwashers, clothes dryers, freezers, etc."

27. Henderson, Bruce D., *Cross-Sectional Experience Curves*, p. 3. "The experience curve phenomenon is as real as gravity. Otherwise, there is little to explain the constant growth in per capita output."

28. Henderson, Bruce D., *Why Costs Go Down Forever* (Boston: Boston Consulting Group, 1974).

29. Falling unit costs and rising productivity are two sides of the same coin. Increasing productivity or efficiency means improving economic performance, using less input (cost) for the same or greater output. In effect, a nation's rising productivity curve (output units per labor hour) is an inverted version of its "composite learning curve" (labor hour per output unit).

30. Rosenberg, "Technological Interdependence," pp. 26–40. See p. 34. Quoting Hunter, Louis, *Steamboats on the Western Rivers* (Cambridge: Harvard University Press, 1949), pp. 121–22:

> The story is not for the most part, one enlivened by great feats of creative genius, by startling inventions or revolutionary ideas. Rather, it is one of plodding progress in which invention in the formal sense counted far less than a multitude of minor improvements, adjustments, and adaptations. The heroes of the piece were not so much such men as Watt, Nasmyth, and Maudslay, Fulton, Evans, and Shreve— although the role of such men was important—but the anonymous and unheroic craftsmen, shop foremen, and master mechanics in whose hands rested the daily job of making things go and making them go a little better.

31. See chapter 1, note 24.

Henderson, *Experience Curve Revisited*, p. 2. "Often products change even though they serve the same needs of the same customers. This would not happen if the changed product was not more cost effective."

Sanger, David E., "Japan to Design Superfast Airliner," *New York Times* (August 10, 1988), p. C1.

32. David, Paul A., "Learning by Doing and Tariff Protection: A Reconsideration of the Case of the Ante-Bellum United States Cotton Textile Industry," *Journal of Economic History* (September 1970), pp. 521–601.

Andrews, Edmund L., "Mach 3 Passengers? No Simple Formula," *New York Times* (January 14, 1990), p. F8.

CHAPTER 18, JAPAN'S SECRET WEAPON

1.

Car/Year	1912$	1958$	1989$
Ford Model T	$600	$2,000	$8,250
Ford Escort	NA	NA	$6,495

2. Abernathy, William J. and Kenneth Wayne, "Limits of the Learning Curve," *Harvard Business Review* (September–October 1974), pp. 115–18.

Henderson, Bruce D., *Why Costs Go Down Forever* (Boston: Boston Consulting Group, 1974), p. 1. "Without growth, cost decline does in fact slowly fade until it becomes imperceptible."

3. Gilder, George, *The Spirit of Enterprise* (New York: Simon & Schuster, 1984), p. 168. "Business magazines [in 1983] intensified their ongoing critiques of the experience curve, as if it were an optional facet of business life rather than the essence of it. . . . No company working in the shadows of Japanese productivity, however, can escape the constraints of the curve."

4. Greenhouse, Steven, "An Anxious Philips: The Electronics Giant Is Struggling to Keep Up with the Japanese," *New York Times* (June 4, 1989), p. F1.

Sanger, David E., "Japanese Electronics Thrive Despite Asian Competition," *New York Times* (December 28, 1988), p. C1.

5. Sanger, David E., "A New Japanese Push on Chips," *New York Times* (November 9, 1988), p. C1.

Sanger, David E., "Contrasts on Chips: As a Joint Venture Collapses in U.S., Japanese Companies Act like a Cartel," *New York Times* (January 18, 1990), p. C1.

6 This section relies heavily on Prestowitz, Clyde V., *Trading Places: How We Allowed Japan to Take the Lead* (New York: Basic Books, 1988), p. 11.

Tolchin, Martin, "Technology Report Finds Japan Leads in 6 Areas," *New York Times* (May 16, 1989), p. C15. Reported on defense technologies only.

Tolchin, Martin, "Crucial Technologies: 22 Make the U.S. List," *New York Times* (March 17, 1989), p. C1.

Freiberger, Paul, "U.S. Fights for Its High-Tech Life," *San Francisco Examiner* (January 8, 1989), p. D1.

7. Powell, B., et al., "Japan Goes Hollywood," *Newsweek* (October 9, 1989), pp. 62–72.

A September 1989 *Newsweek* poll found that 52 percent of Americans think the economic power of Japan is the greatest threat to the United States, while 33 percent think the military power of the Soviet Union is a greater threat.

8. Pollack, Andrew, "Japan's New Farm Belt: Japanese Money Is Pouring into U.S. Farms, Ranches and Food Processing," *New York Times* (May 14, 1989), p. F1.

Hicks, Jonathan P., "The Takeover of American Industry," *New York Times* (May 28, 1989), p. F1.

9. Fallows, James, "Containing Japan," *Atlantic Monthly* (May 1989), pp. 40–54.

10. Gilder, *Spirit of Enterprise*, pp. 176–77.

Barron, James, "Rockefeller Center Stake and Other Japanese Deals Breed Jokes and Anger," *New York Times* (December 18, 1989), p. A17.

11. Schonberger, Richard J., *Japanese Manufacturing Techniques: Nine Hidden Lessons in Simplicity* (New York: Free Press, 1982), p. 2. "Total quality control procedures, implemented in concert with the just-in-time (IT) system and a host of related productivity enhancing techniques, give Japan a decisive edge in industrial management. Catching up with the Japanese depends not so much on changing tax, trade, regulatory, and labor laws and policies as it does on changing our industrial management policies, procedures, and systems."

12. Prestowitz, *Trading Places*, pp. 122, 128.
Scott, Bruce R., "National Strategy for Stronger U.S. Competitiveness," *Harvard Business Review* (March–April 1984), p. 77. "High-level Japanese officials explain the changes [in the structure of their economy] as the result of their rejection of the static theory of comparative advantage, so firmly entrenched in Western economic theory. In its place, they say, they have developed a notion of dynamic comparative advantage. Japan has shown not only that comparative advantage can be shifted but also that the shifts can be created and managed according to a pattern or plan."

13. Scott, "National Strategy." "Unfortunately, the experience curve so familiar to management consultants has not made its way into economic theory; it continues to treat evidence of the curve's existence as anecdotal and suspect. Economists rationalize the demise of U.S. industries such as TV and autos on the grounds that consumers will benefit from lower-cost imports. They assume that those who lose their jobs will automatically find equivalent work. With automatic adjustment, no strategy is needed."

14. Thompson, Donald N., "Pricing and the Experience Curve Effect," in *Macromarketing: A Canadian Perspective*, D. Thompson, ed. (Chicago: American Marketing Association, 1980), p. 109. "Experience curve analysis can be used as a basis for industrial strategy, for both growth and mature stage products. The most successful example historically is that of Japan. Exploitation of product-specific economies, combined with a willingness to sell initially at a very low margin while growth in production experience is taking place, plus a home market protected by non-tariff barriers, has enabled the Japanese to achieve world-wide comparative advantage in shipbuilding, steel, cameras, consumer electronics, and to bid for it in areas like duplicating machines."
Ghemawat, Pankaj, "Building Strategy on the Experience Curve," *Harvard Business Review* (March–April 1985), p. 143. "What distinguishes the winners from the losers in the experience curve game is their grasp of both the logic of the experience curve and the characteristics of the competitive arena that determine its suitability as a strategic weapon."
Hirschmann, Winfred B., "Profit from the Learning Curve," *Harvard Business Review* (January–February 1964), p. 128. Quoting Fred Bucy, president of Texas Instruments: "I think the big difference is that TI is the first major non-Japanese company they have run into that understands and uses the learning curve. . . . In Japan, both government and industries understand this. Most other industries don't. TI has used this concept informally and formally for many years, and this is absolutely mandatory to compete successfully with the Japanese."

15. Porter, Michael E., "Strategic Interaction: Some Lessons from Industry Histories for Theory and Antitrust Policy," in *Strategy, Predation, and Antitrust Analysis*, Steven C. Salop, ed. (Washington, DC: Federal Trade Commission, 1981).
Montgomery, David B. and George S. Day, "Experience Curves: Evidence, Empirical Issues, and Applications," in *Strategic Marketing and Management*, H. Thomas and D. Gardener, eds. (Chichester [West Sussex]: John Wiley, 1985), p. 235. "[A]ntitrust economists and politicians may be ill-advised to use industry profits as an indication of implicit collusion, and thereby an invitation to dismantle concentrated industries."
Matheson, David H. M., "Antitrust Without Economics: A Fresh Approach to Competition and to Potential Competition" (Cambridge: Harvard Law School and Harvard Business School, unpublished thesis, April 1980).

16. Reich, Robert B., "Hi-Tech Warfare: Fixated on Russia, We Risk Losing to Japan," *New Republic* (November 1, 1982), pp. 17–21.

17. Ghemawat, "Building Strategy." But see Ross, David R., "Policy Implications of the Learning Curve" (Chicago: Northwestern University, Ph.D. dissertation, 1984), University Microfilms #8411184, p. 16. "Little support is found for the position that existing antitrust laws unduly limit a firm's ability to take advantage of learning economics. The folk theorem that monopoly is socially optimal along the learning curve is shown to hold only under

extreme circumstances. However, for a wide range of plausible market conditions, models of industry evolution along a learning curve pose the fundamental policy challenge that legitimate learning behavior of predatory conduct undetected in a learning curve environment may result in unassailable market power and monopoly profits well in excess of the reward needed to bring forth the innovation characterized by the learning curve." (Note: Ross overlooks the fact that "monopolies," in the rare instances that they arise, are temporary. Rapid technology sees to that. For example, satellites destroyed AT&T's "natural monopoly" in long distance. And fiber optics are already eroding satellite dominance of international communications.)

Fuller, Charles Baden, "The Implications of the Learning Curve for Firm Strategy and Public Policy," *Applied Economics* (1983), p. 549.

Spence, A. Michael, "The Learning Curve and Competition," *Bell Journal of Economics* (Spring 1981), p. 68.

Henderson, Bruce D., *Henderson on Corporate Strategy* (Cambridge: Abt Books, 1979), pp. 90–94.

18. Prestowitz, *Trading Places*, p. 235.
19. Prestowitz, *Trading Places*, pp. 34, 269. "According to Western economic theories, Japan should have imported these products while producing others that were more competitive. Thus, in targeting IBM, Japan was implicitly rejecting Western theories. . . . [T]he Japanese cannot believe that the Americans can continue to live by an economic doctrine which, in Japanese eyes, has been close to disastrous for the United States."

Fallows, James, "Containing Japan," *Atlantic Monthly* (May 1989), p. 43. Quoting Chalmers Johnson: "If the United States were a well-run country, neoclassical economists would be hanging from the Capitol dome. . . . They predicted that by the time the dollar got down to 190 yen, the trade deficit would have disappeared."

20. Bhagwati, Jagdish, "Japanese-American Trade: Super 301's Big Bite Flouts the Rules," *New York Times* (June 4, 1989), p. F2.

Grayson, Leslie E., "For its Own Good, Japan Needs a Shove," *New York Times* (June 4, 1989), p. F2.

21. Prestowitz, *Trading Places*, pp. 75–76. "Japan's imports of manufactured goods as a percentage of gross national product had been 1.5 percent in 1960. In 1986, they were 1.6 percent despite several rounds of liberalizing trade negotiations in which Japan had made what appeared to be significant concessions. Over the same period, the U.S. numbers had gone from under 1 percent to 4.4 percent, and those for the European Economic Community (excluding intra-European trade) from 1.1 percent to 4.5 percent. Thus the amount of imports had quadrupled in the United States and European economies in response to liberalization, while remaining virtually unchanged in Japan. Moreover, there was the pattern of Japan's trade: whenever a product was manufactured in Japan, imports of it were nearly nil."

22. Dataquest, Inc., San Jose, California.
23. Prestowitz, *Trading Places*, pp. 36–37, 63.

"Who are the copy cats now?" *The Economist* (May 20, 1989), pp. 91–94.

Bulkeley, William M., "Sensitive Area: Long a U.S. Province, Supercomputer Market Feels a Japanese Threat," *Wall Street Journal* (May 24, 1989), p. A13.

Yoder, Stephen Kreider, "U.S. Chips Are Quietly Cracking the Japanese Market," *Wall Street Journal* (March 22, 1989), p. B4.

24. Gilder, George, "The Revitalization of Everything: The Law of the Microcosm," *Harvard Business Review* (March–April 1988), p. 53. "Between 1956 and 1978, when most of the key innovations arose, Japan is estimated to have paid some $9 billion for U.S. technologies that required—depending upon assignment of costs—between $500 billion and $1 trillion to develop."

25. Dataquest, Inc., San Jose, California.
26. Prestowitz, *Trading Places*, pp. 48–49.

Pollack, Andrew, "Computer Makers Decide to Abandon Joint U.S. Venture," *New York Times* (January 13, 1990), p. 1.

27. Sullivan, Jeremiah J. and Ikujiro Nonaka, "The Application of Organizational Learning Theory to Japanese and American Management," *Journal of International Business Studies* (Fall 1986), pp. 127, 129. "Several Japanese theorists offer organizational learning theory as the best descriptor of Japanese managerial behavior. They go even further and claim

that Japanese cognitive skills at carrying out organizational learning are the real source of Japanese managerial success rather than Theory Z's social skills stressing team-building, consensus, and trust (Nonaka and Sato 1981; Kagono, Nonaka, Sakakibara, and Okumura 1983, 1985; Nonaka and Johansson 1985)."

See McMillan, Charles J., "Production Planning in Japan," *Journal of General Management* (Summer 1983), pp. 43–72.

28. Imai, Masaaki, *Kaizen: The Key to Japan's Competitive Success* (New York: Random House, 1986), p. xxix.

Rappaport, Andrew, "Wrong Way to Save the Chip Industry," *Wall Street Journal* (December 15, 1989), p. A10.

29. Berger, Suzanne, Michael L. Dertouzos, Richard K. Lester, Robert M. Solow, and Lester C. Thurow, "Toward a New Industrial America," *Scientific American* (June 1989), p. 42.

In a recent comparative study of industrial research and development in Japan and the U.S., Edwin Mansfield of the University of Pennsylvania found that U.S. companies are still devoting only a third of their R&D expenditures to the improvement of process technology; the other two thirds is allocated to the development of new and improved products. In Japan those proportions in R&D expenditures are reversed. . . .

Maganizer, Ira and Mark Patinkin, *The Silent War: Inside the Global Business Battles Shaping America's Future* (New York: Random House, 1989).

Thurow, Lester C., "A Weakness in Process Technology," *Science* (December 18, 1987), pp. 1659–63.

30. Hirschmann, "Profit from the Learning Curve," pp. 134–36.

Day, George S. and David B. Montgomery, "Diagnosing the Experience Curve," *Journal of Marketing* (Spring 1983), p. 47. "Hollander found that the largest proportion of the technology-driven cost reductions were due to a series of minor technical changes based on a broad consensus that continuous cost reduction was a high priority."

31. Hirschmann, "Profit from the Learning Curve," p. 137. "Merely expecting progress does not bring it about. It is not ordained by fate to arrive on schedule, but must be continuously, vigorously, and resourcefully sought."

Day and Montgomery, "Diagnosing the Experience Curve," p. 48. "Cost reductions due to learning and technology are the result of continuous, planned efforts by management. Cumulative experience does not guarantee that costs will decline but simply presents management with an opportunity to exploit."

Thompson, Donald N., "The Experience Curve Effect on Costs and Prices: Implications for Public Policy," in *Regulation of Marketing and the Public Interest*, Baldertston, Frederick E., James M. Carman, and Francesco M. Nicosia, eds. (New York: Pergamon Press, 1981), p. 62. p. 66. "It has never been assumed that these observed or inferred reductions in cost with volume increases are automatic. They depend on a management under competitive pressure to force costs down as volume increases."

Stevenson, Richard W., "At McDonnell, Growing Pains," *New York Times* (August 15, 1989), p. C1.

32. Hayes, Robert H., "Why Japanese Factories Work," *Harvard Business Review* (July–August 1981), p. 61.

33. Schonberger, *Japanese Manufacturing Techniques*, p. 40. "The typical Western attitude is that learning occurs of its own accord—typically at a 5 to 15 percent rate; the Japanese, by contrast, are improvement oriented. That is, they strive to make learning/productivity/cost reduction happen. The advanced state-of-the-art mechanism for making it happen is the just-in-time production system."

34. Wheelwright, Steven C., "Japan—Where Operations Really Are Strategic," *Harvard Business Review* (July–August 1981), pp. 67–74.

Bacon, Kenneth H., "Rebuilding America: Start at the Factory," *Wall Street Journal* (May 16, 1988), p. 1. A 1987 Department of Defense study reports an 8 to 10 percent defect rate in U.S. electronics products versus a 0.5 to 1 percent defect rate in Japan.

Sanger, David E., "Japan's Luxury-Car Gains Pose New Threat to Rivals," *New York Times* (January 3, 1990), p. 1.

35. Lieberman, Marvin B., "Learning, Productivity and U.S.–Japan Industrial 'Competitive-

ness,' " in *Managing International Manufacturing*, Kasra Ferdows, ed. (Amsterdam; New York: Elsevier Science Publications, 1989), pp. 215–38. "[T]he ascendancy of Japanese manufacturers has been limited to a specific class of industries where the Japanese have achieved more rapid rates of learning and process improvement. The comparatively slow diffusion of manufacturing methods from Japan to the U.S. has enabled this competitive advantage to be sustained over time. . . . Japanese productivity growth has been disproportionately concentrated in industries producing high-volume products where a large number of interdependent processing steps must be coordinated (Abegglen and Stalk, *Kaisha*). Industries with these characteristics include autos, consumer electronics, cameras, watches, and copying equipment. In other industries, the absolute level of Japanese productivity, and the rate of productivity growth, have been comparable to that observed for U.S. firms. This has been true, for example, in capital-intensive process industries such as paper and chemicals, and in relatively simple assembly industries such as textiles and clothing. . . . What might account for the more rapid productivity growth of Japanese firms in these industries? I argue that it stems primarily from two factors: (1) the just-in-time approach to coordinated production flows, and (2) the human resource management policies of Japanese firms."

36. Honzik, C. H. and E. C. Tolman, "Introduction and Removal of Reward, and Maze Performance in Rats," *University of California Publications in Psychology* 4:17 (December 19, 1930), pp. 257–75.

37. Abegglen, James C. and George Stalk, Jr., *Kaisha: The Japanese Corporation* (New York: Basic Books, 1985), pp. 196–97.
    Alston, J. P., *The American Samurai* (New York: de Gruyter, 1986), pp. 10, 201–2.

38. Lieberman, "Learning, Productivity," pp. 215–38.

39. Ghemawat, "Building Strategy." "Cost reductions are almost never automatic; companies must work for them. Incentive programs should reward people for cost-reducing ideas and companies must encourage managers to implement them. Otherwise, costs may stagnate or even increase as time passes." But see "A Lada in Perestroika's Vanguard," *New York Times* (August 10, 1989), p. C10. A $12,000 bonus for a 13-member team helped cut windshield breakage in a Soviet auto plant from 12 percent to 0.3 percent.

40. Abegglen and Stalk, *Kaisha*, pp. 5–6. "The competitive fundamentals chosen by the successful kaisha [Japanese corporation] include:
    A growth bias.
    A preoccupation with actions of competitors.
    The creation and ruthless exploitation of competitive advantage.
    The choice of corporate financial and personnel policies that are economically consistent with all of the preceding.
    The strong bias toward growth of successful kaisha is closely linked to their desire to survive."

41. See McKinnon, Ronald I., "Sound Dollar Tells Business: Think Long," *Wall Street Journal* (June 15, 1989), p. A14.
    Fallows, James, "Getting Along with Japan," *Atlantic Monthly* (December, 1989), p. 53.
    Gilder, George, "American Technology at Fire-Sale Prices," *Forbes* (January 22, 1990), p. 60.

42. Thompson, "Pricing," p. 109. "[A] stable price pattern, where price follows costs and the margin between them remains fairly constant over time as experience accumulates . . . is virtually never found in North American marketing practice. Donald J. Daly of York University has concluded that virtually the only stable price patterns found are those in Japanese industry."
    Henderson, Bruce D., *The Experience Curve Revisited* (Boston: Boston Consulting Group, 1980), p. 1. "The experience curve is a cost relationship. Prices may not parallel cost for long periods of time. In the USA prices parallel costs in only approximately two-thirds of the cases. In the other third there is usually a long period when prices stay unchanged in current dollars while costs decrease steadily. This is then followed by a long period of prices falling faster than cost. This pattern is usually accompanied by significant shifts in the market share and leadership. For some reason this unstable pattern rarely occurs in Japan. In Japan prices seem to parallel costs from the beginning in almost all situations."

43. Lodge, George Cabot, "U.S. Competitiveness: The Policy Tangle," *Harvard Business Review* (January–February 1985), p. 34. "Some economists now recognize that most

trade among industrial countries turns more on dynamic learning-curve effects and scale economies than on fixed-resource endowments, but their new models have not yet been fully integrated into a broader theory."

Hershey, Robert D., Jr., "Tougher Antitrust Stance Expected," *New York Times* (April 4, 1988), p. C1.

Editorial, "Flavors of Capitalism," *New York Times* (January 15, 1990), p. A14.

44. Arthur, W. Brian, "Positive Feedbacks in the Economy," *Scientific American* (February 1990), p. 98.

45. White, Theodore H., "The Danger from Japan Forty Years after the Surrender," *New York Times Magazine* (July 28, 1985), p. 21.

PART V, STRUGGLE AND COMPETITION/CHAPTER 19, ESCAPE THROUGH DIVERSITY

1. Stonehouse, Bernard, *Wideawake Island: The Story of the B.O.U. Centenary Expedition to Ascension* (London: Hutchinson, 1960).

2. Simmons, K. E. L., "Ecological Determinants of Breeding Adaptations and Social Behavior in Two Fish-Eating Birds," in *Social Behaviour in Birds and Mammals*, J. H. Crook, ed. (London: Academic Press, 1970), p. 44.

3. Simmons, "Ecological Determinants," p. 41.

4. Brower, L. P., "Experimental Analyses of Egg Cannibalism in the Monarch and Queen Butterflies, *Danaus plexippus* and *D. gilippus berenice*," *Physiological Zoology* 34 (1961), pp. 287–96.

   Fox, Laurel R., "Cannibalism in Natural Populations," *Annual Review of Ecology and Systematics* (1975), p. 97.

5. Darwin, Charles, *The Origin of Species by Means of Natural Selection or The Preservation of Favoured Races in the Struggle for Life* (New York: Avenel Books, 1979 ed.), p. 127. "As species of the same genus have usually, though by no means invariably, some similarity in habits and constitution, and always in structure, the struggle will generally be more severe between species of the same genus, when they come into competition with one another, than between species of distinct genera."

6. Gause, G. F., *The Struggle for Existence* (New York: Hafner Publishing, 1964), p. v.

7. Pianka, Eric R., *Evolutionary Ecology*, 3d ed. (New York: Harper & Row, 1983), pp. 197, 210.

8. See Pianka, *Evolutionary Ecology*, p. 251–52. "The concept of the niche pervades all of ecology; were it not for the fact that the ecological niche has been used in so many different ways, ecology might almost be defined as the study of niches."

9. Friday, Adrian and David S. Ingram, eds., *The Cambridge Encyclopedia of the Life Sciences* (Cambridge: Cambridge University Press, 1985), p. 133. "Sharing a need for the same resource is a necessary but not a sufficient prerequisite for competition: competition will only occur if the quantity of the shared resource is insufficient to satisfy the requirements of all the consumers of that resource."

   Wilson, Edward O., *Sociobiology—The New Synthesis* (Cambridge: Harvard University Press, 1975), p. 85.

   MacArthur, Robert H., *Geographical Ecology: Patterns in the Distribution of Species* (New York: Harper & Row, 1972), p. 21.

10. Heinrich, Bernd, *Bumblebee Economics* (Cambridge: Harvard University Press, 1979), p. 148.

11. Davies, N. B. and A. I. Houston, "Territory Economics," in *Behavioural Ecology: An Evolutionary Approach*, 2d ed., J. R. Krebs and N. B. Davies, eds. (Oxford: Blackwell Scientific Publications, 1984), pp. 148–69.

12. Buss, Leo W., "Competition and Community Organization on Hard Surfaces in the Sea," in *Community Ecology*, Ted J. Case, and Jared Diamond, eds., (New York: Harper & Row, 1986), p. 521.

13. Oster, George F. and Edward O. Wilson, *Caste and Ecology in the Social Insects* (Princeton: Princeton University Press, 1978), p. 235. "[I]f a species has adopted a successful specialized defense in response to a predator, then it may appear that the predator plays only a small role in the ecology of the species, since it can be observed to inflict relatively small losses on the population."

Pianka, *Evolutionary Ecology*, p. 185. "Because it is always advantageous, when possible, for either party in a competitive relation to avoid the interaction, competition has been an important evolutionary force that has led to niche separation, specialization, and diversification. If, however, avoidance of a competitive interaction is impossible, natural selection may sometimes favor convergence."

14. Pianka, *Evolutionary Ecology*, pp. 309–16.
    MacArthur, *Geographical Ecology*, p. 210.
    Brown, James H. and Arthur C. Gibson, *Biogeography* (St. Louis: C.V. Mosby, 1983), pp. 492–522.
    Eckholm, Erik, "Secrets of the Rain Forest," *New York Times Magazine* (January 17, 1988), p. 30.
15. Hutchinson, G. Evelyn, "The Concept of Pattern in Ecology," *Proceedings of the Academy of Natural Sciences* 105 (1953), pp. 1–12.
16. Diamond, Jared M., "Distributional Ecology of New Guinea Birds," *Science* (February 23, 1973), p. 759.
17. Diamond, Jared M., "The Ethnobiologist's Dilemma," *Natural History* (June 1989), pp. 26–30.
18. Diamond, "Distributional Ecology," p. 764.
19. Diamond, Jared M., *Avifauna of the Eastern Highlands of New Guinea* (Cambridge, MA: Nuttall Ornithological Club, No. 12, 1972), p. 35.
20. MacArthur, *Geographical Ecology*, p. 61. "In human affairs we express it by saying 'a jack of all trades is a master of none.' It tells us that a harvester cannot be simultaneously perfect at several jobs; perfection in one involves reduced efficiency in another, and if an organism must try to harvest in various ways, it must compromise its efficiency in each. But since competition often puts a premium on efficiency, this assumption implies a division of labor among specialists. It is the ultimate reason we have so many species."
21. Diamond, "Distributional Ecology," p. 767.
    Diamond, *Avifauna*, p. 42.
22. Pianka, *Evolutionary Ecology*, p. 201.
    Ehrlich, Paul R. and Jonathan Roughgarden, *The Science of Ecology* (New York: Macmillan, *Evolutionary Ecology*, 1987), p. 248.
23. Pianka, *Evolutionary Ecology*, p. 197. "Perhaps the most far-reaching evolutionary effect of interspecific competition is ecological diversification, also termed niche separation. This in turn has made possible, and has led to, the development of complex biological communities. Another presumed result of both intraspecific and interspecific competition is increased efficiency of utilization of resources in short supply."
    May, Robert M., "How Many Species Are There on Earth?" *Science* (September 16, 1988), pp. 1441–49.

CHAPTER 20, ECONOMY AS ECOSYSTEM

1. Friday, Adrian and David S. Ingram, eds., *The Cambridge Encyclopedia of the Life Sciences* (Cambridge: Cambridge University Press, 1985), p. 135. In biology, "the quantity of a consumable resource may govern the level of consumers, but rarely will the consumers control the amount of their consumed resource."
2. The product is the firm's "phenotype" and its technology is its "genotype." Consumer selection acts on the phenotype, affecting the survival prospects of the genotype only indirectly. By contrast, organisms are phenotype/genotype packages. Destroying one destroys the other.
3. Superficially, resources seem to come from customers rather than suppliers. After all, a firm gets its money from its customers, not its suppliers. But, in and of itself, money has no value. Money is a record-keeping system, a clever counting device that bridges the time gap between receipt of raw materials and the shipment of finished products. But even in primitive economies where no money is used, barter still moves resources up the value-added chain from suppliers to producers to consumers.
   Stevenson, Richard W., "At McDonnell, Growing Pains," *New York Times* (August 15, 1989), p. C1.
4. Emmel, Thomas C., "Adaptation on the Wing," in *The Natural History Reader in Evolution*, Niles Eldredge, ed. (New York: Columbia University Press, 1987), p. 15.

Erlich, Paul R. and Jonathan Roughgarden, *The Science of Ecology* (New York: Macmillan, 1987), pp. 310–18.

Owen, D. F., *Camouflage and Mimicry* (Chicago: University of Chicago Press, 1982).

Gilbert, L. E., "Coevolution and Mimicry," in *Coevolution*, Douglas J. Futuyma and Montgomery Slatkin, eds. (Sunderland, MA: Sinauer Associates, 1983), pp. 263–81.

Wickler, W., *Mimicry in Plants and Animals*, trans. by R. D. Martin (New York: McGraw-Hill, 1968).

5. Mulcahy, David L., "The Rise of Angiosperms," in *The Natural History Reader in Evolution*, Niles Eldredge, ed. (New York: Columbia University Press, 1987), p. 23.

6. Andrewartha, H. G. and L. C. Birch, *The Ecological Web: More on the Distribution and Abundance of Animals* (Chicago: University of Chicago Press, 1984), p. 38.

7. Defining an industry as an "economic species" presents several problems. In nature, a species is a population of organisms that can breed among themselves and produce fertile offspring. Since organizations do not perpetuate themselves by sexual reproduction, this definition is not useful. Instead, one must look to the marketplace in any attempt to define an economic species. Whenever a customer group considers several organizations as viable alternative suppliers, then, at least for that product category, those firms should be treated as members of the same economic species or industry. The definition can never be crisp and precise. One customer may consider two firms as alternatives, while an apparently similar customer may not.

   Most firms, particularly the smallest ones, compete in only one market niche and are therefore members of just one species. But as a firm grows, it will tend to proliferate new subsidiary organizations under the same corporate umbrella. One corporation—a legal entity—may be comprised of several quite distinct economic organizations. In some cases, a single division of a company may have products that span several distinct market niches. Because of this, it is impossible to neatly pigeonhole a company or a division in one industry or another without careful study. Some large conglomerates are active in dozens of unrelated industries. Since nature observes bionomic but not legal principles, biology offers no parallel for such multispecies conglomerates.

8. Ingrassia, Paul and Gregory A. Patterson, "Is Buying a Car a Choice or a Chore? Huge Selection Has Its Pluses and Its Minuses," *Wall Street Journal* (October 24, 1989), p. B1.

9. Henderson, Bruce D., *Perspectives: To Each His Own* (Boston: Boston Consulting Group, 1979).

10. Levin, Doron P., "Minivans: Zippy Hybrids Win a Place in the Family Driveway," *New York Times* (January 14, 1990), p. F10.

    Kanabayashi, Masayoshi and Bernard Wysocki, Jr., "Japan's Auto Firms Stressing Technology in Up-Market Move Against Competition," *Wall Street Journal* (September 26, 1985), p. 38.

11. Swasy, Alecia, "P&G Moves to Revamp its Pampers," *Wall Street Journal* (August 9, 1989), p. B1.

    "This Market Didn't Bottom Out," *Wall Street Journal* (August 30, 1989), p. B1.

    Greenhouse, Steven, "Innovation Key to Diaper War," *New York Times* (November 25, 1986), p. 29.

    Grover, Mary Beth, "A Natural Toothpaste from Maine Seeks its Niche," *New York Times* (November 5, 1989), p. F13.

12. Kleinfield, N. R., "A Squeeze on Margins as Grocers Compete In Bread," *New York Times* (October 15, 1989), p. F15.

13. Rooney, Andy, "Oat Bran Immortality," *San Francisco Chronicle* (December 3, 1989), p. Supplement 3.

14. Carman, John, "Fast Backward—Decade of TV Clicks: The Change in Viewing Habits," *San Francisco Chronicle* (December 6, 1989), p. 295.

    Hershey, Robert D. J. "FCC Votes Down Fairness Doctrine in a 4–0 Decision," *New York Times* (August 5, 1987), p. 1.

15. Periodicals Institute, West Caldwell, NJ (personal communication).

16. Kerr, Peter, "Time Inc. Strategist Gerald M. Levin, A Video Visionary Sees a Future in Print," *New York Times* (September 16, 1984), p. 6. "You have to look at our corporate genes," he says. "We are predisposed to distributing information through magazines and books."

Pianka, Eric R., *Evolutionary Ecology*, 3d ed. (New York: Harper & Row, 1983), pp. 195–97.

17. Prokesch, Steven, "Awaiting the Shakeout on Fleet St.," *New York Times* (January 8, 1990), p. C1.

18. See De Sola Pool, I., H. Inose, N. Takasaki, and R. Hurwitz, *Communications Flows: A Census in the United States and Japan* (Tokyo: University of Tokyo Press, 1984).

19. "Delivery Industry's Happy Marriage," *New York Times* (December 23, 1989), p. 25.
    Sims, Calvin, "Coast-to-Coast in 20 Seconds: Fax Machines Alter Business," *New York Times* (May 6, 1988), p. 1.
    Reibstein, Larry, "Federal Express Faces Challenges to its Grip on Overnight Delivery," *Wall Street Journal* (January 8, 1988), p. 1.
    Calta, Marialisa, "How Delivery-Service Couriers Stitch the Day-to-Day Fabric of Rural Life," *New York Times* (August 23, 1989), p. B8.

20. Pianka, *Evolutionary Ecology*, p. 208. "[F]ossil history is replete with cases of natural invasions and subsequent extinctions. The simplest and most plausible explanation for many of these observations is that surviving species were superior competitors and that niche overlap was too great for coexistence. Before natural selection could produce character displacement and niche separation, one species had become extinct."
    "The Evolution of the Typewriter," *New York Times* (November 17, 1985), p. 8.
    Duke, Paul, and Karen Blumenthal, "CD Recorder Poses Upset for Industry: Tandy's Plan May Shake Recording Business," *Wall Street Journal* (April 26, 1988), p. 6.
    Fisher, Lawrence M., "A Comeback for the Vacuum Tube," *New York Times* (May 18, 1988), p. C6.
    Hicks, Jonathan P., "New Materials Altering the Aircraft Industry," *New York Times* (December 20, 1989), p. C5.

21. Tannenbaum, Jeffrey A., "As Yogurt Craze Waxes, It Taxes Some Shop Owners," *Wall Street Journal* (December 14, 1989), p. B2.
    Charlier, Marj, "Chicken Economics: The Broiler Business Consolidates, and That Is Bad News to Farms," *Wall Street Journal* (January 4, 1990), p. 1.
    Taylor, Robert, "Thrifts' Struggle Is Becoming Darwinian: Strong Turn on Weak in Brutal Consolidation," *Wall Street Journal* (July 5, 1988), p. 6.

22. Clifford, Donald K. and Richard Cavanagh, "From America's Midsize Companies: The New Way to Win at Business," *New York Times* (October 6, 1985), p. F2.
    O'Connor, Matt, "Small but Profitable Farm Gear Firms Respond to Subtleties of Weak Market," *Wall Street Journal* (December 21, 1984), p. 30.
    Russell, Mark, "Small Steelmakers Find Profitable Niches," *Wall Street Journal* (January 8, 1987), p. 6.
    Dyson, Esther, "Self-Organizing Systems," *Release 1.0* (New York: EDventure Holdings Inc., June 27, 1989), p. 31. "Competition and diversity are good—but at the right level: between companies not within them. This leads ineluctably to the conclusion that a company is frequently better off funding a start-up than taking on an innovative, counterculture project itself. . . . Cray Research's decision to split the company in two was a straightforward, clear-eyed recognition of the company's inability to support two conflicting efforts managerially and *emotionally* [emphasis in original]."

23. Goold, Michael, *Perspectives: Specialization or the Full Product Line* (Boston: Boston Consulting Group, 1979).
    Herman, Tom, "Is Financial Product Explosion Perilous for Investors?" *Wall Street Journal* (December 21, 1989), p. C1.
    Crockett, Barton, "What's New in Satellites," *New York Times* (December 24, 1989), p. F13.

24. Kotlowitz, Alex, "Truck Makers' Road is a Rough One—Firms Hurt by Rivalry, Despite Efficiency Steps," *Wall Street Journal* (November 20, 1985), p. 6.

25. Odum, Eugene P., "The Strategy of Ecosystem Development: An Understanding of Ecological Succession Provides a Basis for Resolving Man's Conflict with Nature," *Science* (April 18,1969), pp. 262–70.

26. See "Postscript: Bionomics vs. Social Darwinism."

27. Henderson, Bruce D., *Perspectives: Strategic and Natural Competition* (Boston: Boston Consulting Group, 1980). "The general theory of business competition is almost certainly in its infancy."

28. But see Henderson, Bruce D., "The Origin of Strategy," *Harvard Business Review* (November–December 1989).

CHAPTER 21, DIVIDE AND PROSPER

1. Lewontin, Richard, *Human Diversity* (New York: Scientific American Books, 1982), p. 169.
2. Hölldobler, Bert and Edward O. Wilson, *The Ants* (Cambridge: Harvard University Press, 1990), pp. 1–3.
   Wilson, Edward O., *Sociobiology—The New Synthesis* (Cambridge: Harvard University Press, 1975), pp. 397, 421.
   Sudd, John H. and Nigel R. Franks, *The Behavioural Ecology of Ants* (New York: Chapman and Hall, 1987), p. 161.
3. Wilson, *Sociobiology*, p. 398.
   Dumpert, Klaus, *The Social Biology of Ants* (Boston: Pitman Advanced Publishing Program, 1978), p. 2.
4. See Andersson, Malte, "The Evolution of Eusociality," *Annual Review of Ecological Systems* 15 (1984), p. 182.
   Wilson, *Sociobiology*, p. 399.
   Haskins, Caryl P., *Of Ants and Men* (New York: Prentice-Hall, 1939), pp. 121–127.
   Wheeler, William Morton, *Ants: Their Structure, Development and Behavior* (New York: Columbia University Press, 1910), p. 7.
5. Wilson, E. O., "The Principles of Caste Evolution," in *Experimental Behavioral Ecology and Sociobiology*, B. Holldobler and M. Lindauer, eds. (Sunderland, MA: Sinauer Associates, Inc., 1985), p. 309. "The ultimate currency in the colony fitness equations is energy. The workers appear programmed to sweep the nest environs in such a way as to gain the maximum net energetic yield. . . . Colony design then becomes essentially a problem in economics. I have suggested use of the similar expression 'ergonomics' to acknowledge that work and energy are the sole elements of calculation, and nothing like humanlike transactions with credits and money is involved."
   Oster, George F. and Edward O. Wilson, *Caste and Ecology in the Social Insects* (Princeton: Princeton University Press, 1978), p. ix: "We have chosen to view the evolution and ecology of insect castes from the perspective of ergonomic efficiency. This appears to be the only theme that is both unifying and sufficiently explicit to offer some hope of empirical verification." p. 23: "Colonies of social insects are distinguished from solitary insects less by novel behavior patterns than by increases in the scale and efficiency of their operations. The key to this improvement appears to be the ability to conduct activities concurrently instead of in series." p. 156: "Caste evolution has been guided by conflicting selective forces that promote ergonomic efficiency on the one hand and risk avoidance on the other. We can therefore usefully classify the life styles of eusocial species by the ways in which the compromise between risk and reward is struck."
   Sudd and Franks, *Behaviourial Ecology*, p. 65: "One of the secrets of the success of ants, compared with solitary insects that also have nests and show some parental care, is that different individuals in ant nests can specialize in different tasks so that each can work more efficiently.
6. Wilson, E. O. "The Defining Traits of Fire Ants and Leaf-Cutting Ants," in *Fire Ants and Leaf-Cutting Ants*, Clifford S. Lofgren and Robert K. Vander Meer, eds. (Boulder, CO: Westview Press, 1986), p. 5.
   Wilson, E. O., *The Insect Societies* (Cambridge: Harvard University Press, 1971), pp. 41–48.
   Wilson, *Sociobiology*, p. 423.
   Weber, Neal A., *Gardening Ants: The Attines* (Philadelphia: American Philosophical Society, 1972), pp. 22–26.
   Wilson, E. O., "Clockwork Lives of the Amazonian Leafcutter Army," *Smithsonian* (October 1, 1984), p. 93.
7. Dumpert, *Social Biology*, p. 126.

8. Dumpert, *Social Biology*, p. 214.
   Weber, *Gardening Ants*, p. 63.
9. Dumpert, *Social Biology*, pp. 64–111.
10. Oster and Wilson, *Caste and Ecology*, pp. 6, 124.
   Wilson, E. O., "Behavioral Discretization and the Number of Castes in an Ant Species," *Behavioral Ecology and Sociobiology*, Vol. 1 (1976), pp. 141–54.
11. Wilson, E. O., "Caste and Division of Labor in Leaf-cutter Ants: The Ergonomic Optimization of Leaf Cutting," *Behavioral Ecology and Sociobiology*, Vol. 7 (1983), p. 162.
   Sudd and Franks, *Behaviourial Ecology*, pp. 79–94.
   Wilson, "Principles of Caste Evolution," pp. 320–23.
   Wilson, E. O., "The Relation Between Caste Ratios and Division of Labor in the Ant Genus *Pheidole*," *Behavioral Ecology and Sociobiology*, Vol. 16 (1984), pp. 89–98.
12. Wilson, E. O., "Caste and Division of Labor in Leaf-cutter Ants (*Hymenoptera: Formicidae: Atta*): 1. The Overall Pattern in *A. sexdens*," *Behavioral Ecology and Sociobiology*, Vol. 5 (1980), p. 153.
13. Wilson, "Caste and Division of Labor in Leaf-cutter Ants: The Ergonomic Optimization of Leaf Cutting" (1983), p. 164. "What *A. sexdens* has done is to commit to the size classes that are energetically the most efficient, by both the criterion of the cost of construction of new workers and the criterion of the cost of maintenance of workers."
   Wilson, "Caste and Division of Labor in Leaf-cutter Ants (*Hymenoptera: Formicidae: Atta*)," p. 150.
14. Wilson, E. O., "The Defining Traits of Fire Ants and Leaf-Cutting Ants," in Lofgren and Vander Meer (1986), p. 7.
   Bristow, Catherine M., "Is Diet Choice a Picnic for Leaf-Cutter Ants?" *Trends in Ecology and Evolution*, Vol. 3:7 (July 1988), pp. 153–54.
   Brody, J. E., "Far from Passive, Many Plants Live in a State of War," *New York Times* (May 26, 1987), p. 15.
15. Dumpert, *Social Biology*, pp. 250–54.
16. Dumpert, *Social Biology*, p. 152.
   Wilson, E. O., "Caste and Division of Labor in Leaf-cutter Ants (*Hymenoptera: Formicidae: Atta*)," *Behavioral Ecology and Sociobiology*, Vol. 14 (1983), p. 56. "In sharp contrast to older colonies, beginning colonies have a nearly uniform size-frequency distribution. . . . [T]he queen produces about the maximum number of individuals which together can perform all of the essential colony tasks."
   [Note: In business, newly founded companies tend to hire a few flexible, generalist workers to support the entrepreneurial founders. Company founders typically bring with them expertise or technology from their previous firms.]
17. Dumpert, *Social Biology*, p. 253.
   Sudd and Franks, *Behaviourial Ecology*, p. 36.
18. Wilson, E. O., "The Defining Traits of Fire Ants and Leaf-Cutting Ants," in Lofgren and Vander Meer (1986), p. 5.
19. Haskins, *Of Ants and Men*, p. 51. "Certain similarities between individual ants and men strike us at once. All of them, of course, are in the nature of parallel developments, brought into like channels as the two creatures struggled with the same problems of existence."
20. Sudd and Franks, *Behaviourial Ecology*, p. 35.
   Dumpert, *Social Biology*, p. 249.
21. Wilson, E. O., *Sociobiology—The New Synthesis* (Cambridge: Harvard University Press, 1975), p. 399. "Once a species has crossed the threshold of eusociality there are two complementary means by which it can advance in colony organization: through the increase in numbers and degree of specialization of the worker castes, and through the enlargement of the communication code by which the colony members coordinate their activities. This statement is the insectan version of the venerable prescription that a society, like an organism and indeed like any cybernetic system, progresses through differentiation and integration of its parts. . . . [C]astes tend to proliferate in evolution until there is one for each task."
22. Sudd and Franks, *Behaviourial Ecology*, pp. 40–41. "Ant colonies are in many respects closely analogous to human factories; a division of labor is organized so as to maximize profits, portions of which are reinvested to maintain the production machinery, sustain further growth or set up new factories. An ant colony producing more sexual offspring

than its neighbors is effectively increasing its market share, just as a profitable company might do."

CHAPTER 22, ENDING POVERTY

1. Thurow, Lester C., "Time to Retrain the American Farmer," *Technology Review* (May–June 1987), pp. 22–23.
2. See chapter 4.
   Himmelfarb, Gertrude, *The Idea of Poverty: England in the Early Industrial Age* (New York: Vintage Books, 1985).
3. Rossi, Peter H., *Down and Out in America: Origins of Homelessness* (Chicago: University of Chicago Press, 1989). Estimates of the homeless population range from 300,000 to three million.
4. *Statistical Abstract of the United States, 1989* (Washington, DC: U.S. Department of Commerce, 1988), Table 736: 1987 data, 32.546 million below poverty level. The 1987 "poverty index" for a family of four was set at $11,611. "The poverty index is based solely on money income and does not reflect the fact that many low-income persons receive noncash benefits such as food stamps, Medicaid, and public housing."
5. *Statistical Abstract of the United States, 1989*, Table 734: 1966—28.5 M (14.7 percent of population); 1987—32.5M (13.5 percent of population). Table 738: 1987—12.4M poor children.
   Browning, Edgar K., "Income Distribution and Redistribution," in *Capitalism and Equality in America*, Peter Berger, ed. (Lanham, MD: Hamilton Press, 1987), pp. 87–88.
6. Butler, Katy, "The Great Boomer Bust," *Mother Jones* (June 1989), p. 33.
   Kuttner, Robert, "The Declining Middle," *Atlantic Monthly* (January 1987), pp. 60–72.
   Cyert, Richard M. and David C. Mowery, *Technology and Employment: Innovation and Growth in the U.S. Economy* (Washington, DC: National Academy Press, 1987), pp. 108–11.
   Thurow, Lester, "A Surge in Inequality," *Scientific American* (May 1987), p. 33. "What, then, is the cause of the rising inequality in the distribution of earnings? There are two major forces: (1) intense international competitive pressures, coupled with high unemployment, and (2) a rising proportion of female workers. . . . [N]oncompetitiveness in manufacturing leads directly to more inequality in the distribution of earnings."
   Ash, Timothy G., "Who Will Give East Europe Back Its Lost Years?" *San Francisco Examiner* (December 10, 1989), p. A20.
7. *Statistical Abstract of the United States, 1989*, Table 724: March 1988 data: Money Income of Families—4.4 percent under $5,000; 7.8 percent over $75,000. Table 722: March 1988 data: Lowest fifth—4.6 percent of aggregate income; highest fifth—43.7 percent of income.
   Williamson, Jeffrey G., "Is Inequality Inevitable Under Capitalism? The American Case," in *Capitalism and Equality in America*, Peter Berger, ed. (Lanham, MD: Hamilton Press, 1987).
8. Plattner, Marc F., "The New Egalitarianism," in *Capitalism and Equality in America*, Peter Berger, ed. (Lanham, MD: Hamilton Press, 1987), pp. 259–76.
   Okun, Arthur M., *The Political Economy of Prosperity* (New York: W.W. Norton, 1970), p. 11. "The market generates a distribution of income which is a by-product of its solution of the problems of allocation and production. The solutions to these problems have certain demonstrably ideal properties, but the resulting income distribution has no inherent logic."
   Okun, Arthur, *Equality and Efficiency: The Big Tradeoff* (Washington, DC: Brookings Institution, 1975), pp. 43–44.
9. Campbell, Colin, ed., *Income Redistribution* (Washington, DC: American Enterprise Institute, 1977).
   Greene, Leonard M., *Free Enterprise Without Poverty* (New York: W.W. Norton, 1981).
   Murray, Charles, *Losing Ground—American Social Policy, 1950–1980* (New York: Basic Books, 1984).
10. Browning, "Income Distribution," pp. 91–92. "Many discussions of redistributive policies proceed on the implicit assumption that the income is just 'there,' and the only problem is to see that it is distributed in an equitable or just fashion. Perhaps the most important

contribution economics can make is to emphasize that income must be produced before it can be redistributed, and that redistributive programs tend to undermine the incentives to produce income in the first place."

Cobbs, John, "Egalitarianism: Threat to a Free Market," *Business Week* (December 1, 1975), pp. 62–65.

Cobbs, John, "Egalitarianism: Mechanisms for Redistributing Income," *Business Week* (December 8, 1975), pp. 86–90.

Cobbs, John, "Egalitarianism: The Corporation as Villain," *Business Week* (December 15, 1975), pp. 86–88.

11. Malabre, Alfred L., *Beyond Our Means: How Reckless Borrowing Now Threatens to Overwhelm Us* (New York: Vintage Books, 1987).

12. *Statistical Abstract of the United States, 1989* (Washington, DC: U.S. Bureau of the Census, 1980), Table 690. Real GNP per capita (in 1982 dollars): $11,781 in 1970 to $15,770 in 1987. A 1.73 percent average growth rate.

13. Thurow, "Surge in Inequality," p. 32. "If one leaves aside homes and real estate, the top 2 percent of all families are found to own 54 percent of all net financial assets (stocks, bonds, pension funds and so on), the top 10 percent to own 86 percent and the bottom 55 percent to have zero or negative financial assets."

14. Tuckman, Howard P., "Supply, Human Capital, and the Average Quality Level of the Science and Engineering Labor Force," *Economics of Education Review* 7:4 (1988), pp. 407–8.

15. Stringer, C. B. and P. Andrews, "Genetic and Fossil Evidence for the Origin of Modern Humans," *Science* 239 (March 11, 1988), p. 1264.

Lewontin, Richard, *Human Diversity* (New York: Scientific American Books, 1982), p. 123.

16. But see Rothman, Stanley and Mark Snyderman, *The IQ Controversy: The Media and Public Policy* (New Brunswick, NJ: Transaction Books, 1988).

17. Smith, James P. and Finis R. Welch, *Closing the Gap: Forty Years of Economic Progress for Blacks* (Santa Monica, CA: Rand Corporation, 1986). From 1967 to 1984, due to a rapid rise in education among blacks, the black-to-white poverty rate differential for two-parent families was cut by two-thirds.

18. Connor, Walter D., "Social Mobility and Democratic Capitalism in America," in *Capitalism and Equality in America*, Peter Berger, ed. (Lanham, MD: Hamilton Press, 1987), pp. 117–18.

19. Plattner, "New Egalitarianism," pp. 268–71.

Hooper, Judith and Dick Teresi, *The 3-Pound Universe* (New York: Dell Publishing, 1986), p. 62. Quoting Michael Merzenich: "Your genes don't predestine you to be a surfer, a dreamer, a world-class chess player, a Mercedes mechanic, a Folies Bergeres girl, a drill-bit salesman, or Jean-Paul Sartre. Your accumulated thoughts and actions weave your neurons into the unique tapestry of your mind."

20. Mincer, Jacob, "Human Capital and Economic Growth," *Economics of Education Review* 3:3 (1984), p. 195. "As an economic concept human capital is at least two centuries old, but its incorporation into the mainstream of economic analysis and research is a new and lively development of the past two decades."

Tuckman, "Supply, Human Capital," p. 405.

Wolfe, Dael, *The Uses of Talent* (Princeton: Princeton University Press, 1971), p. 7.

Becker, Gary S., *Human Capital* (New York: Columbia University Press, 1964).

Thurow, Lester, *Investment in Human Capital* (Belmont, CA: Wadsworth Publishing Company, 1970).

Williamson, "Is Equality Inevitable," pp. 62–63.

Schultz, Theodore W., "Nobel Lecture: The Economics of Being Poor," *Journal of Political Economy* 88:4 (1980), p. 642. "A fundamental proposition documented by much recent research is that an integral part of the modernization of the economies of high- and low-income countries is *the decline in the economic importance of farmland and a rise in that of human capital—skills and knowledge* [italics in original]."

21. U.S. Census Bureau, "Dollars for Degrees," *Wall Street Journal* (March 17, 1988), p. 21. Professional degree $3,439, doctoral degree $2,747, master's degree $1,956, bachelor's degree $1,540, associate degree $1,188, vocational degree $990, high-school diploma $415.

22. Cohn, E., *The Economics of Education* (Cambridge: Ballinger Publishing, 1979), pp. 113–19.

23. Cohn, *Economics of Education*, p. 16. "Only a few economists included human capital in their definition of capital, and with the exception of Adam Smith, none have considered human capital to be the center of economic theory and the main source for strength and growth. As Eli Ginzberg (*The Development of Human Resources*) points out, human resources did not seem to be of much import: Ricardo, writing in the early days of the industrial revolution, saw no reason to be concerned with the availability of labor. There was a great number of rural workers at the doors of the new factories looking for employment. The mills of that day had no difficulty absorbing illiterate, unskilled workers so long as they were able and willing to submit to discipline. In Ricardo's view the strategic element in the economy was capital."

24. Mark, Jerome, "Technological Change and Employment: Some Results from BLS Research," *Monthly Labor Review* (April 1987).

25. Cyert and Mowery, *Technology and Employment*, pp. 122–36.
Sheedy, James L., "Retooling Your Workers Along with Your Machines," *Wall Street Journal* (July 31, 1989), p. A12.

26. Connor, "Social Mobility," pp. 108–10.
Neuhaus, Richard John, "Equality in Everyday Life," in *Capitalism and Equality in America*, Peter Berger, ed. (Lanham, MD: Hamilton Press, 1987), pp. 179–222.
Plattner, "New Egalitarianism," p. 264.

27. See Cobbs, "Egalitarianism: The Corporation as Villain," p. 56. Quoting John Rawls in *Theory of Justice*: "In order to treat all persons equally, to provide genuine equality of opportunity, society must give more attention to those with fewer native assets and to those born into less favorable social positions. The idea is to redress the bias of contingencies on the direction of equality."

28. Schultz, "Nobel Lecture," p. 645. "[T]he capital homogeneity assumption is the disaster of capital theory."

29. U.S. Department of Commerce, "What's It Worth? Educational Background and Economic Status: Spring 1984," *Current Population Reports* (Series P-70, No. 11, September 1987), p. 5. "[T]he average monthly income of bachelor's degree recipients in engineering was $2,833, while the average monthly income of persons with an advanced degree in English was $1,945."
Rumberger, Russell W., "The Changing Economic Benefits of College Graduates," *Economics of Education Review* 3:1 (1984), p. 9.

30. Executive Compensation Service, *Technician and Skilled Trades and Office Personnel Report* (Fort Lee, NJ: Wyatt Data Services, 1989), pp. 52–59.

31. Mincer, "Human Capital," p. 198. "[I]n data where age and length of work experience are statistically separable, levels and shapes of earnings curves are mainly a function of experience rather than of age. Moreover, earnings profiles differ by occupation, sex and other characteristics in systematic ways that cannot be attributed to aging. One may also interpret the shape of the earnings profile as a 'learning curve' or a reflection of growth of skills with age and experience known as 'learning by doing.' "

32. Huberman, Bernardo, "The Social Mind," unpublished working paper (Palo Alto: Xerox Parc, 1989). "Highly cooperative systems, when sufficiently large, can display universal individual performance characteristics, independent of the detailed nature of either the individual processes or the particular problem being tackled. . . . This universal feature, which goes under the technical name of log-normal distribution, is expected to apply when the solution of a problem requires the successful completion of a number of nearly independent steps. . . . [A] study of income distribution in families and single individuals in the U.S. and many other economies also shows a log-normal distribution, which can be ascribed to the many necessary steps that lead to the accumulation of wealth by individuals. These examples suggest that there is indeed an underlying universal law describing the behavior of large systems of interdependent entities. Therefore, when studying the way resources are allocated to individual agents in computational ecologies, one expects a consequent wide distribution in their utilization."

33. Conner, "Social Mobility," p. 120.

34. U.S. Department of Labor, *The Dictionary of Occupational Titles, 1986 Supplement to the Fourth Edition* (Washington, DC: U.S. Government Printing Office, 1986).

35. Union Bank of Switzerland, Employment Advertisement, *New York Times* (October 22, 1989), p. F29.
36. *Digest of Education Statistics, 1987* (Washington, DC: Center for Education Statistics, 1987), Table 154.
    Wolfe, *Uses of Talents,* "If we speak of species instead of specialties, if we call their roles niches instead of specializations, and if we say that the number of species increases as the ecosystem matures, then we have described some well-recognized ecological trends."
37. Dressler, Catherine, "USX Steels Itself to Falling Demand," *San Francisco Examiner* (April 29, 1990), p. D6.
    Silvestri, George T. and John M. Lukasiewicz, "A Look at Occupational Employment Trends to the Year 2000," *Monthly Labor Review* (September 1987), p. 61.
38. Rosenthal, Elizabeth, "Innovations Intensify Glut of Surgeons," *New York Times* (November 7, 1989), p. B5.
39. Cyert and Mowery, *Technology and Employment,* pp. 86–99.
    Miller, Krystal, "Repair Industry Struggles to Survive Cars' High Quality," *Wall Street Journal* (January 5, 1990), p. B2.
    U.S. Congress, Office of Technology Assessment, "Technology and Structural Unemployment: Reemploying Displaced Adults" (Washington, DC: U.S. Government Printing Office, February 1986). "The workers hardest hit by displacement are older workers, the less educated, the less skilled, minorities and, in many cases, women."
40. Marx, Karl, *Capital* (New York: International Publishers, 1967 ed.), p. 644. "The greater the social wealth, the functioning of capital, the extent and energy of its growth . . . the greater the industrial reserve army . . . and the greater is official pauperism. *This is the absolute general law of capitalist accumulation* [italics in original]."
41. Mincer, "Human Capital," p. 202. "Human capital, or population quality, was left out of Malthusian theory. The theory actually omits any economic motivation."
42. Reich, Robert B., "Hi-Tech Warfare: Fixated on Russia, We Risk Losing to Japan," *New Republic* (November 1, 1982), p. 21. "All too often, history teaches us, a society's capacity for compassion and civic virtue exists in direct proportion to the rise in its citizens' real incomes."
43. *Statistical Abstract of the United States, 1989,* Table 740: Of 6.196M total poverty families with household heads more than twenty-five years of age, 3.165 (51.1 percent) have three years or less of high school. By personal communication with Census Bureau: 45.3 percent have less than four years of high school, and 36.6 percent are high school graduates.
    Kozol, Jonathan, *Illiterate America* (Garden City, NY: Anchor Press/Doubleday, 1985), pp. 13–22.
    Hunter, Carman St. John and David Harman, *Adult Illiteracy in the United States* (New York: McGraw-Hill, 1979), pp. 23–56.
44. Bennett, Amanda, "Aetna Schools New Hires In Basic Workplace Skills," *Wall Street Journal* (November 10, 1989), p. B1.
45. National Science Board, *Science Indicators—The 1985 Report* (Washington, DC: National Science Foundation, 1985), p. 5.
    Brooks, Harvey, "National Science Policy and Technological Innovation," in *The Positive Sum Strategy: Harnessing Technology for Economic Growth,* Ralph Landau and Nathan Rosenberg, eds. (Washington, DC: National Academy Press, 1986), pp. 137–38.
    Pettit, Joseph M., "Technological Education," in Landau and Rosenberg (1986), pp. 255–62.
46. Berger, S., M. Dertouzos, R. Lester, R. Solow, and L. Thurow, "Toward a New Industrial America," *Scientific American* (June 1989), p. 40.
    Hershey, Jr., Robert D., "As Labor Pool Ebbs, Factories Fish Harder," *New York Times* (December 22, 1989), p. C1.
    Levin, Doron P., "Smart Machines, Smart Workers," *New York Times* (October 17, 1988), p. C1.
47. Cyert and Mowery, *Technology and Employment,* pp. 67–68.
    Kershner, Vlae, "The Payoff For Educated Workers," *San Francisco Chronicle* (December 26, 1989), p. A2.
    "America's Shrinking Middle," *The Economist* (November 12, 1988). "It also turns out that older, well-educated workers have done better than younger, less well-educated ones. As a result the falling earnings of young men with no more than high school education

394 · NOTES

account for most of the shrinkage in the middle of the earnings distribution and for most of the expansion at the bottom."

Magnet, Myron, "The Rich and the Poor: Are the Haves Responsible for the Disquieting Plight of the Have-Nots?" *Fortune* (June 6, 1988), p. 207. "In this explanation, the same global economic forces that benefit the Haves by creating richly rewarded high-skill jobs impoverish the Have-Nots by sending low-skill jobs abroad or abolishing them altogether. If the poor had the necessary skills, there would be no problem. But, says William Woodside, chairman of Primerica's executive committee, 'We're creating a two-tier society. The educational requirement for jobs is going up rapidly, and we're not giving the poor the kind of education required to handle the jobs that are around today.' "

48. "The Value of Education," *New York Times* (November 8, 1989), p. B9. "The gap between the median incomes of 30-year-old male high school graduates and 30-year-old male college graduates has 'opened up like a rocket, from about 15 percent in 1973 to 50 percent now,' said Frank Levy, an economist at the University of Maryland School of Public Affairs and visiting professor at Brown University. . . . It is not that the absolute value of a bachelor's degree has increased, said Professor Levy, who has been studying income distribution in the United States; median earnings for college graduates have remained fairly static since 1973. Rather, he said, income data from the Census Bureau show median earnings of male high school graduates falling precipitously."

49. Thurow, "Surge in Inequality," pp. 36–37. "Regardless of what one thinks about the role of taxes and transfers in limiting inequality, they are clearly not the appropriate means for counteracting the current surge in inequality. The heart of the solution will have to be found in a higher rate of growth of productivity and enhanced international competitiveness. To compete in industries that pay high wages and make goods of high value, a country must ensure that its labor force is as well educated and skilled as any in the world, must keep up with or ahead of competitors in investment in capital equipment and must make sure that the technologies being employed are the most effective. Comparisons with either Japan or Europe reveal that the U.S. is not world class in any of those areas. The problem is not that the U.S. is doing worse than it used to but that the rest of the world is doing much better."

50. Magnet, "The Rich and the Poor," p. 206.

Randle, Wilma, "The Changing Face of the Work Force," *San Francisco Examiner* (January 7, 1990), p. D1.

51. Peterson, Peter G. and Neil Howe, *On Borrowed Time: How the Growth in Entitlement Spending Threatens America's Future* (New York: Simon & Schuster, 1988), p. 81. In 1986, the federal government spent a total of $70.3 billion on means-tested entitlements, $3.4 billion went to Guaranteed Student Loans. The rest went to various forms of consumption support.

Schultz, "Nobel Lecture," p. 648. "Since schooling is primarily an investment, it is a serious error to treat all schooling outlays as current consumption."

Haveman, Robert, *Starting Even: An Equal Opportunity Program to Combat the Nation's New Poverty* (New York: Simon & Schuster, 1988), pp. 22–23. "The War on Poverty and the Great Society began with a worthy rationale . . . . but the rationale of equalizing opportunities that motivated the early War on Poverty–Great Society planners was not sustained by the policies that evolved. Much of the increased spending went for quite a different purpose—to relieve income poverty. . . . The initial commitment to 'even starting line' and 'level playing fields' turned into operational strategies to reduce income poverty, thereby equalizing outcomes.

Long-term and permanent progress against poverty and inequality is possible only through programs that make it possible for individuals to acquire sufficient skills and training to become economically independent, and give them the incentives and hope to make the effort . . . Hence, if less poverty is the objective, efforts to redress the balance need to be directed toward programs that will foster more equal opportunities, self-sufficiency, and independence."

52. See chapter 27.

53. Fallows, James, *More Like Us: Making America Great Again* (Boston: Houghton Mifflin, 1989).

54. Berger, Michael, "Foreign Labor Exploding in Japan," *San Francisco Chronicle* (May 21, 1990), p. C1.

van Wolferen, Karel, *The Enigma of Japanese Power* (New York: Alfred A. Knopf, 1990). Drucker, Peter F., "Japan's Not-So-Secret Weapon," *Wall Street Journal* (January 9, 1990), p. A14.

55. Wynter, Leon E. and Jolie Solomon, "A New Push to Break the 'Glass Ceiling,' But Senior Jobs for Minorities Remain Scarce," *Wall Street Journal* (November 15, 1989), p. B1. "Xerox will be one of the first companies prepared to test the value of American cultural diversity against Japanese homogeneity in the global marketplace."

56. Lehner, Urban C., "Mixed Emotions: Japanese May Be Rich, But Are They Satisfied with Quality of Life?" *Wall Street Journal* (January 9, 1990), p. 1.

PART VI, FEEDBACK LOOPS AND FREE MARKETS/CHAPTER 23, SPONTANEOUS ORDER

1. Whitehead, Alfred North, *Science and the Modern World* (New York: Macmillan, 1925).
2. "Mammals and Amoebae Get the Message," *New Scientist* (September 15, 1988), p. 38.
3. Bonner, John Tyler, "The Life Cycle of the Cellular Slime Molds," *Natural History* (December 1978), p. 70.
4. Devreotes, Peter, "Dictyostelium discoideum: A Model System for Cell-Cell Interactions in Development," *Science* (September 8, 1989), p. 1056.
   Tomchik, K. J. and P. N. Devreotes, "Adenosine 3',5'—Monophosphate Waves in Dictyostelium discoideum: A Demonstration by Isotope Dilution—Fluorography," *Science* (April 24, 1981), p. 443.
   Klein, Peter S., Tzeli J. Sun, Charles L. Saxe III, and Alan R. Kimmel, "A Chemoattractant Receptor Controls Development in Dictyostelium discoideum," *Science* (September 16, 1988), p. 1467.
5. Bonner, John Tyler, "The Society of Amoebas," *Science 84* (December 1, 1984), p. 72.
6. Wheeler, David L., "Investigating the Life Cycle of the Lowly Slime Mold, Ohio Researcher Finds a Marvel of Biological Design," *Chronicle of Higher Education* (April 12, 1989), p. A4.
7. Bonner, John Tyler, "Differentiation in Social Amoebae," *Scientific American* (December 1959), pp. 152–60.
   Devreotes, "Dictyostelium discoideum," p. 1058.
8. Hapgood, Fred, "One's a Crowd," *Science Digest* (April 1982), p. 32.
9. Shevchenko, Arkady N., *Breaking with Moscow* (New York: Alfred A. Knopf, 1985), p. 280.
   Melloan, George, "Only Pluralism Can Bring Communist Reform," *Wall Street Journal* (September 27, 1988), p. 35.
10. Taubes, Gary, "The Body Chaotic," *Discover* (May 1989), p. 64. "[M]ost natural systems are not linear. Often they don't move in a simple straight line from cause to effect but in cycles, with the effect feeding back on the cause and perhaps amplifying it. Or their behavior is marked by abrupt transitions, by effects that are all out of proportion to the cause—the straw that breaks the camel's back."
   See May, Robert M., "Simple mathematical models with very complicated dynamics," *Nature* (June 10, 1976), p. 459.
   Nova: The Strange New Science of Chaos, Episode 1603 (Boston: WGBH Television Foundation, 1989). Jerry Gollub: "The entire universe is filled with fluids in turbulent motion. The atmosphere, the oceans, much of outer space is basically turbulent fluid. So one could take the point of view that you don't understand anything until you understand turbulence."
    Hooper, Judith and Teresi, Dick, *The 3-Pound Universe* (New York: Dell Publishing, 1986), p. 370–75.
11. Gleick, James, *Chaos: Making a New Science* (New York: Viking, 1987), pp. 3–4.
    Pattee, Howard, "Instabilities and Information in Biological Self-Organization," in *Self-Organizing Systems—The Emergence of Order*, Eugene F. Yates, ed. (New York: Plenum Press, 1987), p. 332: "A basic discrepancy, then, between the physicist's and biologist's approach to self-organization is that the physicist's theory recognizes no symbolic restrictions and no historical regularities, whereas the biologist's theory assumes genetic symbol systems with more than 3 billion years of selected historical structures."

Weiss, Rick, "A Flight of Fancy Mathematics: Chaos Brings Harmony to a Birder's Puzzle," *Science News* (March 17, 1990), p. 172.

12. Gleick, *Chaos*, p. 68 "Nonlinear systems with real chaos were rarely taught and rarely learned. When people stumbled across such things—and people did—all their training argued for dismissing them as aberrations."
    Campbell, David, Jim Crutchfield, Doyne Farmer, and Erica Jen, "Experimental Mathematics: The Role of Computation in Nonlinear Science," *Communications of the Association of Computing Machinery* (April 1985), p. 374. "The reason for the nomenclature and for the strong bias toward the study of linear systems is expediency: In the past, nonlinear was nearly synonymous with nonsolvable. Today, thanks in large part to computers, many previously intractable nonlinear problems have been solved, and the field of nonlinear studies has come into its own."

13. Campbell, et al., "Experimental Mathematics," p. 374. "It would be hard to exaggerate the role that computers and numerical simulations have played in the recent progress of nonlinear science."
    Pagels, Heinz R. , *The Dreams of Reason: The Computer and the Rise of the Sciences of Complexity* (New York: Simon & Schuster, 1988), p. 73. "Life is nonlinear, and so is just about everything else of interest. The human mastery of the nonlinear regime will open a vast new realm of existence."
    Hooper and Teresi, *The 3-Pound Universe*, p. 360. Quoting Ralph Abraham, University of California at Santa Cruz mathematician: "Only once or twice in a millennium is there a true scientific revolution, a paradigm shift. Newtonian mechanics and the invention of calculus in the seventeenth century brought about the last one. The current scientific revolution will synthesize the whole intellectual discourse of the species."

14. Hooper and Teresi, *The 3-Pound Universe*, p. 375.
    Gleick, James, "When Chaos Rules the Market," *New York Times* (November 22, 1987), p. 1. When they speak of chaos, scientists mean erratic behavior that appears to be random but is not."
    Pagels, *Dreams of Reason*, p. 54–55. "Complexity . . . is a quantitative measure that can be assigned to a physical system or a computation that lies midway between the measure of simple order and complete chaos."

15. *Nova, The Strange New Science of Chaos*, quoting Jerry Gollub: "Sensitive dependence on initial conditions is the fundamental cause of chaos. It arises from the underlying nonlinearity of the equations describing the motion."
    Monastersky, Richard, "Forecasting into Chaos: Meterologists Seek to Foresee Unpredictability," *Science News* (May 5, 1990), pp. 280–82.

16. Taubes, Gary, "The Body Chaotic," *Discover* (May 1989), p. 66. "Why should a heart need chaos? 'To be healthy,' Goldberger says, 'you need to be able to cope with an environment that's throwing you curveballs and sliders and knuckleballs. And if you're wrapped up in some periodic, monotonous dynamic, you're in no shape to contend with the environment. Chaos is the only mechanism I know for generating that necessary variability and for doing so in a somewhat controlled manner.' "

17. Goldberger, Ary L., David R. Rigney, and Bruce J. West, "Chaos and Fractals in Human Physiology," *Scientific American* (February 1990) pp. 43–44. "The conventional wisdom in medicine holds that disease and aging arise from stress on an otherwise orderly and machinelike system—that stress decreases order by provoking erratic responses or by upsetting the body's normal periodic rhythms. In the past five years or so we and our colleagues have discovered that the heart and other physiological systems may behave most erratically when they are young and healthy. Counterintuitively, increasingly regular behavior sometimes accompanies aging and disease. Irregularity and unpredictability, then, are important features of health. On the other hand, decreased variability and accentuated periodicities are associated with disease."

18. *Nova: The Strange New Science of Chaos*, Alan Garfinkel: "Biological systems, at least in some respects, need to be chaotic. They need to be bubbly. They need to stay loose. And chaos can provide the mechanism whereby it does that."

19. *Nova: The Strange New Science of Chaos*, Paul Rapp: "Constrained randomness is the secret of healthy nerve action." Quoting Alan Garfinkel: "Order is not always good. In

brain waves at least, this kind of order is pathological. And a chaotic-looking EEG [elec-troencepholagram] is a healthy one."
Goldberger, et al., "Chaos and Fractals," p. 49.
20. Hall, Stephen S., "A Molecular Code Links Emotions, Mind and Health," *Smithsonian* (June 1989), p. 64. "Bit by bit, these and other scientists are assembling a mosaic of data suggesting that our anatomical systems, separated by 19th century tradition, routinely communicate with one another. Carrying the messages back and forth, moreover, are small, go-between molecules."
Bonner, John Tyler, "Hormones in Social Amoebae and Mammals," *Scientific American* (June 1969), p. 78.
21. Schaffer, W. M. and M. Kot, "Do Strange Attractors Govern Ecological Systems?" *BioScience* 35:6 (June 1985), p. 349.
Schaffer, W. M. and M. Kot, "Chaos in Ecological Systems: The Coals that Newcastle Forgot," *Trends in Ecology and Evolution* 1:3 (September 1986), p. 58. "Until recently, ecologists have ignored the possibility that chaos may be an important component of ecological systems. With the development of powerful new concepts and techniques for the study and detection of chaotic systems, it is becoming apparent that chaos may be widespread in nature, and may necessitate a fundamental reappraisal of many ideas in community and population ecology."
22. Odum, Howard T., "Self-Organization, Transformity, and Information," *Science* (November 25, 1988), pp. 1132–39.
23. Diamond, Stuart, "Setting Crude Prices in the Pits," *New York Times* (December 9, 1984), p. F4.
Gleick, "When Chaos Rules the Market," p. 1.
24. Waldrop, M. Mitchell, "PARC Brings Adam Smith to Computing," *Science* (April 14, 1989), p. 145.
25. The author wishes to thank Bernardo Huberman for his kind assistance.
Huberman, Bernardo A., "Computing in the Network Age," *Datamation* (September 15, 1989), p. 33.
26. Waldspurger, Carl A., Tad Hogg, Bernardo A. Huberman, Jeffrey O. Kephart, and Scott Stornetta, "SPAWN: A Distributed Computational Economy" (Palo Alto: Xerox PARC Report, SSL-89-18, 1989), p. 2. "[D]ata in the world is distributed and changing too rapidly for a central controller to have available all information needed to effectively plan detailed behavior, even if sufficient computational power is available."
27. See Waldspurger, et al., "SPAWN," for a full description.
28. Waldrop, "PARC Brings Adam Smith," p. 145.
Nova: The Strange New Science of Chaos, Paul Rapp: "One is compelled to ask the question, what functional advantages can chaotic behavior actually provide? One of the areas where it is fairly clear that advantages can arise is in the area of optimization. Essentially, the notion of search for the best solution. What a certain amount of turbulence in that search can do is help you avoid becoming preoccupied with a small-scale solution and possibly lose sight of a much better solution."
29. Waldspurger, et al., "SPAWN," pp. 24–25.
Peterson, Ivars, "Digging into Sand," *Science News* (July 15, 1989), p. 42. "Researchers at the Santa Fe (N.M.) Institute are studying the possibility of applying the concept of self-organized criticality to economic systems. Traditionally, economists tend to describe their systems in terms of simple equations relating a few quantities such as interest rates and employment levels. They usually study the effects of small deviations from an equilibrium situation. . . . Applying the concept of self-organized criticality to an economic system adds a new dimension. In such a state, a small perturbation can create either a small effect or a large one. There's no limit on how long the effect might last or how far it could extend through the system. These fluctuations are much stronger than those possible in an equilibrium model."

CHAPTER 24, RULES VS. PRICES

1. Miller, Mark and K. Eric Drexler, "Comparative Ecology: A Computational Perspective," in *The Ecology of Computation*, B. A. Huberman, ed. (Amsterdam: Elsevier Scientific Publications, 1988), pp. 51–76.

Waldrop, M. Mitchell, "PARC Brings Adam Smith to Computing," *Science* (April 14, 1989), p. 145.

Markoff, John, "In Computer Behavior, Elements of Chaos," *New York Times* (September 11, 1988), p. E6.

Ceccatto, H. A. and B. A. Huberman, "Persistence of Nonoptimal Strategies," *National Academy of Science* (May 1989), p. 3443. "The existence of computational ecologies brings to mind the spontaneous appearance of organized behavior in biological and social systems, where agents can engage in cooperating strategies while working on the solution of particular problems."

Kephart, Jeffrey O., Tad Hogg, and Bernardo A. Huberman, "Collective Behavior of Predictive Agents," unpublished work paper (Palo Alto: Xerox PARC, October 17, 1989), p. 28.

Huberman, B. A., "The Social Mind," unpublished working paper (Palo Alto: Xerox PARC, 1989).

2. Pagels, Heinz R., *The Dreams of Reason: The Computer and the Rise of the Sciences of Complexity* (New York: Simon & Schuster, 1988), p. 42. "Using computers, scientists can build mathematical models of complex phenomena—human learning, unconscious processes, animal and cultural evolution, the cell, violent behavior, the brain—to name but a few applications. In spite of the diversity of these phenomena, the mathematics used to model all of them has elements in common, and that feature is becoming the basis of a new way of integrating the sciences."

Gleick, James, "When Chaos Rules the Market," *New York Times* (November 22, 1987) p. 1. "Economic theorists—if not the practitioners who actually make forecasts and design trading strategies—have recognized the nonlinearity of such systems for some time. Nevertheless, the preferred models of economics have traditionally been linear, meaning they tend naturally to seek a balanced equilibrium or follow regular, periodic cycles. Those model behaviors, many now feel, are misleading. Chaos theory offers a radically new way of working systems of nonlinear equations and discovering the deeper patterns that often underlie them."

Kelsey, David, "The Economics of Chaos or the Chaos of Economics," *Oxford Economic Papers* 40 (1988), pp. 1–31.

Anderson, Philip W., Kenneth J. Arrow, and David Pines, *The Economy as an Evolving Complex System* (Redwood City, CA: Addison-Wesley, 1988).

Pagels, *Dreams of Reason*, pp. 145–46 "The economic system, if it is anything, is a system far from equilibrium like the evolutionary system or the immune response. It is continually making adjustments to keep itself far from equilibrium (although there may be local equilibria). Next to nothing is understood about dynamical systems far from equilibrium."

3. Thurow, Lester C., "U.S. Drug Policy: Colossal Ignorance," *New York Times* (May 8, 1988), p. E29.

4. Goodman, Ellen, "Gorbachev's Slow System Has a Live Private Sector," *International Herald Tribune* (May 9, 1985), p. 4.

5. Reich, Robert B., "Government's Shifting Role: Capricious Regulation is the Market's Foe," *New York Times* (June 11, 1989), p. F3.

6. Bailey, Elizabeth E., "Deregulation: Causes and Consequences," *Science* (December 5, 1986), pp. 1211–16.

Brooke, James, "Ailing Nigeria Opens Its Economy," *New York Times* (August 15, 1988), p. C10.

Davidson, Joe, "African Rebel: Tanzania is Reviving Its Economy by Using Tools of a Free Market," *Wall Street Journal* (January 27, 1988), p. 1.

Asman, David, "Free Market Theories Become Public Policy in Ecuador," *Wall Street Journal* (April 11, 1986), p. 25.

Weisman, Steven R., "The Rajiv Generation," *New York Times Magazine* (April 20, 1986), pp. 18–69.

7. Bovard, James, "Put Agriculture Policy Out to Pasture," *Wall Street Journal* (February 4, 1988), p. 24.

Bovard, James, *Farm Fiasco* (San Francisco: Institute for Contemporary Studies, 1988).

Schneider, Kenneth, "The Farm Economy is Fine, and Can Expect More Aid," *New York Times* (February 4, 1990) p. E4.

Bethell, Tom, "Why Berkeley is Turning into a Commuter School," *Wall Street Journal* (October 11, 1988), p. A20.

8. Maurice, Charles and Charles W. Smithson, *The Doomsday Myth: 10,000 Years of Economic Crisis* (Stanford, CA: Hoover Institution Press, 1984).

9. Waldman, Steven and Rich Thomas, "How Did It Happen?" *Newsweek* (May 21, 1990), pp. 27–32.

Rosenbaum, David E., "A Financial Disaster with Many Culprits," *New York Times* (June 6, 1990), p. 1.

10. Tucker, William, "Marketing Pollution," *Harper's* (May, 1981), pp. 31–38.

11. Postan, M. M., *The Medieval Economy and Society* (Middlesex: Penguin Books, 1972), pp. 45–80.

12. Shabecoff, Philip, "In Search of a Better Law to Clear the Air," *New York Times* (May 14, 1989), p. E1.

13. Naj, Amal Kumar, "Not the Cleanest Ways to Clear the Air," *Wall Street Journal* (June 19, 1989), p. A16.

14. Pollack, Andrew, "Innovators and Investors Hindered in the Business of Pollution Control," *New York Times* (August 29, 1989), p. 1. "The nation's effort to overcome its pressing environmental problems is being slowed by barriers that discourage technologically innovative companies and the people who invest in them, Government officials, investors and executives at the companies say.... The barriers arise because polluters see little reason to spend on new and better technology unless the Government makes them do so. While standards have historically become stricter over time, investors are often reluctant to risk money on how and when the regulations will change. Moreover, the need to obtain permits from several levels of government greatly slows the introduction of technology."

Feder, Barnaby J., "Wringing Profits From Clean Air," *New York Times* (June 18, 1989), p. F1.

15. Umana, Alvaro, "Costa Rica's Debt-for-Nature Swaps Come of Age," *Wall Street Journal* (May 26, 1989), p. A11.

16. But see *Project 88—Harnessing Market Forces to Protect Our Environment* (Washington, DC: Public Policy Study sponsored by Senator Timothy Wirth and Senator John Heinz, December, 1988).

Graff, Thomas J., "Harnessing Market Forces to Protect Our Environment," *Environmental Defense Fund Newsletter* (February, 1989), p. 4.

"Searching for Incentives to Entice Polluters," *New York Times* (October 8, 1989), p. F7.

Passell, Peter, "Private Incentives As Pollution Curb," *New York Times* (October 19, 1988), p. C2.

Hahn, Robert W., "Economic Prescriptions for Environmental Problems: How the Patient Followed the Doctor's Orders," *Journal of Economic Perspectives* (Spring 1989), pp. 95–114.

17. Kristof, Nicholas, "Playing the Market in Pollution Rights," *New York Times* (September 14, 1986), p. E6.

Weisskopf, Michael, "Free Market Strategy Puts Profit in Pollution Control," *Washington Post* (November 12, 1989), p. H1.

Pasztor, Andy, "Market Booms for 'Rights' to Pollute," *Wall Street Journal* (June 18, 1981), p. 25.

Blinder, Alan S., "Why Not Sell Pollution by the Pound?" *Washington Post* (August 8, 1987), p. A15.

18. Passell, Peter, "Sale of Air Pollution Permits is Part of Bush Acid Rain Plan," *New York Times* (May 17, 1989), p. 1.

Hahn, Robert W., "Last Gasp for Bush Clean Air Reforms," *Wall Street Journal* (November 7, 1989), p. A28. "Despite these successes, flexible approaches have been viewed as sacrilege by virtually all environmental groups, with the recent exception of the Environmental Defense Fund. Congress remains distrustful of using markets to solve environmental problems. Markets may improve the environment and save money, but they also reduce the ability of bureaucrats and congressmen to decide how and where resources will be spent."

"The Greening of the Invisible Hand," *The Economist* (December 24, 1989), pp. 107–8.

19. Phone interview with Carl Pope on May 17, 1990.

20. Beardsley, Tim, "Polluting Rights: How to Build a Market for an Unwanted Commodity," *Scientific American* (November, 1989), pp. 76–79.
"A Survey of the Environment: Costing the Earth," *The Economist*, (September 2, 1989), p. 8.
21. Borrelli, Peter, "The Ecophilosophers: A Guide to Deep Ecologists, Bioregionalists, Greens, and Others in Pursuit of Radical Change," *The Amicus Journal* (Washington, DC: National Resources Defense Council, Spring 1988), pp. 30–39.
22. Smith, Jr., Fred L., "Controlling the Environmental Threat to the Global Liberal Order," Paper presented to the Mont Pelerin Society Meeting in Christchurch, New Zealand (Washington, DC: Competitive Enterprise Institute, November 30, 1989). "In recent months, the television screens have shown dramatic scenes of environmental and economic disasters: dead elephants and fleeing East Germans. Yet, the causes of these two disasters were not dissimilar: both the African ecology and the East German economy have been excluded from the world economy. In recent days, the failures of economic central planning have finally forced reform on Eastern Europe. That same inherent flaw will force reform some day in the environmental field."
Horowitz, David, "From Red to Green," Speech to Conservative Leadership Conference, Washington, D.C., December 1, 1989 (unpublished).
"Russia's Greens, The Poisoned Giant Wakes Up," *The Economist* (November 4, 1989), pp. 23–26.
Bramwell, Anna, "The Greening of Mrs. Thatcher," *Wall Street Journal* (October 9, 1989), p. A14. "In ironic contrast to many of their Western counterparts, environmentalists in Eastern Europe blame socialism and the lack of property rights for their ills."

PART VII, PARASITISM AND EXPLOITATION/CHAPTER 25, THE HOOK

1. Swift, Jonathan, "On Poetry: A Rhapsody," in *The Portable Swift*, Carl Van Doren, ed. (New York: The Viking Press, 1948), p. 576.
2. Crosby, Alfred W., *Epidemic and Peace, 1918* (Westport, CT: Greenwood Press, 1976), pp. 207–15, 315.
Anderson, Michael, *International Mortality Statistics* (New York: Facts on File, 1981), p. 66.
3. U.S. Department of Health, Education, and Welfare, *Surgeon General's Meeting on Influenza, February 12, 1979* (Washington, DC: U.S. Department of Health, Education, and Welfare, 1979), p. DO5.
4. Scott, Andrew, *Pirates of the Cell: The Story of Viruses from Molecule to Microbe* (Oxford: Basil Blackwell, 1987), p. 73.
5. Simons, Kai Henrik Garoff and Ari Helenius, "How an Animal Virus Gets into and out of Its Host Cell," *Scientific American* (February 11, 1982), p. 58.
6. Friday and Ingram, *The Cambridge Encyclopedia of Life Sciences* (Cambridge: Cambridge University Press, 1985), pp. 290–91.
Noble, Elmer R. and Glenn A. Noble, *Parasitology: The Biology of Animal Parasites, 5th ed.* (Philadelphia: Lea and Febiger, 1982), p. 3.
7. Radetsky, Peter, "The Ultimate Parasite," *Discover* (August 1989), pp. 20–21.
8. Burnet, Sir MacFarlane and David O. White, *Natural History of Infectious Disease, 4th ed.* (Cambridge: Cambridge University Press, 1972), p. 66.
9. In some cases, there is no "hook" per se. In these situations, the parasite has a means of being injected inside the host's tissues. The parasite that causes malaria is injected into humans by a mosquito. Once inside the body, there is no way to eject the parasite. Effectively, the host is "hooked."
10. Chandler, Asa C., *Introduction to Parasitology, 10th ed.* (New York: John Wiley, 1961), pp. 334, 342.
Noble and Noble, *Parisitology*, p. 228.
Crompton, D. W. T. and S. M. Joyner, *Parasitic Worms* (London: Wykeham Publications, 1980), p. 178.
11. Markell, Edward K. and Marietta Voge, *Medical Parasitology, 4th ed.* (Philadelphia: W.B. Saunders, 1976), pp. 207–19.
Chandler, *Introduction to Parasitology*, pp. 356–59.

Donaldson, R. J., *Parasites and Western Man* (Baltimore: University Park Press, 1979), pp. 115–16.
12. Wardle, Robert A., James A. McLeod, and Sydney Radinosky, *Advances in the Zoology of Tapeworms, 1950–1970* (Minneapolis: University of Minnesota Press, 1974), pp. 163–64.
Crompton and Joyner, *Parasitic Worms*, p. 45.
13. Wardle, et al., *Advances in Zoology of Tapeworms*, p. 238.
Markell and Voge, *Medical Parasitology*, p. 208.
14. Swartzwelder, J. Clyde, "Clinical Taenia Infection: An Analysis of Sixty Cases," *Journal of Tropical Medicine and Hygiene* (August 1, 1939), pp. 226–29.
Donaldson, *Parasites and Western Man*, p. 116.
15. Scott, *Pirates of the Cell*, pp. 97–99.
Augros, Robert and George Stanciu, *The New Biology: Discovering the Wisdom in Nature* (Boston: New Science Library, 1988), p. 104.
16. See Chandler, *Introduction to Parasitology*, p. 115: Quoting Charles S. Elton: "A parasite's existence is usually an elaborate compromise between extracting sufficient nourishment to maintain and propagate itself, and not impairing too much the vitality or reducing the numbers of its host, which is providing it with a home and a free ride."
17. Whitfield, Philip J., *The Biology of Parasitism: An Introduction to the Study of Associating Organisms* (Baltimore: University Park Press, 1979), p. 3.
18. See De Soto, Hernando, *The Other Path: The Invisible Revolution in the Third World* (New York: Harper & Row, 1989).
19. *Statistical Abstract of the United States, 1989* (Washington, DC: U.S. Bureau of the Census, 1989), Table 284.

CHAPTER 26, PRIVATE CORPOCRACY

1. Green, Mark and John F. Berry, *The Challenge of Hidden Profits: Reducing Corporate Bureaucracy and Waste* (New York: William Morrow, 1985), p. 72.
2. Taylor, John, *Storming the Magic Kingdom: Wall Street, the Raiders and the Battle for Disney* (New York: Ballantine Books, 1987), p. 24.
3. Taylor, *Storming the Magic Kingdom*, p. 42.
4. Magnet, Myron, "No More Mickey Mouse at Disney," *Fortune* (December 10, 1984), p. 58.
5. Sloan, Allan, "Why Is No One Safe?" *Forbes* (March 11, 1985), p. 139.
6. Bruck, Connie, *The Predator's Ball: The Junk Bond Raiders and the Man Who Staked Them* (New York: Simon & Schuster, 1988), p. 93.
7. Green, Mark and John F. Berry, "Takeovers, a Symptom of 'Corpocracy,' " *New York Times* (December 3, 1986), p. 31.
8. Stein, Benjamin J., "Who Owns This Company Anyway? Greenmail Leaves Shareholders Out in the Cold," *Barron's* (December 15, 1986), p. 9. "Stockholders are offered the chance to make a significant appreciation on their shares. Management stands to lose their jobs, power and perks if the stockholders get that profit. Thus, management's interests clearly conflict with those of the stockholders."
9. "The High Price Disney Paid to Save Itself," *Business Week* (June 25, 1984), p. 32.
10. Eckhouse, John, "Disney's Financial Wizardry: Under CEO Eisner, the Company Has Gone from the Edge of Disaster to the Pinnacle of Success," *San Francisco Chronicle* (September 18, 1989), p. C1.
Magnet, "No More Mickey Mouse," p. 58.
11. Taylor, *Storming the Magic Kingdom*, p. viii.
12. Rosenberg, Hilary, "Saul Steinberg, Chairman Reliance Group Holdings," *Institutional Investor* (June 1, 1987), p. 45.
13. Scheibla, Shirley Hobbs, "A Mickey for Greenmail? The Disney Affair Spurs Congress to Action," *Barrons* (June 18, 1984), p. 9.
Weidenbaum, Murray, "Strategies for Responding to Corporate Takeovers," in *Public Policy Toward Corporate Takeovers*, Kenneth Chilton and Murray Weidenbaum, eds. (New Brunswick, NJ: Transaction Books, 1988), pp. 141–69.
14. Nathans, Leah, "Takeover Curbs Are Coming: Congress Will Act This Year," *Duns Business Month* (February 1, 1987), p. 43.

Jensen, Michael C., "Eclipse of the Public Corporation," *Harvard Business Review* (September–October 1989), pp. 61–62. "Takeovers, corporate breakups, divisional spinoffs, leveraged buyouts, and going-private transactions are the most visible manifestations of a massive organizational change in the economy. These transactions have inspired criticism, even outrage, among many business leaders and government officials, who have called for regulatory and legislative restrictions. The backlash is understandable. Change is threatening; in this case, the threat is aimed at the senior executives of many of our largest companies."

15. Nader, Ralph, Mark Green, and Joel Seligman, *Taming the Giant Corporation* (New York: W.W. Norton, 1976), p. 54.
   Compact Disclosure and Information on over 12,000 Public Companies (Bethesda, MD: Disclosure Inc., 1988). As of November 1988, 270 of 476 (57 percent) Fortune 500 companies were incorporated in Delaware.
   Geyelin, Milo and Vindu P. Goel, "Pennsylvania Legislators Gird to Battle," *Wall Street Journal* (December 26, 1989), p. A16.

16. Weidenbaum, Murray L., "The Best Defense Against the Raiders," *Business Week* (September 23, 1985), p. 21.

17. See Talner, Lauren, *The Origins of Shareholder Activism* (Washington, DC: Investor Responsibility Research Center Inc., 1983).
   Gray, H., *New Directions in the Investment and Control of Pension Funds* (Washington, DC: Investor Responsibility Research Center, 1983), pp. 29–51.
   "America's Shareholders Break into the Boardroom," *The Economist* (April 29, 1989), pp. 75–76.
   Power, Christopher and Vicky Cahan, "Shareholders Aren't Just Rolling Over Anymore: Institutional Investors Start to Challenge Management," *Business Week* (April 27, 1987), p. 32.
   Regan, Edward V., "Pension Funds: New Power, New Responsibility," *Wall Street Journal* (November 2, 1987), p. 28.
   Dobrzynski, Judith H. and Jonathan B. Levine, "Whose Company Is It, Anyway? Proxy Fights Are Spreading as Shareholders Seek More Power," *Business Week* (April 25, 1988), p. 60.

18. Willcox, Tilton L., "The Use and Abuse of Executive Powers in Warding Off Corporate Raiders," *Journal of Business Ethics* (1988), p. 48.
   White, James A., "Public Pension Funds Increase Pressure In Deciding Roles of Firms They Invest In," *Wall Street Journal* (May 15, 1989), p. A5.
   Sandler, Linda, "Dual Stock Categories Spur Powerful Debate Over Stability vs. Gain Class Struggle," *Wall Street Journal* (May 17, 1988), p. 1.
   Golub, Steven, "Equality for Some Is Still the Rule," *Financial World* (February 10, 1987), p. 23.

19. Laderman, Jeffrey M. and Paula Dwyer, "Coming to Blows over One Share, One Vote," *Business Week* (July 8, 1988), p. 81.

20. Green and Berry, *Challenge of Hidden Profits*, p. 385.

21. "The Forbes 500 Annual Directory," *Forbes* (May 1, 1989), p. 175.

CHAPTER 27, PUBLIC BUREAUCRACY

1. National Commission on Excellence in Education, *A Nation at Risk: The Imperative for Education Reform* (Washington, DC: U.S. Government Printing Office, 1983).

2. Stern, Joyce, ed., *The Condition of Education: A Statistical Report* (Washington, DC: Center for Education Statistics, 1987), p. 26.
   Magnet, Myron, "How to Smarten Up the Schools: Will the Education Crisis Torpedo U.S. Economic Preeminence?" *Fortune* (February 1, 1988), p. 86.
   Bennett, William J., *American Education: Making It Work* (Washington, DC: U.S. Department of Education, 1988), p. 10.

3. Uzzell, Lawrence A., "Education Reform Fails the Test," *Wall Street Journal* (May 10, 1989), p. A20.

4. The statistics comparing Japanese and American students were drawn from the following sources:

Bennett, *American Education*, p. 12.

White, Merry, *The Japanese Educational Challenge: A Commitment to Children* (New York: Free Press, 1987), p. 73.

Rubenstein, Carin, *Working It Out: Chinese Children Concentrate Intently on Their Studies Even in Primary School* (New York: UAL, Inc., 1986).

Magnet, Myron, "How to Smarten Up the Schools."

5. Magnet, Myron, "How to Smarten Up the Schools." Quoting professor Herbert J. Walberg.

6. Magnet, "How to Smarten Up the Schools," p. 86.

7. "Spending on Schools: Pick Your Number," *The Economist* (February 17, 1990), p. 27.

Brimelow, Peter, "Are We Spending Too Much on Education?" *Forbes* (December 29, 1986), pp. 72–76.

Brimelow, Peter, "American Perestroika?" *Forbes* (May 14, 1990), pp. 82–86.

8. Snyder, Thomas D., *Digest of Education Statistics, 1987* (Washington, DC: National Center for Education Statistics, 1987), p. 155.

Bennett, *American Education*, p. 9.

Vedder, Richard, "Small Classes Are Better for Whom?" *Wall Street Journal* (June 7, 1988), p. 34.

"Education Cost Put at $308 Billion in 1987–88," *New York Times* (August 23, 1987), p. 10.

Brimelow, "Are We Spending Too Much," p. 74.

Holusha, John, "Out of Patience: Detroiters Say No to More Taxes," *New York Times* (December 18, 1988), Sect. 4, p. 4.

Stern, *Condition of Education*, p. 35.

9. Brimelow, "Are We Spending Too Much," p. 75.

See *Statistics of State School Systems*—1965–66, 1967–68, 1969–70, 1971–72, 1973–74 (Washington, DC: National Center for Education Statistics).

Statistics of Public Elementary and Secondary School Systems, Fall 1979 (Washington, DC: National Center for Education Statistics).

Digest of Education Statistics, 1987 (Washington, DC: National Center for Education Statistics).

10. See "Chicago Schools: Worst in America," *Chicago Tribune* (May 15–29, 1988).

11. Bell, T. H., *The Nation Responds: Recent Efforts to Improve Education* (Washington, DC: U.S. Department of Education, 1984).

Stern, *Condition of Education*, p. 51.

Putka, Gary, "Teachers Get More Pay and Power in the Wake of Reform Movements," *Wall Street Journal* (September 21, 1987), p. 27.

Maeroff, Gene I., "Education Watch: Teachers Get a Dose of Their Own Medicine," *New York Times* (June 2, 1985), p. E6.

Fiske, Edward B., "35 Pages That Shook the U.S. Education World," *New York Times* (April 27, 1988), p. B10.

12. Daniels, Lee A., "Tests Show Reading and Writing Lag Continues," *New York Times* (January 10, 1990), p. B7.

Carmody, Deirdre, "Blacks Gain Again in College Admission Tests," *New York Times* (September 20, 1988), p.11.

Stern, *Condition of Education*, p. 26.

13. Snyder, *Digest of Education Statistics*, p. 70.

Chodes, John, "Public Education—Dump It," *New York Times* (December 19, 1988), p. A19.

14. Chubb, John E., "To Revive Schools, Dump Bureaucrats," *New York Times* (December 9, 1988), p. A22.

15. Putka, Gary, "Parents in Minnesota Are Getting to Send Kids Where They Like," *Wall Street Journal* (May 31, 1988), p. 1.

16. The author is indebted to Dr. Ruth Randall, Commissioner of Education; Ken Zastrow, Director of Open Enrollment; Dan Loritz, legislative aide to the governor; and Joe Nathan, consultant to the governor, for their cooperation in a series of interviews.

17. Marquand, Robert, "Going to College While in High School," *Christian Science Monitor* (February 27, 1987), p. 21.

18. Bencivenga, Jim, "Multiple Choice: Minnesota Opens Enrollment—and Eyes Reform," *Christian Science Monitor* (June 10, 1988), p. 19.

19. Raywid, Mary Anne, "Synthesis of Research on Schools of Choice," *Educational Leadership* (April 1, 1984), p. 70.
20. Bencivenga, "Multiple Choice," p. 19.
21. Donahue, John D., *The Privatization Decision: Public Ends, Private Means* (New York: Basic Books, 1989).
22. Fiske, Edward B., "Parental Choice in Public Schools Gains," *New York Times* (July 11, 1988), p. 1.
    Nathan, Joe, "Results and Future Prospects of State Efforts to Increase Choice Among Schools," *Phi Delta Kappan* (June 1, 1987), p. 746.
    Van Tassel, Priscilla, "State Weighs Open-Choice Schooling," *New York Times* (March 13, 1988), Sect. 12, p. 1.
    Alexander, Lamar, Bill Clinton, and Thomas H. Kean, *Time for Results: The Governors' 1991 Report on Education* (Washington, DC: National Governors' Association Center for Policy Research and Analysis, 1986).
    "Governors Opt for Choice of Schools," *Wall Street Journal* (August 28, 1986), p. 16.
    Leslie, Connie, "Giving Parents a Choice: Consumerism Comes to the Schoolyard," *Newsweek* (September 19, 1988), pp. 77–82.
    Wells, Amy Stuart, "Milwaukee Parents Get More Choice on Schools," *New York Times* (March 28, 1990), p. B8.
23. Nathan, "Results and Future Prospects," pp. 746–52. At least 15 states have taken formal action to increase parental choice in public schools: Alaska, Arizona, California, Colorado, Florida, Iowa, Louisiana, Massachusetts, Minnesota, Missouri, New York, North Carolina, Virginia, Washington, and Wisconsin.
    Fiske, Edward B., "Parental Choice in Public Schools Gains," *New York Times* (July 11, 1988), p. 1.
    Chubb, John E., "A Blueprint for Public Education," *Wall Street Journal* (June 6, 1990), p. A16.
24. Bacon, Kenneth, "Education Summit Gets a Good Report Card Well in Advance of Next Week's Opening Bell," *Wall Street Journal* (September 20, 1989), p. A24.

PART VIII, MUTUALISM AND COOPERATION/CHAPTER 28, SOVIET CAPITALISM

1. King, Jr., Martin Luther, "Where Do We Go From Here?" *A Testament of Hope: The Essential Writings of Martin Luther King, Jr.*, James Melvin Washington, ed. (New York: Harper & Row, 1986), p. 626.
2. Shmelyov, Nikolay, "Toward a Soviet Market Economy," *Wall Street Journal* (August 26, 1987), p. 20. "Persistent, long-term efforts to overturn the objective laws of economic life and crush the age-old natural incentives to work ultimately brought on results directly opposite to those which we had anticipated. We now have an economy which is out of whack and plagued with shortages, an economy which rejects scientific and technical progress and which is unplanned and—if we want to be totally honest—unplannable. Industry now rejects 80 percent of new technical inventions and decisions. Our level of efficiency is among the lowest in the industrialized countries—particularly in agriculture and construction. What is holding us back? Primarily the ideological fear that we will release the evil genie of capitalism from the bottle."
3. Bynum, W. F., E. J. Browne, and Roy Porter, *Dictionary of the History of Science* (Princeton: Princeton University Press, 1981), p. 407. "The idea of symbiosis first became clear when lichens were shown [to be] mutually beneficial combinations of an alga and a fungus. This was demonstrated by H. A. De Bary (1831–88) in 1866, being followed by successful reconstructions of lichens from appropriate ingredients."
4. Voslensky, Michael and Eric Mosbacher, translator, *Nomenklatura: Anatomy of the Soviet Ruling Class* (London: The Bodley Head, 1984), p. 75.
    Gailbraith, John, and Menshikov, Stanislav, "A Perestroika Primer: Is This the Second Russian Revolution?" *New York Times* (May 29, 1988), p. 46.
5. Shevchenko, Arkady N., *Breaking with Moscow* (New York: Alfred A. Knopf, 1985), p. 174.
    Voslensky, *Nomenklatura*, pp. 178–242.
6. Schmemann, Serge, "Tide of Luxuries Sweeps German Leaders Away," *New York Times* (December 10, 1989), p. 15.

7. Wohlstetter, Albert, "When Empires Are Falling, Daring is Prudence," *Wall Street Journal* (December 12, 1989), p. A14.
8. Bovard, James, "Mail Monopoly Says Happy New Year," *Wall Street Journal* (December 29, 1989), p. A6.
9. Goldman, Marshall I., *Gorbachev's Challenge: Economic Reform in the Age of High Technology* (New York: W.W. Norton, 1987), pp. 86–117.
10. See chapter 11.
11. Greenhouse, Steven, "A Thorny East Bloc Issue: Replacing Hated Managers," *New York Times* (December 12, 1989), p. C1.
12. Brenner, Reuven, "Don't Frighten the East Bloc Bureaucrats," *Wall Street Journal* (December 26, 1989), p. A9.
13. Goldman, Marshall I., *Economic Reform in the Age of High Technology* (New York: W.W. Norton, 1987). Quoting John Stuart Mill (1859): "The Czar himself is powerless against the bureaucratic body; he can send any one of them to Siberia, but he cannot govern without them, or against their will. On every decree of his they have a tacit veto, by merely refraining from carrying it into effect."
14. "Nothing to Lease But Your Chains," *The Economist* (September 16, 1989), p. 51.
15. Friedman, Thomas L., "Baker Says Gorbachev's Economic Plan Lacks Basic Changes," *New York Times* (December 16, 1989), p. 8.
    Clines, Francis X., "Soviet Deputies Fault Gorbachev: Plan is Called the Old 5-Year System in a New Guise," *New York Times* (December 14, 1989), p. 1.
    Gumbel, Peter, "Soviet Premier Offers Modest Economic Plan: Ryzhkov Doesn't Stray Far from Central Planning Despite Aide's Urging," *Wall Street Journal* (December 14, 1989), p. A13.
    " 'Market Socialism' Can Wait: Moscow Seeks Tighter Control Over Economy," *San Francisco Chronicle* [Los Angeles Times News Service] (December 14, 1989), p. 1. "Ryzhkov's distinctly conservative line appeared to reflect the rising fear within the Soviet leadership that unless the shortages—which range from meat, potatoes and vegetables to soap, gasoline, and cotton cloth—are quickly ended and consumer demand satisfied, the reform effort will be in serious jeopardy."
    Silk, Leonard, "Why Gorbachev Delays Reforms," *New York Times* (April 13, 1990), p. C2.
    Keller, Bill, "Soviet Economy: A Shattered Dream," *New York Times* (May 13, 1990), p. 1.
16. Passell, Peter, "New Soviet Blueprint Seeks a Middle Road," *New York Times* (December 9, 1989), p. 19. "The 64-billion-ruble question is whether Mr. Gorbachev can succeed in his mission to find an alternative to capitalism that does not clash with the peculiarly Russian sense of order and economic justice. For all the sudden homage to the merits of the market economy, Kremlin economists seem frozen at the threshold: Ordinary Soviet citizens, they fear, would find the resulting degree of freedom—the freedom to flop or succeed grandly—more than a little unnerving."
    Keller, Bill, "How Gorbachev Rejected Plan to 'Shock Treat' the Economy," *New York Times* (May 14, 1990), p. 1.
17. Abrams, Garry, "How U.S. Marxists Explain Europe," *San Francisco Chronicle* (December 13, 1989), p. 3.
    Doder, Dusko and Susan V. Lawrence, "China the Beacon for Communism," *San Francisco Chronicle* (December 20, 1989), p. Briefing 6. "Publicly, Chinese officials have remained tight-lipped about the radical changes in the Soviet Union and Eastern Europe. But privately, Deng has denounced Gorbachev's politics as 'not in conformity with true Marxism Leninism'—a serious charge in the language of international socialism."
    'Z,' "The Soviets' Terminal Crisis," *New York Times* (January 4, 1990), p. A17.

The whole impossible enterprise of Lenin and Stalin was sustainable only as long as the human and material resources on which the system fed retained the vitality to endure the burden of the regime, and as long as some modicum of material success undergirded the party's monopolistic position.

When these conditions ceased to hold, beginning with Deng Xiaoping's marketization of 1979 and Solidarity's revolt of 1980, the Communist parties' will to power began to flag and their people's habit of fear began to fade. For the Soviet part-state's survival, this development soon made necessary the expedients of perestroika and glasnost. But these are only pale substitutes for the market and democracy, halfway measures designed to square the circle of making the vivifying forces of a resurrected civil society compatible with the party's leading role.

But this circle cannot be squared. If marketization and privatization are the economic goals of reform, then party planning becomes superfluous, indeed downright parasitical. If multiple parties, elections and the rule of law are the political goals of reform, then the dual administration of the party-state becomes supernumerary, indeed positively noxious.

There is no third way between Leninism and the market, between Bolshevism and constitutional government. Marketization and democratization lead to the revival of civil society, and such a society requires the rule of law. But civil society under the rule of law is incompatible with the preservation of the lawless leading role of the party.

18. Uchitelle, Louis, "East Europe Tries a Mild Capitalism: Tentative Ventures into Free Markets," *New York Times* (December 1, 1989), p. C1.
19. Fialka, John J., "Internal Threat: Soviets Begin Moving Nuclear Warheads Out of Volatile Republics," *Wall Street Journal* (June 22, 1990), p. 1.
20. Uchitelle, Louis, "No Economic Model Fits East Bloc," *New York Times* (December 30, 1989), p. 17.
    Greenhouse, Steven, "In Poland, Capitalism Brings Hope Tempered With Worry," *New York Times* (January 1, 1990), p. 1.
21. Greenhouse, Steven, "Eastern Europe Awaits the Storm: As Market Forces Come into Play Social Tensions Are Sure to Rise," *New York Times* (December 17, 1989), p. F4.
22. Clines, Francis X. "Moscow Is Said to Consider Urgent Economic Measures," *New York Times* (March 20, 1990), p. A7.

CHAPTER 29, GLOBAL COEVOLUTION

1. Blaug, Mark, *Economic Theory in Retrospect, 4th ed.* (Cambridge: Cambridge University Press, 1985), p. 711. "The moral of the story is simply this: it takes a new theory, and not just the destructive exposure of assumptions or the collection of new facts, to beat an old theory."
2. "The 1980's: When Information Accelerated," *New York Times* (December 31, 1989), p. 1.
   Wright, Karen, "The Road to the Global Village," *Scientific American* (March 1990), pp. 83–94.
3. "Airlines' Passenger Total Globally Rose 3.4% in '89," *Wall Street Journal* (January 3, 1990), p. B4.
   Kristof, Nicholas D., "Computers Reshape Markets," *New York Times* (October 7, 1985), p. 25.
4. Lohr, Steve, "The Growth of the 'Global Office,' " *New York Times* (October 18, 1988), p. C1.
5. Greenhouse, Steven, "Sweden's Social Democrats Veer Toward Free Market and Lower Taxes," *New York Times* (October 27, 1989), p. A3.
6. Winter, Ralph E., "Research and Development Spending to Rise 4.8% in 1990, Battelle Predicts," *Wall Street Journal* (December 28, 1989), p. A2.
7. "Spending on Schools: Pick Your Number," *The Economist* (February 17, 1990), p. 27.
8. Aschauer, David Alan, "Public Spending for Private Profit," *Wall Street Journal* (March 14, 1990), p. A16.
9. Peterson, Peter G. and Neil Howe, *On Borrowed Time: How the Growth in Entitlement Spending Threatens America's Future* (New York: Simon & Schuster, 1988).
10. Apple, R. W., "Bush-Dukakis Debate: For Workers in Texas, Little to Cheer," *New York Times* (October 15, 1988), p. 9. "Mr. [C. D.] Hooper, the pipe fitters' business manager [Local 211] listened to all this and commented gravely: 'We're heading for a world

economy. The trouble is that they're bringing us down to the foreigners' level, instead of raising them to ours, and I don't want to live in a grass shack and eat fish heads.' "

11. Kristof, Nicholas D., "Deng Appears on Chinese TV, Surrounded by Hard-Liners," *New York Times* (June 10, 1989), p. 1. In a notable exception, Deng Xiaoping said after the Tiananmen Square massacre, "This disturbance was something beyond anyone's control. A very small number of people created turmoil, and this eventually developed into a counterrevolutionary rebellion. They are trying to overthrow the Communist Party, topple the socialist system and subvert the People's Republic of China so as to establish a capitalist republic."

12. King, Jr., Martin Luther, *A Testament of Hope: The Essential Writings of Martin Luther King, Jr.*, James Melvin Washington, ed. (New York: Harper & Row, 1986), p. 619.

POSTSCRIPT: BIONOMICS VS. SOCIAL DARWINISM

1. Wilson, Edward O., *Biophilia* (Cambridge: Harvard University Press, 1984), p. 66.
2. Gould, Stephen Jay, "William Jennings Bryan's Last Campaign," *Natural History* (November 1, 1987), p. 16.
3. Chase, Alan, *The Legacy of Malthus: The Social Costs of the New Scientific Racism* (New York: Alfred A. Knopf, 1977). See chapter 15, "The Old Scientific Racism's Last Hurrah: Six Million One-Way Tickets to the Nazi Death Camps."
4. Bowler, Peter J., *Evolution: The History of an Idea* (Berkeley: University of California Press, 1984), p. 270. According to Bowler, there was a nonaggressive form and an extreme form of social Darwinism. The view of the nonaggressive social Darwinists was, "If the number of unfit individuals at the bottom of the social hierarchy was becoming too much of a burden on the community, the answer was not starvation but government control to restrict their breeding. The extreme form "argued for a policy of complete laissez-faire in order to give free reign to economic competition. The state must withdraw from all efforts to limit the freedom of individual action, leaving everyone to rise or fall according to their ability. Progress would only occur if the fittest were allowed to fight their way to a dominant position in the economy, while those unfit to work would have to take the consequences."
5. Gould, Stephen Jay, *The Mismeasure of Man* (New York: W.W. Norton, 1981).
   Ludmerer, Kenneth M., *Genetics and American Society: A Historical Appraisal* (Baltimore: Johns Hopkins University Press, 1972).
   Also see Rothman, Stanley and Mark Snyderman, *The IQ Controversy: The Media and Public Policy* (New Brunswick, NJ: Transaction Books, 1988).
6. *World Development Report 1987* (Oxford: Oxford University Press, 1987), pp. 256–57.
7. Wilson, Edward O., *Sociobiology: The New Synthesis* (Cambridge: Harvard University Press, 1975), p. 5. "The principal goal of a general theory of sociobiology should be an ability to predict features of social organizations from a knowledge of these population parameters combined with information on the behavioral constraints imposed by the genetic constitution of the species."
8. Wilson, *Sociobiology*, p. 121.
9. Caplan, Arthur L., ed., *The Sociobiology Debate: Readings on the Ethical and Scientific Issues Concerning Sociobiology* (New York: Harper & Row, 1978).
10. Schemeck, Harold M., Jr., "Schizophrenia Study Finds Strong Signs of Hereditary Cause," *New York Times* (November 10, 1988), p. 1.
    Franklin, Deborah, "What a Child Is Given," *New York Times Magazine* (September 3, 1989), p. 36. "The question today is no longer whether genetics influence personality, but rather how much, and in what ways?"
11. Sahlins, Marshall, *The Use and Abuse of Biology: An Anthropological Critique of Sociobiology* (Ann Arbor: University of Michigan Press, 1976).
12. Bonner, John Tyler, *The Evolution of Complexity by Means of Natural Selection* (Princeton: Princeton University Press, 1988), pp. viii–ix. "The important point, however, is that there is an enormous difference between the mode of inheritance of flexible behavior and of structure. The latter is directly controlled by genes, while the former is passed from one individual to another by nongenetic or behavioral transmission. These are two kinds of inheritance which operate by totally different mechanisms, but dovetail with one another and are both under the direct influence of selection. . . . [B]oth are ultimately controlled

by genes, but the connection between flexible behavior and the genome is remote; what is inherited is a capacity to learn and invent and instruct."

13. Deevey, Jr., Edward S., "The Human Population," *Scientific American* (September 1960), p. 195.

14. Lewin, Roger, *Thread of Life: The Smithsonian Looks at Evolution* (Washington, DC: Smithsonian Books, 1982), pp. 64–65.
    Gould, Stephen Jay, *An Urchin in the Storm: Essays About Books and Ideas* (New York: W.W. Norton, 1987), pp. 221–22.
    Bock, Walter, "Principles and Methods of Comparative Analyses in Sociobiology," in *The Sociobiology Debate: Readings on the Ethical and Scientific Issues Concerning Sociobiology*, Arthur L. Caplan, ed. (New York: Harper & Row, 1978), p. 405.

15. Mayr, Ernst, *The Growth of Biological Thought: Diversity, Evolution, and Inheritance* (Cambridge: Harvard University Press, 1982), p. 465. "One important aspect of the evolutionary redefinition of homologous is that it is applicable not only to structural elements but to any other properties, including behavioral ones, which might have been derived by inheritance from a common ancestor."

16. Staddon, J. E. R., *Adaptive Behavior and Learning* (Cambridge: Cambridge University Press, 1983), p. 7. "Functional explanations do one thing that no mechanistic explanation can: They can explain similar outcomes produced by different means. For example, the eyes of vertebrates and octopi are very similar in many ways: Both have lenses, a retina, and some means of limiting the amount of light that can enter. This convergence cannot be explained by a common ancestry or any similarity of developmental mechanisms. The *only* explanation we can offer for this astonishing similarity is the common function of these organs as optical image-formers."

17. See preface, note 2.

18. Stuart-Harris, Charles H. and Geoffrey C. Schild, *Influenza: The Viruses and the Disease* (Littleton, MA: Publishing Sciences Group, Inc., 1976), pp. 16–20.

INDEX

ABC, 219
Abegglen, James C., 383*n*40
Abraham, Ralph, 396*n*13
Abstract of British Historical Statistics (Mitchell), 355*n*24
Acquired characteristics, heritability of, 28–29
Adams, John, 13
Adenine, 2
Aerospace industry, 128
Agricola, Georg, 9
Agriculture, 31
   ancient, 31, 46, 231–32, 235, 253*n*19
   during Industrial Revolution, 233
   and "law of diminishing returns," 49–50
   learning curve in, 177, 183, 187
   no-growth era of, 245
   pricing and, 269, 270
AIDS, 285, 289
Aircraft industry, 178–79, 202
Altruism, instinctive, 346
Amaya, Naohiro, 192
Amoebas, slime-mold, 255–59, 261, 263
American Economic Review, The, 52–53
American Economics Association, 52
American Museum of Natural History, 55

Amino acids, 2, 83, 84
Ammonites, 62
Analogy, 349, 408*n*16
Animalens, Inc., 176, 375*n*7
Antitrust laws, 193, 194, 201, 249, 380*n*15
Ants, 226–32, 235, 239–41, 346, 365*n*13, 370*n*21, 388*n*5, 389*nn*13, 16, 19, 389–90*n*22
Apartheid, 290
Apple, R. W., 406–7*n*10
Apple Computers, 264
Arvida Corporation, 300
Arrow, Kenneth J., 182, 375*n*1, 377*n*18
Arthur, W. Brian, 377–78*n*21, 378*n*24
Ascension Island, 205–6, 209
Asimov, Isaac, 353*n*28, 354*n*8
Atmospheric engines, 21–25, 31, 73, 75, 233, 362*n*9
ATP, 85, 86, 363*n*11
Australian aborigines, 5
Australopithecines, 65, 66, 68, 69
Automated egg production, 173–74
Automobile industry, 188, 217–18
   corpocracy in, 305
   labor/management relations in, 291

Babbage, Charles, 87
Bacon, Francis, 9